DIGITAL FILMMAKING HANDBOOK

Ben Long and Sonja Schenk

CHARLES RIVER MEDIA

CHARLES RIVER MEDIA, INC.
Rockland, Massachusetts

Publisher: Jenifer Niles
Production: Publishers' Design and Production Services, Inc.
Cover Design: The Printed Image

CHARLES RIVER MEDIA, Inc.
P.O. Box 417
403 VFW Drive
Rockland, Massachusetts 02370
781-871-4184
781-871-4376(FAX)
chrivmedia@aol.com
http://www.charlesriver.com

This book is printed on acid-free paper

Digital Filmmaking Handbook
by Ben Long and Sonja Schenk
    ISBN: 1-58450-017-4
    Printed in the United States of America

00 01 02 03 7 6 5 4 3 2

CHARLES RIVER MEDIA titles are available for site license or
bulk purchase by institutions, user groups, corporations, etc. For
additional information, please contact the Special Sales Department
at 781-871-4184.

DIGITAL
FILMMAKING
HANDBOOK

CONTENTS

Acknowledgments

Sonja Schenk wishes to thank Hank Clay of in:sync, Rod Finley, Julie Gordon of Gordon Images and Communications, John Hanish, Jeff Kress, Ken Musen, Jacob Nassim, Jane Perratt from DPS, Benoit Rossel from Swiss Effects, Gregg Rossen, Wes Sewell, Carl Stanza from 4MC, Pamela Soper, Michael Wynses, Gibert Yablon from Film Out Xpress, and most of all, Ralph Smith. Also thank you to DeeDee Halleck for starting me off on the right foot as a video maker.

Ben Long would like to thank the many vendors who generously contributed software and support, especially Susan Doering at Adobe; Andy Baum, Keith Hatounian, Ralph Fairweather and Jean Grandy at Apple; Eric Dohnlinger at Newer Technology; and Charles McConathy at ProMax. I would also like to thank Larry Jordan and the users of *www.2-pop.com* who are a great resource for digital videographers of all skill levels. As always Craig Lyn generously answered loads of special effects-related questions while Sean Safreed expertly fielded countless video-related questions. I also wish to thank Mike, Gary, Fred and Byron, my first (and best) production teachers.

Also, special thanks to Sean Wagstaff, and Rick LePage for getting us started and supporting us during this whole writing "thing."

Introduction

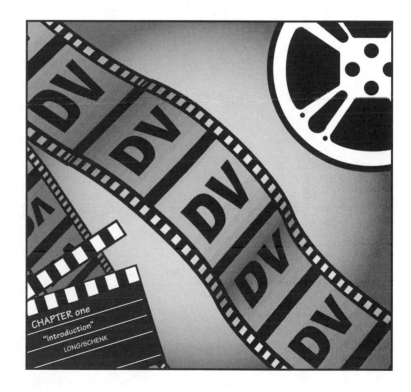

CHAPTER one
"introduction"
LONG/SCHENK

Several years ago, actor/monologist Spalding Gray was sent with a small video crew to Los Angeles to conduct an interesting experiment. While spending a day in the city, he chose random people—cab drivers, clerks, waiters, people on the street—and asked them a simple question: "Hi," he said. "I was hoping you'd talk to me about your screenplay." Invariably, each person responded the same way: "How did you know I was writing a screenplay?"

It seems that just about everyone these days has an interest in making movies. But, as everyone knows, movie-making is colossally expensive, and Hollywood is something of a closed community. Since getting that "big break" isn't easy, more and more filmmakers are going independent and producing movies on their own.

"Indie" films are nothing new, but the number of independent productions has increased dramatically since the 70s and 80s when people like John Cassavettes, John Sayles, and Spike Lee scraped together shoestring budgets and begged and borrowed equipment and talent to produce their films. In 1998, more than 1,000 films were submitted to the famed Sundance film festival, and four of 1997's Best Picture Oscar nominees were independent productions.

Though independent filmmaking is cheap by Hollywood standards, the independent filmmaker still has to come up with tens or hundreds of thousands of dollars to pay for sets, actors, locations, and, most of all, equipment. In the past, cameras, lights, film-stock, editing facilities, special effects, and post-production were the most expensive items in an indie film budget. But with new digital video technology, that is starting to change. New standards and tape formats ranging from MiniDV to DVCPro allow filmmakers to shoot high-quality footage for far less money.

With DV technology, it's possible to get a polished, edited feature "in the can" for substantially less than if you were shooting on film. Once your feature is finished, you can use your final, edited digital videotape to shop around for a distributor who will pay for a transfer to film.

Even if you're not interested in becoming a movie mogul, you may find yourself facing more and more of a demand for video production. With new Web-based streaming technologies and faster desktop computers, more and more businesses are finding corporate and industrial applications for high-quality video production tools. Whether it's live webcasting or producing a CD-ROM-based annual report, you might have recently found yourself needing to wear the video producer hat.

While there has been plenty written about how famous, monied producers like George Lucas use high-end proprietary equipment to create digital special effects, there has been very little about how non-famous, less-monied individuals can use inexpensive new DV technology, their desktop computer, and off-the-shelf software to create fully-realized, marketable feature films. *The Digital Filmmaking Handbook* is targeted at anyone who wants to use their desktop computer and DV camera to create professional-quality productions (Figure 1.1).

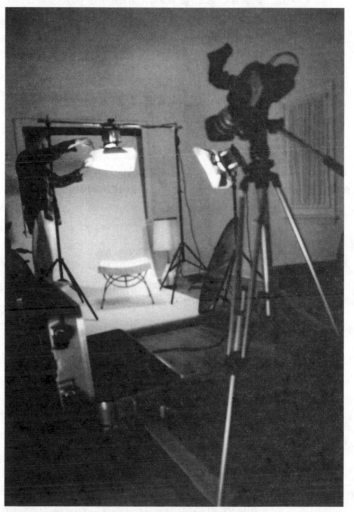

FIGURE
1.1 *Using a small, DV-equipped film crew doesn't mean you have to sacrifice quality. Modern DV equipment can deliver results that are a good substitute for expensive analog video or film.*

Although this book covers everything the independent filmmaker needs to know to get a feature-length film made, it's also ideal for industrial and corporate producers who need to create training videos or trade show presentations. Multimedia developers, meanwhile, will find answers to all of their video-production questions, ranging from how to shoot special effects to how to optimize video for distribution via CD-ROM or the Web.

This book is meant to be both a start-to-finish production guide and a reference for learning more about particular tasks. While we can't spend too much time covering the artistry of writing, shooting, and editing, we will give you some suggestions of where to learn more about such non-technical issues. For more experienced users, we've included details on the latest technologies, tips and guidelines for transitioning from older video or film technology, and suggestions and strategies for using digital equipment and digital workflow to reduce your production costs. From sophisticated titles to complex compositing, *The Digital Filmmaking Handbook* will show you how to create shots and effects that are rarely associated with low-budget production.

What Kind of Equipment Do I Need?

This book assumes you will be using a Macintosh or Windows-compatible computer. Some familiarity with your operating system of choice will be required, as well as a video camera of some kind. Guidelines for selecting equipment are provided in Chapters 5, 6, 10, and 11 (Figure 1.2).

We also assume that you are familiar with some basic computer terms—RAM, kilobytes, megabytes, clock speeds, etc. A glossary is included in Appendix A.

Finally, though we assume no formal training in video or film production, we might—on occasion—use production-related terms. These are also included in the glossary. You might be surprised to learn how much you already know about video production. Watching movies is the best way to learn the visual literacy required of a good filmmaker, and most people have seen a lot of movies. At times, we may illustrate a concept by referencing movies available at your local video store. Careful study of these materials is a great way to learn.

What Is Digital Video?

The phrase *digital video* is very confusing because there are many things that are, technically, "digital video." A QuickTime movie downloaded from the Web is digital video, as is an animation generated by a computer graphics program. A video hobbiest may use an inexpensive digitizing board to pour

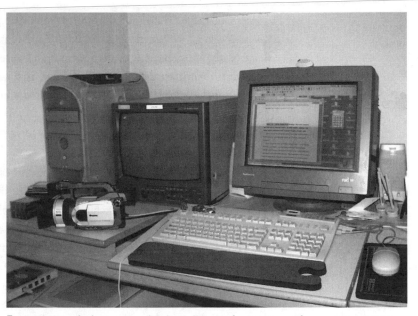

FIGURE   *Typical editing setup showing a Macintosh computer with a computer monitor,*
1.2   *an NTSC monitor, speakers, and video camera connected to the computer*
          through a Firewire cable.

video from her home video camera into her computer, while a big film studio may use special scanners to transfer 35mm motion picture film into
high-end graphics workstations. The results are all "digital video."

Things get even more complicated when you consider that some people
use the term "digital video" to refer to very specific pieces of equipment (a
"DV camera," for example), while others use "digital video" as a broader
term that encompasses any type of digitized video or film.

If your computer has a *Firewire* interface built into it, your computer sales-
man may have said something like "with this Firewire interface, this computer
is a great 'digital video' machine." But what does this really mean? Can you
plug any old camera into it? Is the machine ready to create a great new digital video feature-length movie? Unfortunately, the answer to both of those
questions is no. However, such a computer can be used as one component of
a system that can take video from a video source, edit it, add special effects
and graphics, and then output the results to a video or film recorder. In some
cases, your source video will be a special digital video camera or tape deck. In
other instances, it might be a traditional analog camera or deck. The main
difference between a digital and an analog camera is that a digital camera dig-

itizes video *while* you shoot, and stores it on tape in a digital format, while an analog camera stores video and audio on tape as analog waves.

For the most part, when we say "digital video," we're referring to the broadest definition: a process wherein your source video is "digitized" at some point so that it can be manipulated and edited on the computer.

WHAT IS DIGITIZING?

A digital video camera is a lot like a flatbed scanner, in that both devices "digitize" an image. A flatbed scanner, for example, divides a page into a grid of tiny pixels and then *samples* each pixel. Each sample is analyzed and assigned a numeric value—a digit, or series of digits—that represents the pixel's color.

A frame of video can be digitized using the same process. However, since one video frame is composed of an average of 720×480 pixels (or 345,600 pixels), and each second of video requires 30 frames, you need a fast computer with a lot of storage.

A digital video camera digitizes video on-board and simply stores the resulting numbers on a tape. Consequently, if you use a Firewire connection to transfer video from a DV camera into your computer, you don't technically "digitize" the video, because the camera has already done that for you. Rather, you simply copy the numbers (which represent the digitized images) from the tape into your computer.

On the other hand, if you're using an analog video camera, the digitizing process will happen inside your computer, rather than inside your camera. You will need special hardware in your computer that can change the analog video signal from your camera into digital information and store it on your computer's hard drive. These "video capture boards" also compress the video before storing it and decompress it when you're ready for playback. Video capture boards can be expensive and require a fast processor and very fast hard drives (Figure 1.3).

We'll discuss the details and merits of both systems later in this book.

Why Digital Video?

Obviously, video technology has been around for a while and has been working just fine, so what's all the fuss about all this new digital video stuff? Digital video technology has three advantages over traditional video editing and production equipment: quality, function, and price.

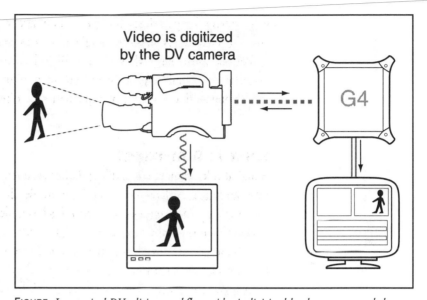

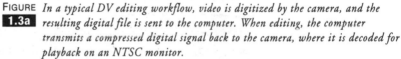

FIGURE
1.3a *In a typical DV editing workflow, video is digitized by the camera, and the resulting digital file is sent to the computer. When editing, the computer transmits a compressed digital signal back to the camera, where it is decoded for playback on an NTSC monitor.*

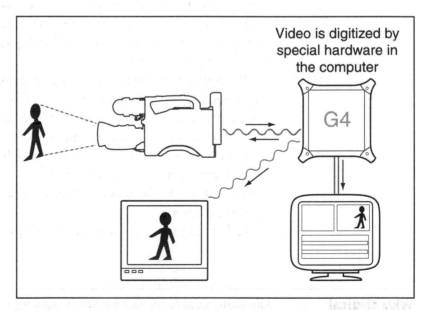

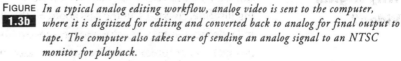

FIGURE
1.3b *In a typical analog editing workflow, analog video is sent to the computer, where it is digitized for editing and converted back to analog for final output to tape. The computer also takes care of sending an analog signal to an NTSC monitor for playback.*

Price Check

The following chart shows two rough price comparisons (circa January, 2000) between feature production using analog video, digital video, and film. In the first chart, we present a rough "ideal" situation: analog production using high-quality BetaSP, digital production using MiniDV format and a three-chip camera, and 16mm film production.

In the second chart, we present a more affordable comparison: analog video production using a single-chip Hi8 camera, digital video production using a single-chip MiniDV camera, and film production using a pre-owned 16mm camera. Note that although there may be changes in quality from system to system, all of these are suitable for feature-film or documentary work.

Rough Production Hardware Costs
Ideal

	Analog	Digital	Film
Computer	$4,000*	$2,800**	$4,000***
Analog digitizing card	$1,000–$5,000	N/A	$1,000
Camera	$30,000	$4,000	$6,000
Analog deck	$12,000	$1,000	$2,000
Speakers, NTSC monitor, cables	$500–up	$500–up	$500-up
Editing software	$400–$1,000	$400–$1,000	$2,000
Stock	$700	$300	$10,700 ?
Telecine transfers	N/A	N/A	$5,000
Total:	**$48,600+**	**$9,000+**	**$31,200+**

*Macintosh 350 MHz G4 computer with 128MB RAM, 36GB Ultra2 SCSI with interface, 17″ Apple monitor, Zip drive, DVD-ROM drive, 56K modem, three built-in Firewire ports.

**Same as analog system, but with a 27GB Ultra ATA hard drive instead of a SCSI drive.

***Figures based on film projects using analog-based editing systems as described in * with the lowest quality digitizing card and additional film matchback software.

Really Low Budget			
	Analog	Digital	Film
Computer	$4,000*	$1,300**	$1,300***
Analog digitizing card	$1,000–$5,000	N/A	N/A
Camera	$750	$1,300	$2,000
Analog deck	$2,000	N/A	$1,000
Speakers, NTSC monitor, cables	$500–up	$500–up	$500–up
Editing software	$2,300	$400	$1,400
Stock	$300	$300	$10,700
Telecine transfers	N/A	N/A	$4,000
Total:	**$10,850–up**	**$3,800–up**	**$19,900-up**

*Macintosh 350 MHz G4 with 128MB RAM, 18GB Ultra2 SCSI with interface, 17″ Apple monitor, DVD-ROM drive, three built-in Firewire ports.
**iMac DV with 400 MHz G3 processor, 64MB of RAM, 56K modem, 10GB drive, two Firewire ports, DVD.
***Figures based on a film project using a DV-based editing system as described in **, a used 16mm camera, and additional film matchback software.

Though "inexpensive" may not be the first word you'd use to describe the thousands of dollars you'll need for a computer and digital video equipment, trust us, it's **much** cheaper than what you'd spend on traditional video or film. With digital video, you don't have the film stock and processing costs that you'd face if you were shooting film, and your computer can take the place of whole racks of equipment you'd need if you were shooting traditional analog video. And, digital video formats can potentially deliver much higher quality than traditional analog formats, and can be edited and copied with no loss in quality from generation to generation.

In addition to being less expensive than film or video, your desktop computer can perform functions that are normally not possible using traditional technology (or only possible with very expensive dedicated equipment and teams of skilled craftsmen). The difference between digital and analog video production is as profound as the difference between using a typewriter and using a word processor.

Finally, with digital video, you no longer have to think in terms of pre- and post-production. With laptop computer-based editing systems, for example, you can edit as you shoot, trying out rough edits on-set, making it easier to ensure that you've shot what you need.

Linear versus Non-Linear

The non-linear editing that computers make possible is a great boon, but don't get confused by the linear and non-linear nature of different media. The digital media that you "digitize" or "capture" into your computer is non-linear, which means you have random access to any part of it. Digital video*tape* is a different story. Because it's on a piece of tape, it's linear. To access a given point in your digital videotape, you have to roll forward or backward through the tape, just like you do on analog VHS tape.

What this Book Covers

This book follows the traditional filmmaking stages of pre-production, production, and post-production. Throughout the book, we'll show you how to throw out the traditional approach and begin to mix and match the different stages of production to take advantage of DV technologies.

Chapters 2–7 cover the traditional stage of "pre-production," the part of the process where you make all the decisions necessary to start shooting: writing, planning, financing, budgeting, scheduling, storyboarding, and choosing basic equipment.

Chapters 8–10 cover the traditional stage of "production," the principal shoot of your project: lighting, set design, shooting and recording production sound, including tips for special shooting situations such as blue-screen photography.

Chapters 11–18 cover the traditional stage of "post-production": editing room equipment, advanced editing techniques, sound design, special effects, and delivery of the finished product—everything from streaming video for the Web to getting your 35mm release print.

Pop Quiz

If you're seriously thinking of embarking on a video production, you're about to begin a very complicated process. The more you know before you start, the more smoothly things will go for you. Before you dive in, you should know the answers to these questions:

- What is your final product? Projected 35mm film? Home video? Broadcast television? DVD? Live Webcast? CD-ROM? Foreign release? Corporate/educational use? (Chapters 4 and 18 can help you understand the technical specifications for these different formats).
- What peripheral products will you be creating? Work-in-progress VHS copies, trailers, press kits? Outputting different formats requires more planning than a project that sticks to one type of output.
- What equipment do you already own or have access to that you can use to produce your project? Consider this question carefully, as some older equipment might be more of a hindrance than a help.
- How much time and money do you want to spend in post-production?

If you take the time to make some hard decisions before you shoot, you'll save time and money throughout the process. You don't have to know all the answers, but you should at least know the questions that will come up during the course of your production.

CHAPTER

2

Planning Your Project

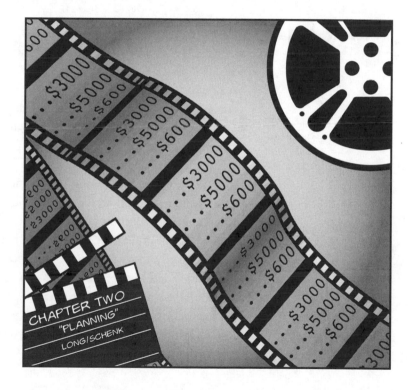

CHAPTER TWO
"PLANNING"
LONG/SCHENK

IN THIS CHAPTER

- Before you start
- Writing for DV Projects
- Scheduling Your Project
- Budgeting
- Paying As You Go
- Budgeting Can Be Fun

Before You Start

All video productions begin, of course, with a well-written script and a lot of planning. Good planning involves everything from pitching your idea and scheduling your shoot to budgeting your production. Because pre-production is where you'll determine much of the look and quality of your project, good planning weighs heavily on your production and post-production success. Fortunately, there are a number of digital tools available to help with all aspects of pre-production.

This chapter is divided into three sections: writing, scheduling, and budgeting. In the writing section, we'll cover some basics of preparing your script. In the scheduling section, we'll go over the all-important schedule, the anchor that keeps your production from getting out of hand. Finally, we'll help you understand some of the basic issues around budgeting your project.

Unfortunately, the "writing-scheduling-budgeting" model is a drastic oversimplification of the pre-production process. In reality, each of these processes affects the others, and all three are intertwined and interrelated. Our goal is to help you understand what questions you need to ask yourself, and where you might be able to find some answers before you dive in.

Writing for DV

No matter what your finished product will be—feature film, documentary, corporate training video—you have to start with a written script. A script is more than just a description of what people will say and do during your shoot. Your script is also a description of what locations and props you'll need, as well as what special effects, graphics, and sets you'll have to create. A finished script is required to start pre-production budgeting and scheduling and will serve as a reference point that you will follow all the way through post-production.

Don't skimp on this all-important first step. *No amount of production can save a poorly written script!*

WRITING

No matter what type of production you're planning, your first writing task is to decide what your story is about. Industrial and corporate presentations, music videos, documentaries, and marketing or advertising pieces usually have simple, well-defined goals. If you articulate these ideas before you start, you'll have an easier time focusing on what needs to be written. It's equally important to have a clear thematic idea when writing a fictional piece or feature. Though these themes or goals are often more abstract or complicated than in a simple industrial video, you still need to have some idea of what it is you want to say.

Before you start writing your script, consider your overall story. It will be much easier to write the actual scenes and dialog if you have a sense of the whole story before you start. Obviously, in a character-driven piece, it can sometimes be difficult to know what the ending will be before you've taken the character through the beginning and middle, but you should still, at least, have an idea of the overall tone and structure of your story.

TIP

Treatments
If you've worked out the details and structure of your story, you might want to consider writing a "treatment" before you begin writing the script. A treatment is the telling of your story in prose. Sometimes your treatment will have some dialog, at other times it will simply be a description of what's happening in the story. Treatments help you organize your thoughts, get any initial images and dialog down on paper, and serve as a way to present your story to other people. If you've got a producer or investor who's interested in your story idea, showing them a treatment might help you secure some funding.

Once you're comfortable with the idea of telling your story visually, it's time to start thinking about the structure of your story. Hollywood screenplays typically have a three-act structure. In act one, the characters and major conflicts are introduced. In act two, the conflicts are complicated and in act three, the conflicts are solved. An easier way to look at this is to say that the story has a beginning, middle and end. This simple structure is a good form to use for any type of script-writing and you should carry the beginning/middle/end form all the way through your script. Each act, every scene, even individual shots should have a sense of beginning, middle and end.

Doing It Write

Whether or not you're an experienced writer, crafting a good shooting script is a daunting challenge. Screenplays are very different from other types of writing, and you'll want to devote a good amount of study and practice to your script writing. For more on the craft of writing, check out `www.dvhandbook.com/writing.html`. There you'll find essays and suggestions on the craft of writing, as well as recommendations of books, classes, and Web links to learn more.

SCRIPT FORMAT

Traditional movie screenplays have a very specific format that has been designed and refined to convey much more than just dialog and scene descriptions. Screenplay format makes it easy to quickly judge budget and scheduling concerns in a script. No matter what type of project you're working on, writing screenplays in this format will make your production job much easier. There are a number of programs to assist in the writing and formatting of your screenplay. Many of these programs also offer interfaces to automatic budgeting and scheduling programs.

Screenplay Format

One of the biggest advantages of screenplay format is that it makes it easier to determine the length and pacing of your script. If you follow standard screenplay margins and layouts, your script will average one minute of screen time per page. In reality, there is a lot of variation, of course. A one-page description of an epic sea battle might actually take five minutes of screen time, while a page of witty banter might fly by in 20 seconds. On average, the one-page-per-minute rule is a good guideline to follow.

If you follow traditional screenplay format, your script will be divided into scenes delineated by *sluglines*. A slug tells whether the following scene is INTerior or EXTerior, the location of the scene, and whether the scene takes place during the day or night. For example:

```
INT. MAD SCIENTIST'S PANTRY -NIGHT
```

These sluglines make it easy to count and reorder your scenes, and make it simple for a producer to quickly arrive at a rough idea of cost. If your script has a lot of EXT scenes at NIGHT, then it's going to be more expensive (lights, location shots, and overtime add up quickly). Similarly, if your slugs all run along the lines of:

```
EXT. UPPER ATMOSPHERE OF MARS —NIGHT
```

then it's pretty obvious that your script is effects-heavy and, therefore, expensive.

Standard screenplays are always typed in 12-point Courier with the margins shown in Figure 2.1.

Top margin: .75" - 1"

Dialog
   Left margin: 3"
   Right margin: 2.3"

Parenthetical Description
   Left margin: 3.7"
   Right margin: 3"

Slug-line and Action
   Left Margin: 1.5" - 2"
   Right Margin: 1"

```
                                                          87.
CONTINUED:

walks in the front door, still sweaty and still carrying his
plastic bag.
                          RICHARD
                        (yelling)
                Who's got the purple rig out here?
A particularly beer-gutted, cowboy-hat-wearing, scruffy-
looking truck driver turns around from the bar.
                      TRUCK DRIVER
                Yo.
Richard whips THE PEARL-HANDLED PISTOL out from behind his
bag and points it squarely at the man's face. A few yelps go
up from the customers as everyone hits the floor. Except for
the music, the place is suddenly silent.
                          RICHARD
                Get over here right now! Move!
The man does, looking both scared and angry as he approaches
Richard with his hands held up ever-so-slightly.

AT THE DOOR

Richard grabs the man's shoulder and jabs the pistol into his
back.
                          RICHARD
                C'mon, let's go.
                        (to the restaurant)
                If any of you move in the next five
                minutes, I'm blowin' him away!
                                                    CUT TO:
EXT. TRUCK STOP PARKING LOT  - NIGHT
The purple truck being the closest to the truck stop door,
Richard and the driver are almost immediately at the

CAB OF THE TRUCK

Gun still pointed at the man, Richard motions the man into
the cab. Once the man is seated, Richard LOWERS THE GUN and
reaches into his pocket.
                          RICHARD
                Look, man, I'm sorry, but the cops are
                screwin' me around and I need a hand.
                Here's 100 bucks. Get on the Interstate
                and drive south for ten minutes, that's
                all I need. When they stop you tell em
                        (MORE)
                                              (CONTINUED)
```

Bottom margin: .5" - 1.5"

FIGURE   *Although measurements can vary, if you use the margins shown you'll have a*
2.1   *script formatted in "standard" screenplay format.*

Standard screenplay format has a number of other conventions as well. For example, if a scene continues from one page to the next, then "CONT'D" is placed at the bottom of the first page. Similarly, if a character's dialog jumps to another page, then "MORE" is placed below the flowing dialog. Through the years, screenplay conventions have been refined and standardized as a way of making script breakdown, budgeting, and scheduling much simpler. It's safe to say that if your screenplay is not formatted according to standard conventions, no one in the film industry will read it. A poorly formatted screenplay is an instant indication of a very "green" screenwriter.

Two-Column Formats

If you're writing a script for a news, industrial, corporate presentation, or advertising production, then you'll most likely want to use a two-column, A/V script format. Much simpler than screenplay format, A/V formats are ideal for planning and scripting live broadcasts, short subjects, and other multi-camera, multi-source shoots.

A/V scripts use a simple, two-column layout, with the talent's dialog in the right-hand column and simple storyboards/camera descriptions in the left-hand column. A/V scripts are used by the talent to read or learn their lines and by the director and technical director who will be shooting the script (Figure 2.2).

Sides

Sometimes it is useful to create "sides" for your talent, especially when recording dialog or voice-over narration. "Sides" are a version of your script that only contain the actors' lines, making it easier to read.

TIP

SCREENWRITING SOFTWARE

A whole range of writing software exists that not only makes it easy to render your scripts in standard screenplay format, but also provides some valuable tools for editing and restructuring your script.

For standard screenplay formats, programs like BC Software's *Final Draft* format your scripts as you write (Figure 2.3). Anyone who has tried to add all the MOREs and CONTINUEDs manually will find this one feature worth the investment. In addition to formatting, Final Draft provides a lot of automation. Character names can be entered by simply typing the first few letters of a name, and the program does a very good job of anticipating what the next character's name will be, making it simple to type back-and-forth dialog. Final Draft pro-

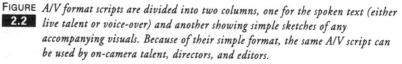

ACME STUDIOS

Project Title: Pocket Stonehenge Demo Video
Producer: I.S. Whelthie
Director: Cecil B. DeMilo   Date: Aug 9, 1999

VIDEO	AUDIO
STOCK FOOTAGE: TRACTOR/COMBINE	(VO continued) would ever dispute the incredible technological breakthroughs in modern agriculture. But for some tasks
LONG SHOT: STONEHENGE	the old ways are still the best ways.
MED SHOT: FARMER LOOKING AT A FIELD	When you're getting ready to plant, you need valuable, accurate information.
OVER-THE-SHOULDER: FARMER LOOKING AT CALENDAR	You need to know--with certainty-- when seasons begin and end.
PRODUCT SHOT: FIRST STILL, IN PALM. THEN CLOSE-UP OF POCKET STONEHENGE BEING UNFOLDED AND DEPLOYED.	You need...the Pocket Stonehenge. Collapsible. Portable. And backed by technology that's stood the test of time. With the Pocket Stonehenge, you can be certain that you're getting accurate, up-to-the-minute solstice information with none of the expensive batteries or messy sacrifices required by other technologies.

FIGURE 2.2   *A/V format scripts are divided into two columns, one for the spoken text (either live talent or voice-over) and another showing simple sketches of any accompanying visuals. Because of their simple format, the same A/V script can be used by on-camera talent, directors, and editors.*

vides other utilities, including a Scene Navigator that lets you see your scenes as a series of index cards that can be easily rearranged (Figure 2.4).

Other good scriptwriting programs include Screenplay Systems *Scriptwriter*, which, in addition to a set of tools similar to Final Draft's, includes a number of features aimed at writers of non-linear stories. If you're scripting an interactive multimedia presentation, game, or Website where your story might branch and change, Scriptwriter is a good solution.

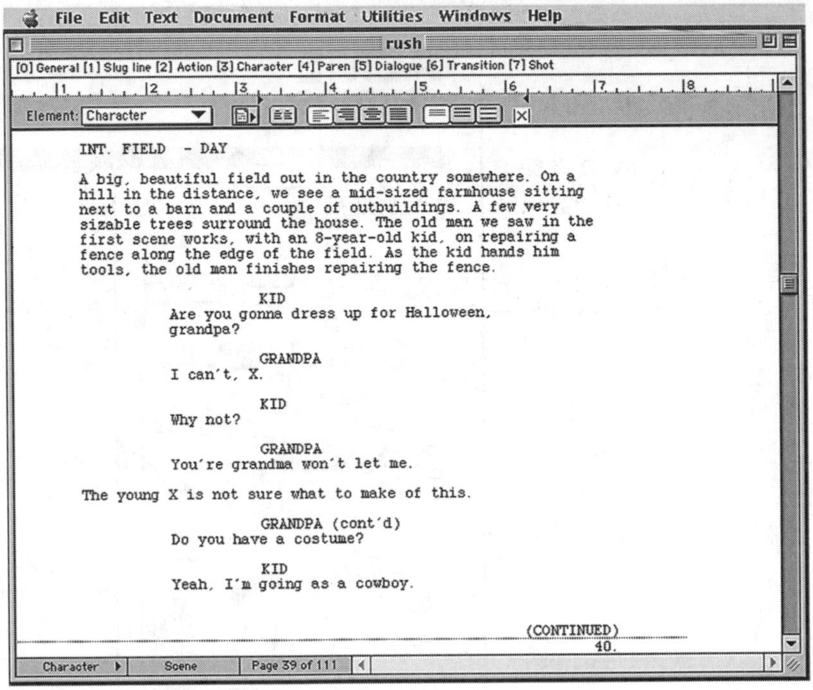

FIGURE 2.3 *Final Draft provides a complete, automated screenplay-writing environment. Character names, scene locations, and other repeating elements can be automatically entered by the program. Most importantly, Final Draft automatically indents and paginates your screenplay according to standard, accepted specifications.*

For A/V scripts, BC Software also sells *Final Draft A/V,* a program designed specifically for writing two-column scripts. In addition to the same automation features as Final Draft, Final Draft A/V also offers simple storyboard tools.

If you're already comfortable using Microsoft Word, you might consider *ScriptWizard* and *Side By Side,* add-on formatters that process your Microsoft Word files.

Before you make a final choice as to which program to use, consider that some packages work in tandem with other software to automate your budgeting and scheduling tasks. If you can afford it, it's worth considering packages that work together to create a complete pre-production toolbox.

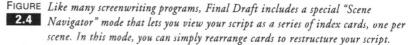

File   Edit   Text   Document   Format   Utilities   Windows   Help

Navigator - shuttle thing

Display Scenes

EXT. DESERT - NIGHT	EXT. SPACE CAMP - DAY	INT. CLASSROOM - DAY
Title: "One month later. Morocco." The camera pans across a BARREN DESERT LANDSCAPE swept with moonlight, finally arriving at a well-lit, smallish air force base. A small cluster of buildings--bristling with antenae and satellite dishes--sits beside a vast	A low-slung, school-yard-like complex is bordered by a parking lot over which the words "NASA Space Camp, Atlanta GA" are SUPERIMPOSED. PARKER: (voice over) Since I've only got one day here at the camp, I thought I'd cut to the chase...	At the front of a classroom of happy-looking teenage students stands Parker. Behind him, on a chalkboard, we see his name. He's got the kids eating out of his hand. PARKER: ...and show you one of NASA's most important secret documents.
They laugh PARKER: Now, this is good and gross and all but I brought The List because you guys think you want to be astronauts some day and you need to understand what being an astronaut is about. In 1986, there were 7 people who knew what it was about. And	INT. WOODS' CAR - DAY Woods and Parker are driving down a highway somewhere. Over the course of this conversation, they approach and enter an air force base. PARKER: This is crazy. We're not s'posed to go up for 18 months and now they want us to go in three? Why?	INT. BRIEFING ROOM - DAY Parker, Woods, Eastman, Dr. Something and three other people--STACK, a fit man of roughly the same age and build as Parker, BAKER a smaller, somewhat shy-looking man and MCCRAW, an attractive woman in her mid-30s--sit behind a table at a press conference. Behind and around them stand the usual
EXT. SERVICE ROAD - DAY A large NASA semi-truck, accompanied by several vans is making its way toward a building somewhere at Cape Canaveral. INSIDE THE TRUCK Baker and Parker ride in the cab along with the driver. Both men are sorting through handfuls of folders.	INT. BIO-LAB - DAY A huge, hectic lab full of shelves of experiments. Microscopes, beakers and all sorts of lab stuff are interspersed with terrariums full of frogs and insects. There's also a good amount of engineering going on. Guys working on frog feeding machines and special treadmills and pieces of equipment.	INT. UNDERWATER TRAINING FACILIT For practicing spacewalks and other zero-gravity activities, NASA uses a special facility containing a huge tank of water. In it, astronauts can practice tasks in a less-weighty environment. UNDERWATER we see two men in spacesuits surrounded

FIGURE
2.4
Like many screenwriting programs, Final Draft includes a special "Scene Navigator" mode that lets you view your script as a series of index cards, one per scene. In this mode, you can simply rearrange cards to restructure your script.

FINISHING UP

Eventually, after many rewrites, you'll have a "finished" script. (The script won't really be finished as you'll make loads of changes in production and post-production, but you'll at least have something you can use to start shooting.) Presumably you've already gotten some feedback at this point, either from friends, former friends, or relatives. Now you're ready to start thinking about assembling your cast and crew and, more importantly, raising money for your shoot.

Writing Software

In addition to screenwriting software, there are a number of other computer-based writing aids ranging from rhyming dictionaries to brainstorming tools. Check out www.dvhandbook.com/writingtools.html for comprehensive lists of screenwriting software and utility programs.

TIP

The Pitch
Unfortunately, you can't expect your script to speak for itself. Most potential backers and crew members won't have the time or patience to read an entire script, so you'll have to win them over through a good pitch. For more on pitches, check out www.dvhandbook.com/pitching.html.

Scheduling

Scheduling and budgeting are very closely related. In fact, because they are so intertwined, there's a saying in the entertainment industry: "Good, Fast, and Cheap: You can only have two of these things."

Assuming you want your project to be good (we hope!), then your production will have to be either slow or expensive. Are you going to choose *slow,* and have a three-month shoot that only takes place on weekends? Or are you going to take the *expensive* route and shoot for 14 consecutive days?

To succeed at the "good and fast" model, you'll need a full crew and all the equipment advantages possible. To succeed at the "good and cheap" model, you'll need the time to wait for free or cheap equipment and manpower.

In the simplest terms, your goal in creating a schedule is to keep from wasting your cast and crew's time (which equates to wasting your money). A good schedule is flexible and ensures maximum efficiency of shooting costs.

TIP

Don't Spend It All in One Place
If you know there are some scenes that you absolutely, under no circumstances, are willing to skimp on, then shoot those scenes first. Most likely, compromise will come because you're running low on money. With those crucial scenes in the can, you won't be tempted to alter them or scale them back when you start to run out of cash.

Chaos Theory

Perhaps the best way to understand how complicated a production schedule can be is by example. Consider the following production schedule scenario for a medium-budget DV production with a union cast and crew:

You're shooting a Western on location in Arizona. Everything's good to go, you've got a bunch of extras, four actors, and a union crew. After getting everyone from the airport to the location—which counts as a day of paid labor plus per diem money for cast and crew—you awake at your desert location the next day to a giant thunderstorm. It's short-lived, but now the dusty town isn't very dusty. Luckily you've prepared for just such an event by scheduling alternate "cover sets" throughout your shoot. So, you move everyone into the saloon to shoot the gambling scene. Unfortunately, you don't need your lead actress for this scene, but you'll have to pay her anyway, since anything less than a 10-day break is considered a "holding" day in a SAG (*Screen Actor's Guild*) agreement. To "hold" her, you'll have to pay her.

Because of the delays due to changing locations, you're only going to shoot one page of script instead of the three that you were aiming for that day. Also, you have a very early, 3:00 A.M. call tomorrow for some crew members, and you have to give them 10 hours of "turnaround"—the time between the "wrap" of one day's shoot and the "call" of the next day's shoot. This means your lighting crew and art department must leave the set at 5:00 P.M., to have enough turnaround time before you need them at 3:00 the next morning.

It's hectic, and you're patting yourself on the back for having it all under control, when your lead actor takes you aside and explains that shooting the gambling scene out of sequence is a big problem for him, motivation-wise, so he'd prefer to shoot the scene in the barn where he has a heart-to-heart talk with his horse. Unfortunately, the horses don't arrive until tomorrow.

SOMETHING OLD, SOMETHING NEW

Shooting schedules for feature films follow a formula developed long before the advent of computers. The shooting schedule provides a method for tracking a very large amount of information in a way that's modifiable and portable. You start by filling out script breakdown sheets, (Figure 2.5) and production strips (Figure 2.7). Production strips are then placed in a set of production boards (Figure 2.6). The result is a spreadsheet with rows of cast member names and other important elements and columns of scene information.

At the intersections of the rows and columns, each cast member can see which scenes they will be involved in, and when those scenes will be shot. The final set of production boards is a hard-backed folder that is taken onto the set for easy reference.

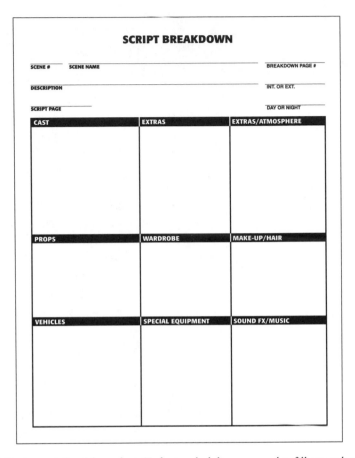

FIGURE   *A sample breakdown sheet. To begin scheduling, you need to fill out such a sheet*
2.5   *for each scene in your script (a template for this breakdown sheet is included on*
         The Digital Filmmaker's Handbook CD-ROM).

Using Movie Magic Scheduling Software

No matter what your project, film production scheduling software like Movie
Magic's *Scheduling* can be invaluable. Movie Magic Scheduling can import
properly formatted screenplays and automatically create breakdown sheets
(Figure 2.5) and production strips (Figure 2.7). You can print these strips out
and place them in special plastic sleeves for placement on your board. Screenplay Systems also makes production boards and paper for printing production
strips. Because each scene is on a separate strip, you can easily rearrange the

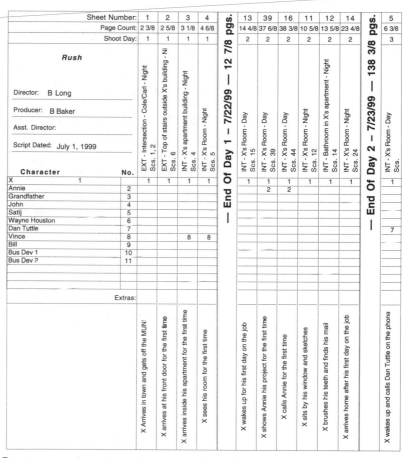

Sheet Number:	1	2	3	4		13	39	16	11	12	14		5
Page Count:	2 3/8	2 5/8	3 1/8	4 6/8		14 4/8	37 6/8	38 3/8	10 5/8	13 5/8	23 4/8		6 3/8
Shoot Day:	1	1	1	1	— End Of Day 1 — 7/22/99 — 12 7/8 pgs.	2	2	2	2	2	2	— End Of Day 2 — 7/23/99 — 138 3/8 pgs.	3
Rush Director: B Long Producer: B Baker Asst. Director: Script Dated: July 1, 1999	EXT - Intersection - Cole/Carl - Night Scs. 1, 2	EXT - Top of stairs outside X's building - Ni Scs. 6	INT - X's apartment building - Night Scs. 4	INT - X's Room - Night Scs. 5		INT - X's Room - Day Scs. 15	INT - X's Room - Day Scs. 39	INT - X's Room - Day Scs. 44	INT - X's Room - Night Scs. 12	INT - Bathroom in X's apartment - Night Scs. 14	INT - X's Room - Night Scs. 24		INT - X's Room - Day Scs.
Character No.													
X 1	1	1	1	1		1	1	1	1	1	1		1
Annie 2							2	2					
Grandfather 3													
John 4													
Satij 5													
Wayne Houston 6													
Dan Tuttle 7													7
Vince 8			8	8									
Bill 9													
Bus Dev 1 10													
Bus Dev 2 11													
Extras:	X Arrives in town and gets off the MUNI	X arrives at his front door for the first time	X arrives inside his apartment for the first time	X sees his room for the first time		X wakes up for his first day on the job	X shows Annie his project for the first time	X calls Annie for the first time	X sits by his window and sketches	X brushes his teeth and finds his mail	X arrives home after his first day on the job		X wakes up and calls Dan Tuttle on the phone

FIGURE
2.6   *A sample production board from a feature film created in Movie Magic
Scheduling. In a real production board, the strips would be color-coded as to
whether they were day or night, and would be placed in movable holders
mounted on a large strip board.*

scene order in the event an actor gets sick or a location gets rained out. Production boards allow for the sort of "thinking on your feet" that is always necessary during a shoot.

TIP

Scheduling According to Page Count
*Most shoots aim for a certain number of pages per day. Studio films often shoot
about two pages a day, whereas many independent filmmakers must opt for a less
luxurious schedule, shooting upwards of four pages a day. Of course this all depends on the content of the pages you are shooting. An effects-intensive scene will
require much more time than a dialogue scene*

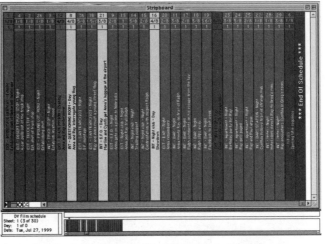

FIGURE *A set of production strips created in Movie Magic Scheduling.*
2.7

TIP

Pick-Ups
After you're done with your principal shoot, you may find that you need to reshoot or add new scenes. These "pick-ups" are usually shot after a first rough cut has been finished. Maybe there was a video drop-out in the only good take of a key scene, or maybe you decided that the way an actor played a scene isn't working. Most projects schedule a few days or a week for pick-ups to reduce the likelihood of cast and crew availability problems.

Good scheduling requires a lot of imagination. To be well-prepared, you need to envision all the possible things that might go wrong. Experience is the best tool for scheduling. In lieu of that, check out *www.dvhandbook.com/schedulingbooks* for a list of some very good books on production scheduling.

Budgeting

Budgeting any sort of film or video project is a complicated and time-consuming process that goes hand in hand with scheduling—you can't figure out how much your shoot will cost if you don't know how long it's going to take. Unfortunately, you don't know how much time you can afford if you don't know what your budget is. To get started, you'll need to create a preliminary budget to give you a ballpark figure of the kind of financing you need, and then a revised budget once you have an idea of the real amount of cash you'll have on hand. You'll need to prepare both your budget and schedule with the idea that unforseen circumstances—both good and bad—will require you to make a lot of changes. Unfortunately, budgeting is a complicated process and we can't cover it in-depth in this book. However, there are a lot of good books on the subject, and several of our favorite budgeting resources are listed at www.dvhandbook.com/budgeting. Fortunately, there's plenty of good software available to help ease your budgeting headaches (Figure 2.9).

BUDGETING SOFTWARE

Typically, budgeting programs are integrated with scheduling programs, and many can work in conjunction with screenwriting programs. Movie Magic Budgeting works in tandem with Movie Magic Scheduling, which can take a screenplay from Final Draft to create a set of breakdown sheets. You can then

Acct #	Category Title	Page			Total
02-00	WRITING	1			250
03-00	PRODUCER & STAFF	1			500
05-00	TALENT	1			123
	TOTAL ABOVE-THE-LINE				873
07-00	PRODUCTION STAFF	1			0
08-00	PRODUCTION DESIGN	1			1,000
10-00	SET OPERATIONS	2			6,088
11-00	CAMERA DEPARTMENT	2			5,100
12-00	SPECIAL EFFECTS	2			100
13-00	WARDROBE	3			250
14-00	MAKE-UP & HAIR	3			240
15-00	ELECTRICAL	3			4,420
16-00	TRANSPORTATION	3			540
17-00	LOCATION EXPENSES	4			700
18-00	PRODUCTION SOUND	4			1,370
19-00	VIDEOTAPE STOCK	4			200
	TOTAL PRODUCTION				20,008
20-00	EDITORIAL	4			15,460
21-00	MUSIC	5			100
22-00	POST-PRODUCTION SOUND	5			2,500
23-00	TITLES & GRAPHICS	5			0
24-00	SPECIAL EFFECTS	5			0
25-00	PICK-UPS	6			1,000
26-00	RELEASE PRINT	6			54,000
	TOTAL POST PRODUCTION				73,060
28-00	DISTRIBUTION COSTS	6			5,000
	TOTAL OTHER				5,000
	Total Below-The-Line				98,068
	Total Above and Below-The-Line				98,941
	Contingency				9,894
	Grand Total				108,835

FIGURE *A budget summary or "top sheet" for a $100,000 DV feature film.*
2.8

take these breakdown sheets and import them into Movie Magic Budgeting to create your categories and budget line items (Figure 2.9). The final budget for any feature film can run a pretty long page count; to give you an idea, we've included several sample budgets at www.dvhandbook.com.

Another advantage of Movie Magic Budgeting is a feature called *subgroups*. With subgroups, you can create three sample budgets based on different shooting media: 16mm film, BetacamSP, and DV. After entering budget figures for all three subgroups, you can choose one to be active. Movie Magic will then calculate the budget for that subgroup. The other subgroups will still be visible as gray text, but they won't factor into the budget totals. With this feature, you can have three potential budgets in one file until you determine what format you'll use to shoot your project (Figure 2.10).

Movie Magic Budgeting also helps you easily create a budget topsheet—a simple, easy-to-read summary of your budget that you can give to investors and include in proposals and pitches (Figure 2.8). On the other hand, if you're shooting a very low-budget production or one with less complicated budgeting concerns, then a simple spreadsheet program like Excel or even personal finance software like Quicken might be all you need.

Paying as You Go

Most filmmakers want to do just that: make a *film*. Unfortunately, shooting film is expensive. Shooting digital video with the idea of ultimately transferring to film is not necessarily any cheaper, but with DV you can "back-end" your costs. This means that the cost of your shoot is going to be much cheaper than a film shoot, since you won't be paying for film stock and processing. Your post-production will also be significantly cheaper because you won't have to pay for costly telecine sessions, lab fees, and negative cutting (all of which will be explained later).

The cost of your final delivery will vary, depending on the format of your end product. If your final output will simply be copies from your editing system, your cost will be little more than the price of the tapes. If you want higher-quality video output, you'll have to use a professional facility whose services cost around $20,000. If you want to release on film, a feature film release print could run upwards of $45,000.

In other words, if your end product is video, your budget will be significantly lower than shooting on film. If your end product is film, your overall budget might be about the same as if you'd shot on film, but your production

DVfilmbudget

Acct #	Category Title	Page		Total
07-00	PRODUCTION STAFF	1		0
08-00	PRODUCTION DESIGN	2		1,000
10-00	SET OPERATIONS	2		6,288
11-00	CAMERA DEPARTMENT	2		26,800
12-00	SPECIAL EFFECTS	2		100
13-00	WARDROBE	3		250
14-00	MAKE-UP & HAIR	3		240
15-00	ELECTRICAL	3		4,220
16-00	TRANSPORTATION	3		540
17-00	LOCATION EXPENSES	4		700
18-00	PRODUCTION SOUND	4		1,370
19-00	VIDEOTAPE STOCK	4		562
	TOTAL PRODUCTION			**42,070**

11-00 -- CAMERA DEPARTMENT

Acct #	Account Title			Total
11-01	Director of Photography			12,500
11-03	First Assistant Camera			7,200
11-05	Camera dept Production Asst.			2,000
11-06	Camera dept. expendables			100
11-07	Camera package purchase			5,000
	Total			**26,800**

11-01 -- Director of Photography

Description	Amount	Units	X	Rate	Subtotal
$2500/week - principal	4	weeks	1	2,500	10,000
1 week pick-ups	1	week	1	2,500	2,500
Total					**12,500**

FIGURE **2.9** *Three layers from a DV feature film budget created in Movie Magic Budgeting. (a) The budget topsheet with subtotals for the production section of the budget. (b) The next level down with details for the camera department budget. (c) Details about the director of photography's schedule and salary.*

budget will be much lower and you will need less money at the outset. You'll be able to shoot all or most of your project and possibly even do a rough cut or trailer, which you can then use to raise more money to finance a final transfer to film.

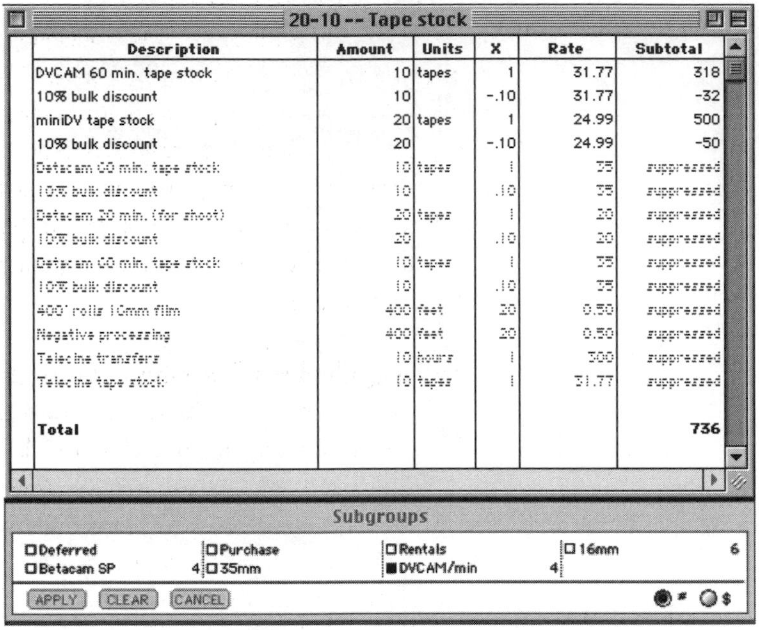

Description	Amount	Units	X	Rate	Subtotal
DVCAM 60 min. tape stock	10	tapes	1	31.77	318
10% bulk discount	10		-.10	31.77	-32
miniDV tape stock	20	tapes	1	24.99	500
10% bulk discount	20		-.10	24.99	-50
Betacam 60 min. tape stock	10	tapes	1	35	suppressed
10% bulk discount	10		.10	35	suppressed
Betacam 20 min. (for shoot)	20	tapes	1	20	suppressed
10% bulk discount	20		.10	20	suppressed
Betacam 60 min. tape stock	10	tapes	1	35	suppressed
10% bulk discount	10		.10	35	suppressed
400' rolls 16mm film	400	feet	.20	0.50	suppressed
Negative processing	400	feet	.20	0.50	suppressed
Telecine transfers	10	hours	1	300	suppressed
Telecine tape stock	10	tapes	1	31.77	suppressed
Total					**736**

Subgroups

| ☐ Deferred | ☐ Purchase | ☐ Rentals | ☐ 16mm | 6 |
| ☐ Betacam SP | 4 ☐ 35mm | ■ DVCAM/min | 4 | |

[APPLY] [CLEAR] [CANCEL]

FIGURE **2.10** *Screenplay Systems' Movie Magic Budgeting uses subgroups to help you try out different scenarios in a single budget file. In this figure, the tape stock portion of the budget is detailed with the DV subgroup active and the Betacam SP and 16mm subgroups grayed out.*

The low cost of DV effectively removes a lot of the financial risk in an independently funded project. If you don't succeed in finding a theatrical distributor for your film, you won't have to make a release print, thereby saving yourself about $45,000. You can still distribute your film on video for broadcast television, home video, or as a pitch reel for yourself as a director or your next project. If that sounds depressing, just think how much more depressing it would be if it had cost $80,000 instead of $15,000.

Even if you are planning on financing as you go, you still need to create a budget so that you know how much money you need/want. Then, as your project progresses, revise your budget for each phase of production as you learn what your financial assets will be. No matter how "no budget" your project, you should know the minimum dollar amount you need to get your project shot, whether it's $500 or $500,000.

BIG, BIGGER, OR BIGGEST

In Hollywood, "low-budget" means a total budget of $500,000 to $1,000,000; in other words, their idea of low isn't very low. But this is partly because these figures include the costs of paying union actors and crewmembers, and doing everything by the book. Budgets go even higher when you factor in publicity. Independent producers can get away with much less. Their budgets tend to fall into three categories: *no budget, ultra-low budget,* and the bottom end of *low budget.* You should determine where you want your project to fall before you start creating a budget.

> **No-budget budgets.** The history of independent productions is rife with examples of "creative" financing, from directors selling their bodies to science (Robert Rodriguez for "El Mariachi"), to directors charging productions on their credit cards (Robert Townsend for "Hollywood Shuffle"). Fortunately, with digital video technology, you don't necessarily have to resort to such extreme measures because your budget can be fairly small. Typically, low-budget DV productions will start at around $10,000 to $20,000, and will shoot on digital videotape with the goal of a tape finish. If you fall into this range, you'll most likely be using a small cast and crew, many of whom might be working for free or for deferred payment. You'll be back-ending your expenses in hopes of finding a distributor to pay for the tape-to-film transfer.

> **Ultra-low budgets.** Typically, ultra-low budget projects range from $50,000 to $300,000. Producers can afford to pay key crewmembers and actors. As a mid-range producer, you'll want to consider higher-quality formats such as DigiBeta or Betacam SP, or you might even be shooting 16 or 35mm film. If you're shooting film, your post-production will be more expensive because of lab costs and film-to-tape transfers. If you can afford it, you may want to hire more people and equipment to make your production take less time. As with no-budget productions, DV technology can help your ultra-low budget go farther, especially during post-production.

> **Low budgets.** If you're lucky enough to have access to half a million dollars or more, then you're in the realm of the "low" budget producers. For this kind of money, you've probably got an all-union crew complete with drivers and caterers, and you're most likely shooting on film, either 16mm or 35. However, DV can still play a big role in your pro-

duction and can still help you keep your budget down in post-production. If you can afford a high-quality film scan, you can bring in high-res scans of your film footage, perform sophisticated effects and composites in your computer, and then output your altered scenes back to film. High-quality film scanning and output can be expensive, but for some effects, the cost of scanning and printing will still be less than achieving effects through traditional methods. Many of the big-budget special effects you see at the movies are created on desktop computers and equipment easily affordable to the low-budget producer with the right talent at hand.

Ask and Ye Shall Receive
For his independent feature, π, Darren Aronofsky raised part of his budget by simply asking everyone he knew for 50 bucks. Then he asked some of his principal cast members to do the same. Although it was a simple idea, it wasn't long before he'd raised several thousand dollars. The lesson here is that there's no set way to raise money for your feature, and as we've seen in the past couple of years, a Hollywood-scale budget isn't always necessary for success.

Budgeting Can Be Fun

Budgeting and scheduling are more than just the process of determining costs and organizing your shoot; they are the blueprints for the creative part of making a film. Creating a budget is the first instance where you will take your script apart into all of its separate pieces and components. The scheduling breakdown process is where you will begin to make your first creative decisions about your script. From choosing locations and design elements (choices that usually require a balance of desire against cost), to types of equipment and number of crew members, the decisions you make during pre-production will determine everything from the look of your sets to the types of shots and effects you can achieve. The rest of this book should give you a good idea as to what will be different about using DV technology versus film or analog video in terms of equipment and workflow. With a little technical knowledge, you'll be able to make good budgetary and scheduling decisions throughout the filmmaking process.

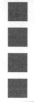

CHAPTER

3

Previsualization

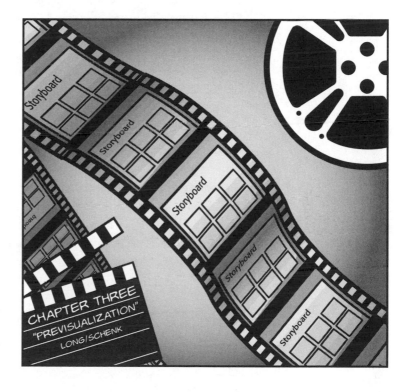

IN THIS CHAPTER

- Storyboarding
- Location Scouting
- Production Design
- Video Storyboards

Y ou may have heard stories about how Alfred Hitchcock meticulously planned which cars would drive by in the background of some of his scenes. Or perhaps you've read about the maniacal detail that Stanley Kubrick demanded in any of his productions. You can argue at length about whether such concern contributes to the viewer's experience, but there's a another lesson to be learned from both examples: Prepare!

As a director, you're responsible for everything the viewer sees on screen, whether it's good or bad. With a little preparation, you can improve your odds that the viewer is seeing something good.

Your main tool for preparing for your shoot is the *storyboard*. Because storyboarding requires you to perform the first serious visualization of your project, the storyboarding process forces you to answer some questions that you may not have dealt with during the writing of your script. From choosing locations to the look of your production to how your project will be edited, storyboarding is where you'll make many practical decisions about how you'll shoot your script. Furthermore, storyboarding will force you to think of your script as a series of images. Because images are the essence of cinema, the sooner you start planning your visuals, the better off you'll be.

TIP

Coverage
The term coverage *refers to how much cover footage you shoot for a particular scene. No matter how much you plan, you can't always think of everything. Once you start editing, you may realize that the way you had originally conceived a shot doesn't work. If you were fortunate to have shot a number of takes—some from different angles—then you can find a way to use this extra cover footage to get a good edit.*

Storyboarding

Storyboards are comic-book like representations of the images in your production (Figure 3.1). How well they're drawn and what they look like doesn't matter, just as long as they convey to you and your crew a reasonable

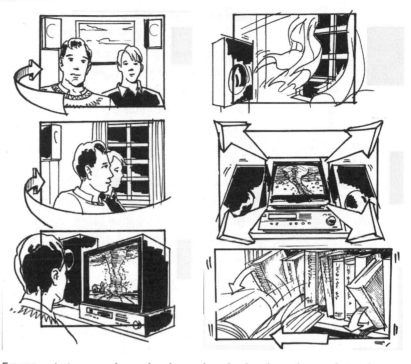

FIGURE
3.1   *A picture can be worth a thousand words when drawn by a professional story-*
       board artist.

approximation of how the composition, framings, and cuts in your production
will play out. The amount of detail in your storyboards will depend on the
type of scene you are creating. For a scene of three people talking around a dinner table, your storyboards will probably be less detailed and will serve more
to help you plan framing and cutting. For a special effects-heavy shot of a
spaceship flying into a spaceport on a faraway, alien world, your storyboards
will include more detail to help your art department and visual effects crews
plan and prepare for their work.

It doesn't necessarily matter if you shoot exactly what you planned in your
storyboards. More important is the information that you will learn while storyboarding. Until you meticulously start to plan things on paper, you may not
know how much *coverage* you need for a particular shot, or that you're going
to need a particular set piece or prop.

Whether or not you choose to draw storyboards, you still need to go
through a "storyboarding" process. That is, you need to methodically plan the

visual images and details that you will use to create your final product. This planning ranges from deciding how to frame and shoot a scene, to choosing a location, cast, set, and props for your shoot.

As you've probably already guessed, there are a number of software packages that can help you create storyboards. Before we get to those, however, let's take a quick look at some of the other tasks that will be part of your pre-production visualization.

LOCATION SCOUTING

The locations and sets on which you choose to shoot will convey some of the most vital visual information in your story. Sometimes, set and location will convey even more than your script or your actors.

There's no real rule for finding a location, you simply have to get out of the house and start looking around. There are, however, some things to remember and some questions to ask when looking for and selecting a location. And, depending on the type of equipment you will be using, your location needs may vary. Consider the following when scouting locations:

- **Is the location available?** Obviously, you'll have to talk to the owners and see if you can work a deal—either for cash or donations of improvements to the property.
- **Do you need both the inside and outside?** You can always shoot your interiors on a set, or in a building to which you have better, less expensive access. Storyboard carefully for these situations.
- **Can you find the same type of location in a cheaper town?** The inside of an office is the inside of an office. See if you can find office space nearby, but in a cheaper location.
- **Is the location a reasonable distance from the rest of your shoot?** Lugging equipment, cast, and crew to faraway locations can quickly become prohibitively expensive, particularly on a union shoot.
- **Does the location require redressing or modification?** Removal of signs, addition of new signs, changing the look or "period" of the environs. This can be done through practical set dressings or through digital "dressing" and post-processing.
- **Does the location afford the coverage you need?** If the shots you plan on shooting require many different angles, you'll need to consider your location carefully. For example, though your location may look great, be

Film Crew in the 'Hood

For his movie "Do the Right Thing," Spike Lee made major modifications to an entire city block in Brooklyn. With a clear idea of the storefronts he needed for his set—as well as their proximity to each other—his set designers set about modifying existing buildings to fit his needs. In addition to getting the individual storefronts he needed, he got all of the "in-between" locations (sidewalks, street corners, etc.), and all within walking distance of each other. In the process of preparing the set, his location security guards cleared out and renovated a crack house, a set change that, obviously, made a lasting improvement in the neighborhood.

sure you can you shoot it from multiple angles and reverse angles without getting unwanted scenery (Figure 3.2a-c).

- **Similarly, make sure your location has the physical space required for the size of your shoot.** In addition to your equipment, don't forget the support needs of your crew (trucks, catering, porta-toilets, etc.) (Figure 3.3).

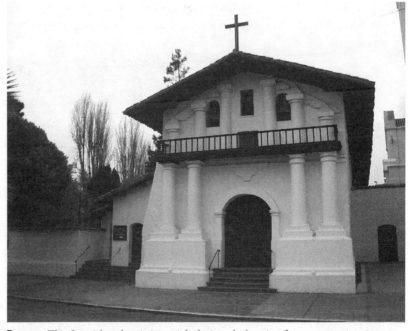

FIGURE
3.2a
This Spanish-style mission might be just the location for some exteriors in your turn-of-the-century drama . . .

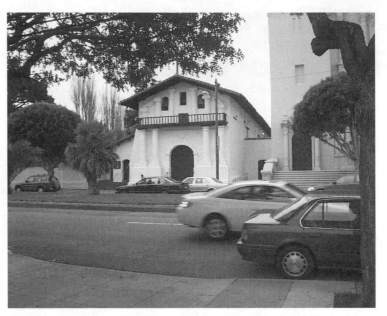

FIGURE   *. . . unfortunately, it sits on a very busy, four-lane thoroughfare, which*
3.2b   *will make shooting clean audio very difficult . . .*

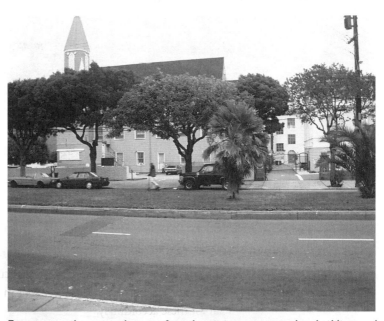

FIGURE   *. . . also, across the street from the mission are very modern buildings and*
   parking lots, which will make reverse angles difficult. (On the other hand, this
location—San Francisco's Mission Dolores—was good enough for Hitchcock! He
featured it prominently in Vertigo. Of course, it wasn't a period piece, and
there was much less traffic in 1958.)

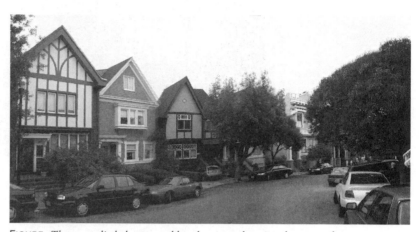

FIGURE **3.3** *These cozy little houses could make a great location; however, the narrow street could make things difficult if you're expecting to use a large crew. Also, clearing the street of cars could require expensive city permits, making what seemed like a cheap location into a big expense.*

- **Does the location have access to sufficient practical resources such as power?** Remote locations pose other logistical problems, such as access to restrooms and refrigeration.
- **Is the location too noisy?**
- **What are the location requirements of your equipment?** If you are shooting at night, you may be able to get away with more or less lighting depending on the type of camera you are using. Also, video cameras can have difficulty dealing with certain repeating patterns and textures. Closely spaced horizontal or vertical lines can create annoying interference patterns on your screen. Does your location contain such textures? If so, can you shoot around them?
- **Don't forget about light and sound.** Can you adequately light and mic your location for the needs of your particular equipment? Different cameras and formats have different needs in regard to light and sound. Plan for these accordingly.
- **Can you improve the authenticity of your set with sound effects?** Adding some simple ambient sounds to a shot—adding the cries of a circus barker to a shot of a tent, for example—can improve the authenticity of your set.

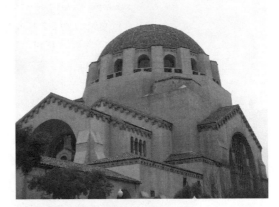

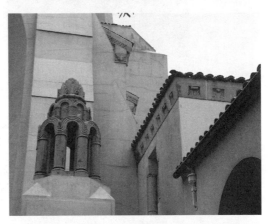

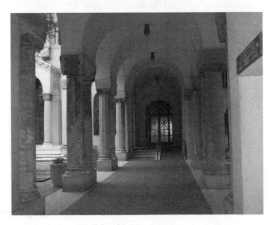

FIGURE   *A few well-planned establishing shots combined with the right audio can*
3.4a-c   *quickly establish a Mid-Eastern location . . .*

- **Can you fake it?** Cutting from a good, convincing establishing shot of a sun-dappled vineyard with appropriate ambient sound effects to an interior set that's been properly decorated might be all you need to make your audience believe that you paid for a long shoot in the hills of Tuscany (Figure 3.4a-d).

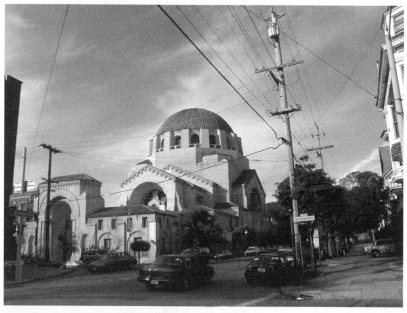

FIGURE   *. . . when, in fact, you've only gone as far as a busy American street corner.*
3.4d

Talk to your principal crew members when scouting locations. Does the production designer agree with your assessment of the feel of the set? Can he or she dress it accordingly? Does the cinematographer feel he or she can shoot it in the way that you want? And can it be done affordably? Does your gaffer think the set can be outfitted? Careful storyboarding will be help you explore these issues and formulate questions to present to your crew.

PRODUCTION DESIGN

The visualization/storyboarding phase is your chance to work with your crew to create the "look" of your movie—from the look of the objects, set, and cast, to the way the movie will be shot and cut, a process also known as "production design."

Whether you do it yourself or attach a professional production designer to your project, defining the look is more than just creating a style, it's a chance to explore how all of the elements at your disposal can be used to strengthen your visual image and, consequently, your story. (For more about production design and art direction, see also Chapter 8.)

CREATING THE STORYBOARD

What and how you choose to storyboard depends largely on the nature of your script. For dialog-heavy scenes, storyboarding is less crucial—simply storyboard a few scenes to get a feel for the location and pacing. For action scenes, you'll want to include details such as the duration of each cut (or special effects sequence) and detailed explanations of how fast objects will be moving and in what direction. You might also want more detail in any type of scene where you need to convey visual details to production designers and set builders.

In addition to visualizing the movement of your camera, you'll also use storyboards to explore the motion of elements within your scene. For complicated effects or action shots, your storyboards will be your first opportunity to choreograph your scenes.

Camera Angles

Here's a list of the types of shots or camera angles you can use to compose a scene. Figure 3.5 shows samples of each type of shot, and how you might represent such shots, framings, and cuts within your storyboards.

Master shot. A master shot is a relatively wide, static shot that covers all the action in a scene. Often it is used more as a "safety" shot or a back-up in case the planned coverage doesn't work. Master shots "establish" the scene—its location, participants, and tone. They are what gives the viewer their first, big hit of information in a scene.

2-shot. A shot used to cover a dialogue scene between two actors. Both actors are visible, usually from mid-torso up.

Over-the-shoulder (OS). Also used to cover dialogue scenes between two actors. The shot focuses on one actor but contains the silhouette or partial view of the second actor in the foreground.

FIGURE   *Camera angles.*
3.5

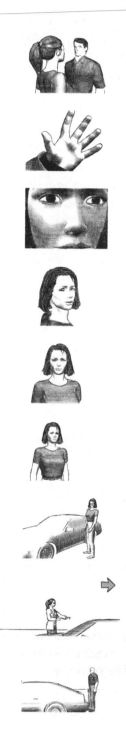

Reverse. A view 180 degrees from the previous shot. Usually used in combination with a Point of View shot or an Over the Shoulder shot.

Point of view (POV). A shot where the camera shows the point of view of one of the characters. Often a dolly move.

Extreme close up (ECU). A very tight close-up, such as a shot of someone's eyes or a bug on his or her nose.

Close-up (CU). A tight shot where the subject fills the whole frame. If the subject is a person, a shot of his or her head.

Medium close-up (MCU). A slightly wider shot than a close-up. Usually like a sculptured "bust"; i.e., head, neck, shoulder, upper torso.

Medium shot (MS). On a person, usually a waist up view.

Wide shot (WS). A shot that shows a whole area, usually full-figure in the case of people.

Tracking (or dolly). A moving shot that uses a camera dolly (a wheeled cart that travels along special tracks) to push the camera through the scene. Often an opening shot or a POV. Depending on how they're designed, dolly shots can travel from side to side or forward and back.

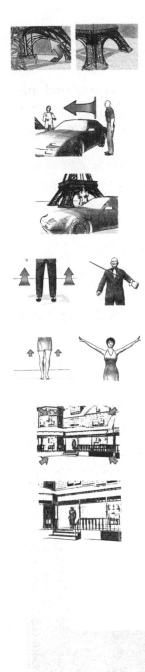

Crane. A moving shot that uses a camera crane to move the camera through the air, allowing movement on an X-Y-Z axis.

Pan. A side-to-side movement of the camera, where the camera rotates around its base. The resulting motion is what you would see if you stood in one place and turned your head from side to side. Often used to follow a figure across frame.

Tilt. Similar to a pan, but the camera tilts up and down. Analogous to tilting your head up or down. Usually used to reveal something, like a character who has just ripped his or her pants.

Pedestal. Raising or lowering the camera, usually by adjusting the tripod on which the camera is mounted. Creates a "rising periscope" point of view. Very rarely used in features.

Zoom. A lens movement from a tight to a wide shot (zoom out), or a wide to a tight shot (zoom in).

Dolly counter zoom. A shot where a dolly and a zoom are performed at the same time. In the resulting shot, the framing of the image stays the same, but the depth of field changes dramatically. Objects in the background foreshorten and appear to float backward. The most famous example is in "Jaws," when Roy Scheider sees the shark in the water on the crowded beach. His POV of the shark is a dramatic dolly counter zoom.

Slow reveal. Usually a pan, tilt, or dolly that reveals something that at first wasn't apparent. A woman laughs at a table, pan over to reveal that her husband has just spilled his wine.

COMPUTER-GENERATED STORYBOARDS

Programs like *Storyboard Artist* and *Storyboard Quick* provide simple drawing tools and libraries of characters, props, sets, and camera motion symbols that allow you to create storyboards quickly and easily. Though they may not look as good as hand-drawn storyboards drawn by a professional storyboard artist, these programs provide many advantages over handmade storyboards. With their object-oriented nature, storyboarding programs make it simple to pick up objects and move them around, providing for easier revisions.

If you've already scouted and found some of your locations, you can shoot photos and import them into your storyboard program, letting you create storyboards containing images of your actual locations. Some programs even let you add sound and define sequences to create slide-shows complete with dialog from your actual cast (Figure 3.6).

Of course, there's no reason you can't use your favorite image editor or paint program to create your storyboards. Whether you draw directly into the computer, or work on paper and then scan your drawings, preparing final storyboards in a program like Photoshop will let you easily create mixes of location photos, and simple sketches or clip art.

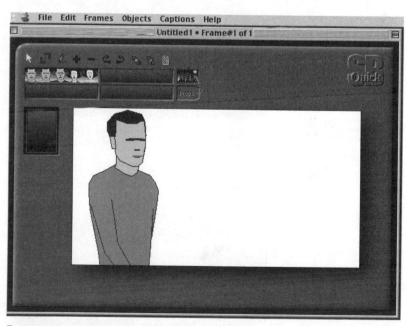

FIGURE *The Storyboard Quick interface.*
3.6

MetaCreations' *Poser* is a very good tool for storyboarding, visualization, and planning. With Poser, you can quickly and easily create 3D figures, props, and sets that can be posed and manipulated to create complex choreographies and scenes. Because you can move your camera and characters in true 3D space, you can view your scene from different angles to block character and camera position as well as choreography. If your set designers have been designing or modeling in a 3D package, you can import their set models into Poser to better visualize your scene (Figure 3.7).

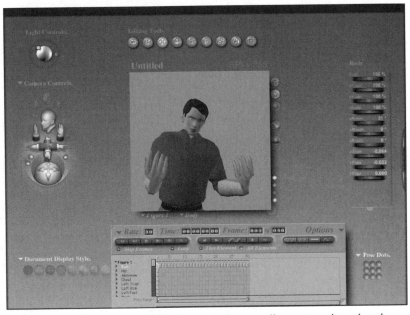

FIGURE *Poser 4 lets you pose and block scenes to create still or animated storyboards.*
3.7

Less Is More

Remember, storyboards are a visualization tool, not an end product. If you show crew members detailed, photorealistic storyboards, they'll be inclined to think that those images are what your final scene will look like. Better to give designers, costumers, set builders, and actors rough, sketchy storyboards. Let them use their expertise to design and create the details that they're responsible for.

If you are shooting photographs, scanning pictures, or creating 3D renderings, look for ways to simplify your pictures. Many 3D programs, including Poser, offer special "toon" rendering modes that will render your images as cartoony outlines with flat color fills. These are ideal for storyboarding. For scanned photographs, try using Adobe Photoshop's *Graphic Pen* or *Photocopy* filters to reduce your images to black-and-white, "sketchier" renderings.

ANIMATICS

Moving, animated storyboards, or "animatics," are a great—sometimes essential—way to plan complex action and motion. Animatics can provide good visual references for everyone, from designers to effects crews to actors. For example, you can use a program like Poser to create animatics that can be shown to actors and crew and that can even be used as placeholder video while you're editing.

If your feature will require complex effects shots such as 3D animation or compositing, talk with your effects crew about building your animatics in a way that can be reused later. For example, if your 3D team is building complex choreographies for animatics, maybe they can reuse the same files as the starting point for their final renderings.

CREATING VIDEO STORYBOARDS

If a paper storyboard is not enough for you to work out your visualizations, consider using any kind of video camera to create video storyboards.

Gather your cast in a rehearsal space, grab some props and set pieces if you can find them (and if not, pantomime will do just fine), and begin to block and stage some scenes. This will give your cast a chance to rehearse, and help your director and cinematographer work out details of lighting and shooting.

If you have access to equipment for digitizing this footage, go ahead and perform some rough edits. These rough takes can be much more than work copies: If you save your edit project files, you can later swap out this rough footage for your real footage and not have to re-edit.

CREATING ROUGH EFFECTS SHOTS

If your feature will contain complex effects shots—battling spaceships, giant flying insects, waving computer-generated cornfields—you'll want to start preparing such shots early in production. There's no reason you can't have your effects department quickly rough-out low-res, low-detail animations that can serve as animated storyboards. With these rough animations, you can more easily plan and direct shots. Having low-res proxy footage also means that you can go ahead and start editing before your final effects are rendered.

Summary

Filmmakers have always had to engage in meticulous planning before rolling their cameras. As a DV filmmaker, you have a decided advantage. With digital tools for storyboarding, you can more easily try out different visualizations. And, with digital editing, your storyboards, animatics, and early work files can actually be repurposed to save time in your final post-production. These are all topics we'll discuss in more detail later. And, these are all processes that require a lot of hardware. Choosing the right equipment will be your next task.

CHAPTER

Choosing a Videotape Format

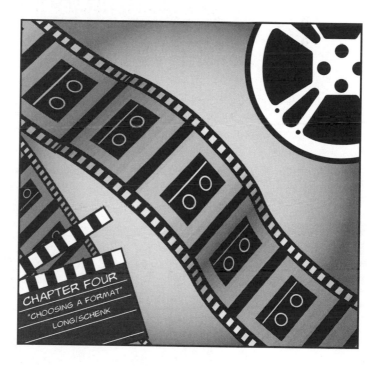

CHAPTER FOUR
"CHOOSING A FORMAT"
LONG/SCHENK

IN THIS CHAPTER

- Delivery Is Everything
- Video Basics
- Video Format Features
- Videotape Formats

If you don't already own digital video equipment, you're going to have to choose a video format. You may have thought you'd already done this—after all, you've decided to shoot digital video, right? Unfortunately, the digital video world has become increasingly complicated over the last few years as more and more hardware companies have released more and more formats (Figure 4.1).

If you already own—or have access to—equipment that you plan to use for your production, then your format choice has been made by default. However, it's still important to understand the workings of your format so that you can avoid its limitations. Also, just because you've decided to shoot on one format, doesn't mean you won't have to use some others during your production. From creating VHS copies for test screenings and promotion, to dubbing to high-end formats for transfer to film, you may end up using two or three formats before you deliver your final product.

If you've already chosen a format, you might be tempted to skip some of the technical discussions introduced in this chapter. However, because many of

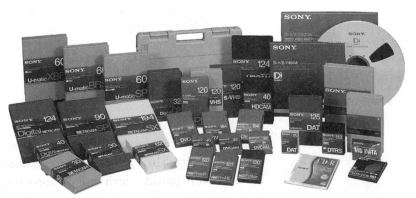

 FIGURE 4.1   *A quick glance at the Sony family of tapes gives an indication of the number of tape formats that exist today. This photo also includes audio tape formats.*

these concepts and terms will come up during production, we recommend that you at least skim this chapter.

Delivery Is Everything

Before you look at formats, it's important to know what your end product is going to be. A projected feature film? A home video release? A Webcast? Delivery medium is an important consideration when choosing a format, as some formats are better-suited to certain types of delivery.

You might be thinking "I'll just shoot the best quality that I can and then I'll be able to adapt my project to any medium." Unfortunately, for any number of technical (and financial) reasons, this is not a practical way to think. It's better to make some decisions now about delivery so that you can choose the highest quality, most-affordable format for your intended delivery medium.

Web/Multimedia

The compressed video that is used for Web and multimedia projects is very low quality, but this doesn't mean that you should just get that old VHS camcorder out of the closet and start shooting. Although low quality, Web video is still good enough to reveal artifacts such as light flares and noise. Similarly, if you're planning on night shoots or special effects such as blue-screen compositing, you will need a higher-quality format. And, shooting better quality affords you the option of repurposing your footage later.

Home Video

If you're planning a "straight-to-video" release, or are preparing a corporate presentation or trade show video, you can count on your project being distributed and viewed on VHS. This means that you can get away with shooting in any tape format that's better than VHS; that is, all of them. As with Web video, you'll need to pick a quality that suits the type of shooting you plan on doing.

Broadcast Television

Although almost any of today's digital formats pass the muster for being broadcast, broadcasters all have different criteria for what they will accept. In general, you will have to provide a high-quality master, usually Digital Betacam or D2 with a stereo audio mix. In addition, you'll probably have to provide additional copies with special audio tracks. Depending on the network you're producing for, you'll be required to deliver either a digital videotape output from a non-linear editing system like Avid's Media Composer or a videotape Master created in a linear (digital or analog) online session. We'll discuss the details of these processes in Chapter 18.

Projection

Any format can be used for projection, but there is one important thing to keep in mind: People will be seeing your video footage at 10 to 50 times the size of your video monitor. Noise and digital compression artifacts can be enlarged to the size of someone's head. Consequently, you should try to work at the highest quality you can afford.

TIP

Digital Projection

High-end digital projection systems are being developed with the eventual goal of replacing film projection in theaters. Although it's probably too early to be considering digital projection, if you have a project that you know will be projected digitally, you'll want to be very careful about shooting with narrow depth of field and pay close attention to any special effects compositing, as these factors are frequently criticized in digital projection screenings.

If you ultimately want your project to be projected from a film projector—in a movie theater, ideally—your final video will have to be transferred to film. Because of the technical concerns around video-to-film transfer, choice of format is very important. We'll cover these issues in more detail later in this chapter.

TRYING TO CHOOSE

Once you have a better idea of how you will deliver your final product, you can begin to think about the best video format for the job. Whether or not you already have equipment, an understanding of the workings of digital video formats will make much of your work easier. That understanding begins with a discussion of some video basics.

Video Basics

Although digital tape specs are much different from analog specifications, digital videotapes have a lot in common with the analog tapes of old. Just like audio tape, videotape works by manipulating magnetic particles that are suspended in a medium applied to a thin piece of celluloid.

And, as with analog formats, the head of a digital tape deck is actually a metal housing that contains multiple record and playback heads. Videotape is pulled out of the tape cassette and wrapped part-way around this spinning housing. Wear on the tape caused by rubbing it against spinning metal is one of the things that causes *dropouts* and other image degradations.

Currently, the video that feeds your TV—whether broadcast through the air or fed from a video deck—is *interlaced*. For each frame of video, your TV first displays all of the even-numbered scan lines—from top to bottom—and then goes back and fills in all the odd-numbered scan lines. Interlacing was invented in the early days of television as a way to stop the image from flickering.

Your computer monitor—and many new digital television formats—uses *progressive scan*. They actually draw each line, in order, from top to bottom. This results in a cleaner-looking image and, potentially, higher resolution. We'll discuss progressive scanning as it relates to cameras in Chapter 6 (Figure 4.2).

Making Tracks
Like analog tape, the information stored on a digital tape is laid down in separate "tracks" along the tape. For more on the type and arrangement of digital video tracks, take a look at www.dvhandbook.com/tracks.html.

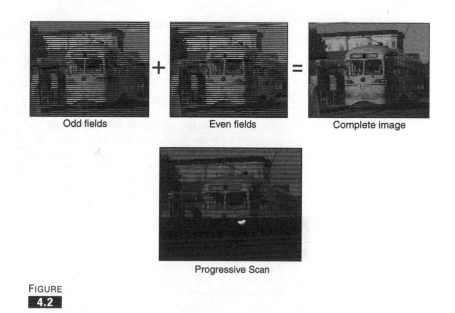

Odd fields   +   Even fields   =   Complete image

Progressive Scan

FIGURE
4.2

VIDEO STANDARDS

Unfortunately, we now have to tell you the big lie of digital video: it's really analog.

Okay, we're being dramatic, but, ultimately, all video gets turned into an analog signal because that's the type of signal your TV understands. So, even though your deck and camera may be storing information digitally, that information is converted to an analog signal before it's ever broadcast through the air (as from a TV station) or sent through a wire (as from a VCR) to your television.

There are different standards for these analog signals (Table 4.1). When your digital video camera plays to your television, it converts its digital signals into the standard *analog* signal that your TV understands. *NTSC* is the standard in the U.S. and Japan, while *PAL* is the standard for video in most of the rest of the world (*SECAM* is used in France, Russia, and Asia).

NTSC video consists of 525 interlaced scan lines running at 29.97 frames per second. PAL is slightly higher resolution with 625 interlaced scan lines, and it runs at 25 frames per second. PAL also uses a better method of handling color.

Most likely, you'll choose the standard that is used wherever you live. Obviously, if you live in the U.S. but are producing a video for distribution in the U.K., you should work in PAL. However, no matter where you live, you might want to consider PAL if your ultimate goal is a transfer to film.

At 25 frames per second, PAL video is much closer to film's 24 fps rate than is NTSC. This will make for easier transfer to film, with fewer motion artifacts. And, PAL's higher quality will result in a better film image than NTSC.

On the downside, all your equipment has to conform to the video standard you've chosen. So, if you choose PAL, you'll have to buy PAL-compatible

TABLE 4.1   **Different television standards have different frame rates, numbers of scan lines, and horizontal line resolutions. We've included relevant film specs for the sake of comparison.**

Standard	NTSC	PAL	HDTV	Film
Frame rate	29.97	25	24 or 30	24
Fields	2 fields	2 fields	No fields	No fields
Vertical res.	525	625	1080	N/A
Scanning method	Interlaced	Interlaced	Progressive	N/A
Aspect ratio	1.33:1	1.33:1	16:9 or 1.78:1	1.33:1*

* 35mm film has an aspect ratio of 1.85:1 when projected.

monitors, decks, digitizing equipment, and editing software. This is no big deal if you live in a country where PAL is the standard. But if you don't, finding equipment and the general cost and hassle of using a different standard may be a hurdle.

Digital Television

If you've got a lot of money, your choice of standard is a bit more complicated, as you might want to choose one of the new digital TV standards. *DTV* is confusing because there are so many different formats, specifications, and names that all fall under the "digital television" umbrella. "DTV" includes ATV (Advanced Television), a transmission system for broadcast; HDTV (High Definition Television), a subset of DTV; and SDTV (Standard Definition Television), a digital broadcast standard for existing analog video.

If you're going to try to shoot in a DTV format, it will most likely be HDTV, which has a resolution of 1920×1080 pixels with a 16:9 aspect ratio and either 24 or 30 progressive scan frames per second.

Expect to see more HDTV projects as we near the 2006 F.C.C. deadline when all U.S. broadcasters are required to switch from NTSC to DTV. HDTV's advantage to a project with a film finish is its higher quality and 16:9 aspect ratio, which is closer to that of wide-screen film.

TIP

Changing Your Video Standard
It is possible to convert from one standard to another, either through expensive tape-to-tape conversions, or through special software. However, changing standards in the middle of a project is going to cost time, money, and possibly image quality.

TIMECODE

One of the most common questions about video is, "why is timecode so important?"

If you've ever scrolled through a six-hour VHS tape looking for that TV show you missed a couple of weeks ago, you can appreciate the value of timecode. As you might have noticed, every time you remove the tape or turn the power off on your home VHS deck, the time counter resets itself to zero. As you scroll forward through a few hours' worth of tape, the counter advances as expected. But, if you eject the tape and then put it back in, the counter will read zero, *even though the tape is wound forward to the two-hour mark!*

With timecode, if you're two hours into the tape when you insert it, the counter on the deck will read two hours. Or, if you're two hours, ten minutes, three seconds, and twenty frames into the tape, the counter will read 02:10:03:20. Every time the counter displays that number, you'll see the exact same image. Not only does this make it easier for you and your NLE to find stuff on your tapes, it also makes it possible for the video deck to access any individual frame on the tape. Such fine control means you can accurately insert scenes onto any point on the tape.

Timecode allows you to reconstruct your edited work at any time. For moving a project from one computer to another, recreating a project after a computer crash, or performing a higher-quality "online" editing session, timecode is essential. (We'll talk more about online editing in Chapters 12 and 18). That said, here are some further clarifications about timecode.

Choosing a Brand of Tape

Although heady engineer types can spend hours arguing the merits of particular brands of videotape, odds are the average user won't be able to tell the difference (between tapes, not heady engineers). Your camera manufacturer probably recommends that you use their specially manufactured tapes. Although this may seem like a scam to sell videotape, using your camera maker's tapes is probably not a bad idea. Because they know the exact chemistry of their tape, they can engineer heads that respond better to their unique tape formulation.

Some people claim that certain brands of tape contain lubricants that can react chemically to the lubricants in your camera, or from other tapes, and gum up your camera. We have seen no compelling evidence for this, but you can safely eliminate this concern by consistently using tapes of the same brand.

For the most part, the difference between cheap and expensive tape is only a few dollars per cassette. Because you'll only get one shot at some scenes in your feature, don't scrimp—go ahead and pay the extra few dollars.

Drop Frame versus Non-Drop Frame

Because the frame rate of NTSC video is an odd 29.97 frames per second, *drop frame timecode* was developed to help round off the fractional frames to less awkward whole numbers. With drop frame timecode, the frame itself is not dropped, just the number in the counter. In other words, the frame rate is still 29.97 fps, but the counter is counting at 30 fps.

Drop frame timecode is usually indicated with semicolons separating the hours, minutes, seconds, and frames, so one hour is 1;00;00;00. Non-drop frame timecode is indicated by colons, so one hour is 1:00:00:00. Unfortunately, this is not a standardized feature, and not all VTRs display timecode in this manner.

Drop frame timecode is the standard for broadcast television in America, but if your project somehow ends up being non-drop frame, don't panic—just make a note on your tape. Whether you choose to work in drop frame or non-drop frame doesn't matter. Just make sure everyone working on the project is aware of which one you're using.

Types of Video Timecode

There are several standards of timecode, and a deck or camera can only read timecode that it has been designed to understand.

- **SMPTE** timecode is the professional industry standard set up by the Society of Motion Picture and Television Engineers (SMPTE). All professional equipment can read SMPTE timecode, so if you need to work with existing professional equipment, you'll need to use SMPTE timecode.
- **DV timecode** is the format developed for the DV format. If you plan on using *only* DV-format equipment, DVTC will be an acceptable alternative to SMPTE timecode. As the popularity of the DV formats increase, DVTC is becoming more integrated into the realm of professional video editing equipment.
- **RCTC** (Rewriteable Consumer Time Code) is a format Sony developed for use with consumer Hi8 equipment. As with DVTC, if you are planning on remaining in an RCTC equipment environment, it should serve its purpose well, but, unlike DVTC, you'll have a hard time finding any support for RCTC outside your own editing system.

Where the Timecode Is Stored on the Videotape

Timecode can be stored in a number of physical locations on a videotape: on the **address track,** on an **audio track,** or as **window burn** (sometimes called "vis" code), which is a visible counter that is superimposed over your video. The address track is the preferred place to store timecode—it's invisible, accurate, and leaves all the audio tracks available for audio. Audio track timecode offers a way to add SMPTE timecode to a tape that doesn't have an address track, such as VHS tape. Or, if you're using a DV tape and need SMPTE timecode, but don't want to corrupt the native DVTC timecode track, audio track timecode allows you to have both.

Window burn timecode (Figure 4.3) is usually reserved for work copies of master tapes. Some producers make VHS viewing copies of their camera original tapes with window burn timecode that matches the source masters' timecode for logging and taking notes on a VHS deck away from the editing room.

Most digital video formats uses address track timecode, but, in special situations, you might need to resort to window burn or audio track timecode. We'll discuss these situations later in the book.

Timecode for Film Sources

Film has different methods for keeping track of time: keycode and Aaton timecode. **Keycode** refers to a number on each frame of the film itself that is put there by the film lab. When a film-to-video (or telecine) transfer is made, you

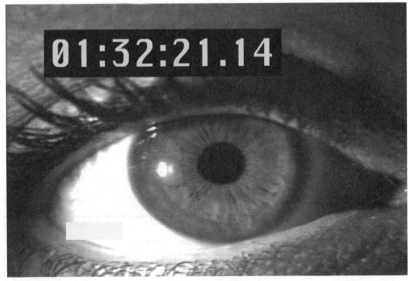

FIGURE   *A video image with window burn SMPTE timecode.*
4.3

can have the keycode numbers added to your videotapes in the form of window burn. Since this code is permanently superimposed over the video, this option is only viable if you are planning to eventually go back to film. **Aaton timecode** is an electronic timecode for film developed by the camera manufacturer Aaton. Electronic pulses are stored on the film itself and can be added to telecine transfers as window burn timecode. The *only* reason you need to keep track of keycode or Aaton timecode is if you shot on film with the idea of finishing on film.

3:2 Pulldown

If you're not going to be transferring film to video, you don't need to worry about 3:2 pulldown. 3:2 pull-down refers to the way that 24 fps film footage is transferred to 30 fps (i.e., 60 fields per second) NTSC videotape. The first frame of film is "pulled down" to the first two fields of video, the second frame of film is pulled down to the next *three* fields of video, and so on (Figure 4.4). Unfortunately, in the resulting video, a clean edit can only be made at every fifth video frame. In addition, to achieve the 29.97 native frame rate of NTSC video, the film picture and audio is slowed down .1% during the telecine process. This can lead to some complications in editing, and especially rotoscoping and other special effects. See Chapter 13 for more on 3:2 pulldown.

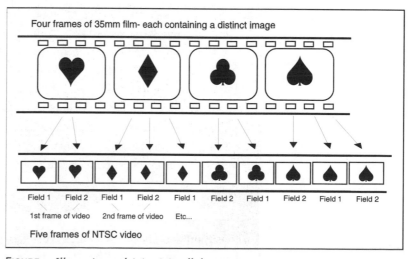

FIGURE   *Illustration explaining 3:2 pull-down.*
4.4

**Video Format
Features**

Those heady engineer types that we mentioned earlier love to throw around arcane terms when discussing digital video formats (or anything else, for that matter). As you begin looking into the specifications of different formats, you're going to hear a lot of talk about compression ratios, data rates, and color sampling ratios. Although you may have already chosen a format, either because of cost or availability, understanding your format's specifications can help you maintain the highest quality throughout your production process. If you haven't chosen a format, a close examination of format specs might make the choice obvious.

Note that many formats have particular types of hardware associated with them, so you will need to consider how a format's associated hardware fits into your workflow. For example, if you want to shoot using a particular aspect ratio, or use a specific hardware interface to move your footage into your computer, you'll need to choose particular formats.

On the following pages are explanations of what all those arcane specifications mean.

COMPRESSION

To fit more data onto a tape and to better facilitate digital post-production, most digital video formats will use some kind of data compression. This compression process can greatly affect the quality of your image. Uncompressed video has a compression ratio of 1:1, while compressed video can range anywhere from 10:1 to 1.6:1. Video compressed at a 10:1 ratio has 10% of its original data. Although video with a low compression ratio seems like it would look better, this isn't always the case, because some compression schemes (or algorithms) are better than others.

Most compression algorithms work by reducing unnecessary, redundant color information in each frame. Most of the information that your eye perceives is light versus dark, or *luminance*. In fact, your eye is not very good at perceiving color information, or *chrominance*. Because your camera can capture more color than your eye can perceive, compression software can afford to throw out the colors that your eye is less sensitive to, resulting in less color data and, therefore, smaller files.

Video is compressed using a piece of software called a *codec,* or COmpressor/DEcompressor. The most common types of digital video compressions are DV-based compression, DCT-based compression, MPEG-2, and M-JPEG. Although there are a lot of arguments about which type of compression is better, in the end you should simply try to look at footage compressed with different formats, and decide for yourself which looks better.

Color Sampling Ratio

As previously mentioned, the human eye is more sensitive to differences in light and dark (luminance) than to differences in color (chrominance). When a digital camera is sampling an image, the degree to which it samples each primary color is called the *color sampling ratio*. A fully uncompressed video signal—also known as RGB color—has a color sampling ratio of 4:4:4. The first number stands for the luma signal (abbreviated y'), and the second two numbers stand for the color difference components (Cb and Cr) which together add up to the full chroma signal. 4:4:4 means that for every pixel, four samples each are taken for the luma signal and the two parts of the chroma signal.

A color sampling ratio of 4:2:2 means that for every 4 luma samples, there are 2 color difference complete samples. This results in the loss of half the color detail. Because this is color detail that the human eye cannot perceive, it's worth throwing it out for the sake of saving storage space. 4:2:2 is the color sampling ratio of D1 video and ITU-BR 601.

DV formats use 4:1:1 color sampling, which is an amount of color reduction that is considered visible to the viewer. However, you should compare for yourself to see if the amount of degration is acceptable.

Because PAL video handles color differently, a color sampling ratio of 4:2:0 in PAL is equivalent to 4:1:1 in NTSC.

RESOLUTION

Video resolution is measured by the number of vertical lines that fit across the image horizontally. This is also called the *horizontal line resolution*. Due to the way the eye works, a set of alternating black and white lines, like those in Figure 4.5 will look like grey mush if the lines are small enough. Horizontal line resolution measures how many alternating black and white lines can fit in a video image before turning into an indistinct gray mass.

Due to its subjective nature, the horizontal line resolution is not a hard-and-fast figure: It varies according to such factors as the monitor or TV, the camera hardware, how bright the room where the monitor is, how far you are from the monitor, and how good your vision is. The *vertical line resolution* is fixed and inherent to each video standard: 525 lines for NTSC, of which 485 are visible, and 625 lines for PAL, of which 575 are visible.

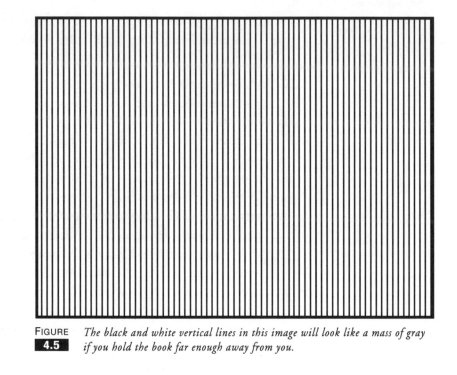

FIGURE   *The black and white vertical lines in this image will look like a mass of gray*
4.5   *if you hold the book far enough away from you.*

ASPECT RATIO

The ratio of the width of an image to its height is called the *aspect ratio* (Figure 4.6). Television and most computer monitors have an aspect ratio of 4:3. HDTV and most film formats have a much wider aspect ratio. Typically, wider is more "cinematic." In the larger scheme of things, we're a short species and we tend to build and orient horizontally across the ground, rather than up. Consequently, shooting in a wider format lets you put more information on screen and is a truer representation of the way our field of vision works.

If you can afford to be choosy, aspect ratio is an important consideration. If you're going to do a final output to film, you'll want to choose a video format with an aspect ratio close to that of your target film format.

Changing aspect ratios is difficult, time-consuming, and, ultimately, a compromise. If you're not sure of your final aspect ratio, choose the narrowest possible.

An Aspect Ratio by Any Other Name . . .
The 4:3 aspect ratio of television and most computer screens is sometimes referred
TIP   *to as a 1.33:1 ratio. This is to allow for easier comparison to film ratios (Table 4.2).*

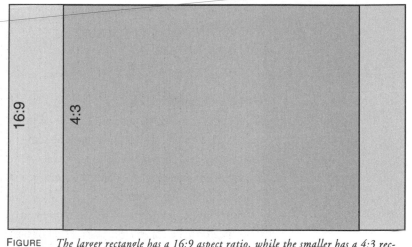

FIGURE 4.6 *The larger rectangle has a 16:9 aspect ratio, while the smaller has a 4:3 rectangle. Most formats only provide a 4:3 aspect ratio.*

Table 4.2   Film and Video Aspect Ratios

Video Formats	Video Aspect Ratios	Film Formats	Film Aspect Ratios
NTSC, PAL, or SECAM Television	1.33:1	Super 8mm	1.33:1
640 × 480 pixel computer screen	1.33:1	16mm	18:13
MiniDV	1.33:1	Super 16mm	5:3
DVCPro	1.33:1	35mm (projected):	3:2
DVCAM	1.33:1	35mm full	1.33:1
DVCPro50	1.33:1	Vistavision	3:2
DigitalS	1.33:1	65mm	16:7
Digital Betacam	1.33:1	IMAX	6:5
Betacam SP	1.33:1	70mm	2.19:1
D1	1.33:1	Techniscope	2.35:1
HDTV	16:9 or 1.78:1		

TIP

DV by Any Other Name
Don't let "DV" and "MiniDV" confuse you; these are actually exactly the same format, the only difference being the size of the tape cartridges. Traditionally, professional video formats have different cassette sizes—large ones for editing, and

smaller ones for shooting. So, the DV format offers small MiniDV tapes for shooting, and larger DV tapes for shooting and/or editing (though there's no reason you can't edit with MiniDV tapes).

PIXEL SHAPE

While your computer screen and a frame of video might have the same 4:3 aspect ratio, they won't necessarily have the same pixel dimensions because, unfortunately, not all video formats use pixels of the same shape. Yes, on top of all the other concerns and complications, you also have to think about the shape of the individual pixels!

Your computer screen—as well as many video formats—uses square pixels. This means that a screen with a resolution of 640×480 pixels will have an aspect ratio of 4:3. DV, DVCAM, DVCPRO, and D1 (sometimes incorrectly referred to as CCIR-601) all use rectangular pixels and require pixel dimensions of 720×486 pixels to achieve the same 4:3 aspect ratio. But wait, it gets worse. NTSC D1 formats use vertically oriented rectangular pixels, while PAL D1 formats use horizontally oriented rectangular pixels.

The trouble with the difference in pixel shapes is that images will become distorted when you move from a rectangular-pixel format to the square-pixel format of your computer screen (Figure 4.7 a–d).

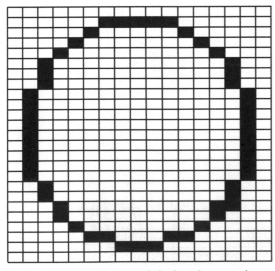

FIGURE **4.7a** *(a) Converting a circle built with rectangular pixels into square pixels . . .*

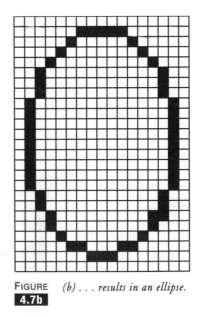

FIGURE **4.7b** *(b) . . . results in an ellipse.*

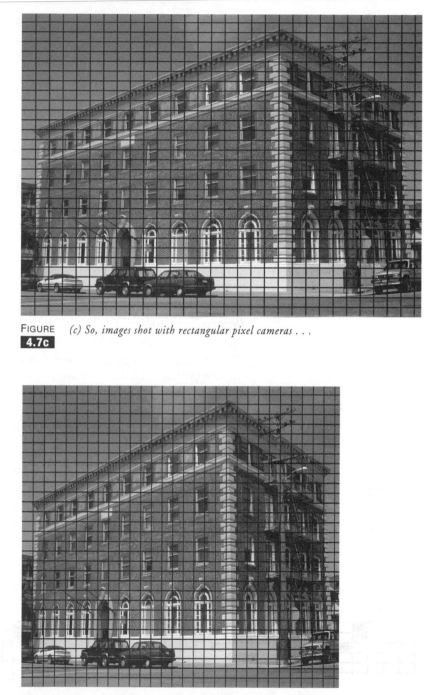

FIGURE
4.7c   *(c) So, images shot with rectangular pixel cameras . . .*

FIGURE
4.7d   *(d) . . . will look distorted and squished when displayed on your square pixel computer monitor.*

Because you can work around different pixel shapes through software, pixel shape shouldn't really be a concern when choosing a format. But, if you're planning on a lot of graphics or special effects, pixel shape can become more of a hassle. If you've already created a bunch of graphics at 640×480 on your computer screen and don't want them horizontally distorted when you go out to tape, you might want to pick a format with square pixels. Later, we'll discuss how to handle differing pixel shapes.

ANALOG COLOR

Even though your video hardware may be digital, all digital formats use analog connections to connect to monitors and often to other types of decks or your computer. There are three types of analog video connections, and each treats color differently. (See Chapter 11 for more on cables and connectors.) In ascending order of quality, they are:

- **Composite video** bundles all of the luminance and chrominance information into a single signal (i.e., a composite signal). Composite video typically connects to a deck or monitor through an *RCA* connector or a single *BNC* connector.
- **Y/C video:** (aka S-Video) In Y/C video, the video signal is broken down into two parts: luminance and chrominance. This results in better signal quality than composite video, but not as high a quality as component video. Y/C video connects using a proprietary connector.
- **Component video** divides the video signal into four different parts: YRGB, where Y = luminance; R = red; G = Green; and B = Blue. This results in a higher quality signal than composite or Y/C video. Component video typically connects using four separate BNC connectors, one for each video signal.

DATA RATE

As we've discussed, a digital video camera digitizes its video signal and stores the resulting data on tape as a digital file. The amount of information that a particular format stores for each second of video is measured by its *data rate*. For example, the MiniDV format has a data rate of 25 megabits per second (Mbps). This means that 25 Mbps of information are stored for each second of video. (If you factor in audio, timecode information, and the other "housekeeping" data that needs to be stored, MiniDV actually takes up about 36 Mbps.) DVCPro50, on the other hand, stores about 50 Mbps of information for each second of video. As one would expect, more information means a better picture, and the 50 Mbps data rate is one of the reasons that DVCPro50 has higher quality than MiniDV.

AUDIO

Many digital formats offer a choice of audio sampling rates, which is a measure of the resolution of the audio. As with an image, higher resolution is better. While professional digital audio is sampled at either 44.1 kHz (CD quality) or 48 kHz (DAT quality), there is little appreciable quality difference to the listener. It's pretty safe to say that all digital video formats will offer at least 44.1 kHz, CD-quality audio. However, it's important to know the sampling rate of your sound so that you can maintain it throughout your production and post-production processes.

TAPE LENGTHS, SIZES, AND SPEEDS

Each tape format has its own set of available tape lengths, though not all tape formats have tapes that are longer than 90 minutes. If your final project is going to be more than 90 minutes, you may need to use two tapes for your master. For television broadcast, this is rarely a problem, since you will probably build commercial breaks into your master edit. For feature films, you need to be aware that you'll have to find a break in your movie to allow for a "reel change." Generally, shorter tapes are used for shorter projects such as commercials, training, and industrial videos.

Learn by Watching
For the ultimate demonstration of how to use short tape lengths, go rent Alfred Hitchcock's Rope. *Because Hitchcock wanted to preserve the feel of the stage play upon which the film's story was originally based, he decided not to edit the movie. Instead, he kept the camera running as long as the film would last—10 minutes. When each reel of film neared its end, he would subtly zoom or pan across the back of a coat or prop, stop the camera, reload, and start up again. Surprisingly, you'll rarely notice these "edits" when watching.*

Just as your VHS deck at home supports different recording speeds to trade quality for longer recording times, some formats allow for SP or LP recording modes. Variable record speeds are not features you should be concerned about. You want the best quality possible, and so should always record at the higher quality SP speed.

Different formats typically use equipment that is built around different digital interfaces. These interfaces (either firewire of SDI) are what you will use to get video into and out of your computer. Depending on the computer hardware you can afford, you may need a particular interface. We'll discuss digital I/O in detail in Chapter 5. For now, keep in mind that you'll need to consider I/O when making a format choice.

Videotape Formats

Hopefully, if you've read the previous section, you now have a better idea of the factors that separate one format from another. In the following list, we've listed the advantages and disadvantages of many different video formats. Take a look at the list to get a better idea of how you can use each format.

Analog consumer formats. Most people are familiar with VHS, S-VHS, Betamax, 8mm, and Hi8, all of which were developed for home video. These formats are very inexpensive, but their lack of image quality should deter most serious video producers. Spend a little more money and shoot DV.

Digital 8. Digital 8 is an 8mm consumer format intended to replace analog Hi8. It can use Hi8 or its own Digital 8 tapes. It has a 25 Mbps data rate, a 4:1:1 color sampling ratio, and 5:1 DV-based compression, but is slightly lower-resolution than DV. For longer projects, DV is a better choice.

DV. Intended as a digital replacement for the home video formats mentioned previously, DV has far surpassed the manufacturers' expectations. It has a 25 Mbps data rate, a 4:1:1 color sampling ratio, and a 5:1 compression ratio. The image quality is frequently rated higher than Betacam SP and has the advantage of being less subject to generation-loss.

The Right Format for the Job
All of the 25 Mbps formats—Digital 8, DV, DVCPro, and DVCAM—use the same codec. Therefore, any differences in image quality are hardware dependent; i.e., due to camera technology, lenses, etc. The reason DVCPro and DVCAM are

considered superior formats is due to their reliability in editing-intensive applications such as news gathering, and due to the higher quality cameras and lenses available for these formats (Figure 4.8).

DVCAM. DVCAM by Sony offers a higher tape speed than DV, but not quite as high as DVCPro, and it uses the same metal tapes as DV. The resulting higher-quality image is aimed at industrial users, but appears to be quickly becoming the low-end format of choice for broadcast.

DVCPro. With a faster tape speed than DV and DVCAM JVC's DVCPro sports a more stable image that is less prone to drop-outs.

3/4″ U-matic. Developed in the 1960s, analog 3/4-inch tape is still widely used in government, educational, and industrial productions. It provides much lower quality than any DV format (Figure 4.9).

Betacam SP (BetaSP). Developed by Sony in the 1980s, Betacam SP is still the most popular format for broadcast television (Figure 4.9).

D-9. Developed by JVC as a digital upgrade of S-VHS, D-9 offers high, 4:2:2 image quality and a cheaper price tag than Digital Betacam. But "cheaper than DigiBeta" can still be very expensive (Figure 4.10)!

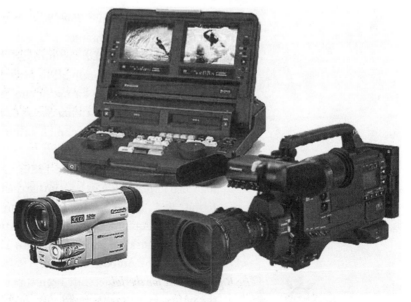

FIGURE
4.8
Equipment from the DV-based formats ranges from consumer handycam models like this Panasonic PY-DV900 (left) to professional-level equipment like this DVCPro50 camcorder (right) and portable editing system (top).

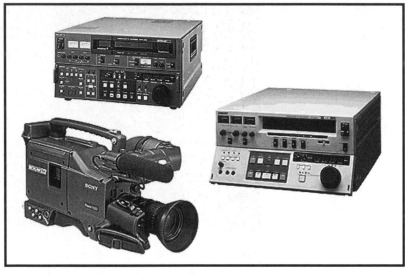

FIGURE   *Professional analog formats: 3/4 inch and Betacam SP.*
4.9

Betacam SX. A digital format aimed primarily at SNG (satellite news gathering) and ENG applications.

Digital Betacam (DigiBeta). Sony introduced Digital Betacam in 1993 as a digital upgrade of Betacam SP. Its extremely high quality has made it the broadcast mastering format of choice. Many high-budget digital films, such as *The Buena Vista Social Club,* are shot on Digital Beta. Digital Betacam decks can also play (but not record) analog Betacam SP tapes.

D-1. Introduced by Sony in the mid-1980s, D-1 was the first practical digital video format. With its high image quality, it is mostly used for mastering and broadcast graphics, compositing, and animation production. Equipment and tapes are extremely expensive, and it isn't used much outside the studio (Figure 4.11).

D-2. Developed by Ampex in the mid-1980s, D-2 is a composite digital tape format that has recently been superceded by Digital Betacam as the most popular mastering format for American broadcast television.

D-3, D-5. Very high-quality digital studio mastering formats developed by Panasonic.

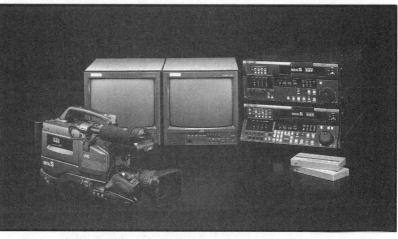

FIGURE   *JVC's D-9 is one of several broadcast-oriented digital video formats.*
4.10

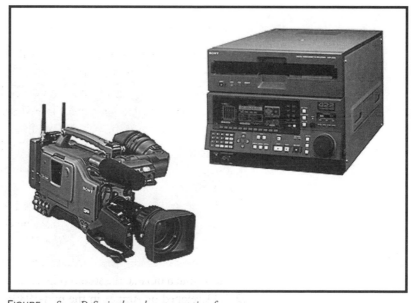

FIGURE   *Sony D-Series broadcast mastering formats.*
4.11

D-5 HD. A high-definition version of D-5, D-5 HD allows for the 1.2 gb/sec data rate and 1080 line interlaced (1080i) or 720 line progressive scan (720p) video of the American HDTV video standard.

D-9HD. The high-definition version of JVC's D-9 format, D-9HD (Figure 4.12).

HDCAM. Sony's contender in the high-definition formats, HDCAM is NTSC/PAL switchable and has an optional 24 fps frame rate. It is aimed at high-end film to digital video uses.

Choose Carefully

The movie The Cruise *was shot on NTSC using a Sony VX1000 MiniDV format camera, but the director was so unhappy with the frame rate issues that resulted from the transfer to film that he ended up going back to his sources and remastering onto a Sony uncompressed HDTV format and then going to film. The process of changing from one digital video format to another is called "transcoding." It is not a lossless process and should be avoided, if possible.*

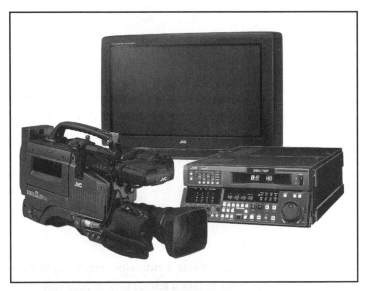

FIGURE

4.12   *High-definition D-series videotape formats, like the D-9 HD equipment shown in this photo, feature widescreen, progressive scan digital video.*

**So Which One
Do I Choose?**

Going back to our original question of how your project will eventually be output, we recommend the following formats:

> **Web output.** Though the low-quality of streaming Web video means you could get away with consumer VHS or Hi8, go ahead and spend a little extra money and shoot DV. The higher quality will yield a better image, and provide more shooting and effects flexibility.
>
> **Video.** DV, DVCAM, or DVCPro are all great choices for a video release, as they provide all the quality you'll need to create a master.
>
> **Broadcast.** Ideally, the format of choice is one of the broadcast standards such as BetaSP or Digital Betacam. However, you can certainly get away with shooting DV, DVCAM, or DVCPro, but expect to do an expensive transfer to DigiBeta.
>
> **Film projection.** In theory, you can shoot any video format for eventual film transfer. We've seen a number of excellent documentaries shot on Hi8. However, if quality is your primary concern, you'll want to choose a higher-end digital format and shoot using the PAL standard. DVCAM or DigiBeta are the preferred choice, though MiniDV or DVCPro are fine alternatives.

**Or, Maybe
It Doesn't
Matter . . .**

In the 1980s, video artists scrambled to buy Fisher-Price Pixelvision cameras that were intended as toys for children. These cameras recorded video onto standard audio cassettes, and the resulting extremely grainy, low-resolution, black-and-white images were (and still are) considered fascinating in ways that perfectly clear Digital Betacam video could never be. You don't need 4:2:2 video to make an interesting project. If the content is compelling, no one's going to complain about the compression artifacts dancing around in the darker parts of your image. But, you do need to decide early on what's right for your project and your intended workflow, as that decision will determine your equipment choices and have a profound effect on how you shoot. If you've made a videotape format decision, or at least narrowed it down, it's time to take a serious look at hardware.

5 Building a Workstation

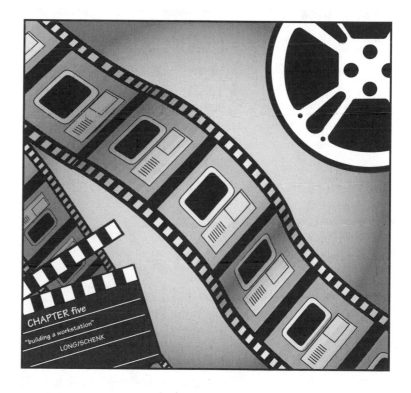

IN THIS CHAPTER

- Choosing a Platform
- Choosing a Video Interface
- Choosing a Computer
- Formatting Your Hard Drives
- Managing RAM

First Things First

Now that you've decided on a videotape format, it's time to start thinking about your workstation—the computer you will use for your editing, special effects, and production. Odds are you already have a computer of some kind. However, your current system may need some upgrades and add-ons to get it up to digital video snuff. If you are starting from scratch, or buying a whole new system, you may have an easier time than the user who's trying to upgrade an existing system, as you can buy a package of components that are guaranteed to be compatible. In this chapter, we'll cover all the questions you need to answer to build the right digital video workstation for your needs.

Choosing a Platform

Your first hardware decision is one you have probably already made: What operating system do you want to use? Mac, Windows? Be? Unix? Because you probably already have an OS of choice, we're not going to spend a lot of time on this question. However, if you are starting from scratch, or if you are wondering what may be in store for you, we'll quickly go over the pros and cons of each OS.

Macintosh OS. As with desktop publishing, video and film production is still somewhat Mac-heavy in its OS preference. Consequently, Mac users will have an easier time finding post-production houses that support (or possibly, *demand*) Macintosh compatibility. In general, setting up and configuring a Macintosh to recognize and use various cameras, interfaces, and storage options will be much easier than configuring any other platform. Firewire DV support is built-in to many new Macs, and the current OS/QuickTime combination provides thorough, robust support for Firewire-based DV I/O and device control.

On the negative side, if you need to use a particular application for your project—such as special Webcasting software, or a sophisticated 3D animation package such as SoftImage or Maya—then you'll need to consider a platform that supports those packages.

Windows 95/98. Windows 95 and 98 machines are typically less expensive than other platforms and are ubiquitous, so you should be able to easily find tech support. In addition, you'll find a number of different software and hardware options in a variety of price ranges, making it simple to fill every niche in your production process.

Unfortunately, neither Win 95 or 98 provides low-level, OS support for Firewire-based digitizing, which means you might have more trouble combining different pieces of hardware and software. Windows machines are much more difficult to set up and maintain, and are not as well-established in post-production houses as Macintosh systems. So, if you are planning on moving your data to a post-production facility for additional editing or film transfer, you'll want to be sure that they can support your hardware and file formats. If you want to attach multiple monitors, you'll need to go with Windows 98.

Windows NT. If you are committed to Intel-compatible hardware and you know you want to use some higher-end software such as Alias' Maya, then you'll need to use Windows NT. While NT has all of the same disadvantages as Windows 95/98, it offers special effects and 3D software that are not available on other platforms. Windows NT does not support multiple computer monitors, though third-party solutions are available. If you're purchasing a new computer, NT is a better choice for video applications than Windows 95 or 98.

BeOS, Unix, Linux. There are already a number of good DV apps for the Be OS, as well as many flavors of Unix and Linux. You can find links and articles about these OSs at www.dvhandbook.com/unix.

You might be more concerned about using a particular piece of software than a particular platform. For example, if you already know Adobe Premiere and want to do your editing there, then you can choose either Mac or Windows. Which platform to choose will depend on your OS preference, budget, and hardware/software requirements. Or, perhaps you already know Final Cut Pro, in which case you will need a Mac, or Speed Razor, which requires Windows. In either case, the software you are comfortable with—editing, painting, compositing, special effects, custom compressors, and so forth—should be the driving force behind your OS choice.

Choosing a Video Interface

Your biggest concern when building a workstation is ensuring that you have a way to get video into and out of your computer. The method you choose to do this will inform all of your other buying decisions, from processor speed to type of disk storage.

There are two ways to transfer video to your computer, either through an analog digitizing process or through a direct digital transfer. Which method you choose will depend mostly on the video format you have chosen.

CODECs Revisited

Video and audio data must be compressed before they can be played and stored by your computer (unless you've got special hardware for playing uncompressed video). The software that handles this task is called a CODEC, for COmpressor/DECompressor. CODECs are usually managed by the video architecture—QuickTime, Video for Windows, Real Media, and so forth—that you are using.

If you have ever created a QuickTime movie on your computer, you have probably been presented with a choice of the different compression options that QuickTime provides. Video, Sorenson, Animation, Cinepak, and many others are all CODECs that are used to compress video for storage, and then to decompress it for playback.

Different CODECs are used for different purposes. You'll use high-compression/low-quality CODECs for Web or CD-ROM delivery, and low-compression/high-quality CODECs for higher-quality playback. Other CODECs are used if you are using special video hardware.

CODECs can be either *lossy* or *lossless;* that is, they either degrade the image quality, or leave it unaffected. Many CODECs take longer to compress than they do to decompress (these are called asymmetrical). Most of the CODECs that ship with QuickTime are asymmetrical. For example, though it may take hours to compress a QuickTime movie using Cinepak or MPEG, the computer can decompress it and play it back in real-time.

When you compress a piece of video, QuickTime hands the video stream to your chosen CODEC, which performs the compression calculations, and then writes out the compressed information to a file. Similarly, when you are ready to play back, QuickTime reads the compressed data and hands it to the appropriate CODEC, which decompresses it into video that the computer can display.

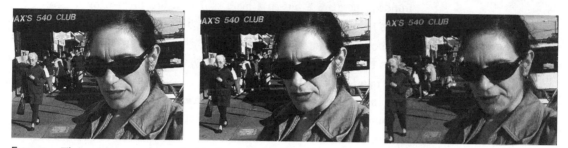

FIGURE
5.1

The same image compressed with, from left to right, DV compression, Sorenson compression, and Cinepak compression. As you can see, image quality varies a lot between different compression algorithms.

DIGITAL VIDEO INTERFACES

One of the great advantages of any DV format is that it's already digital; the camera digitizes the video before it ever writes it to tape. So, to edit, all you have to do is move that digital file into your computer. This process is typically done through either a Firewire or SDI interface. Both interfaces can transfer video and audio, as well as provide device control, through a single cable.

Which interface your camera or deck supports is determined by its tape format. DV, DVCAM, and DVCPro typically provide Firewire interfaces, while D-9, Digital Betacam, D-1, and the HD formats usually sport SDI interfaces.

Firewire

Firewire was developed by Apple in 1986 as a replacement for serial, parallel, SCSI, and to a lesser degree, Ethernet. In the future, computers will likely only have two interfaces for connecting peripherals: USB for slow devices such as keyboards, mice, and printers, and Firewire for high-speed connectivity to mass storage, cameras, scanners, and even networks.

Firewire allows you to daisy-chain up to 64 devices, with none of the settings or ID concerns that you have with SCSI. In addition, Firewire devices are true *peers;* that is, they don't need a computer to know how to talk to each other. So, you can easily connect two cameras together via Firewire to create digital dubs, or even edit!

The Firewire that is present on most computers and cameras today can transmit data at 100 Mbps, *megabits per second*). This is equivalent to 12.5MB per second, or *mega*bytes *per second*—note the capital *B*. (For the techno-minded, there are 8 bits in a byte, so 100 Mbps divided by 8 yields 12.5 MBps.) Since DV only requires a sustained transfer rate of about 3.6 MBps, 100 megabit Firewire is plenty fast. And by the time you read this, 200 or 400 Mbps Firewire—or even 1 gigabit Firewire—may be available. These will allow transfers of 25, 50, or 125 MBps!

If you're going to use Firewire to digitize your video, check to see if your computer has Firewire ports on its motherboard. If not, you'll need to get a Firewire interface for your computer. There are two kinds of Firewire connectors: 6-pin and 4-pin (Figure 5.2). The larger, 6-pin connectors can carry power as well as data, making it possible to have a single cord that provides everything a device needs. Most video cameras have 4-pin connectors, which take up considerably less space than a 6-pin connector. Your computer probably has a 6-pin port, in which case you'll need to get a 6-pin to 4-pin cable.

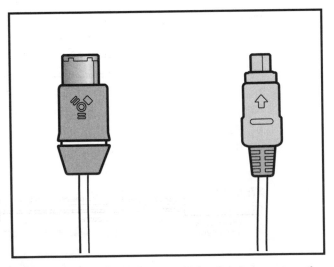

FIGURE   *Firewire connectors come in either 6 or 4-pin versions. 6-*
5.2   *pin versions carry power as well as data.*

SDI

Developed by Sony as an interface between high-end digital video formats and non-linear editing systems, SDI (for Serial Digital Interface) clocks in at 200 Mbps, only double the speed of current Firewire. With SDI being overkill for most DV users, and with 200 Mbps Firewire just around the corner, the main advantage to SDI is that it supports much longer cables than Firewire's four-foot limitation. If you're wiring a full-blown post-production studio, this can be a huge plus. The average user will probably not encounter the need for SDI I/O unless he or she plans on working with D-1, Digital Betacam, Betacam SX, D-9, or HD format equipment. Some very high-end DVCPro and DVCAM video decks also offer SDI I/O.

CAPTURING DV

When you press "play" on a DV deck (or camera), the compressed digital information is read from the DV tape. The deck does two things with this information. First, it decompresses the signal into analog video, which is output through the unit's analog outputs—usually either S-Video or composite. These outputs can feed an external video monitor, an analog tape deck, or an analog digitizing system. Simultaneously, the camera or deck sends the raw, compressed digital stream out through its digital interface. If you have a computer attached to the other end of that digital interface, you can capture that compressed stream (remember, it's *capturing*, not *digitizing*, because the video has already been digitized) and store it on a hard drive. Because of the way the DV CODEC works, the only way to view a full-resolution playback of your captured video is on an external video monitor. The image played on your computer monitor is a low-res proxy of your video (Figure 5.3).

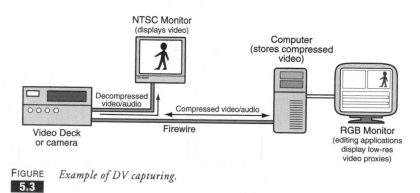

FIGURE
5.3   *Example of DV capturing.*

Because video is passing into and out of your computer in a raw digital form, it is possible to shoot, edit, and print back to tape with no loss of quality (unlike analog systems, which experience generation loss each time you make a new copy). Note that we said "it is *possible*." Depending on the type of effects and edits you are making, you might inadvertently recompress your video, resulting in loss of quality through recompression. In later chapters, we'll discuss how to avoid recompression.

One Video, Hold the Compression

Digital Origin's EditDV Firewire/editing software package avoids recompression trouble by never decompressing your video. Instead, the EditDV software keeps your video in the YUV color space all the time. Because it never converts video to RGB, there's never a need—or concern—for recompression. The downside to this system is that you can only use plug-ins and effects that ship with EditDV.

Manufacturer's Recommendations

No matter what platform you're using, you'll need to be concerned about compatibility between your computer and video hardware. Fortunately, most vendors are diligent about publishing compatibility lists. Such lists include approved drives, interfaces, and CPUs. Before you make any purchases, you'll want to be sure to check out each vendor's compatibility claims. In addition, make sure that your dealer has a good return and exchange policy.

ANALOG DIGITIZERS

Not all cameras have a digital interface. Hardware for older analog formats such as Hi8, and Betacam SP lack any kind of digital I/O, meaning you can't, for example, plug those cameras into a Firewire port on your computer. Even some DV format hardware lacks digital I/O. If you find yourself using hardware without a digital interface, you'll want to consider buying an analog digitizing system to get video in and out of your computer. Or, if you are using video from a number of different formats and sources, an analog digitizer might be the easiest way to handle all your different media.

Analog digitizers (such as the Targa 2000, Canopus Rex, Media 100, and some Avid products) take an analog signal from your camcorder or deck and digitize it using a video card installed in your computer (Figure 5.4). After digitizing, this same video card compresses the video signal for storage on your

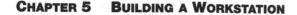

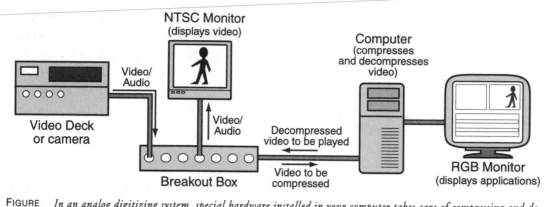

FIGURE
5.4   *In an analog digitizing system, special hardware installed in your computer takes care of compressing and de-*
compressing video in real-time.

hard drive. Specs and quality vary from system to system, but most analog digitizing boards use Motion-JPEG compression, which provides a 4:2:2 color
sampling ratio. However, though their technical specs might be the same, different systems don't all produce the same image quality. You'll want to research
your purchase carefully and, ideally, look at sample output. Some systems
come with different CODECs that can apply more or less compression to fit
more footage, or better-quality footage, onto your hard drive.

Special analog cable connections—such as composite RCA, S-Video, or
BNC connectors for video and audio—are usually provided through a special
"break-out box" that attaches to the video card itself. Many analog video cards
also offer Firewire I/O, but be aware that the video signal that is coming
through the Firewire cable is still being digitized with the analog CODEC. Remember that digital video is compressed by the DV camera before it's recorded
to tape. Consequently, if you digitize this video into an analog video system,
you will be compressing the video *again* and possibly introducing compression
artifacts.

TIP

Look for the QuickTime CODEC
If you want to be able to move video from your editing application into other
programs such as compositing or rotoscoping applications, you should choose an
analog system that provides a QuickTime CODEC. This will let any Quick-
Time-based app interface with your digitizing hardware. In addition to its nor-
mal CODECs, Media 100 also provides a special QuickTime CODEC that

allows playback on computers that don't have Media 100 hardware. If you need an analog digitizer and are planning on moving your video from one machine to another (to go from editing to effects, for example), then Media 100 might be a good choice.

Choosing a Computer

Once you've decided what sort of video interface you'd like to use, you need to buy a computer. You have two options when selecting a workstation: piece together your own system, or buy a "turnkey" system from a vendor that packages equipment.

If you piece together your own system, you'll be able to use any hardware you may already have, and you'll be able to create a system that is tailored to the exact needs of your project. However, depending on your experience and the complexity of your intended project, building your own system may take a lot of time and experimentation. If you're not comfortable with installing hardware and software in your computer, this is not the best choice.

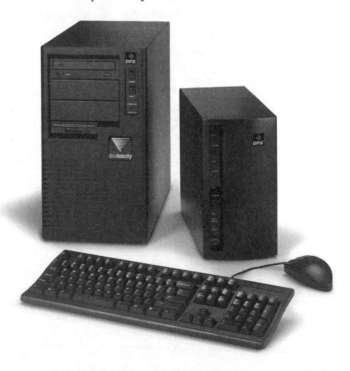

 FIGURE 5.5   *DPS Velocity Pentium III-based turnkey editing system featuring dual-stream uncompressed video and a SCSI drive array.*

With a turnkey system, you'll get a computer that will work properly right out of the box, with no compatibility questions or installation troubles. Avid and Media 100 offer several cross-platform turnkey systems. Promax Systems (www.dvhandbook.com/promax) packages excellent Mac-based turnkey systems that have been preconfigured and pretested. If you've got the money, buying a turnkey system may be the simplest solution to your hardware needs.

No matter which approach you decide to take, it's important for you to understand the issues discussed next. A firm grasp of these concerns will make your current purchase, as well as any future expansion, much easier.

Standalone Editors

There is a third choice when choosing an editing system: standalone editing hardware. Systems like the DraCo Casablanca provide full DV editing with storage, editing software, and digital I/O in a single, plug-and-play video appliance. Such systems are great for the user who absolutely does not want to hassle with a computer.

CPU

Working with video requires a lot of processing power. How much depends largely on the type of video interface you're using. If you're using an analog digitizing card, you can often get away with a less powerful CPU than if you're using a digital video interface. Check the requirements of your video system for more details.

Don't forget that you'll be doing more than just editing video. Be sure to get enough computing muscle to run the various image editors, compositing, and special effects programs that you'll want to use.

Also, consider the other hardware that you might want. If you plan on adding accelerator cards, real-time video processors, or special audio cards, you'll need a system with a good number of expansion slots.

RAM

Fortunately, video editing is more disk intensive than RAM intensive, so you don't need a huge amount of memory for simple editing tasks. A safe bet is 64 to 128 MB of RAM for most editing applications.

However, if you're doing much beyond simple editing with basic dissolves and effects, you should spring for extra memory. To prepare titles and special effects, you'll be depending on an image editor like Photoshop. And, specialized applications that load video segments into RAM—After Effects and Commotion, for example—want *lots* of memory.

So, shoot for 128 MB, but if you can swing it, go ahead and spring for 256 or more. We guarantee that no one who edits video has ever said "gosh, I wish I hadn't bought all that extra RAM."

STORAGE

Just accept right now that you can't buy enough storage. However, with recent changes in technology and pricing, you can get real close. How much storage you'll need depends largely on the nature of your project.

If you are shooting a feature that's two hours long, odds are your shooting ratio will be around 3:1; that is, you'll shoot three times as much video as you'll use in your final product. So, you'll need enough storage for at least six hours of footage. But, you'll also need storage for project files, graphics, special effects, and audio editing. Better to play it safe and increase your storage estimates to something like 8 to 10 hours' worth of storage. Check your video interface manufacturer's specs for information on how much disk space is needed for storing an hour of video. Don't forget that you'll also need space for your OS and your applications. If you are shooting a documentary, keep in mind that your shooting ratios are probably much higher—10:1 or more—but effects and graphics needs might be lower.

Different video input systems have different storage requirements. If you are planning on using a Firewire interface to capture your video, you're in luck! Since Firewire has relatively low throughput requirements, you can get away with using slower, IDE drives. If you are using an analog digitizing system, odds are you'll need faster storage—usually some kind of fast SCSI—configured into an array. Consult your system's documentation for details.

MONITORS

Video applications tend to consume a lot of screen real estate. Consequently, you may want to opt for a video card and monitor that can work at a higher resolution. If you are a Mac or Windows 98 user, you may want to add a second monitor, but be sure you can spare the slot required by a second video card. (External video monitors are discussed in Chapter 11.)

Drive Definitions

SCSI. The Small Computer Systems Interface has been around for a while, and now exists in several flavors such as SCSI-2, Fast and Wide SCSI, and UltraWide SCSI. Video users will need to consider purchasing multiple UltraWide SCSI drives with a spin rate of at least 7200 RPM. Whether you're using a Mac or Windows computer, you'll need to buy a special UltraWide SCSI interface. Up to seven SCSI devices (including the computer) can be chained off of one SCSI interface. Obviously, you'll need drives that are UltraSCSI compatible.

RAIDs and Arrays. A Redundant Array of Independent Disks—usually referred to simply as an *array*—consists of two identical hard drives—usually SCSI—that have been logically *striped* with indexing information so that they can be treated as a single drive. For video, the advantage of an array is speed. Because the computer can *interleave* information between both drives, one drive can be reading or writing while the other drive is preparing to read or write.

EIDE, UltraDMA, ATA, and UltraATA. All variations of the same spec, these drives are much cheaper than SCSI drives. Though not always as fast as a SCSI drive or array, they provide all the throughput you'll need for Firewire-based DV editing. You can chain two devices off of one of these interfaces. Look for drives with a spin rate of at least 5400 RPM and as much capacity as you can afford.

Firewire. As of this writing, Firewire drives are just becoming available in quantity. Fast, and frequently tiny, Firewire drives are currently more expensive than their IDE or SCSI competition, but this will likely change in the future. Hot-swappable, with up to 63 drives per Firewire chain, and no termination or ID issues, these drives are definitely the wave of the future.

2D or Not 2D

If your production will include a lot of 3D animation, you'll want to consider a video card with 3D acceleration features. These cards typically include extra RAM and processors for storing textures and rendering information, and can provide a mammoth increase in 3D rendering performance. However, such boards can run into thousands of dollars. If 3D is not a part of your production, don't spend the extra money for such a video card.

ACCESSORIZING

The hardware we've discussed so far, combined with the right software, will provide you with a good, full-featured post-production facility. However, depending on your application, it might be worth adding on some extra hardware.

Special co-processor cards can be installed that accelerate the rendering of complex effects filters, while other co-processors can be added that will provide real-time transitions and effects. Such co-processors can be expensive, so you'll want to take a close look at your workflow to decide if custom acceleration will save you any money.

For audio-intensive projects, or simply for more audio control, you might want to consider the addition of professional audio editing hardware. Systems like ProTools from DigiDesign provide multichannel, high-quality digital recording with real-time effects and editing. We'll discuss these products more in Chapter 14.

TIP

Uncompressed

Nowadays, there's lots of fancy hardware on the market—everything from accelerator cards, cards that offer dual stream processing, and cards that digitize uncompressed D-1 quality video. For most independent filmmakers, these are overkill, but if you're bent on learning, check www.dvhandbook.com/hardware.

BUILDING A MACINTOSH SYSTEM

If you want to build a Mac-based system from the ground up, your choices are fairly simple. You'll need at least a 300 MHz G3 processor with a Firewire port and a fast hard drive. At the time of this writing, all of Apple's desktop machines ship with at least a 350 MHz G4 processor, two built-in Firewire ports, and a fast Ultra ATA hard drive, so any new desktop Mac will be DV ready.

Your RAM needs will vary depending on your software, but we recommend a system with at least 128 MB of RAM. As Apple's systems ship with, at most, a 20 GB hard drive, you'll probably want to add some extra storage. If you'll be using a Firewire-based editing system, the easiest way to add storage is to chain an additional drive off of the Mac's internal ATA drive. See your instruction manual for details. If you'll be using an analog digitizer, then you'll need to add a fast-SCSI card and an array of fast-SCSI drives. Be aware that the blue and white G3s do not have serial ports, so you'll have to add a USB to serial port adaptor to allow for remote deck control of non-Firewire decks.

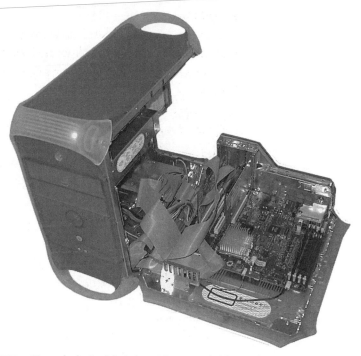

FIGURE

Not only do Apple's desktop Macs provide blazing fast processors and plenty of room for multiple drives, but their easy-opening case is ideal for configuring and reconfiguring a complex video editing workstation.

Co-processors, audio cards, or additional monitors can be added if you need them, but remember that you only have three slots available.

If you don't think you're going to need to add co-processors or huge amounts of storage, the iMac DV is a great editing solution. Because it lacks expansion slots, you won't be able to add additional drive controllers or accelerators, but you can always add Firewire drives, or replace the system's internal hard drive with a larger capacity drive if you need more storage.

If you've already got at least a 300 MHz G3, you need to be sure you have enough RAM and storage. However, note that you may have trouble installing multiple internal drives on blue and white G3s manufactured before June, 1999. Check out www.dvhandbook.com/multipledrives for details.

If you have a slower G3 such as a 233 or 266 MHz and want to use it in a Firewire workflow, you can install a faster processing card such as a Newer Technologies' MaxPowr G4 card. You'll also need a Firewire card, some storage, and possibly more RAM. However, depending on your host machine, such a system still might not provide the throughput required for DV. Given the cheap price of a new G3, it might be more time and cost-effective to simply buy a new computer. An analog system, on the other hand, might work fine with a pre-G3 Mac. If you are interested in a particular analog digitizing system, check with the vendor for system requirements.

Finding a Mac Slot Machine

If you're a Mac user who wants to add a lot of peripheral acceleration or A/V cards, you're going to have to do some planning. Apple's current Mac offerings max out at three slots. However, if you can find an old PowerMac 9600 (which sports six PCI slots) you can easily outfit it with a Newer Technologies' G3 or G4 card and have a speedy, five-slot editing system.

However, as with any piece of hardware, you'll need to do a little investigating to ensure that the Newer accelerator cards are compatible with your other hardware. And, just because a Mac has a G3 or G4 card added to it, there's no guarantee that it will be fast enough for all video applications. Check with your software manufacturer to learn more about compatibility.

BUILDING A WINDOWS SYSTEM

Assembling a Windows system yourself is more complicated than assembling a Mac system, largely because you have more options. If you've used Windows for very long, you've probably already discovered that in the Windows world there are a zillion manufacturers for every type of component and accessory. Getting all of these different components to work together can be difficult. If you're not comfortable with such arcana as setting IRQs or moving jumpers and switches on peripheral cards, then you'll definitely want to consider buying a preconfigured, turnkey system.

Configuring a Windows machine for DV can be complicated. The trouble stems from the fact that your system has to be finely tuned to deal with the requisite throughput required by a video editing program. Because you don't want to drop one frame, you need to be sure that you have no bottlenecks in your hardware.

To begin with, you'll need a fast machine with at least a 350 MHz Pentium II. Next you'll need to decide if you're going to use an analog or Firewire-based editing system. If you opt for an analog system such as Targa or Media100, you'll need to check the specifications of those products to determine your other hardware needs.

If you're going to go with a Firewire-based setup, your first choice will be to pick a Firewire card. Because support for the Firewire interface is not built-in to any Windows OS, Firewire cards for Windows typically come packaged with drivers and editing packages. Digital Origin's EditDV system, for example, is a good Firewire card bundled with all necessary drivers and EditDV.

Once you've selected a Firewire system, it's time to move on to storage. Your computer probably already has an IDE drive of some kind, so you may be able to slave additional IDE drives to your internal host drive.

Of course you'll need a good amount of RAM, as well as a sound card, and any accelerators and co-processors that you might desire. Be sure to plan and manage your slot usage before you start buying equipment, and remember that DV requires fast throughput, meaning that you'll need to use PCI slots for expansion rather than slower ISA or EISA slots.

Once you've gathered all your equipment, it's time to start installing. Go slowly and install one piece of hardware at a time. Don't confuse the situation by throwing a bunch of cards into your PC and then seeing if they work. Debugging such a complex system can be time-consuming and perplexing.

If you are buying a completely new system, consider a pre-assembled turnkey system or a machine with built-in Firewire support. Sony's line of intel-based systems provide hardware designed from the ground up for DV editing. Similar systems from Intergraph and Silicon Graphics provide easy installation and fast video performance (Figure 5.7).

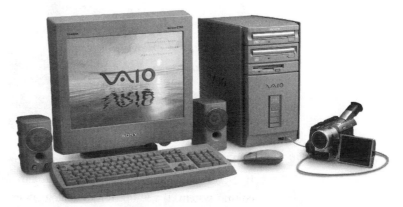

FIGURE

Sony's desktop, Intel-based workstations provide built-in Firewire, and all the hardware and software you'll need to perform DV editing and output.

PORTABLE EDITING

Though unimaginable just a few years ago, the era of portable video editing is here. In addition to allowing you to edit your feature at the beach or in the park, portable editing systems mean you can try rough edits of a scene while you're still on set! With this kind of immediate post-production feedback, you can quickly and easily determine if you've gotten the coverage and performances you need.

Because they're based around laptop computers, assembling a portable system will be much costlier than putting together a desktop system. And, you may not be able to get all the storage and acceleration features you'd have on a desktop.

Macintosh

Mac-based portable editing starts with a 300 MHz G3 (or better) Powerbook and a Firewire PC card such as Newer Technologies' Firewire-2-Go card (Figure 5.9). Though the internal drive in your Powerbook is fast enough for DV, it's probably not too big. If you need more space, consider a Firewire drive (which will require another Firewire PC card) or an expansion bay drive from VST technology.

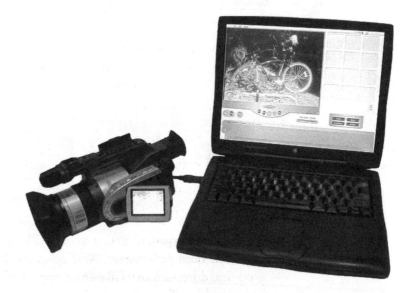

FIGURE
5.8
With the addition of a Firewire card, this 300 MHz G3 PowerBook becomes a fully-functional, portable editing system.

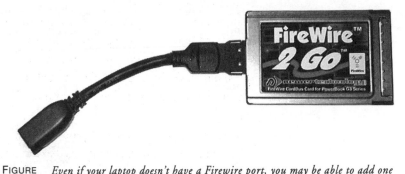

FIGURE
5.9   *Even if your laptop doesn't have a Firewire port, you may be able to add one
with a product such as the Newer Technologies Firewire-2-Go PC Card.*

Windows

There are several vendors that make Windows-based laptop editing systems. Sony makes several VAIO systems that ship with fast processors, a good amount of storage, built in Firewire (though Sony calls it iLink) and a varying assortment of software. When looking for a portable Windows NLE, you'll do better if you buy a pre-configured system.

TIP

Portable Turnkeys
Both Avid and Media 100 make portable versions of their professional, analog digitizing systems. Packed with the same features as their desktop cousins, these systems provide a true portable solution to the die-hard Avid or Media 100 editor. As you might expect, these systems are pricey and probably only for the big-budgeted user with special editing needs.

Formatting Your Drives

Once your computer is set up, you'll need to spend some time partitioning and formatting your hard drives to ensure maximum performance and to ease housekeeping.

The information stored on your drive falls into three main categories: the operating system, data, and applications. Careful planning will allow you to keep these files separate, make it easier to recover from crashes, and ensure maximum video performance. We're assuming that you've got at least two good-sized drives (at least 9 GB each), though the following plan can also work with one drive. The following advice assumes you're using a DV/Firewire workflow. If you're using an analog system, you'll need to consult your documentation for storage details.

Partitioning is a process of logically formatting a single drive so that the computer treats the drive as multiple, discreet drives. Any good drive formatting package will include partitioning software, and your OS probably includes utilities for partitioning. You'll need to plan and create your partitions all at once, and before you install any software, as partitioning will erase everything on your drive.

First, you'll want to create a partition on a bootable drive for your operating system. This will make it easy to re-install or upgrade your OS without having to re-install applications or move data. Remember that you'll need room for the OS, its utility applications, fonts, and drivers for any special hardware. We recommend about a gigabyte.

Next, on the same drive, create a partition for your applications. As with the OS, installing applications on their own partition makes it easy to update or replace a program without having to create space or backup data. Having your applications on a separate drive from your video data will ensure better performance. Three to five gigabytes should be plenty of space.

Finally, partition the rest of that drive as a space for data. You won't use this partition for video data, but for project files, supporting graphics, titles, and so on. This partition will be anywhere from 5 to 20 gigabytes, depending on the size of your drive.

Leave your second drive formatted as a single partition and use this as your video capture drive. This is where your video will be stored while you're editing. Assume 13 megabytes per hour of DV captured video (Figure 5.10).

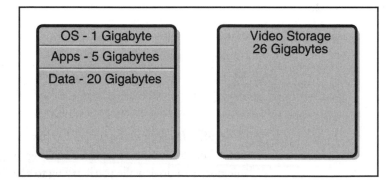

FIGURE **5.10**   *For maximum video performance in a DV editing system, it's best to configure two drives into multiple partitions for OS, applications, program data, and video data.*

TIP

Scratch Disks
While you're working, Adobe Photoshop will sometimes cache information on your hard drive. This scratch disk lets Photoshop sock away data that it can't fit in memory. A large, fast scratch disk can greatly improve Photoshop's performance. If you've got the room, you might consider creating a whole partition just for Photoshop's scratch files. You can specify this drive as your primary scratch disk through Photoshop's Preferences dialog. Remember, Photoshop ideally wants three times the RAM as the size of the image you're editing.

As you use a drive (or partition) it can become *fragmented;* that is, its contents can get spread all over the drive. Even individual files—such as a clip of video—can become fragmented across an entire drive. This can slow down throughput, as the computer will have to spend extra time moving the read/write head around to find the next chunk of data. *Defragmenting* (or *defragging* if you're hip) or *optimizing* the drive will re-order the contents of a drive so that the computer can read as quickly as possible. (If you're using an analog digitizing system, check your manual before optimizing a drive. Some software, such as Avid's Media Composer, fragments the drives on purpose.)

Drive optimizing software is a good way to defragment a drive that's full of data or applications, but the fastest and most thorough way to optimize a drive is to reformat it. Because you may not have a place to stash your data in the meantime, reformatting is not always practical. However, reformatting your video storage drives before you start a new project is always a good idea.

Managing Your RAM

In addition to making sure your computer has enough RAM to run your editing software and support applications, you also want to turn off any operations that will slow down throughput when capturing or digitizing.

Though different editing packages, whether analog or digital, will have guidelines for maximizing your RAM and tweaking your system, we can offer these general guidelines:

- **Turn off virtual memory.** If your OS has a virtual memory feature, turn it off! You don't want the computer taking the time to dump a chunk of memory to a drive while you're trying to sustain a video transfer.
- **Free up as much RAM as you can.** Turn off RAM disks and other processes that gobble up RAM.

- **Turn off unnecessary processes.** Screen savers, file serving software, e-mail programs, network backup systems, and other programs and operations that periodically try to do things should be quit or disabled. You don't want these operations trying to interfere with your digitizing or capturing. Mac users should actually shut down networking altogether, by going to the Chooser and switching AppleTalk to Off.

Managing Macintosh Memory

While Windows 95, 98, and NT dynamically manage memory, Macintosh users still have to manage their RAM by hand (at least until OS X ships). Each application that you run consumes a certain amount of memory. You can see how much by switching to the Finder and selecting **About this Computer** from the Apple menu.

To change the memory allocation for an application, click once on the application's icon to select it, then choose **Get Info** from the Finder's File menu. In the resulting dialog box, change the **Show** pop-up menu to memory. You can now tell the computer how much memory to grab when launched.

You may want to change your allocation to allow more programs to be open at the same time, or to provide more memory to a particularly RAM-hungry application.

TIP

AppleScripting RAM Changes
To speed up changing memory allocations, create AppleScripts that automatically change a program's memory allocation before launching. You can use the AppleScript Editor that ships with your Mac to create these AppleScripts.
For example, we have a script that allocates all of our RAM to Photoshop and then launches it, and another script that allocates half of our RAM to Photoshop and then launches it. We can run these scripts to launch Photoshop with the configuration we need at the moment.
For more details, check out www.dvhandbook.com/applescript.

Conclusion

There are a lot of products and options out there for the digital video user. As a feature filmmaker, you don't need to worry about most of them. Relative to some DV tasks, your needs are fairly simple, so don't go overboard in building your system. Stick with what will work best for your production, and aim for a system that can support the software that you prefer to use.

CHAPTER

6

Choosing a Camera

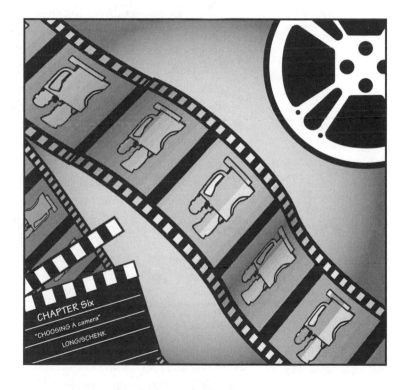

IN THIS CHAPTER

- Evaluating Image Quality
- Camera Features
- Accessorizing
- Camera Compared

As we discussed in Chapter 4, new digital video formats deliver much better quality than most of the older analog formats. But, it doesn't matter how good your format is if your camera shoots lousy images. Outside of format choice, the camera you choose will have the biggest effect on the quality of your final footage.

Fortunately, along with the proliferation of affordable digital video formats, the last few years have also seen the release of many high-quality, inexpensive DV cameras. The DV film-maker can now buy an affordable camera that rivals professional cameras of just a few years ago. Understanding the features and trade-offs of different cameras is essential to selecting a camera and using it to its full potential.

In this chapter, we'll explain the various features and functions of a DV camera, with details of how these features work, and guidelines for evaluating and selecting the right camera for your project.

Choosing a camera is a process of weighing three factors: image quality, price, and features. As a feature filmmaker, you should be most concerned about image quality, particularly if you are planning on transferring to film.

Image Quality

Portability and cool features are nice, but if that lightweight camera with the cool special effects produces images with lousy color and distracting artifacts, your audience is going to be less inclined to pay attention to your story.

Two factors contribute the most to your camera's image quality (or lack thereof): the camera's lens, and the number of chips the camera uses to create an image. Your first choice, then, will be to decide between single-chip and three-chip models.

CCD

In the old days, video cameras used vacuum tubes for capturing images. Today, video cameras use special imaging chips called *CCDs,* or *charge-coupled devices.* Just as their tube-based predecessors used either one or three tubes to capture an image, CCD-based cameras use either a single CCD to capture a full-color image, or three chips to capture separate red, green, and blue data, which is then assembled into a color image (Figure 6.1).

A CCD looks like a normal computer chip, but with a sort of light-sensitive "window" on top that is divided into a grid. The circuitry controlling the CCD can determine the amount of light striking each cell of the grid and use this data to build an image. The finer the grid, the higher the resolution of the CCD.

Single-chip cameras have red, green, and blue filters arranged over clusters of cells in the CCD. These filter the light coming through the lens and allow the camera to record color images. A single-chip camera uses one chip to gather all of its color information; when compared to a three-chip camera, a single-chip image might show strange color artifacts or bleeding, smeary colors as well as a softer, lower-resolution image.

In a three-chip camera, a series of prisms splits the incoming light into separate red, green, and blue components, and directs each of these components onto a separate CCD. Because the camera is dedicating an entire sensor to each color, color fidelity and image detail are much improved (Figures 6.2 and 6.3).

The image data gathered by the CCD is passed to an on-board computer that processes the data and writes it to tape. How the computer processes the

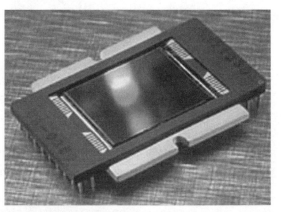

FIGURE
6.1   *A Kodak KAF-1302E(LE) CCD.*

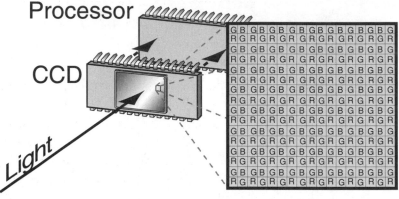

FIGURE
6.2
In a single-CCD camera, light is focused by the lens onto the CCD. Red, green, and blue filters placed over alternating cells of the CCD enable it to calculate color. Notice that there are far more green cells. The resulting data is passed on to the camera's processor.

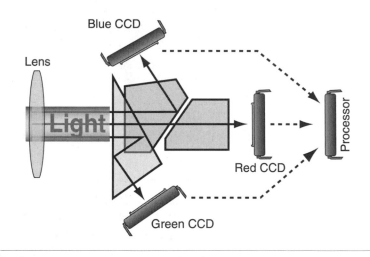
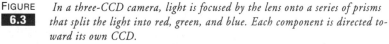

FIGURE
6.3
In a three-CCD camera, light is focused by the lens onto a series of prisms that split the light into red, green, and blue. Each component is directed toward its own CCD.

data can have a lot to do with how images differ from camera to camera. Canon cameras such as the XL-1, GL-1, or Elura, for example, tend to produce warmer images, with stronger reds and magentas. Sony cameras such as the VX1000, DCR-TRV900, or DCR-PC1, tend to produce cooler, less-saturated images with stronger blues. One approach is not better than the other, but you may find that you have a personal preference, or that one is better-suited to the tone of your project.

Evaluating a CCD

You shouldn't have any trouble determining if a camera is a single or three-chip device, as vendors tend to clearly tout their extra chips in writing on the side of the camera. Typically, three-chip cameras start at around $2,000–$2,500.

Though three-chip cameras are definitely better than single-chip units, the difference is not as extreme as it used to be. If a single chip camera is all you can afford, don't worry, there are plenty of good single-chip units out there. As an example, Thomas Vinterberg shot *The Celebration*—which went on to a wide theatrical release and a special jury prize at the Cannes Festival—using a Sony PC7, a $1,000 single-chip camera that has since been replaced by the PC1 and PC100.

When evaluating a camera, first look at its color reproduction. If you're a stickler for accuracy, you'll want to see if the camera can create an image with colors that are true to their originals. Whether or not you're concerned with color accuracy, look for color casts or odd shifts in color.

You'll also want to check the camera's response to different lighting situations. Unfortunately, your average electronics store is not the best place for testing a camera. However, if you can manage to point the camera out of a window, or into the dark recesses of a shelf or cabinet, you should be able to get an idea of the CCD's color response under different lighting. In addition to color consistency, and casts or shifts in color, look for additional noise.

CCD-based cameras can have a tendency to create vertical white bands when exposed to bright elements in a scene. Different cameras employ different techniques to deal with this problem, and some are better than others. When evaluating a camera, point it at a bright light (but never at the sun!) and then quickly tilt the camera down. Look for vertical banding and smearing during the camera move. Vertical banding is not a reason to reject a camera, as you can always work around it, but it is important to know if your camera has this tendency.

Stay Sharp

Many cameras try to improve image detail by applying sharpening filters to each frame of video, just as you might apply a sharpen filter to an image in Photoshop. While these features are great at improving fine detail in a shot, they are often too much of a good thing. Apply too much sharpening, and diagonal or curved lines will appear jagged, or *aliased*.

Oversharpening is easiest to spot on moving objects or during camera movements. When testing a camera, pan it about and look at objects that have very high-contrast edges. Look for "moving," jagged edges. Next, point the camera at an object with a thin, high-contrast horizontal line across it. Look to see if the line is stable or if it flashes on and off. Tilt the camera off-axis and watch how much the edges of the horizontal line change and alias (Figure 6.4).

Sharpening can also be a *good* thing, so as you are watching for aliasing, also pay attention to how sharp the camera renders fine detail. If you are testing in an electronics store, shooting objects with buttons, switches, and LEDs make great tests.

Higher-end cameras such as the Canon GL-1 often have a sharpening control. If the camera in question has such a control, play with it and see if you can use it to resolve oversharpening problems. Pay attention to how fine detail changes as you adjust the sharpening. Also look for any color shifts or changes as you adjust sharpening controls (Figure 6.5).

White Balance

To accurately represent color, your camera needs to know what objects in your image are white. Once the camera is calibrated for white, it can more accurately reproduce other colors. Most cameras can automatically adjust their *white balance* once they've been told what kind of light is being used to light the location. We'll discuss white balance in detail in Chapter 9. When evaluating a camera, though, see what white balance options are provided. At the least, a camera should provide separate settings for indoor or outdoor. Better are cameras that provide presets for specific kinds of lights. The ideal white balance control is a fully manual control that takes a reading off of a white object that you hold in front of the camera.

LENSES

Just as a film camera works by using a lens to focus light onto a piece of film, a digital video camera uses a lens to focus light onto the imaging window of a CCD (or group of CCDs). And, just as the quality of lens on a still camera can mean the difference between a good or bad photo, the quality of the lens on your video camera can mean the difference between sharp images with good color, and soft images with muddy color.

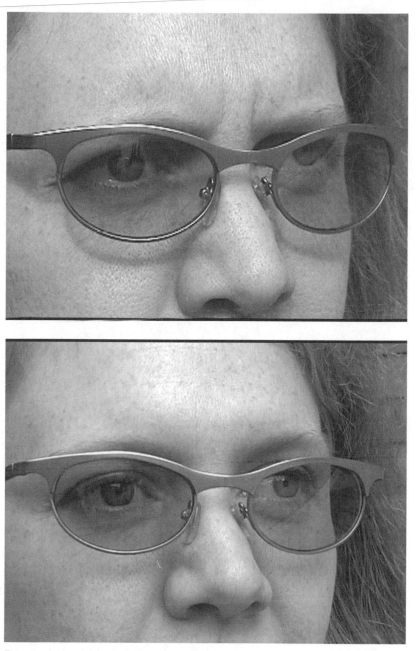

 FIGURE *Oversharpening can create annoying artifacts that jump and slide around*
6.4   *your image. In the top image, (shot with a Sony DCR-PC1) notice the strong*
        aliasing around the top of the glasses. The bottom image (shot with a Canon
        GL-1) lacks the aliasing around the glasses.

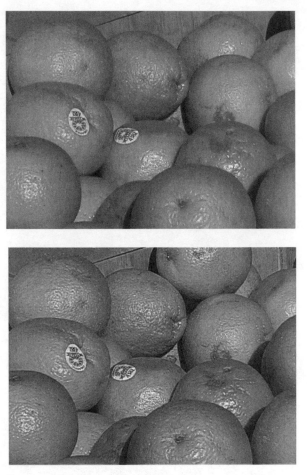

FIGURE   *If your camera has a manual sharpness control, you can decide how much*
6.5   *sharpening is appropriate for your image.*

At the prosumer and low-end professional level, most DV cameras have fixed, zoom lenses; that is, you can't change the camera's lens as you might do on your 35mm SLR camera. At the higher end, DV cameras have interchangeable lenses that let you select from a variety of zoom ranges, wide angles, and telephoto options.

Lens Quality

When evaluating lens quality, look for changes in brightness across the image. Does the lens produce images that are brighter in the middle than at the edges?

As you zoom the lens in and out, does the image get darker as the lens goes more telephoto?

Look for distortion around the edge of the image, particularly at wide angles. Does the image bow in or out as you zoom the lens back and forth? Similarly, look for changes in sharpness and detail throughout the lens's zoom range.

Chromatic aberration occurs when the lens does not equally focus all wavelengths of light. This problem is usually worse in single-chip cameras, though three-chip cameras with lower-quality lenses can also suffer from chromatic aberration. You can spot chromatic aberration by looking for fringes of red or green in high-contrast areas or around dark lines.

Lens Features

Depending on the quality of their controls, some lenses are easier to use than others. To make sure your lens provides controls that let you get the kind of camera movements and effects that you want, consider the following:

- **Zoom control.** Is the zoom control well-positioned, and does it provide for smooth zooming at variable speeds?
- **Manual focus.** If your camera has manual focus, where is the control? Whether electronic or mechanical, test the camera's manual focus for ease of use and reliability. Also be sure it holds focus when set. If the lens in question has a focusing *ring* (like what you'd find on a 35mm SLR camera), check to see if it has distances marked on it.
- **Aperture.** As with focus rings, some higher-end lenses have manual rings for controlling the lens aperture (apertures are discussed later in the chapter). Check for f-stop markings, ease-of-use, and accuracy.

Though lower-end cameras tend to have lenses built right in to the camera's body, this doesn't mean that they're necessarily low-quality lenses. Canon and Sony both include very high-quality lenses on cameras priced all the way down to $1,200. We'll discuss manual camera operation in more detail later in this chapter.

Never Mind the Reasons, How Does It Look?

At some point, you need to take a step back and look at the images produced by the cameras you are considering. You may find that you like one image bet-

Digital Zoom

Most consumer video cameras include a *digital zoom* feature. When digital zoom is activated, the camera will begin to digitally enlarge the image after you have zoomed to the optical limit of the lens. The results of this "fake zoom" are often terrible. At extreme zooms, shapes become blobby mosaics of muddy color, and even a minor amount of digital zoom can introduce noise and ugly artifacts. Unless you are intentionally going for a grungy look, digital zoom is a useless feature—turn it off and leave it off! (If you *are* going for a grungy look, shoot non-grungy footage and grunge it up in post-production. You'll have much more flexibility.)

ter than another, and you may have no idea why. That's okay. If you prefer one image over another, but can't find a technical reason for your preference, don't worry about it. In the end, your subjective opinion is more important than any technical benchmarks or specifications.

Camera Features

You may find that you see little difference in quality between cameras. If this is the case, then you can make your buying decision based on the features that you need and want. As a filmmaker, your feature requirements are different than the casual home user, so examine each camera's features carefully.

ERGONOMICS

Currently, there are DV cameras ranging from the size of a personal stereo all the way up to large, shoulder-mounted units. Choosing a "style" of camera means balancing features and shooting style, with cost.

Smaller cameras typically lack high-end inputs such as XLR audio jacks (more about audio jacks in Chapter 10). They also usually don't have as many manual features and practically never include such niceties as lenses with aperture and focus markings. And, if you opt for a really small camera like the Canon Elura or Sony PC-1, then you'll only get a single CCD.

On the other hand, small size makes a camera easier to carry, and ideal for surreptitious shooting. For documentaries, a low-profile camera might help you to get candid footage (nothing shuts up an interview faster than sticking

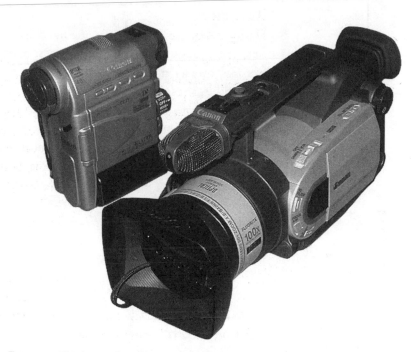

FIGURE 6.6   *The design of your camera not only dictates how comfortable the camera is, but what types of shots you'll be able to get. While a small hand-held may be more portable, a larger camera will facilitate more complex cinematography.*

a big lens in his or her face) or to shoot clandestinely in locations that wouldn't normally allow a camera (Figure 6.6).

Similarly, if you're shooting a feature, a smaller camera makes it easier to shoot scenes without being seen (drawing a crowd with your production can often slow things down). If you're shooting without a city permit or permission, the "tourist" look of a smaller camera may be just what you need to keep from getting hassled.

Larger cameras usually sport three CCDs for better image quality while their heavier weight makes for easier shooting and smooth, steady camera moves. And, let's face it, they look cooler.

Don't ignore the camera's physical feel. To get the footage you need, you must be able to move the camera with great precision. If a camera is too heavy (or light) or too bulky for you to pan and tilt comfortably, you may not be able to get the shots you want. The camera's weight can also have budgetary consequences, as a heavier camera will require a more sturdy—and therefore more expensive—tripod.

BATTERIES

Having a battery die during a shoot is more than just an inconvenience, it's a time and money waster. Unfortunately, most cameras ship with batteries that won't last over a long shoot. When purchasing, find out what other batteries are available, and how long they will last.

Ideally, you'll want enough battery life for several hours of shooting. Battery cost should be factored into your assessment of final camera cost. Note that using an LCD viewfinder will consume your batteries faster. If you know you'll be using the LCD a lot, you'll need to assume shorter battery life.

TIP

Third-Party Batteries

For extra-long life, consider a battery belt such as those made by NRG Research. With enough juice to power a camera and light for several hours, a battery belt is a great—though bulky and costly—solution to short battery life.

MANUAL OVERRIDE

The most important feature for the serious videographer is manual override. Controls for manually setting the camera's focus, aperture, shutter speed, audio levels, and white balance are essential for flexible shooting.

The problem with automatic mechanisms is that they're not too smart and they have no artistic flair. Rather, they are designed to produce a good picture under common, ideal shooting situations.

With manual focus controls, you can choose what to focus on, and compose your shots the way you choose (Figure 6.7). Similarly, manual aperture controls (sometimes called *iris* or *exposure*) let you compensate for difficult lighting situations such as harsh backlighting.

Lower-end cameras typically provide electronic manual controls that are accessed through a menu system or from buttons on the camera's control panel. Higher-end cameras will have lens-mounted rings just like the rings on a 35mm still camera.

Lower-end cameras usually don't have values marked on their focus or aperture controls; instead, they display simple slider graphics in the camera's viewfinder. While this is effective, the lack of quantifiable settings can make it difficult to get the same settings from shot to shot. Such electronic controls are not necessarily suited to changing aperture or focus on-the-fly, making it difficult to do *rack focus* or *pull focus* shots (see Chapter 9 for more on these types of camera moves).

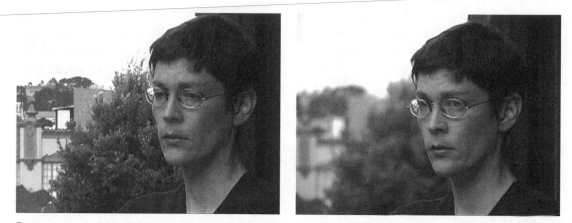

FIGURE
6.7   *Manual controls give you more freedom for composition. In this example, we used manual focus and aperture controls to go from an image with a sharp, focused background, to one with a soft, blurry background.*

Manual What?
We'll discuss the theory and use of manual iris and shutter speed in Chapter 9.

TIP

Shutter Speed

Most cameras automatically select a shutter speed based on their aperture setting, a process called *shutter priority*. Many cameras also provide manual shutter speed control, which provides you with another degree of creative control. By switching to a higher shutter speed—1/200th to 1/4000th—you can stop fast-moving action such as sporting events. A faster shutter is great for picking out fine detail, but faster speeds eliminate most motion blur, which can result in an image with very strobic, stuttery motion (Figure 6.8).

Unfortunately, though vendors frequently provide fast shutter speeds, they often skimp on slower ones. If you are ultimately planning to transfer your finished video to film, it's a good idea to look for a camera that can be forced to shoot at 1/60th of a second. At this speed, you'll tend to get a better film transfer.

AUDIO

After manual controls, your next concern should be the camera's audio facilities. It's pretty safe to say that the microphones included on all camcorders are

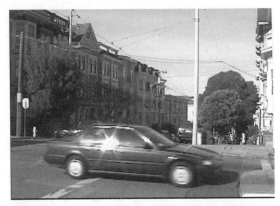

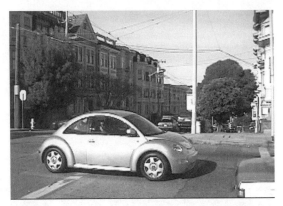

FIGURE
6.8a   *At a somewhat "normal" shutter speed of 1/60th of a second, the moving car has a pronounced motion blur.*

FIGURE
6.8b   *At 1/4000th of a second, moving objects in each individual frame are frozen. When played back, the video can have a somewhat "stroboscopic" look.*

lousy. Low-quality to begin with, their usefulness is further degraded by the fact that they often pick up camera motor noise, as well as the sound of your hands on the camera itself. Consequently, an external microphone jack and a headphone jack are essential for feature production. In addition to replacing the lousy on-board mic on your camera, an external mic jack lets you mix audio from a number of mics, and feed the result into your camera. We'll discuss audio hardware more in Chapter 10. When evaluating a camera, first check what kind of mic connectors it has—XLR, or mini—and make sure the connectors are positioned so that mic cables and connectors won't get in the way of moving the camera and shooting (Figure 6.9).

A headphone jack is a must-have to ensure that you're actually recording audio (you'll be surprised how easy it is to forget to turn on a microphone).

Manual audio gain controls let you adjust or *attenuate* the audio signal coming into the camera, making it easy to boost quiet voices, or lower the level on a roaring car engine.

PROGRESSIVE SCAN

As we discussed in Chapter 4, current video standards such as PAL and NTSC are interlaced; that is, each frame of video consists of two sets of scan-lines, or *fields,* which are separately painted onto the screen every 60th of a second. Progressive scanning—painting the scan lines on, in order, from top to bottom—

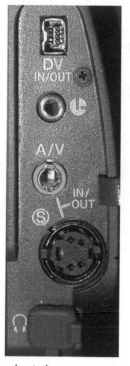

 FIGURE **6.9**   *Be sure to determine what jacks your camera provides. This Canon GL-1 provides a headphone jack (bottom) on its rear panel, and a mini mic jack on a side panel (not shown).*

is what your computer monitor does, and it typically produces a clearer, less-flickery image.

Because of interlacing, normal video effectively has a frame rate of 60 half-frames per second and is subject to motion artifacts such as jittery motion.

Some cameras can shoot in a non-interlaced, progressive scan mode, which presents frames that are much clearer than those of interlaced video. (Some companies refer to this as "Movie mode.") However, the clarity of the frames also means that fast-moving images can have a strange, stroboscopic quality to their motion.

Progressive-scanned video often looks much more "film-like" than interlaced video. Not because of grain or texture, but because it is, in some ways, a lower frame rate than interlaced video. Since progressive scanned video is running at 29.97 whole frames per second, it's closer to film's 24 fps than interlaced video's 60 half-frames per second.

Some film transfer houses claim that progressive scan yields a better film transfer, and many transfer houses recommend shooting progressive. Others are more comfortable with interlaced, because that's what they're used to transferring. Be sure to do a lot of test shoots before you commit to shooting in progressive scan mode.

IMAGE STABILIZATION

Because it's difficult to hold a one- or two-pound camcorder steady, most cameras now provide some sort of image stabilization feature to smooth out bumpy, jittery camera movement. Five years ago we would have told you to deactivate these features and leave them off. But today's image stabilization technology—though no substitute for a tripod—is very effective and (usually) has no ill side effects.

There are two kinds of image stabilization: electronic and optical. Electronic image stabilization (sometimes called *digital image stabilization*) requires a CCD with a larger imaging size than the actual image size that is displayed. EIS works by detecting camera motion, analyzing it to see if it's intentional or not, and then digitally moving the image to compensate for unwanted motion. Because the camera is overscanning the actual field of view, there are enough extra pixels around the edges to allow for this kind of movement (Figure 6.10).

Since the camera is constantly moving the image about the screen to compensate for shake, electronic stabilization can often result in softer, slightly blurred images. We've also seen some cameras show a slight color shift when

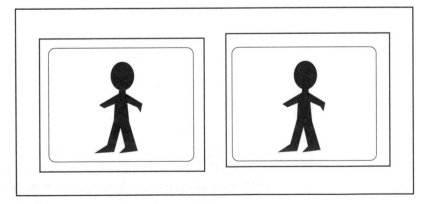

 FIGURE **6.10**   *In electronic image stabilization, the camera scans an oversized area and then pans about that area to compensate for shake.*

using EIS. However, most EIS functions in use today do an excellent job of stabilizing your image without noticeably degrading its quality.

Optical image stabilization doesn't alter your image, but instead, changes the internal optics of the camera to compensate for motion. Rather than solid prisms, cameras with optical stabilization use prisms composed of a transparent, refractive fluid sandwiched between two flat pieces of glass. Motors around this prism sandwich can move the glass panels to reshape the prism. Light passing through this mechanism can be redirected onto the correct part of the CCD to compensate for camera shake (Figure 6.11).

Since OIS doesn't ever touch your image data, there's no chance that it will corrupt your image. On the downside, because it's more complicated, optical stabilization costs more than electronic stabilizing. Also, because the stabilization is tailored to a particular lens, if you add wide angle or other attachments that change the focal length of your lens, OIS will stop working.

When evaluating a camera, try some motion tests—both slow and smooth, and fast and jittery—to see how each camera's stabilization feature affects overall image quality.

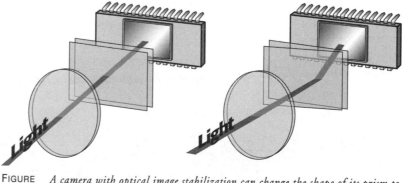

FIGURE **6.11**   *A camera with optical image stabilization can change the shape of its prism to redirect light to the right position on the CCD.*

WIDESCREEN

Many cameras include a "widescreen" mode that lets you shoot in a 16:9 aspect ratio à la HDTV or wide-screen film. These features work by cropping the top and bottom of the frame to letterbox the image down to 16:9.

The downside to this "hacked" 16:9 effect is that you lose a lot of vertical resolution. If your CCD only has 360,000 pixels and you're using a third of them for black areas above and below your image, you're effectively shooting with much lower resolution than your camera is capable of (Figure 6.12).

Some formats, such as Digital Betacam can shoot a true 16:9 aspect ratio because they use rectangular CCDs that actually have a full 16:9 ratio's worth of pixels. DV, MiniDV, and other formats that don't provide a "true" 16:9 mode, can usually output a wide-screen, non-letterboxed image to a widescreen TV, but this is hardly useful unless you know that your project will be delivered and viewed on a widescreen device. (Editing widescreen footage also presents technical issues in regards to editing software and hardware. We'll discuss these in chapter 13.)

Another route to shooting wide screen is to leave your camera in its normal shooting mode, and do what film users do: get a special lens.

An *anamorphic* lens optically squeezes the image horizontally to fit a wider image onto the CCD. If you look at an individual frame of film shot with an anamorphic lens, you'll see a squished image that's greatly distorted. But project that image back through a projector that's been fitted with an anamorphic lens, and you'll get an undistorted, really wide picture. Similarly, you can use your editing software to unsqueeze your anamorphic footage to create a true widescreen image (Figure 6.13).

Several manufacturers make anamorphic attachments for camcorders. If you're determined to use one of these, however, you'll need to make sure it works with your camera. Check with your vendor for compatibility. Also, if you're planning on transferring to film, check with your service bureau.

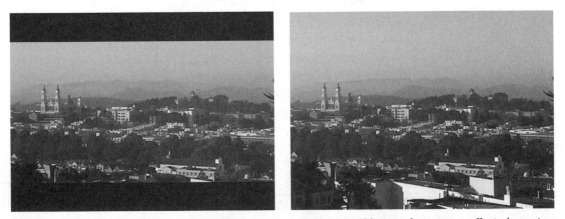

FIGURE
6.12   *The "widescreen" feature on many cameras simply masks the top and bottom of your image, effectively wasting a third of your vertical resolution!*

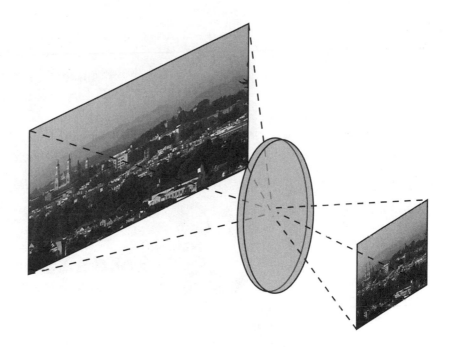

FIGURE
6.13
An anamorphic lens optically squeezes a wide image down to the aspect ratio of your CCD. To look right when viewed, it must be correspondingly desqueezed..

VIEWFINDER

Most video cameras have two viewfinders, an eyepiece viewfinder and a flip-out LCD viewfinder. Curiously, some higher-end cameras such as the Sony VX1000 and the Canon XL-1 have only eyepiece viewfinders.

Because you can tilt an LCD into different viewing angles, flip-out LCDs afford you a wider range of shooting options. However, because an LCD drains your battery quickly and can be difficult to see in bright light, you might not be able to use it all the time. Yes, you want a high-quality LCD, but don't let LCD quality weigh too heavily when choosing a camera.

Some higher-end cameras include a feature called Zebra that displays diagonal black and white lines in areas of your image that are overexposed. These lines are not recorded to tape, they only appear in the viewfinder. If you're manually setting your shutter and iris, Zebra is a must-have for situations when you don't have an external monitor to look at (Figure 6.14).

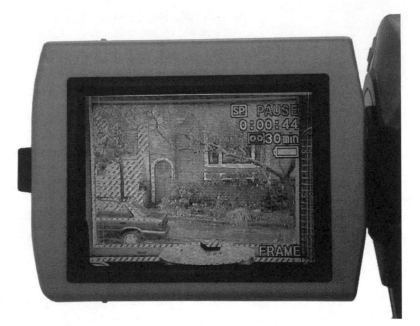

FIGURE   *The diagonal lines in this viewfinder are the "Zebra" marks that indicate*
6.14   *overexposure.*

SPECIAL EFFECTS

Most video cameras, especially lower-cost prosumer cameras, include a number of special effects and wipes ranging from sepia tinting to "arty" posterizing looks. We don't recommend using any of these features. It's better to shoot unprocessed video so as to have the greatest flexibility when you post.

Similarly, many cameras also provide a number of wipes and dissolves. If you plan on editing your entire project in the camera, or without using a computer (by hooking two cameras together), then these wipes and dissolves might be useful. But, as with effects, better to shoot clean footage and add transitions in post-production.

VIDEO STANDARD

In Chapter 4 we discussed NTSC, PAL, SECAM, and DTV, the different video standards. In the process of choosing a format, you probably chose a video standard. Since most camera vendors make separate versions of their cameras for different video standards, you'll want to make sure you get a camera that conforms to your chosen standard. Note that some vendors make cameras that are available in one standard, but not others.

Also note that, because of special tariffs, many PAL cameras have their *DV In* functions disabled. This means you won't be able to lay edited video back out to tape on such a camera. Vendors usually sell separate, more expensive, *DV In* versions of their PAL cameras. There is a strong lobby to get this changed, so it may not be an issue by the time you read this.

USE YOUR DIRECTOR OF PHOTOGRAPHY

If you have already chosen a director of photography, talk to him or her about your camera needs. Your D.P. may have ideas about how to shoot your project that will not only make for better-looking video, but help enhance the emotional impact of your scenes. Depending on what sort of effects you want to achieve, some cameras might be better than others. If you'll be shooting your feature yourself, then consider the same questions you would ask a D.P.:

- **Is there a particular "look" that you are striving for?** Grungy old film? Super saturated and glossy? Muted and subtle?
- **Are you planning on certain camera movements?** If you know that you will be shooting from a Steadicam or other specific camera mount, you'll need to consider the size and weight of your camera.
- **Do you have special post-production needs?** If you know, for example, that you will be shooting blue-screen footage, then you'll want the best image quality you can afford.
- **Does your shoot require more than one camera?** If so, you may need to consider going with cheaper cameras.
- **Are you going to rent a high-end, professional camera?** If so, you may need to hire a professional operator. Consider this in your budget.

Still Images

Most, if not all, digital video cameras include a still image function that lets you use your DV camera like a still camera. Typically, these features grab an individual frame and write it to tape for 5 to 7 seconds (with audio). With your editing software, you can grab a single frame from this 7-second chunk and use it as a still image.

If you really need still image capabilities, either for your video production or for other work, a DV camera is not the best answer. Any digital still camera (or a film camera and a cheap scanner) will yield better still quality than a DV camera, and without using up videotape.

Accessorizing

As with any piece of gear, there are loads of accessories available for your DV camera. And, while many are fun frivolities, others are necessary for a serious DV production. Pick out your camera before you start shopping for any of the following items, though. Different cameras have different needs, and you don't want to buy an expensive accessory only to find it has the wrong type of connector, or is the wrong shape for your camera.

TRIPODS, STEADICAMS, AND BRACKETS

If you need a stable image, there is absolutely *no* substitute for a good tripod. A tripod is also essential for some complex camera motions such as smooth pans with simultaneous zooms. Camera movement is part of your visual vocabulary, and most camera movements require a tripod. Shooting without one limits your vocabulary.

The ideal tripod has a fluid head for smooth movement, and easy-to-find handles for locking and unlocking each axis of the tripod's motion (pan, tilt, and pedestal). Check for stability and sturdiness and make sure the tripod can support the weight of your camera, along with anything else you may need to have onboard (audio mixer, microphones, small lights, etc.).

Many vendors sell special "video tripods" that use a *pistol grip* for positioning. We unequivocally do not recommend this type of tripod. Because you cannot unlock individual axes, pistol grip tripods are unsuited to smooth pans or tilts.

Steadicams/Glidecams

Normally, when you want to move the camera through a scene—rather than having it pan and tilt from a fixed location—you must lay tracks along which your crew will slowly push a camera dolly. In addition to the hassle of laying tracks and smoothly moving the camera, you have to be sure you don't capture the tracks in your shot.

Nowadays you can—if you have enough money—perform such shots with a Steadicam. A clever arrangement of gimbals and counterweights, Steadicams, Glidecams, and other similar stabilizers work by mounting the camera on an apparatus that has a lot of rotational inertia, but little reason to rotate. Though the physics are complicated, the result is simple: a camera that mostly floats in place, but that can be adjusted and moved in simple, tiny movements.

Both Steadicam and Glidecam produce a number of different types of units for cameras of different weights. These devices are not cheap, and if you really need one, you'll probably do better to rent. Note that if you have a very large camera that requires a large Steadicam, you'll also need to spring for a trained Steadicam operator.

Brackets

As we discussed earlier, today's tiny camcorders can be difficult to hold steady because of their low weight. A simple bracket not only provides you with more handholds, but can give you places to mount lights and microphones.

There are a number of inexpensive metal brackets that are normally used by videographers or still photographers to attach external flashes. Brackets provide extra stability and configuration possibilities that can greatly expand the repertoire of what you can do with an otherwise simple camera (Figure 6.15).

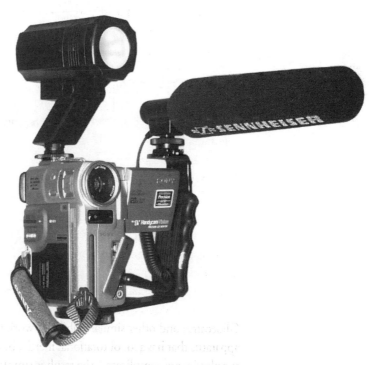

FIGURE

6.15

With the addition of a bracket, this tiny Sony DCR-PC1 becomes much easier to handle.

Microphones

All video cameras—even at the higher end—have marginal microphones, so you'll need to replace these with professional units designed for the type of shooting you'll be doing. We'll discuss mics in Chapter 10.

Filters

You can use filters to change the color or optical properties of the light in your scene. Most filters screw directly onto the threads on the end of your lens, though some have special mounting brackets.

At the very least, you'll want to get a UV filter which, in addition to filtering out some UV light, will serve to protect the lens on your expensive new video camera. Depending on the type of shooting you are doing, you might also want to get a polarizing filter, which will do much to improve your shots of skies, clouds, or reflections. Color tints and optical effects such as starbursts or lens flares can also be added using filters.

Finally, you might also want to use special filters to soften your image to remove some of that hard video "edge." If you are really striving for a film look, such filters can really help. We'll discuss filters more in Chapter 9.

All that Other Stuff

There are any number of other cool and useful accessories ranging from bags and trunks for protecting and transporting your camera, to housings for shooting underwater. For a full round-up of these sorts of items, check out www.dvhandbook.com/accessories.

Cameras Compared

Now that we've looked at the features you'll be seeing on different cameras, let's see how the most popular cameras compare. All of the cameras listed in the next section use the MiniDV format and are well-suited to feature or documentary productions that will be delivered on video or transferred to film.

THREE-CHIP CAMERAS

Sony VX-1000 (street price $3,200). Released in 1995, the VX-1000 was the very first high-quality MiniDV camera and it's still a good choice today. Used on innumerable films (*The Cruise, The Saltmen of Tibet,* Spike Lee's *Bamboozled, Windhorse,* Lars Von Trier's *The Idiots*), the VX-1000's biggest limitations are its price and lack of an LCD viewfinder. But, the unit's image quality, manual controls, and comfortable feel make it an excellent choice.

Canon XL-1 (street price $3,800). Nearly as popular as the VX-1000, the XL-1's interchangeable lenses give it more shooting flexibility than any of its competitors. In addition to the XL-1's excellent image quality, the camera provides good manual controls, and a progressive scan mode, but lacks an LCD viewfinder. Most users either love or hate the XL-1. Frequent complaints include trouble controlling the unit's zoom and focus, while others find the camera uncomfortable and difficult to hand-hold because of the front-heavy weight of the lens. Try before you buy (see Figure 9.4 in Chapter 9).

Canon GL-1 (street price $2,200). With a body similar to the VX-1000 and image quality that's identical to the XL-1, the GL-1 is a great, lower-cost alternative to its high-end cousins. The GL-1's excellent flourite lens reduces chromatic aberration, while the whopping 20x zoom lens delivers excellent image quality. Packing an LCD viewfinder, full manual controls, and a progressive scan mode, the GL-1's biggest drawback is its lack of manual audio gain controls. Though it sports good automatic gain control, the discerning audio engineer might prefer a camera with manual controls. The GL-1 also provides an S-Video input for dubbing from other video sources, letting you use the GL-1 as a video transcoder (refer back to Figure 6.9).

Changing Colors

TIP

In general, Canon cameras tend to saturate colors more than Sony cameras. Images from Canon cameras weigh heavy on the reds and magentas, while Sonys lean toward blues.

Sony TRV-900 (street price $1,900). It may look like a somewhat typical consumer video camera, but the TRV-900 is actually a very capable three-chip DV camera. Though its lens is not up to the quality of the GL-1, the TRV-900 still provides very good image quality, and the camera packs very good manual controls including manual audio control. Unfortunately, the TRV-900 lacks manual sharpness control, meaning you'll have to rely on filters and post-processing if you want to reduce the camera's hard-edged image.

JVC GY-DV500 (street price $6,000) Currently the most full-featured, truly professional MiniDV camera available, the DV500 looks like a traditional high-end, shoulder-mounted camcorder. In addition to its rugged 11 lb, design, the camera features such high-end features as standard 1/2″ bayonet-mount interchangeable lenses, built-in dual XLR balanced mic connectors, and built-in genlocking. No doubt about it, if you've got the money and want the a professional camera, this is the unit of choice.

Sony Progressive Scan

Be aware that the progressive scan feature on many Sony cameras (such as the TRV-900) uses a 15fps shutter rate. So, though your images will be progressively scanned, they'll have a very slow-shutter look.

TIP

SINGLE-CHIP CAMERAS

Sony DCR-PC100 (street price $1,800). A tiny marvel of a DV camera, the PC-100 sports an upright design that makes it ideal for run-and-gun shooting. With good manual controls, S-Video in and out, and good image quality, the PC-100 is a good choice if you need a small camera. Note that Sony single-chip cameras sometimes have curious banding artifacts, so if you can swing the extra $200–$300, the TRV-900 will yield better image quality, but in a somewhat larger package. The PC100's only real advantage over the smaller, cheaper Sony DCR-PC1 is better still quality.

Canon Elura (street price $1,400). Similar in size and shape to the PC100, the Canon Elura sports slightly better image quality, optical image stabilization, S-Video in and out, and a true progressive scan mode, making it one of the best values for the money of all of the single-chip cameras. On the downside, the Elura has no built-in external mic jack or headphone jack, meaning you'll have to add a separate, external docking station to get these necessary features. Unfortunately, adding a docking station somewhat compromises the unit's small size, though if you're always shooting from a tripod, this is less of a concern.

Sony DCR-TRV10 (street price $1,400). A good, all-around camera, the TRV10 provides image quality comparable to the PC1 or PC100, but in a larger body with bigger LCD screen and full complement of jacks (though the camera lacks S-Video in). As with Sony's other cameras, the TRV-10 has occasional image artifacts, but the overall combination of price, performance, and quality makes for a good value.

Sony DCR-PC1 (street price $1,300). The tiniest DV camera of all, the PC1 packs the same video quality as the PC100, but without that camera's improved still quality and S-Video in. Unlike the Elura, it provides mic and headphone jacks onboard, making it the best choice if portability and small size are your primary concern. Unfortunately, running the camera off of wall current produces an intolerable hum when using an external microphone. Plan to buy a lot of batteries with this camera (Figure 6.15).

As you can see, finding the right balance of image quality, manual controls, inputs, progressive scan mode (if you want it), and price can be tricky. Because each camera has at least one limitation, we can't wholeheartedly recommend any one of them. Which one is right for you will depend on your needs and shooting conditions. At the time of this writing, these represent the market leaders in cameras. For updated listings and coverage of more models, check out www.dvhandbook.com/cameras.

7 Non-Linear Editing Software

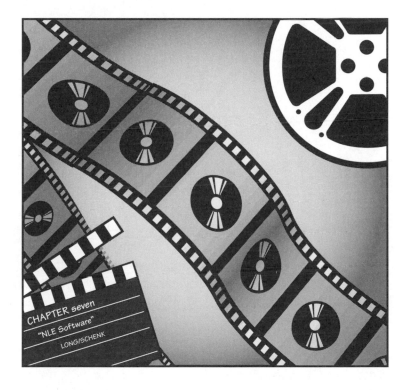

CHAPTER seven
"NLE Software"
LONG/SCHENK

IN THIS CHAPTER

- You Say On-Line, I Say Off-Line
- Non-Linear Editing Software Basics
- What's in an NLE
- Getting Media into Your Project
- Effects and Titles
- Audio Tools
- The Final Output
- NLEs Compared

Now that you've assembled your computer, it's time to choose the editing software that you'll run on your new workstation. Though editing is a *post*-production task, we've chosen to talk about it now because it's a good idea to select your editing package *before* you start shooting. If you know what your editing program is capable of before you shoot, you'll have a better idea of how certain scenes need to be shot, and what you can and can't fix "in post." This is especially true for effects-intensive projects where planning weighs heavily on your shooting. Also, if you select your editing package now, you can start learning the ins and outs while you work your way through pre-production and production.

In this chapter, we'll cover all of the issues, concepts, and terminology you'll need to understand when choosing a non-linear editing package. Your NLE will be the heart of your post-production system, so you'll want to choose carefully.

You Say On-Line, I Say Off-Line

Though you may be used to the terms "on-line" and "off-line" when talking about the Internet, those terms have a very different meaning to a video editor. Understanding the difference between on-line and off-line editing is essential to understanding how to get the best possible quality when editing.

On-line editing means that you're working with the media that will end up in your final master. If you capture high-quality video, edit it, add special effects, and finally lay it off to a videotape final master, you're editing *on-line*. Outputting from your computer directly to film using a special film recorder is also considered editing on-line, as is editing streaming media clips for a Web site. In these examples, each project is destined for a very different media, but in each case the editor is creating the final master output. *Off-line editing,* on the other hand, occurs when you are using low-quality, or *proxy,* footage to create a rough draft of your project.

On-line editing does not refer to a specific level of quality, nor does it refer to specific equipment. It is assumed, however, that because you are working with the footage that will be your master, you are probably working with the highest-quality video your system can produce, and with the highest-quality video equipment to which you have access.

THE CONFORMIST

Why wouldn't you always perform an on-line edit on your computer? Let's say you were able to afford to shoot your feature using expensive Digital Betacam equipment, but you can't afford $45,000 for a DigiBeta deck to connect to your computer. To edit your footage on your computer, you'll need to go to an on-line editing suite and pay to have your DigiBeta masters dubbed to another format, such as MiniDV. You can then edit the MiniDV tapes using your computer (this is your off-line edit).

When you're done editing, your editing software can output an *edit decision list,* or *EDL,* which is just that: a list of the edits you decided to make, organized by timecode and tape numbers. You can now take the EDL and your original DigiBeta tapes back to the on-line suite for an on-line session. There, you'll pay to have your original DigiBeta tapes edited according to the instructions in your EDL, a process called *conforming*.

Because an on-line session creates a final edit from your *original* tapes, any color correction, dissolves, or titles that you may have set up in your NLE are irrelevant. Though your EDL can specify certain types of dissolves, it can't specify proprietary, non-standard effects such as wacky page turns and subtle color corrections. These effects will need to be added using the facilities in your on-line suite.

For less-expensive formats such as DV, you can probably afford the equipment you'll need to perform an on-line edit yourself. Note that no matter what type of format you use, if you're creating a lot of computer-generated effects, you'll probably need to on-line edit those yourself to whatever format you can afford.

If you are using a digital interface to get video into your computer, then you will usually be capturing full-quality, on-line footage unless you have multiple resolutions available with your codec. If you are using an analog video interface, as discussed in Chapter 5, your editing system will probably provide options for lower-res digitizing for rough-cuts, and high resolution digitizing to create your final master.

Television Editing and EDLs

If you're still confused about the off-line/on-line workflow, consider how a professional TV show is edited. After the project is shot, the master tapes are given to the off-line editor, who digitizes the footage into an off-line editing system, usually an Avid Media Composer, at a low-quality resolution. The off-line editor edits the final cut and then generates an edit decision list.

The EDL and the master tapes are then handed off to the on-line editor, who conforms the tapes using one or more source decks linked to a Digital Betacam D-1 or D-2 record deck via an edit controller. Or, the on-line editor might use a very high-end non-linear editing system, like Quantel's Edit Box, which will recapture your video from your source masters using your EDL as a guide. Either way, each piece of video that goes onto the final master tape is meticulously monitored for quality and corrected if necessary.

What's in an NLE

A typical non-linear editing program is a very complicated piece of software. However, by identifying the features you need for your project, you can more easily sort through the specifications of different packages. The following are factors you'll need to consider when choosing an editing program.

THE INTERFACE

Most editing applications share a similar interface. A project window contains *bins* or folders, which hold video clips and other media. Double-clicking on a clip will open it in the *source monitor,* a window on the left side of the screen. The source monitor lets you view the shot and select the part of it that you want to use in your final edited *sequence.*

You assemble shots into a sequence using a *timeline* window that displays representations of your clips in their edited order. Separate tracks are used to represent your project's video and audio. When editing, you can *target* particular tracks, letting you choose to edit the audio and video from a clip, or just the audio *or* video. For example, by targeting the video track, you can perform a *cutaway* from one piece of video to another, while the underlying audio keeps playing. We'll cover the different methods of getting clips into the timeline in the next section.

On the right side of the screen is the *record monitor,* a window that displays the video from the timeline—that is, your edited sequence. Figure 7.1 shows the editing interface in Adobe Premiere.

Most editing programs follow this same setup, though some simpler, lower-end programs like Apple's iMovie use a less-complicated, more direct approach. For maximum flexibility, look for a package with robust editing controls (many of which are described next). For faster learning, look for a program with a more streamlined interface, but beware: You may not get all the tools you need to produce high-quality audio and video.

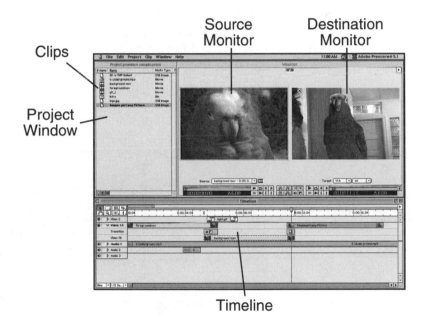
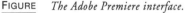

FIGURE
7.1   *The Adobe Premiere interface.*

EDITING FEATURES

One of the best things about a good non-linear editing package is that there are many different ways to make an edit. Following are descriptions of the editing tools found in most NLEs. If you are new to editing, selecting a package with lots of these features will assure the most editing flexibility. If you've got some experience editing, you'll want to be sure to find a package that provides the editing controls that you prefer.

Drag-and-Drop Editing

With drag-and-drop editing, you use the mouse to drag shots from a bin and into the timeline window. Once there, shots can be rearranged by dragging them into the order you prefer. Drag-and-drop editing is often the best way to build your first rough string-up of a scene.

Many editing programs offer *storyboard editing,* which lets you arrange and select multiple shots and drag them into the timeline all at one (Figure 7.2). The result is a sequence built in the order that your selected shots were sorted in your source bin; for example, by take number, by timecode, etc.

Three-Point Editing

Three-point editing lets you define which part of your source clip will be used, by selecting a beginning, or "in-point," and an ending, or "out-point," within the clip (two points), and then selecting where the clip will begin *or* end in your edited sequence (the third point). This allows for a more precise edit than drag-and-drop editing. After defining your points, you press the Edit button and the selected part of your source clip (as defined by the first two points) will be placed on the timeline at the defined destination (the third point) (Figure 7.3).

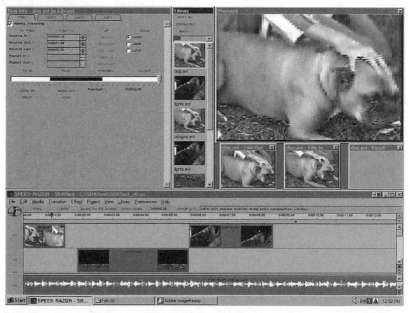
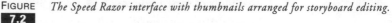

FIGURE 7.2   *The Speed Razor interface with thumbnails arranged for storyboard editing.*

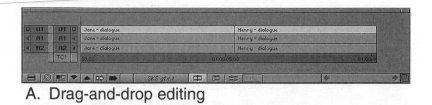

A. Drag-and-drop editing

B. 3-point editing

FIGURE **7.3**   *The two-shot sequence in timeline A was created using drag-and-drop editing, the two-shot sequence in timeline B was created using three-point editing.*

JKL Editing

If your program provides JKL editing controls, the J on your keyboard will play your video in reverse, the K will pause, and the L will play forward. This simple mechanism allows you to quickly shuttle around a video clip to find an in or out point. Since you can usually select an in-point with the I on your keyboard and an out-point with the O, JKL turns your standard keyboard into an efficient one-handed edit controller (Figure 7.4).

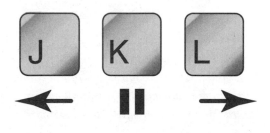

FIGURE **7.4**   *JKL editing provides a simple one-handed editing interface.*

Insert and Overwrite Editing

Whether you're using drag-and-drop, three-point editing, or switching between the two, your editing package should provide for *Insert* and *Overwrite* editing modes. These two options allow you to make a choice as to *how* your footage is added into an already-cut sequence.

When inserting, all of the footage after your in-point is moved down the timeline to accommodate the footage that is being added. In this way, the new footage—whether audio, video, or both—is inserted into the timeline.

Conversely, overwrite leaves all clips in place, but writes the new clip over any existing video or audio (depending on which tracks are targeted) (Figure 7.5).

V1	V1	Jane – dialogue		Dog barks	Henry – dialogue
A1	A1	Jane – dialogue		Dog barks	Henry – dialogue
A2	A2	Jane – dialogue		Dog barks	Henry – dialogue
	TC1	00:00	01:00:05:00		01:00:10:00

SKS gfx.1

A. Insert edit

V1	V1	Jane – dialogue		Dog cutaway	Henry – dialogue
A1	A1	Jane – dialogue		Henry – dialogue	
A2	A2	Jane – dialogue		Henry – dialogue	
	TC1	00:00	01:00:05:00		01:00:1

SKS gfx.1

B. Cutaway

FIGURE **7.5** *Insert edits allow you to add a shot between two existing shots (A), while overwrite edits allow you to easily add a cutaway (B).*

Linear Editors Beware!

If you've got experience editing on a linear editing system, be sure to note that insert editing on a non-linear system has no correlation to insert editing on a dedicated, linear edit controller (where insert means to overwrite a particular audio or video track).

TIP

Trimming

Once you've got a decent rough cut of a scene, you'll want to fine-tune it. For example, you might want to add beats of silence between certain lines of dialogue to show a character's hesitation, or you may want to extend a shot of a character to show his reaction as another character speaks. One way to do this is by *trimming* the edit. A trimming interface has a familiar two-monitor window, but instead of source and record monitors, you see the last frame of the outgoing shot and the first frame of the incoming shot of the edit that you are going to trim. When you're in trim mode, you can extend or shorten the end of the outgoing shot (the "A-side" of the edit), or you can extend or shorten the incoming shot (the "B-side" of the edit).

Ripple, Roll, Slide, and Slip

There are a number of different types of edits that you can make to an existing sequence. The following are four advanced ways to fine-tune your edited sequence. Depending on your software, they can be created in the timeline, in trim mode, or both (Figures 7.6 and 7.7).

- **Roll and Ripple** are two ways to change an existing edit between two shots. *Ripple* allows you to extend or shorten either the outgoing shot (the A-side) or the incoming shot (the B-side). All of the shots in your

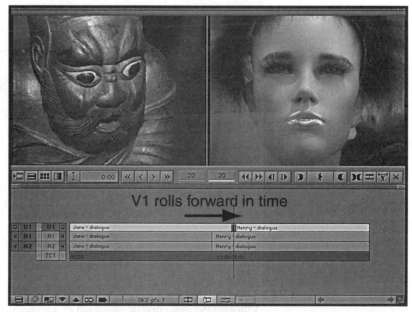

 FIGURE 7.6   *This dialogue overlap was created using a rolling edit, shown here in Avid Media Composer's timeline and trim mode windows. The edit in the video track rolls right as the A-side of the edit is extended and the B-side is simultaneously shortened.*

FIGURE
7.7
By using a slide edit, you can move the center shot in A to the right (B) or to the left (C) without changing the length of your overall sequence.

sequence will move farther down in the timeline to accommodate these added frames. *Roll* lets you extend the outgoing shot and tighten the incoming shot simultaneously (or vice versa). The overall length of the sequence will remain unchanged, which makes Rolling edits well-suited to creating overlapping edits as in Figure 7.6.

- **Slip and Slide** edits involve three shots, like in Figure 7.07 A. If you use a *Slide* edit to drag the middle shot forward in time, the first shot will automatically be extended to fill the gap, while the last shot will be automatically shortened to keep the overall length of the three shots the same. (Figure 7.7b and c) *Slip* allows you to change the footage contained in the middle shot, starting it at a different place without affecting the shots surrounding it, or the duration of the sequence.

Multicamera Editing

If your software allows multi-cam editing, you can "group" shots from different cameras together in your timeline and then select which video you want to see at any given time. Though most independent films are shot with one cam-

era, multicamera editing can be useful if you recorded audio and video separately. You can group the audio and video for each shot using either matching
timecode or a slate sync mark. Figure 7.8 shows multicamera editing in Avid's
Media Composer.

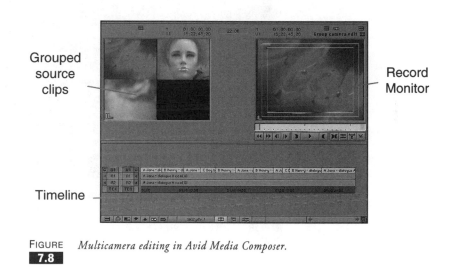

Grouped source clips

Record Monitor

Timeline

FIGURE
7.8   *Multicamera editing in Avid Media Composer.*

EDITING NICETIES

In addition to their editing methods, there are a number of interface and utility features that you should look for when choosing an editing package.

Good keyboard controls are a must as it's much easier to develop an editing rhythm by punching keys than by moving a mouse. Also look for multiple undos (at least 32 levels) and auto save/auto backup features, all of which
will help you recover from the mistakes that will inevitably be made.

Don't be taken in by packages that provide for dozens (or even a hundred)
audio and video tracks. For most features, three or four video tracks and four
to eight audio tracks are all you'll need (Figure 7.9). If you're worried about
keeping your timeline organized, a good *nesting* feature is better than a huge
number of tracks.

With nesting, you can place one edited sequence inside another. That sequence can, in turn, be nested inside yet another. By organizing your project

FIGURE   *Edit DV's interface with multiple video and audio tracks. Note that each*
7.9   *audio track is actually a stereo pair.*

into discreet sequences that are nested inside each other, you can quickly and easily make changes to one piece without a lot of confusing navigation through your timeline.

In addition, look for the following features when assessing an NLE:

- **Matchframe.** Instead of having to search through all your bins and shots looking for a source file that you've already added to your timeline, you simply park your cursor on a frame of the shot in your timeline and press the *matchframe* button. The source clip appears in your source monitor. Related to matchframe is the *find clip* command that opens the bin a shot is located in.

- **Audio scrubbing.** Most digital non-linear editing systems let you *scrub* through the audio, which means that as you slowly scroll through a clip, the audio plays back in slow motion along with the video. This helps you easily find a particular sound, such as a pause in a line of dialogue or the beat in a piece of music.

- **Lockable tracks.** Locking a track can prevent you from making accidental edits. If you follow the traditional motion picture workflow and

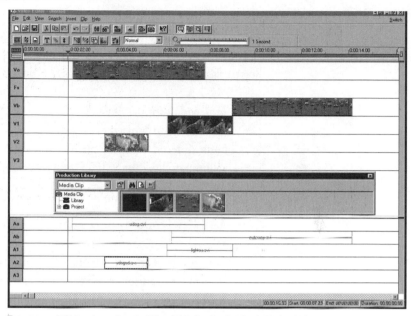

FIGURE   *Editing interface in Ulead Media Studio Pro's Video Editor.*

7.10

lock picture before you begin fine-cutting your sound, actually locking the picture track in your software will help ensure that the edited picture doesn't get changed.

The tools listed provide extraordinary flexibility when cutting your footage. However, non-linear editing is more than just splicing together bits of video. In addition to editing tools, you'll need to consider a package's input, output, and media management tools.

Getting Media into Your Project

Most editing packages offer an internal capture utility for using your video input hardware, whether analog or digital, to get video into your computer. (See Chapter 5 for more on video input hardware.) Some programs, like EditDV, use an external capture utility; in this case, MotoDV. The simplest packages will work like a tape recorder: tell them to start recording and they'll record any video that's fed into them. More sophisticated applications will let you specify which sections of a tape to capture, and will let you capture whole batches of clips. In addition, because your project might involve other types of media (audio, stills, animations), you'll want to be sure a particular package supports the file formats and specifications you need. When looking at an editing package's capturing interface, consider the following:

- **Timecode support.** If you plan to move from one system to another, reconstruct your project, or create an EDL, you need a package that supports timecode. If you plan to integrate with existing professional equipment, look for SMPTE timecode support. If you're going to stick with DV sources and equipment, make sure you have DV timecode support.
- **Audio level controls and meters.** For maximum quality, you need to be able to see audio levels and adjust them while you capture. Look for meters with dB marks and sliding gain controls.
- **Waveform monitors and vectorscopes.** A software waveform monitor and vectorscope are used to fine-tune your video signal to get the best quality possible (see Chapter 12 for more details).
- **Batch capturing.** Batch capturing lets you log an entire tape and then capture all your logged clips in one, unattended operation. This feature

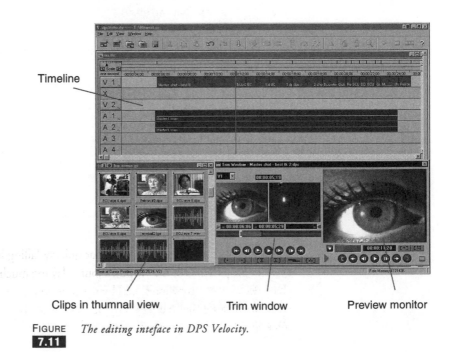

Timeline

Clips in thumnail view   Trim window   Preview monitor

FIGURE   *The editing inteface in DPS Velocity.*
7.11

is also extremely useful if you plan to reconstruct your project on a different system or at a later date.

- **Importing files.** Most editing systems can import and export a number of different graphics and sound formats. If you are dependent on a particular file type, be sure your app supports it.

- **Pixel aspect ratios.** Depending on your video format, you need to make sure your editing app supports the right pixel aspect ratios. Chapter 4 covers the different formats and pixel aspect ratios in detail.

- **16:9 support.** If you shot widescreen footage be sure your package supports 16:9

- **PAL support.** If you shot PAL footage, you'll need an NLE that supports PAL.

ORGANIZATIONAL TOOLS

A good non-linear editing system will provide you with tools that will help you keep track of all the media in your project. In most NLE software, the organizational tools are centered around the bins that contain your source media.

In more sophisticated programs, your bins will display columns showing information about your media: start and end timecode, source tape number, frame rate, number and types of tracks, audio sampling rate, and more. For long projects, you'll want editing software that lets you customize and add columns for your own comments, keywords, and so on. You should be able to *sort* and *sift* your bins according to your needs, and use *search* or *find* commands to find particular clips (Figure 7.12).

EFFECTS AND TITLES

Most NLEs come packed with all sorts of fancy transitions and wipes. However, for a dramatic feature, you probably won't use anything more complex than a cross-dissolve. (Just think of those tacky wipes and iris transitions in *Star Wars* and you'll see what we mean.) But, if you're working on a project that's more stylized, or on a commercial or corporate presentation, fancier transitions may be a necessity.

Because transitions are notorious for quickly falling in and out of fashion, don't let the presence of the "wipe du jour" play too much of a role in your purchase decision—it may look tired by the time you're up and running. Instead, look for software that has a good practical effects package—color correction, internal titling, motion effects, and compositing.

FIGURE   *In Final Cut Pro you can add customized columns and headings when you*
7.12   *view your clips in text view.*

No matter what your taste in effects, look for software that supports effects plug-ins so that you can add effects as needed. And if you're really serious about special effects, look for software that easily integrates with dedicated effects applications such as Adobe After Effects. The following are basic effects features to look for:

- **Plug-ins.** Because there are plug-in effect filters that do everything from sophisticated compositing to special effects such as lightning and "film-look," plug-in support is essential. On the Mac and Windows, most plug-ins conform to the Adobe After Effects or Premiere specifications. Some packages, including most Avid systems and EditDV, have their own proprietary plug-in specifications.
- **Keyframes.** Keyframes allow you to change the parameters of an effect—either plug-in or internal—over time. For example, if you are adding a superimposed video image of a ghost in your shot, you can use

keyframes to make it fade up halfway, hold for a second, flicker a few times, move across the frame, and disappear. The screen position, movement, and transparency of your ghost image are all controlled by keyframes that allow you to choose exactly when and how you want the image to look at each point in time.

- **Rendered vs. real-time effects.** Most non-linear editing programs require that you render each effect and transition before you can play them back in full-motion. Some programs support special hardware that can render effects in real-time. Though expensive, if your project is effects-heavy, the extra hardware can be worth the cost.

TYPES OF EFFECTS

Nowadays, there is a mind-boggling number of effects available in even the cheapest editing packages. In fact, sometimes the cheaper the software, the more effects you get! Nevertheless, they all fall into one of the categories discussed next.

Transitions

Transition effects create a bridge from one shot to another. The most often-used transition is the *cross-dissolve*. Others include various *wipes* and *pushes, page turns,* and *white flashes,* to name only a few. If you're planning on using lots of these, look for software with plug-in support and keyframing (Figure 7.13).

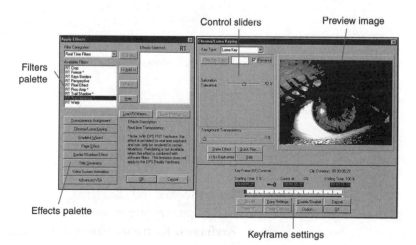

Control sliders   Preview image

Filters palette

Effects palette

Keyframe settings

FIGURE **7.13**   *The effects editor showing Luma keying and keyframes in DPS Velocity*

Image Enhancement Effects

There's a limit to how much you can improve poorly shot video, but your editing software should offer some control over the *brightness, contrast, saturation,* and *hue* of your footage (Figure 7.14).

Motion Effects

One of the most basic video effects is the ability to freeze, slow down, or speed up a shot. If you're going to do lots of motion effects, look for software that lets you set a variable frame rate from 0% (freeze frame) to 400% (the maximum that most programs will allow).

Compositing

Compositing tools are used for everything from complex titling and video collage, to sophisticated special effects including virtual sets and locations. The compositing tools offered by most editing applications (*luma keying, chroma keying,* and *matte keying*) are good enough for creating simple composites, but they lack the precision and control needed for serious special effects (Figure 7.15).

3D Effects

Another hot property these days is the ability to move a video layer in true 3D space. Used primarily for fancy transitions and simple effects, the feature

FIGURE
7.14 *Color correction in Adobe Premiere. If you're used to Photoshop, you'll recognize this standard Levels dialog for adjusting tone and color balance.*

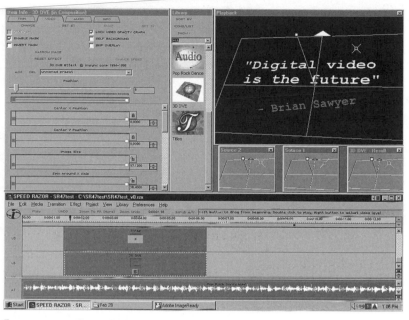

FIGURE   *3D effects editing in Speed Razor.*
7.15

filmmaker will find little use for these features. If you want to create true 3D objects and environments, you'll have to use a 3D animation application like SoftImage or Maya.

TITLES

Most film projects need three types of titles: the opening title sequence, the credit roll, and subtitles. Most editing software can create a credit roll, and subtitling is so basic, it's not even worth worrying about. An opening credit sequence is another story. Complicated title sequences like the one in *The Matrix* or the famous title sequence of *7even* are really more like short animated films and will probably require using a dedicated 2D animation application like Adobe After Effects.

Audio Tools   Audio editing can often make or break a film. Good audio can enhance atmosphere, create drama, and provide reason for what would otherwise seem

FIGURE   *The title tool in DPS Velocity.*
7.16

like a bad edit. Editing software can tend to skimp on audio features, but here are some things to look for that will help you create better sound tracks.

Equalization

Good equalization features (or "EQ" if you want to sound professional) let you do everything from removing the hiss from a bad tape recording to adding presence to someone with a weaker voice.

Audio Effects and Filters

Just like video effects, audio effects and filters let you change the nature of the sound in a clip. And, just like video effects, many programs support audio plug-ins for adding everything from echo, reverb, delay, and pitch-shifting, to specialized effects that make a voice sound like it's coming through a telephone. When selecting an NLE, you'll want to assess what filters are built in, and whether or not the package supports audio plug-ins. See Chapter 14 for more on audio editing.

Audio Plug-In Formats
Though there are a number of audio plug-in formats including TDM, Sound-Designer, and AudioSuite, it's best to look for editing packages that support Premiere's format.

TIP

Mixing

No editing system is complete without the ability to set the audio levels on each individual piece of sound in your sequence, a process called *mixing*. Look for software that has a mixing interface with gain sliders and dB markings. Some editing packages offer real-time mixing, which allows you to adjust audio levels while your sequence plays. This can be a timesaving way to get a rough mix that you can later fine-tune (Figure 7.17).

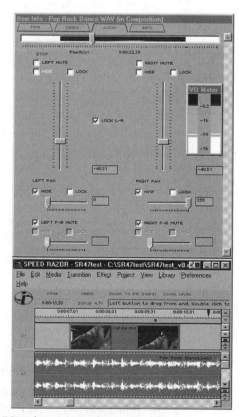

FIGURE   *Audio EQ and mixing interface in Speed Razor.*

The Final Product

Finally, your editing software needs to be capable of outputting your final product, whatever that may be. Outputting can be very complicated, and we've dedicated an entire chapter to it at the end of this book, but here are some guidelines for ensuring an editing package can create the output you need.

Videotape Masters

Be aware that videotape output involves both your hardware and your software—your editing software may claim that it can perform a certain kind of output, but your hardware may not be up to the job.

If you're using an all-digital Firewire or SDI-based system, then output quality is not a concern. But, if you're using an analog video I/O system such as Media 100 or Targa, then you need to make sure your software is capable of playing back your entire project as full-motion and full-screen video. Some systems may have a hard time playing a 90-minute feature in its entirety, requiring you to break it up into smaller sections to do your video output.

We'll cover how to output to tape in more detail later. If you think you might be needing to lay off your feature in segments (which is a good workaround if you don't have enough disk space to hold all your footage), then make sure your software is capable of frame accurate device control and editing to tape. Be aware that these capabilities are dependent on having the right kind of video deck. (Video hardware is covered in Chapter 11.)

Exporting Files

If your video is destined for the Web, DVD, or CD-ROM, you'll need to export your video in whatever format—usually QuickTime files—you need to author your project. Depending on the requirements of your target media, you may need to compress your files with a special CODEC. We'll discuss multimedia and Web output in more detail in Chapter 18.

EDLs

As we discussed earlier, you may need to generate an edit decision list if you plan on finishing your project in an on-line editing suite.

When you're done editing your project, you output an EDL to a special format disk that you can take to your post-production facility. You need to know what sort of editing system they'll be using so that you save your EDL in the proper format. If you haven't selected an on-line house yet, you should be aware that the default format for EDLs is called CMX format. If you think you may need an EDL, be sure that your software at least supports CMX format EDLs. As you can see in Figure 7.18, there are a lot of variables to choose from when you create your EDL. Always talk to your post facility and check their EDL specifications—doing so can save you hundreds of dollars.

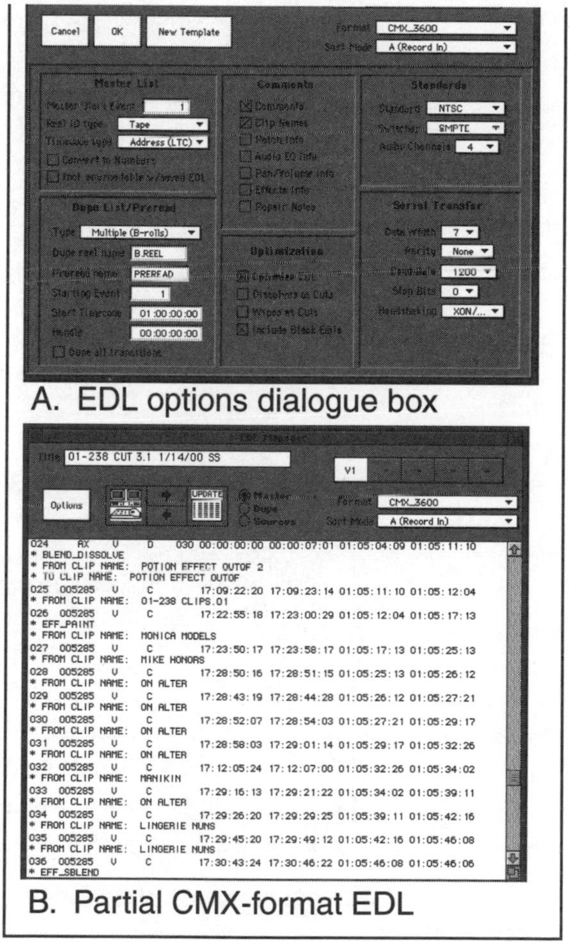

FIGURE 7.18   *Avid Media Composer comes with the Avid EDL Manager utility for creating custom EDLs.*

Film Editing and Cut Lists

Projects shot and finished on film but edited on videotape have a different workflow than projects shot on video or finished on video

After film is shot and sent to the lab for processing, the film is transferred to video through a process called *telecine*. Each frame of the film negative has a number on it, called the *keycode*. These keycode numbers are recorded onto the videotape image along with the picture itself. Since the frame rate of film is 24 frames per second and NTSC video is 29.97 fps, the telecine machine uses a process called *3:2 pulldown* as it transfers the film to videotape. (See Chapter 4 for a technical description of how 3:2 pulldown works.)

The video worktapes that result from the telecine transfer are then edited on a film non-linear editing system that can handle the frame rate issues involved in film editing—Avid's Film Composer, for example.

Once the film is edited and "locked," a *cut list* is generated by the editing system to give to the negative cutter. A cut list is the film equivalent of an edit decision list (EDL) and lists each edit by film roll and keycode numbers. The process of generating the cut list is called *film matchback*. If the film was edited on a *video* non-linear editing system, like those discussed in this chapter, film matchback software such as Filmlogic or Slingshot is used to generate a cut list.

The negative cutter (yes, this is a person) then takes the computer-generated cut list and conforms the negative to match the final edit created on the non-linear editing system. Unfortunately, film matchback is a complicated process and highly prone to errors. Many film labs actually charge extra if the cut list is computer generated.

NLEs Compared   Based on the criteria just discussed, we'll quickly run through the most popular NLE software for Macintosh and Windows to give you an idea of the pros and cons of each. For system requirements, availability, and other details, check out www.dvhandbook.com/nles.

Adobe Premiere 5.1c. The original QuickTime editing program, Premiere recently went through a complete re-write to bring it to version 5. With a re-worked interface and improved audio/video sync, Premiere is finally a respectable system for long-form projects. Though weak on the audio editing and compositing side, Premiere's editing tools are powerful and robust. Premiere's capturing utility is weak, but plug-ins like Pipeline's ProVTR can bring it up to snuff.

Apple Final Cut Pro 1.2. Apple's editing/compositing combo, Final Cut is a very complete, high-end, professional editing system. Packing a full collection of high-end editing tools wrapped up in an interface with excellent mouse *and* keyboard support, Final Cut also includes a fully keyframable compositing module integrated directly into the program. Though no substitute for a compositing package like Adobe After Effects, Final Cut's compositing tools provide plenty of power for most users. Final Cut is weak when it comes to audio editing and rendering is a tad slow when compared to other systems. Also, the program is plagued with some video artifact troubles, though these can easily be avoided.

Apple iMovie. At the time of this writing, iMovie is only bundled with the iMac DV (which, incidentally, is an excellent choice for a DV workstation). Though incredibly simple, iMovie provides most of what you'll need for editing a feature. Though it lacks robust editing controls, a lot of great movies have been made using far less editing power. If you're looking for fine editing controls as well as audio EQ, special effects, waveform monitors, and other utilities, look elsewhere. But, if you wouldn't use such features even if you had them, iMovie's small RAM footprint and simple interface might serve you well.

In:sync SpeedRazor is a popular Windows-based editing package that offers real-time dual stream playback and, when combined with the right hardware, uncompressed D1 NTSC or PAL video in the Video for Windows AVI format. Speed Razor offers a full-range of professional tools including RS-422 deck control, SMPTE timecode support, low and high resolutions, and EDLs. Speed Razor has all the editing tools you need: multiple levels of Undo, keyboard shortcuts, storyboard editing, up to 20 tracks of realtime audio mixing, and field-rendering for effects and transitions. When packaged with Newtec's Video Toaster and Lightwave, Speed Razor rounds out a top of the line 3D system.

EditDV is a great Mac or Windows standalone editing package for DV-based projects. If you plan on doing all your post-production work within EditDV, you'll find it easy to use yet sophisticated. Now a part of the Media 100 family along with Media Cleaner Pro, look for excellent multimedia authoring integration. However, if you need to integrate with other software applications, EditDV is not for you. Because video in EditDV is kept in a YUV color space (which is a good thing, as far as image quality is concerned), EditDV is not compatible with any of the major plug-in architectures.

Media 100 has always been ahead of the competition in terms of ease of integration with QuickTime-based applications. With Media Cleaner Pro and EditDV added to the Media 100 family of products, look for Web-oriented features in the future, including streaming media tools. The dual stream video option offers real-time effects and excellent image quality, although the editing software interface is a bit clumsy compared to packages with Avid-like interfaces (EditDV, Final Cut Pro, and of course, all the Avid products).

Ulead Media Studio Pro is a Windows-based editing system that is actually a group of applications: Video Editor, Audio Editor, Capture, CG Infinity, and Video Paint. This makes Ulead Media Studio Pro very easy to use for the novice non-linear editor. Ulead Video Editor offers a robust selection of editing tools but the Audio Editor, with its simplistic waveform-style editing, and Capture, which offers only the out-of-date VISCA and V-LAN device control protocols, will leave a little to be desired for those used to professional systems.

Avid Xpress & Xpress DV are turnkey systems from Avid that offer a scaled-down version of the Avid Media Composer interface. At the time of this writing, Xpress DV for NT is still in beta testing but Avid Xpress for Macintosh is full-featured and easy to use. The software differs from its high-end cousin by cutting out professional features like multicamera editing, and stripping down the customizability of the interface. That said, the keyboard is nonetheless filled with commands for fast and intuitive editing. Full EDL support, multiple resolution MJPEG codecs, component analog video inputs, solid audio editing tools and support for Quicktime importing and exporting make Avid Xpress a great solution for those who don't want to build their own system and don't need Firewire compatibility.

Avid Media Composer offers all the features discussed in this chapter and then some. Designed for multiple users and large project management, Avid Media Composer sticks to the high-end market with optional support for SDI I/O but no support for Firewire. Avid offers products for Macintosh and NT that differ significantly. Unfortunately, this professional tool comes with a professional price tag. Despite recent price cuts, a turnkey Avid costs upwards of $30,000, not to mention a hefty annual fee for minor upgrades and technical support. A complete rental system, including office space, storage, video decks, other hardware and technical support usually runs $2,000–$2,500 a week.

DPS Velocity is a Windows-based Pentium III turnkey editing system capable of capturing and outputting uncompressed, D1 quality video. Velocity offers realtime, dualstream playback and effects in the Video for Windows AVI format. The editing interface is similar to Media 100 and has everything you need to edit long-format, complex projects: unlimited video and audio tracks, full-featured audio equalization and mixing, and multiple levels of Undo. Velocity's true strength lies in its professional palette of realtime and rendered effects, including realtime color balancing adjustment through a waveform monitor and vectorscope. Add to that the full array of digital and analog input and output formats on the optional breakout box and the responsiveness of the system and you've got a great solution for projects that need lots of effects. You can also purchase a non-turnkey DPS Reality board and Velocity software to install yourself.

Keeping up with the Joneses
The list of available editing products changes constantly. Go to www.dvhandbook.com/NLEs *for comparison charts and up-to-the minute product details.*

OTHER SOFTWARE

Finally, don't expect your NLE package to do everything. Depending on the nature of your production, you'll probably need to buy some additional packages. Logging applications like The Executive Producer, capture utilities like Pipeline's ProVTR, and software waveform monitors and vectorscopes like Videoscope will help you get ready to edit; compression apps like Media-Cleaner Pro, and film matchback software like FilmLogic will help with your output.

Finally, if you're serious about special effects and image enhancement, you'll likely need packages like Adobe After Effects, Ultimatte, and Puffin Design's Commotion. We'll discuss these products in later chapters.

Summary

Your editing system is the hub of your production. Everything you record will go into it and come out of it in some way or another. While it's important to get the features you need, don't get too hung up with "NLE-envy." In the end, if you can get the results you need from your package, then it's probably the right package for you.

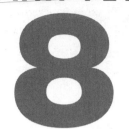

8

Lighting and Art Directing

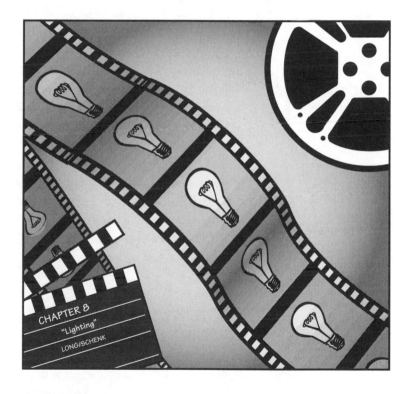

CHAPTER 8

"Lighting"

LONG/SCHENK

IN THIS CHAPTER

- Lighting Basics
- Types of Light
- The Art of Lighting
- Tutorial
- Interior Lighting
- Exterior Lighting
- Special Lighting Situations
- Art Directing
- Rolling . . .

Lighting Basics

Although it's important to choose a good camera for your shoot, the one thing that will have the greatest impact on the quality of your image has nothing to do with your camera. Lighting your scene will have more to do with the quality of your image than any other factor (well, any other factor that you can control, that is). Lighting conveys mood and atmosphere, and is also the key to a successful video-to-film transfer. In this chapter, we will discuss tips for film-style lighting, basic lighting set-ups, lighting for different exterior and interior situations, and lighting for special situations, such as blue-screen photography. Because lighting is intrinsically tied to the set location itself, we'll also discuss set dressing and art direction.

FILM-STYLE LIGHTING

If you've done any research on using video to shoot features, you've probably encountered this piece of advice: "If you want your video to look like film, you need to light it like film." So what's so different about lighting for film?

Traditionally, shooting on film has been technically more challenging than shooting video because film stocks need to be exposed properly, and proper film exposure requires lots of light. Film lighting specialists, known as cinematographers or directors of photography (D.P.s), have taken advantage of the limitations of film and turned them into ways of precisely controlling the final image. Cinematographers do more than use lots of lights, they use special equipment to control the path of the light, the quality of the lights, the brightness of the lights, and the color of the lights. The amount of light coming from every light source is meticulously measured with a *light meter* in order to

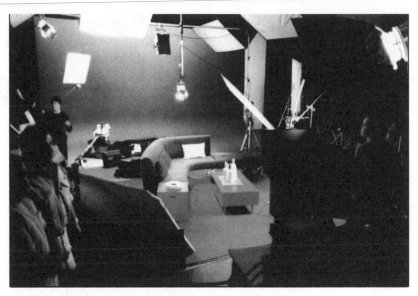

FIGURE   *A digital betacam professional shoot on a soundstage.*
8.1

achieve the desired contrast ratio between the lights and shadows. By controlling these elements, the cinematographer is able to direct the viewer's eye
within the frame.

Lighting, along with focus and framing which we will cover in Chapter 9, all
add up to the visual vocabulary used in filmic storytelling. Film-style lighting is
not so much a distinct visual style as an artistic choice that helps tell the story.

Shooting Video for Film
*If you are going to finish your project on film, you should research and find a film
recordist now. Chapter 18 covers the most popular film recordists for independent
features at the time of this writing. Each film recording company uses a different
process, and they'll have specific tips for how to light and shoot in order to achieve
the best look for your project.*

TIP

Types of Light

Knowing the types of lights available for shooting is like knowing what colors
of paint you have available to paint a portrait. Professional lights fall into two
basic categories: Tungsten balanced (or indoor lights) and daylight balanced
(or sunlight). These two categories represent two very different areas of the
color spectrum. The light from a conventional indoor light bulb tends to look
orange or yellow, whereas the light outside at mid-day tends to appear more
white or blue. Your camera probably has a setting that lets you choose a light

bulb icon (for tungsten) or a sun icon (for daylight). By informing your camera whether you are in daylight or tungsten light, you are letting it know the overall color-cast of the scene. Setting this control is known as *white balancing*. We discuss white-balancing in Chapter 9, but in order to understand it, you first need to understand how light and color are related.

COLOR TEMPERATURE

First, a quick science lesson: Light is measured in terms of *color temperature,* which is calculated in *degrees Kelvin* (K). Indoor tungsten lights have a color temperature of 3200° K, whereas daylight has an approximate color temperature of 5500° K.

Color Plate 1 shows the color difference between tungsten light and typical daylight. As you can see, tungsten light at 3200° K is heavily shifted toward the orange part of the spectrum, which results in the warm, golden cast of household lights. On the other hand, daylight at 5500° K is heavily biased toward the blue part of the spectrum, which results in more of a bluish-white light. Be aware that as the sun rises and sets, its color temperature changes and it decreases into the orange part of the spectrum.

While you may not be able to discern that household light looks orange and sunlight looks blue, the main thing to realize is that daylight is much stronger. (Think of the hotter, blue flames in a burning fire.) Daylight balanced lights are over 2000° K stronger than tungsten lights, and if you try to mix them together, the daylight will certainly overpower the tungsten light. If you can't avoid mixing tungsten and daylight—for example, if you're shooting a day interior scene that absolutely requires that a real window be in the shot—you need to account for the color temperature differences by *balancing* your light sources. Balancing your light sources means that you'll use special lighting accessories to change the color temperature of some of the lights so that they are all either tungsten-balanced or all daylight-balanced. We'll talk more about the specific tools you can use to balance your light sources later on.

Other Types of Lights

Tungsten lights and daylight balanced lights aren't the only types of lights. *Fluorescent* lights have a color temperature that ranges from 2700–6500° K, and *sodium vapor* lights, with a color temperature of about 2100° K, are yellow-orange. *Neon* lights vary wildly in temperature. All of these lights introduce special challenges.

Fluorescents are notorious for flicker and for having a greenish tint, which can be exacerbated on film or video. You can buy or rent special Kino-flo tubes that fit into normal fluorescent fixtures, and get rid of the flicker and the green color. Yellowish-orange sodium lights use a very limited section of the visible color spectrum. The result is an almost monochrome image. If you try to color correct later, you'll have very little color information to work with. Neon lights can easily exceed the range of NTSC color, especially red and magenta neon. Even though they tend to be quite dim in terms of lux or footcandles, they appear bright and overexposed due to their extremely saturated colors. (See color plate 10 and Figure 12.13).

WATTAGE

Lights are also measured in terms of the amount of electric power they require, or the *wattage*. The more wattage, the brighter the light. Typical film lights range from 250 watts to 10K (10,000 watts). The powerful HMI lights used

---

Measuring Light

The intensity of a light stays the same no matter how far the subject is from the light; what changes is the amount of *illumination* given off by the light. Illumination is measured in either *footcandles* (based on the English measurement system) or *lux* (based on the metric system) as expressed in these formulas:

$$\text{Illumination in footcandles} = \frac{\text{Intensity (in candelas)}}{D^2}$$

Where D is the distance in *feet* between the light source and the subject.

$$\text{Illumination in lux} = \frac{\text{Intensity (in candelas)}}{D^2}$$

Where D is the distance in *meters* between the light source and the subject.

Light meters are devices that measure light in footcandles and/or lux, and translate the measurements into *f-stops*.

If you've ever used an SLR camera, you're probably familiar with f-stops. F-stops are defined as the ratio of the focal length of the lens to the aperture of the lens. The aperture is the hole that governs how much light passes through the lens and onto the imaging surface, or *focal plane*. When you adjust the f-stops on an SLR camera, you are opening or closing the aperture of the lens. Many better video cameras also have f-stop marks on their lenses, or in their viewfinder displays. Because of how they relate to exposure in film, f-stops are often used in video to describe increments of light.

to mimic the sun and to light night exteriors have as much as 20,000 watts, whereas a typical household light has a mere 60 watts. The professional lights best-suited for use with video are those with a wattage of 2K or less. Figures 8.2 and 8.3 show some typical professional lights.

TIP

Camera Mount Lights

Camera mount lights, also called "sun guns," are a great quick fix for run-and-gun photography. But if a film look is your goal, save the camera mount light for your next documentary-style project. If you do need to use them, try adding some diffusion fabric to reduce the "hot spot."

CONTROLLING THE QUALITY OF LIGHT

In addition to having different color temperatures, lights have different *qualities*. They can be direct or *hard,* they can be soft or *diffuse,* or they can be *focused,* like a spot light. Figure 8.4 shows the same subject lit with a diffuse key light (a) and a hard key light (b).

There are all sorts of lighting accessories that can be used to control the quality of professional lights. A special *fresnel* lens attachment lets you adjust

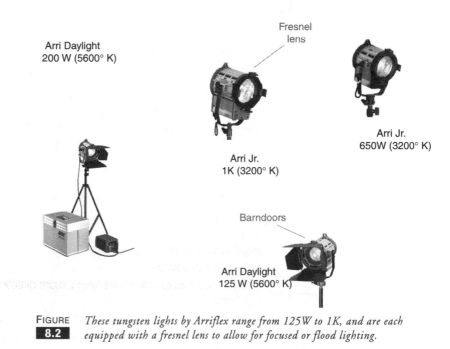

FIGURE **8.2** *These tungsten lights by Arriflex range from 125W to 1K, and are each equipped with a fresnel lens to allow for focused or flood lighting.*

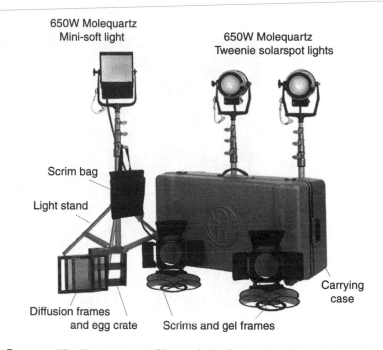

650W Molequartz
Mini-soft light

650W Molequartz
Tweenie solarspot lights

Scrim bag

Light stand

Diffusion frames
and egg crate

Scrims and gel frames

Carrying
case

FIGURE
8.3   *This Teenie-weenie/Softlite combo kit from Mole-Richardson is a good exam-*
ple of a typical video lighting kit.

The Basic Light Kit for Video

A basic light kit for video provides the minimum lighting equipment necessary for three-point lighting. The typical cinematographer won't be happy
with it, but it's a considerable step above single source lighting. A basic
video kit costs around $40 a day to rent and includes something like the fol-
lowing:

    2 650-watt lights (with fresnel lenses)
    2 single scrims
    2 half single scrims
    2 double scrims
    2 half double scrims
    2 sets of barn doors
    1 1K or 650W softlight
    1 egg crate (used to make the softlight more directional)
    3 gel frames
    3 light stands

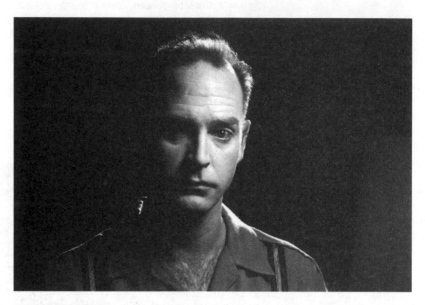

A. Soft key light

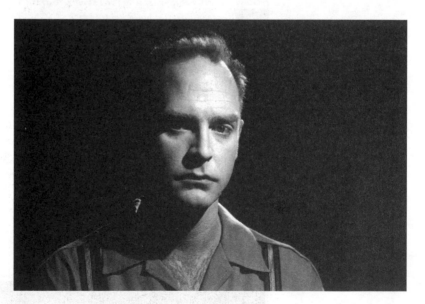

B. Hard key light

FIGURE
8.4   *The choice between a hard or diffuse key is an aesthetic one—this actor is lit with a diffuse key (a) and a hard key (b).*

the angle of the light beam from flood to spot light (Figure 8.2). *Barn doors* attach to the light itself to help you control where the light falls. Round *scrims* fit into a slot between the light and the barn doors and allow you to decrease the strength of a light without changing the quality. Single scrims (with a green edge) take the brightness down by one half f-stop, and double scrims (with a red edge) take it down a whole f-stop. (See the tip on "Measuring Light" for more about f-stops.)

Lighting gels are translucent sheets of colored plastic that are placed in front of the light not only to alter the color of the light but to decrease the brightness (Color Plate 2). The most common use of lighting gels involves converting tungsten to daylight, or vice versa. *Diffusion* gels are usually frosty white plastic sheets that make the light source appear softer. *Gel frames* allow you to place lighting gels behind the barn doors, but it's easier to use clothes pins to attach gels directly to the barn doors.

Bounce cards (often just pieces of white foam core) are also used to create soft, indirect lighting, while *reflectors* (shiny boards) are used to re-direct lighting from a bright light source, such as the sun.

C-stands (short for Century stands) hold *flags, nets,* and other objects in front of the lights to manipulate and shape the light that falls on the subject (Figure 8.5). We'll talk more about how to use these items as we cover traditional interior and exterior lighting.

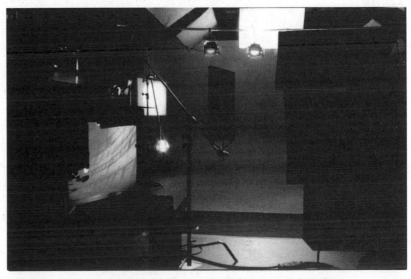

FIGURE   *A soundstage with lots of flags on C-stands to control the light.*
8.5

Lighting Gels

Gels are an indispensable tool if you're serious about lighting. Rosco and Lee make swatch books like the one in Color Plate 2 that contain samples of the different gels they produce. Gel swatch books are usually available at any professional camera store.

Colored gels You can use colored gels to add just about any color in the rainbow to your light sources. It's a good idea to have a choice of colors on hand. Remember that the brighter the light shining through the gel, the less intense the color will be. Adding colored gels will always decrease the brightness of the light.

Color temperature orange (CTO) and color temperature blue (CTB) gels can change the color temperature of a daylight-balanced light to tungsten, or tungsten to daylight.

Neutral density gels cut down the intensity of light without changing the color temperature. These gels are extremely useful when shooting video and come in handy when it's necessary to shoot out windows.

The Art of Lighting

Lighting is one of the most powerful yet subtle filmmaking tools available. *Film noir* classics, like *The Maltese Falcon,* are known for their creative use of light and shadow, while modern comedies often feature a bright, simple lighting style more similar to that of television. No matter what your film is about, creative lighting can add an extra layer to enhance the mood and emotion of your story.

THREE-POINT LIGHTING

Three-point lighting is usually the basic, jumping-off point for more complicated lighting set-ups. Three lights are used in a three-point light set-up. The primary light source, called the *key light,* is used to illuminate the subject and is usually positioned at an angle (Figure 8.6). The key light is a strong, dominant light source and is often motivated by some existing light source in the scene (Figure 8.7a).

A second light, called the *fill light,* is used to "fill in" the strong shadows caused by the key light. Usually the fill light is quite a bit dimmer and more diffuse than the key light (Figure 8.7c). The idea is not necessarily to get rid of

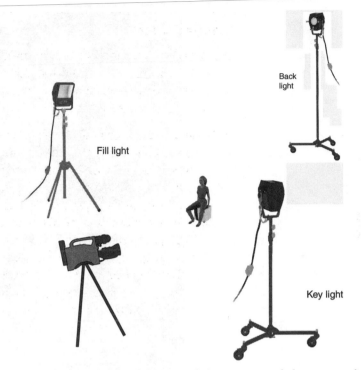

Back
light

Fill light

Key light

FIGURE
8.6
*A diagram of a typical three-point lighting set-up, including camera place-
ment and subject.*

the shadows, but to achieve a pleasing ratio between the lights and shadows on
the subject.

The third light, called the *back light* or sometimes the *kicker,* is positioned
behind the subject and is used to separate it from the background. This separa-
tion lends a sense of depth to the image and helps make your subject "stand
out" better. Sometimes the back light is a different color—bluish or orange (Figure 8.7b). Making choices about the relationship between the key, fill, and
back lights is part of the art of cinematography. After we present a few more key
lighting concepts, you'll be ready to try your hand at the tutorial on page 167.

LIGHTING YOUR ACTORS

Lighting a person is always a bit more challenging than lighting an object—the
human face has a lot of angles and it's easy for bright lights to cast strange and
unflattering shadows. In addition, bright lights can magnify every little flaw on

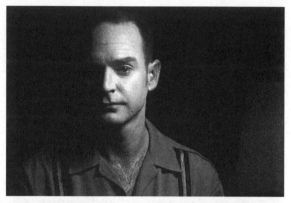

A. Key light only

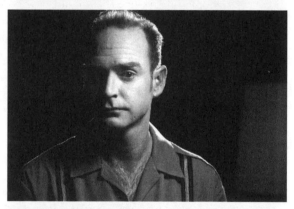

B. Key light and back light

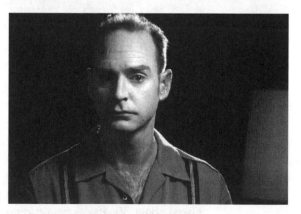

C. Key light, back light, and fill light

FIGURE
8.7   *In this example of three-point lighting, the actor is first lit with a diffuse key light (a), then a hard back light is added (b), and a soft, subtle fill light brings out the left side of his face without losing the high contrast look.*

a person's face, while the wrong color lighting can result in an unnatural looking skin tone. Whether your goal is to make your actors look beautiful or ugly, the right lighting will enhance your characters and story. The following three-point lighting tutorial provides a tried-and-true method for lighting an actor.

Tutorial

THREE-POINT LIGHTING

This tutorial assumes you have a typical video light kit (like the one described in the previous tip), a selection of gels (see the tip on page 164), and a suitable subject to light, preferably a person. If possible, you should also have your camera set up on a tripod in order to see how the different lighting possibilities look through the lens. If you have a field monitor, you should use that too. If you don't have a field monitor, consider recording a test videotape as you experiment with the lights so that you can later view your results on a full-size monitor. You'll also need a pair of work gloves for handling hot lights. Finally, you should start with a large, dark room. A soundstage is ideal, but any dark room will work. If you're doing this tutorial at home, take a look at page 168 for tips on how to avoid blowing a bulb.

STEP 1

To begin, set up your key light. Take one of the 650-watt lights from your kit and set it up on one of the stands. Attach the barn doors to the light itself—they usually just slide into place. Direct the light toward your subject and turn it on. Don't worry about the background yet, we'll deal with that later. Just focus on lighting your subject as best you can.

Now that you've got light on your subject, find a pleasing angle at which to place the light. Try extending the stand to its full height and aiming the light down at your actor. Try lowering it. Try placing the light at different distances from your subject. Does it look better close or farther away? Since this is video, you can set up the lights any way that looks good to your eye. Just make sure that the light is not so bright that it overexposes in your viewfinder. (If your viewfinder provides a zebra display, turn it on to help identify hot spots.)

Because of the shadows cast by a person's nose, the key light is usually placed about 30–45 degrees off-center from the person's face. This position gives definition to the features of the face and allows the shadow from the nose to fall to the side without becoming huge or distorted. The diagram back in Figure 8.6 shows a typical three-point lighting set-up. Once you're happy with the angle, play with the focus knob on the fresnel lens. Does it look better tightly focused or flooded? (Figure 8.4 shows the difference between a hard key and a soft key.) Try adding some diffusion. Play around until you find a look you like, then move on to the next step.

TIP

Don't Waste Expensive Light Bulbs
Avoid touching high-wattage light bulbs, or globes, as they are professionally known. The oil from your fingers can overheat and cause them to explode (the globes, not your fingers).

STEP 2

Now it's time to add the back light. As with the key light, set it up on the stand and play around with different positions. Back lights are usually quite bright and often filtered with lightly colored gels. Usually, the best position for a back light is either high overhead pointing down at the back of the subject's head or way down near the ground pointing up at the back of the subject's head. The reason for this is that you need to avoid both having the light itself visible in the shot and having the light pointed directly at the camera (which will cause a lens flare). Figure 8.8 shows the actor illuminated with the back light only, and Figure 8.7b shows that actor illuminated with the back light and key light.

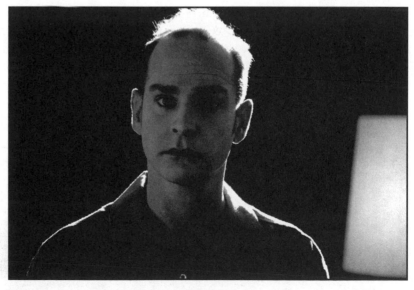

FIGURE   *The same actor lit with a back light only.*
8.8

TIP

Fire Hazards

Avoid putting diffusion gels, lighting gels, and any flammable materials too close to professional light globes—you might end up with a stinky, smoldering mess stuck to your light, or worse, you might start a fire!

Also, use your gaffer's tape to tape down your light's power cords. It can be easy to trip over cords and pull over your lights as you working around them.

STEP 3

Now you are ready to set up the fill light. Take the 1K soft light from the kit and set it up on the stand. Your goal with the fill light is to make the shadows cast by the key light less severe. Usually this means placing the light on the opposite side of the subject from the key light, typically at a 30–45 degree angle directed at the unlit side of the actor's face (see the diagram in Figure 8.6).

The brightness of the fill light is very important, since this is how you control the contrast ratio of your scene. Remember that video doesn't handle high-contrast lighting as well as film does. Try placing the light at different distances from the subject to see how the contrast ratio changes. It's often nice to have a fill light that's a different color than the key light. Experiment with different colored gels until you're satisfied with the fill light. Figure 8.9 shows the actor

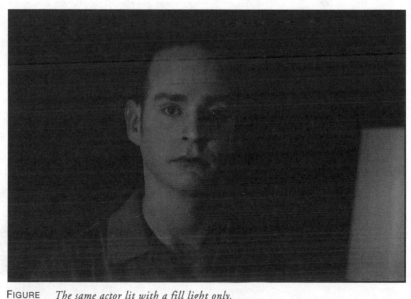

FIGURE   *The same actor lit with a fill light only.*
8.9

illuminated with a soft 1K fill light only, and Figure 8.7c shows a subject lit with key, back, and fill.

STEP 4

Now that you have your three lights set up, it's time to look at the overall scene. Are colored areas washing out too white? Are there hot spots, bright reflections from cheekbones or foreheads? In other words, is it overlit? Try adding single or double scrims to the lights that seem too bright.

How does the background look? It's pretty hard to light the subject and the background with only three lights, but see if you can move the fill light so that it fills in the background as well as the shadows on the subject. Is there too much light falling on the background? Try using the barn doors on the key light to direct the light onto the subject only. If you have barn doors for the fill and back lights, adjust them as well. Remember to wear gloves when you're adjusting lights that have been on for awhile—they get very hot. If your lights are still too bright, try moving them further from the subject, or add more scrims or diffusion to your set-up.

Lighting for Darker Skin Tones
When an actor has darker-toned skin, it can be hard to get enough light on the person's face without overlighting the background because darker complexions simply require more light. If you can, keep the actor farther away from the background so that the light falls on the actor but not the background.

EXPOSURE

As with film, videotape has to be properly exposed to produce a good image. The art of lighting involves choosing an acceptable exposure. Video is much more sensitive to light than is film, and video has less *latitude* (see the following tip), so it's easy to over- and underexpose. However, unlike film, with video you use your field monitor to immediately see if your image is properly exposed. We recommend *always* using a field monitor when shooting video— think of it as your first and only line of defense against poor image quality.

With a field monitor, you can make an immediate decision as to whether or not an overexposed image is acceptable for your project. You may decide, for example, to purposely overexpose the sky, in favor of keeping a good exposure on your actor's face. Be aware that the auto-exposure mechanism in your camera will make exactly the opposite decision, and will properly expose the sky, causing your actor's face to fall into shadow. While well-planned overexposure can often look interesting on videotape, underexposure usually leaves you with a dark or muddy-looking image. Remember, there's almost always some area of overexposure in a properly exposed video image—usually reflective highlights and bright white areas. As a rule, it's better to have more light than not enough light.

Recognizing Proper Exposure
If your video camera has a zebra *feature, overexposure will be particularly easy to spot. On the other hand, underexposure can be hard to see, especially in a tiny viewfinder. Ideally, every image will have a balance of very dark areas and very light areas, even if you're shooting at night. If your overall image looks dark in your viewfinder, chances are it's underexposed.*

Latitude and Video-to-Film Transfers

Latitude refers to how many gradations of gray there are between the darkest black and the brightest white. When you stand in an unlit room in the day and look out the window, you can probably see details in the room, as well as in the bright sunlit areas outside and the outside shadows. In other words, your eye sees all the shades of gray from black to white. Because the latitude of film and video is too narrow to handle both bright areas and the dark areas, you'll have to choose to expose one range: either the sunlit areas or the shadows. Film has more latitude than video, but neither comes anywhere near what your eye is capable of seeing. The challenge for cinematographers is to shoot so that the resulting image looks more like what the human eye would actually see.

If you're planning on eventually transferring your video to film, latitude will be an important consideration. Because the latitude of video is smaller than that of film, any overexposed whites or underexposed blacks will look *clipped*. In other words, they will appear as a solid area of black or white. (If you know how to read a waveform image, take a look at Color Plate 7 and Figure 12.10 for an example of clipped white levels.) The effect of clipped whites or blacks is especially distracting when a filmed image is projected.

Interior Lighting

Lighting an interior scene can present all sorts of challenges, not the least of which is choosing a location that can facilitate your lights. Ideally, you would use a soundstage with overhead lighting grids, lots of available power, and plenty of space for setting up lights as far from your subject as needed. Shooting in a normal house or office building will save you the trouble of having to build a realistic set, but you'll be hampered by less space, a limited power supply, and less control over how much exterior light enters the set.

Power Supply

If you're using professional lights at a real location, you'll have to be careful not to overload the electrical circuits. A little pre-shoot prep work can save lots of headaches later. First you need to map out the electrical circuits at the location. Arm yourself with some masking tape and a socket tester or an easily moveable household lamp. Plug the lamp into the first outlet and turn it on. Go to the breaker box and turn the circuits on and off until you find the one that controls the lamp. If the circuits aren't labeled, use the masking tape to label each one with a number. Then take some masking tape and label the outlet to correspond with the circuit number. Work your way around until you find and label several outlets on different circuit breakers. To be safe, use one light for each 10-amp circuit. Most household circuits range from 10–40 amps, and the amperage of each circuit should be clearly engraved on the switches in the breaker box.

Mixing Daylight and Interior Light

Because of the different color temperatures of daylight and interior light, mixing them together can present a challenge. The simplest solution is to choose which light source you wish to have dominant and balance the other light sources to match the color temperature of that source.

For example, if the dominant light source in your scene is the light streaming through the window, you should balance your light sources for daylight by using daylight balance lights. You can also use Color Temperature Blue (CTB) lighting gels on tungsten lights, but remember that CTB gels decrease the intensity of the lights and may render them useless. If your dominant light source is a 650W tungsten light, you should balance your light sources for tungsten light using Color Temperature Orange (CTO) lighting gels on daylight balanced lights and windows with daylight streaming through. You may also need to add ND (neutral density) gels to control the brightness of the day-light coming through the window. In general, shooting a daytime interior against a window is best avoided.

Using Household Lights

Because video requires less light than film, you can often get away with using normal household lights. Generally, household lamps are less than 3200° K and lean more toward the orange side of the spectrum.

Unfortunately, ordinary household lights are not directional, which makes it harder to control where the light falls in your scene. There are a couple of ways to make household lights directional. You can buy directional or "spot" light bulbs, or you can surround the bulb with tin foil or some other light-proof material. Filter manufacturers like Rosco and Lee sell black wrap, a heavy duty tin foil with a black matte coating that can be used to create makeshift barndoors.

Even if you're not concerned with the light being directional, replacing low-wattage light bulbs with brighter bulbs is a good way to create "practical" lights. "Practical" lights are those that are actually visible in the scene, such as a household lamp that the actor turns on. You can hide diffusion materials or gels in the lamp shade for more lighting control. By using a low-wattage bulb and keeping it several feet away from the actor, the household lamp in the background of Figure 8.7 does not cast any light on the subject.

Clamp Lights

Cheap clamp lights available at any hardware store can be a good way to get some extra, budget illumination. Replace the bulbs with high-wattage directional bulbs, and use black wrap to make them even more directional.

Dealing with Overlit Situations

Whether you're shooting a daytime or a nighttime interior scene, it can be hard to avoid over-lighting the set, especially if you're in a small room. "Flat" lighting means there is not enough contrast between your key and fill lights, which will result in a lack of sculpting. Here are some ways to deal with an overlit scene:

- **Block out entering sunlight.** Because sunlight is so powerful, it may be what is making your scene look overlit. *Duvetine* is a black light-blocking fabric that can be used to cover windows. A cheaper alternative is to cover them with black plastic garbage bags. If the windows are in the shot, you can use *ND gels* (see the Lighting Gels tip on page 164) to tone down the light coming through the windows.

- **Turn off lights, especially overhead fixtures.** If your space is small, you simply may not be able to use all the lights you want without overlighting the scene.

- **Move lights away from the subject.** If space allows, move your lights back. The farther they are from your subject, the less illumination they'll cast on your subject.

- **Black nets and black flags.** Black nets and black flags attach to C-stands and are versatile tools for controlling and blocking light (Figure 8.5).

- **Studio wall paper.** Shooting in a room with white walls is like having four giant bounce cards surrounding your scene. You can buy different colors of studio wall paper to tone down the walls or to create blue/green backdrops for compositing. If you're shooting a night scene, use black studio wallpaper to make a room look bigger than it is—but be careful not to allow any light or hot spots to fall on the black paper.

- **Scrims.** If one or more of your lights are too bright, add scrims to take them down. Most lights will take at least two scrims at once.

- **Barn-doors.** Narrow the opening between the barn doors to make a light more directional.

Exterior Lighting The concept of exterior lighting might sound silly—who needs lights outside when you've got the sun? But if you're bent on a film-style look for your project, you'll need to do more than just point and shoot. Daylight, defined as a combination of skylight and sunlight, is an intense source of light—often too intense for video, especially if you're going for a video-to-film transfer. Think of the sky as a big giant bounce card reflecting the sun. It's a powerful light source in its own right, comparable to a 30,000 watt fixture on the ground and more than 50 times the illumination of a 650W tungsten light. Your light kit will be useless on an exterior shoot unless you've got at least a 2K. The art of exterior "lighting" has to do with blocking, diffusing, filtering, reflecting, and controlling the light of the sun and sky.

Lighting Equipment Checklist

You should have the following items on-hand and easily accessible during your shoot:

- 2″ cloth tape—to tape down cables so that people won't trip over them.
- Power cables and heavy-duty extension cords (25′, 50′, 100′).
- Three-prong to two-prong adapters for older locations.
- Clothespins—used to attach lighting gels or diffusion to barn doors, etc.
- Heavy work gloves—for handling light globes and hot equipment.
- Lighting gels.
- Diffusion materials.
- Reflectors.
- Bounce cards—often nothing more than a big piece of white foam core, bounce cards can help you get more mileage out of your lights.
- Duvetine, black felt or black garbage bags for blocking windows.
- Kino Flo bulbs—these color temperature-corrected, flicker-free light bulbs are used to replace standard fluorescent light tubes in location fixtures.
- Clamps with rubber handles—similar in function to clothespins but with more grip.
- Extra light globes—650W and 1K bulbs to go with your light kit, household bulbs in high wattages, etc. You should have at least one extra globe for every light in your kit.
- C-stands.
- Flags and nets.

Enhancing Existing Daylight

If you're shooting outside on a sunny day at noon, you'll get a brightly-lit image with very harsh shadows. If you're armed with the items listed in the Lighting Equipment Checklist above, you will be able to exert some control over the harsh conditions of bright daylight. Here are a few tips for brightening up those dark shadows:

- Try positioning a piece of foam core below your subject and off to one side, so that the light of the sun bounces off the white foam core and up into the shadows on your subject's face. This is a variation of three-point lighting—think of the sun as your key light, and the bounced light as your fill. Use a C-stand to secure the foam core.

- Use flags, black screens, and diffusion to cut down the intensity of the sun on the subject.
- Use a reflector or a bounce card to create a back light.
- If the contrast ratio is still too high, you need a stronger fill light. Try placing the sun behind your subject and use the bounce card as a soft key light from the front.
- Change locations. If you can't get the look you want in direct sunlight, try moving to a shadier location and using a bounce card to add highlights or positioning a large silk over your subject.

TIP

Golden Hour

The hour or so before sunset, also known as "golden hour," is one of the best times of day to shoot exteriors. The warm cast of the light is very flattering to human skin tones, and the chance of your scene being overlit is reduced. In addition, the low angle of the sun creates sharp, dark shadows, throwing everything in your scene into sharp relief. Unfortunately, you'll have to work fast to take advantage of this quality of light, as it does not last long.

Dealing with Low-Light Situations

The modern video cameras today can do a good job of producing an image with very little light. Unfortunately, they accomplish this by boosting the gain, which adds noise. If you turn off the gain boost, you'll have noise-free video, but probably little or no image. The only solution in this case is to use lights. You'll have to weigh the benefit of noise-free video against the difficulty of lighting. If your eventual goal is a video-to-film transfer, noise should be avoided at all costs. (More on gain in Chapter 9, "Shooting Digital Video.")

TIP

Battery-Operated Lights and Generators

Renting a generator might be out of your league, but for those situations where electrical power is unavailable, try using battery-operated lights.

Special Lighting Situations

Lighting does more than illuminate actors and locations. It also plays a key role in creating a believable setting, pulling off some types of special effects, and producing successful blue or green screen photography.

USING LIGHTS TO CREATE A SCENE

With a little imagination, lights can be used to suggest a location. Here are a few typical ways to create a scene with lights:

- **Car interiors.** A nighttime driving scene can be shot on a soundstage using a few focused lights placed outside the car, along with a fill light. The focused lights should be gelled to match the lights of passing cars, street lights, and brake lights. Each light (except the fill) needs to be manned by a grip who will move the light past the car at irregular intervals to replicate passing lights.
- **Day-for-Night.** Use slightly blue-colored gels to create light that looks like nighttime, and ND filters on your camera to make the image darker. Later, use digital compositing tools to matte out the sky and tweak the contrast ratio.
- **Firelight.** Dark orange gels can make your light source the same color as firelight. Wave flags in front of the light source to create a fire-like flicker. A fan with paper streamers in front of the light can add hands-free flicker.
- **Other illusional spaces.** Carefully flagged lights in the background can create the illusion of space, such as a doorway.

TIP

Smoke and Diffusion
Fog machines and diffusion spray are used to create an atmospheric haze in a scene, which can be very heavy or very subtle.

LIGHTING FOR BLUE AND GREEN SCREEN

If you will be shooting blue or green screen shots for later compositing with other elements, it's critical that you light your screen smoothly and evenly. For best results, consider the following:

- **Choose your compositing software before you shoot.** Different apps have different needs. Taking the trouble to become familiar with your compositing software and its specific needs will save you time and headaches later. See Chapters 16 and 17 for more on compositing apps.
- **Place your subject as far from the blue/green background as possible.** If your subject is too close to the background, you'll end up with *blue spill* (or *green spill*)—reflective blue light bouncing off the blue

screen and onto the back of your actor, resulting in a bluish backlight. This can make it extremely difficult to pull a clean matte later. If you can't avoid blue spill, try to make up for it by adding a hotter orange back light to cancel it out.

- **Light your subject and the background separately.** This also helps avoid blue spill and makes it easier to create the matte. The set in Color Plate 3 shows how much trouble a professional crew has to go to in order to light the set and the green screen separately.

- **Light to minimize video noise.** Video noise can make pulling a matte difficult. Be sure the scene is well-lit so that there's no need for gain-boosting on your camera. If you can, disable the automatic gain boost feature.

- **Try to make sure the blue/green screen is evenly lit.** Because it is important when shooting blue screen that the screen be consistently exposed (or lit), a spot meter can come in handy. A spot meter reads reflective light instead of incident or direct light and can be a real asset when trying to even out the light levels on your blue screen. Most camera shops rent them on a daily or weekly basis.

- **Art direct to avoid blue or green in your subject/foreground.** This may seem obvious, but blue can be a hard color to avoid, which is why the option of green screen exists, and vice versa. In Color Plate 4, the warm oranges and browns of the set lay in sharp contrast to the green screen in the background.

- **Dress the floor.** If you're going to see the actor's feet in the shot, it will be much easier to dress the floor with something like carpeting rather than attempting to composite it later.

- **Screen correction shots.** Most compositing software apps use a screen correction shot to make creating a matte easier. Either before or after every take, get a few seconds of footage of the empty blue/green screen with the same framing as the action. Refer to your compositing software documentation for other specific tips regarding screen correction shots.

- **Have a visual effects supervisor on set.** They may see problems you won't notice.

- **Pay attention to shadows.** Shadows can tend toward blue, which can make creating a matte difficult.

- **Light to match your CGI material.** If you're going to be compositing live action and CGI environments, be sure the live-action lighting matches the CGI environment lighting. If your digital background has an orange hue, it will look strange if your subject is lit with a blue back-light. The green screen set in Color Plate 4 is lit to match a CGI back-ground.

Art Directing

As with lighting, the goal of art directing is to enhance the story by adding to the available visual palette. In *Trainspotting*, every wall is painted a striking color often covered in a thick layer of grime: turquoise, red, green, mustard yellow. This dark, rich palette conveys an atmosphere of opiate sensuality ap-propriate to the film. In the film *Red*, the color palette is biased toward occa-sional touches of bright reds against a background of charcoal grays and rich dark browns. In *American Beauty*, the sets are dressed in typical suburban fur-niture just verging on "kitsch." The comfortable excess of the main family's house lies in sharp contrast to the austere, traditional Americana furniture in house of the family next door. In *Do the Right Thing*, bright reds in the sets and clothing are used to increase both the feeling of hot summer, and the emotional intensity of the drama.

Just as the director of photography is head of the camera department, the production designer is head of the art department. The production designer usually starts working early in the process, helping to generate storyboards and an overall "look" for the project. The title of this position may vary—you may use an art director or a set designer instead of a production designer, but their duties will be relatively the same. On a big movie, the production designer is responsible for the overall vision, while the art director implements that vision and manages the art department crew, which includes set designers, set dressers, prop masters, modelers, scenic painters, set construction workers, and production assistants.

ART DIRECTING BASICS

Good art direction is a combination of the symbolic and the practical. If your story is about a young girl growing up in Kansas in 1850, you'll be limited to certain types of buildings, furniture, and clothes. But you still have the choice of giving her a sunlit, whitewashed bedroom with furnishings upholstered in bright calico fabrics, or an age-darkened room with no direct sunlight and dull, dark fabrics. These simple details tell two very different stories.

One of the easiest ways to add visual symbolism to a scene is via lighting, as discussed earlier in this chapter. Colors also have strong connotations for people. Black symbolizes death; red symbolizes blood and violence, but also love and passion; blue is peaceful and calming, but also indicates sadness, and so on. Similarly, styles of furniture and clothing can say a lot about a character. An elderly woman living alone in a house decorated in sparse Eames furniture from the 1960s might indicate someone who won't let go of the past. Change the character to a young man, and the same furniture indicates a retro-hip sense of style. Clutter can be comfortable or claustrophobic, sparsity can be clean or indicative of emotional emptiness. In addition to externalizing the themes of the story, production design should also aid in focusing the viewer's eye, a challenge that goes hand in hand with lighting and framing the shot.

Building a Set

If your location needs are very specific, it may be easier to build a set than to find the right location. Whether you build your set on a stage or at a location, you'll need to spend some extra effort to make it look real. Sets are usually built out of *flats*, large, hollow wooden walls that are held up from the rear with supports. If you rent a soundstage, you may find that several flats come with the stage rental. You can paint them the color of your choice.

Typically, a room built on a stage will have three solid walls and a fourth wall on wheels for use when needed. Many flats have doors or windows built into them. When shopping for a soundstage, look for one that has the sort of flats you need. If your needs are very specialized, you may need to built your own flats, and color or texture them appropriately. For example, you can easily create a stucco or adobe look by gluing foamcore to a flat and then spraypainting it (spraypaint dissolves foamcore). Hiring a set carpenter can save lots of time and trouble.

TIP

Retail Therapy
Good set dressers and wardrobe people spend a lot of time browsing in the shops in their city. A thorough knowledge of where to buy odds and ends is one of the secrets of their profession.

Set Dressing and Props

Whether you have a found location or a built set, the next step is to dress it. Dressing a built set may take a little more work because it will be completely empty. On the other hand, your options may be limited when dressing a found location because you'll want to avoid disturbing the occupants or ruining their property. Either way, a good prop (short for property) can really sell a weak location. A giant gilded Victorian mirror, a barber's chair, a mirrored disco ball— the mere presence of these objects tells you where you are and makes the location believable. Props can be very expensive to rent, but if you can find that one key piece, it might be worth the money. In addition to prop rental houses, you can sometimes rent props from retailers. Usually this will involve a hefty deposit and the requirement that it be returned in perfect condition.

If your film involves weapons and fight scenes, you'll need special props like breakaway furniture and glass, fake knife sets, and realistic looking guns. Fake knife sets usually include a real version of the knife, a rubber version, a collapsible version, and a broken-off version. Renting a realistic-looking gun usually involves some extra paperwork and you are required to keep it concealed at all times. If you have a really specialized object that you need—like the Get Smart shoe-phone—you'll probably need to have a fabricator or modeler make it for you.

Art Director's Tips and Tricks

Distressing gives objects a patina of age. You can use any number of products to make something look brown or yellow with age: water-based wood stains, soaking objects in tea or coffee, fabric dyes, and rinse-out hair dyes, like Streaks and Tips, which washes off non-porous surfaces. You can use household *contact paper* to cover up flat surfaces that don't work with your production design. Spraying the object with window cleaner first will make the contact paper easy to remove. Clear contact paper can also be used to protect flat surfaces.

Mirrors can look great, but create special problems for lighting and shooting. Work with the director of photography before putting a mirror in a set. Extremely *saturated colors* look great to the human eye, but not to the video camera. Take care to avoid highly saturated reds in particular. *Stripes* and other detailed patterns also look bad on video, usually resulting in a distracting moire effect. If you're eventually going to transfer to film, some of these problems will actually diminish after your video is transferred to film.

Art Directing Equipment Checklist

Staple gun
Hammer, screwdriver, and other tools
Nails, tacks, and push-pins
Various types of glue
House paint and spray paint, various colors including black
Paint brushes and rollers
Bucket
Dark brown and amber water-based stains, Streaks and Tips, etc.
Dulling spray (to take the shine off reflective objects)
Contact paper
Window cleaner (with ammonia)
Cleaning products
Rags, towels, cheese cloth
Dust mask

TIP

Maintaining Continuity

Big movies have a person in charge of continuity on set at all times. His or her job is to keep track of any changes in set design, props, or costumes, so that later footage of that scene will look the same. Usually this is done using a polaroid or digital still camera, but if you're using a DV camera, you can also use its still frame mode.

Rolling . . .

Lighting and production design provide the backdrop in which your story will take place. Once you've tackled them, you're ready for the most important step of all: shooting the action.

CHAPTER

9 Shooting Digital Video

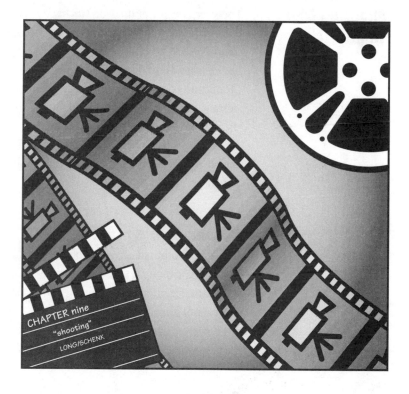

CHAPTER nine
"shooting"
LONG/SCHENK

IN THIS CHAPTER

- Shooting Digital Video
- The Tools of the Trade—the Camera
- During the Shoot
- Special Shooting Situations
- Quiet on the Set, Please

Shooting Digital Video

The sweeping panoramas of *Lawrence of Arabia,* the evocative shadows and compositions of *The Third Man,* the famous dolly/crane shot that opens *A Touch of Evil*—when we remember great films of the past, striking images usually come to mind. Digital technology has made visual effects and other post-production tasks a hot topic, but shooting your film is still the single most important step in a live-action production. Shooting good video requires more than just taping pretty images. As a director, the ability to unite the actors' performances with the compositions of the cinematographer, while managing all the other minutia that one must deal with on a set, will be key to the success of your project.

BEFORE YOU START

As a "digital filmmaker" you probably would like your feature to look as "cinematic" as possible. If you want your DV feature to look more like a film than a home-movie, then you're going to have to shoot it like film. Film-style shooting requires lots of advance planning and preparation. If you've already storyboarded your script and planned your effects shots, you've done about 80% of the prep work. Here's how to do the other 20%.

Rehearsals

Film productions are notorious for scheduling little or no rehearsal times for the actors. But you can never have too many rehearsals before going into production. For *The Saint,* director Phillip Noyce, actor Val Kilmer, and actress Elizabeth Shue improvised dialogue during rehearsals and in initial takes and then worked those lines and scenes into the final shoot.

How you decide to work with actors is up to you, but at the very least, plan on spending some time choreographing the movement of the actors, also known as *blocking*, for the camera. The more action you have in your scene, the more time you should spend blocking. Blocking a fight scene in a way that looks realistic but also fits with the visual look of your film can be a big challenge. If your film has an important fight scene, consider using a *fight choreographer*. Also, consider shooting your rehearsals to get a feel for the flow of the scene, and for planning your shot list. Whatever you do, don't wait until the day of the shoot to start blocking. Because you'll be under pressure to not waste precious time and money, you will very likely do a bad job. Lastly, if you have complicated lighting effects and camera moves for action or special effects scenes, schedule some time with the camera and lighting crew for technical discussions and rehearsals.

Camera Diagrams and Shot Lists

Take a look at the storyboards for a simple scene in Figure 9.1. (Storyboarding is covered in Chapter 3.) These storyboards show that the scene needs a master shot, three close-ups, and a two-shot. The script for this scene, in Figure 9.2, is *lined* and *numbered*, with each number representing a different camera angle, and each line indicating its duration.

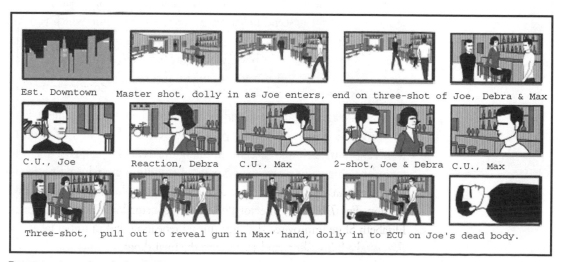

Est. Downtown   Master shot, dolly in as Joe enters, end on three-shot of Joe, Debra & Max

C.U., Joe   Reaction, Debra   C.U., Max   2-shot, Joe & Debra   C.U., Max

Three-shot,   pull out to reveal gun in Max' hand, dolly in to ECU on Joe's dead body.

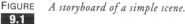

FIGURE
9.1   *A storyboard of a simple scene.*

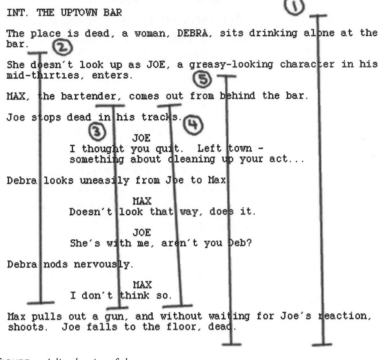

INT. THE UPTOWN BAR

The place is dead, a woman, DEBRA, sits drinking alone at the bar.

She doesn't look up as JOE, a greasy-looking character in his mid-thirties, enters.

MAX, the bartender, comes out from behind the bar.

Joe stops dead in his tracks.

              JOE
    I thought you quit. Left town -
    something about cleaning up your act...

Debra looks uneasily from Joe to Max

              MAX
    Doesn't look that way, does it.

              JOE
    She's with me, aren't you Deb?

Debra nods nervously.

              MAX
    I don't think so.

Max pulls out a gun, and without waiting for Joe's reaction, shoots. Joe falls to the floor, dead.

FIGURE   *A lined script of that same scene.*
9.2

In this particular scene, the coverage is designed *master shot* style. A master shot covers the entire scene and serves as the foundation into which you will edit the cut-aways and other shots. The shot numbers on the lined script are detailed in the *shot list* at the bottom of Figure 9.3. Each shot in the list corresponds to the camera angles and movements diagrammed in the top portion of Figure 9.3.

Camera diagrams can also include information about light placement. Even if a camera diagram is overkill for your scene, you should always arrive on set with a shot list. A simple checklist detailing the day's plan can go a long way toward helping you achieve your goals and communicate your vision to the crew. Without a shot list it can be very easy to forget a close-up, or to not cover the scene properly.

TIP

Planning a Test Shoot
If you're really worried about how your footage is going to turn out, you should plan on a simple test shoot. Schedule the test shoot prior to going into production.

This will give you a chance to look at the quality of your footage and determine if you need to make any changes in your shooting plan. If you're transfering to film, you may also want your film recordist to do a film print of your test shoot (approx. $200–$500).

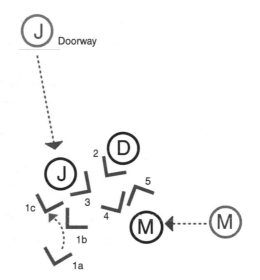

1. Master shot of scene: Wide shot (1a) , dolly in, hold on 3-shot (1b), dolly in to ECU of Joe (1c).
2. C.U. of Debra
3. C.U. of Joe
4. Two-shot of Debra and Joe
5. C.U. of Max

Cutaways: E.C.U. of gun, details of bar, etc.

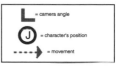

FIGURE
9.3
The corresponding camera diagram and shot list.

PREPARING YOUR EQUIPMENT

Video equipment is relatively easy to use compared to film equipment. Nonetheless, you'll need to do a little equipment preparation before your shoot.

Preparing the Videotape

Before you shoot or edit onto a new videotape, you should fast-forward it to the end and then rewind it. This ensures that the tape has been stretched as much as it will stretch under normal use, and that it is tightly and evenly spooled. Just as an audio cassette tape can get loose inside the cartridge, the tape in a video cassette can become slack. Stretching and winding the tape will reduce the risk of dropouts, tape jams, and even tape breakage.

Crewing Up

If you're a novice director, having a big crew might prove to be more of a hindrance than a help. On the other hand, having an extra person on set just might save the day. Here's a list of the almost militaristic hierarchy of camera and lighting crewmembers you'll find on a typical union film set:

Director of photography (D.P.), aka cinematographer—this is the person in charge of all camera operations and lighting. With a skeleton crew, the D.P. may operate the camera, with a bigger crew the D.P. will hire a . . .

Camera operator This is the person behind the camera, who works in tandem with the d.p.

First assistant camera (A.C.) The first A.C. is responsible for loading the film camera, setting up the lenses and filters for each shot, and making sure the shot is in focus.

Second A.C. The second A.C is responsible for keeping camera reports, slating each shot, and sometimes loading film into the magazines.

Gaffer The gaffer is the head electrician on the set and is responsible for directing the set-up of the lights and other electrical equipment.

Best boy and electricians The best boy is the first assistant under the gaffer. As with other first assistant positions, the best boy manages the other set electricians in the setting up of lights, etc.

Key grip The key grip assists the gaffer with lighting, and is responsible for coordinating the placement of grip equipment (flags, nets, etc.), special riggings, and the hardware used to move the camera.

Dolly grip Big movies have special grips who are employed to operate cranes, dollies, and other heavy equipment.

Camera department production assistants The camera department often needs a p.a. or two to run errands to the equipment rental house, purchase film stock or videotape, and so on.

Conserving Your Batteries

Certain camera features require a lot of power to run. These include power zoom controls, LCD displays, rewinding and fast-forwarding tapes, and playing back tapes. Always try to use A/C power when using these functions. Also, most cameras have a standby feature that shuts the camera off when not in use.

If your camera is capable of generating color bars and audio reference tone, you should record at least a minute of bars and tone onto the head of the tape before you shoot. Refer to your camera user manuals for instructions. You should *always* avoid recording anything important on the first minute or two of your tape—this is the part of the tape that is most prone to damage. Also, if your camera allows you to set the timecode hour, go ahead and do so. It may be useful in post-production to have your timecode set at different hours on different tapes. You can even have the hour correspond to the tape number, usually starting with hour 01, which will make it very easy for your editor (or yourself!) to find tapes later on. (If you're wondering why you'd want timecode at all, read the timecode section in Chapter 4, "Choosing a Videotape Format.") Finally, don't forget to label your tapes as you use them, and depress the record inhibit tabs—you don't want to accidentally record over an already-used tape because it looked like new stock!

Environmentally Incorrect

Even though you can re-use videotape stock, you should avoid doing so. Videotape gets physically worn the more you use it, and becomes more susceptible to dropouts and degradation. If you must recycle tapes, be sure to "degauss," or magnetically erase, your tapes. Also, avoid using the end of a tape from a previous shoot. This reduces the risk of accidentally recording over your previously shot footage. It sounds silly, but it happens all the time. Tape stock is relatively cheap—budget some extra money and avoid the potential pitfalls of used tape.

Preparing Your Camera

Before you start rolling, you should check all the controls and settings on your camera to make sure they are all set appropriately. Make sure that any features you don't want (16:9 shooting, progressive scan, etc.) are turned off.

If your camera allows for manual white balancing, now is the time to do it. Once your lights are set up, place something white in-frame, like a piece of foamcore or a white wall. Make sure the white card is illuminated by the dominant light source in your scene. Frame the camera so that only white shows in the viewfinder, and press the *white balance* button. You've just told your camera how to render the color white for your scene. You'll need to white balance every time you significantly change the lighting, especially if you switch from daylight to tungsten light, or vice versa. Newer cameras have pretty good automatic white balance controls, and in some cases it may be more efficient to use the auto white balance. However, the only way to determine if you're happy with the white balance is to look at the image on a field monitor.

TIP

Alternative White Balancing
You can use the white balancing feature on your camera to achieve different color effects. White balancing against a bluish surface will result in a warmer-looking image, while balancing against an orangish surface results in a cool-looking image. Since white balancing affects the scene's overall color temperature, it is sometimes easier to adjust the white balance than it is to place colored lighting gels on all your light sources.

If you are shooting from a tripod or some other image stabilizing device, be sure to turn off any electronic or optical image stabilization features on your camera. Electronic image stabilization algorithms typically shoot at higher shutter speeds. In addition to producing a harsher image, you'll also see a reduction in gain. Some EIS mechanisms will also soften your image, even when they're sitting still.

Optical image stabilization mechanisms won't change your image quality, but they will drain your battery life. Since you won't need stabilization if you're using a tripod, go ahead and turn off your optical stabilization.

Preparing the Audio Equipment
Finally, you need to make sure all your audio equipment is hooked up and working properly, and that you're getting good audio levels. Chapter 10 covers everything you need to know about production sound.

The Tool of the Trade—The Camera

The camera is the central piece of equipment in any sort of production. DV cameras, like the Canon XL1 in Figure 9.4, have been a hot topic among independent film-makers for a while now. We're biased toward cameras that offer manual override of all key camera functions: zooming, focus, white balancing, f-stop/iris control, variable shutter speeds, and gain controls. Each of these features plays an important role in successful shooting.

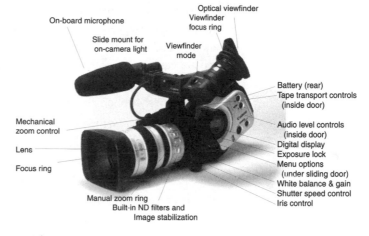

Optical viewfinder
Viewfinder focus ring
On-board microphone
Slide mount for on-camera light
Viewfinder mode
Battery (rear)
Tape transport controls (inside door)
Audio level controls (inside door)
Mechanical zoom control
Lens
Focus ring
Digital display
Exposure lock
Menu options (under sliding door)
White balance & gain
Shutter speed control
Iris control
Manual zoom ring
Built-in ND filters and Image stabilization

FIGURE
9.4   *The Canon XL-1.*

Camera Equipment Checklist

You should keep these items in your camera case for easy access at all times:

- Your camera's original owner's manual
- Lens tissue
- Lens cleaning fluid
- Measuring tape
- Rain cover, umbrella, or plastic garbage bags
- Sun shade
- Head cleaning cartridge
- Extra lenses (if applicable)
- Lens filters
- Extra batteries (charged)
- A/C adapter
- Flashlight
- Standard tool kit
- Slate (see Chapter 10)
- White pencil (for temporarily marking settings on the lens)
- Colored tape (for marking blocking, camera and light placement)

THE LENS

Camera lenses fall into two categories: *prime* lenses and *zoom* lenses. Prime lenses have a fixed focal length, measured in millimeters, which determines their angle of view. Prime lenses are known for producing a sharper image than zooms, and D.P.s who work in feature films are used to having a selection of high-quality prime lenses for their 35mm film cameras. However, most video cameras are equipped with zoom lenses (Figure 9.5), which offer a range of focal lengths from telephoto (or close-up) to wide angles, and are more suitable to documentary-style photography.

All Lenses Are Not Alike
There is about a 7x factor when figuring what a DV lens correlates to in terms of millimeters on a 35mm lens. The 5.5–88mm zoom lens that comes with the XL1 is the equivalent of an approx. 39–600mm lens on a 35mm still camera.

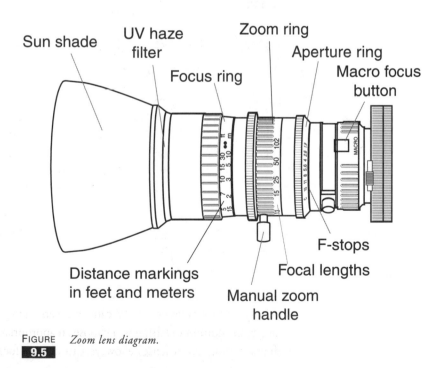

FIGURE
9.5   *Zoom lens diagram.*

This means that a 50mm Canon EOS lens will look about like a 350mm lens on your DV camera.

Telephoto Lenses

A lens is considered "telephoto" (Figure 9.6d) if it magnifies the image at least 50% more than a normal lens (Figure 9.6c). As a lens gets more telephoto, its angle of view gets narrower and the sense of perspective in the image gets shallower. This shallow perspective results in images that have a very compressed sense of depth.

In addition to allowing you to shoot close-up shots of faraway objects, telephoto lenses allow you to shoot with a very shallow depth of field, as we'll explain later.

TIP

Care of the Lens

Always keep your lens cap on when your camera is not in use. Keep a UV haze filter on your lens as a protective layer. Avoid touching the lens with your bare hands, since the oil from your fingers can etch a permanent mark on the glass. Never clean a lens with dry fabric or tissue. Instead, use a lens tissue dampened with lens cleaning fluid to wipe it off.

Wide Angle Lenses

A wide angle lens provides a wide field of view, allowing you to get closer to your subject, or display more background (Figure 9.6b). A wide angle lens is handy when you're shooting in a small space and don't have room to back away from your subject. However, as we'll see later, wide angle lenses are not especially flattering, as they can add distortion around the edges, an effect that may or may not be desirable. An image shot with an extremely wide angle lens, or *fish-eye lens,* will be very distorted, resulting in a rounded looking image, as if seen through a peep-hole.

Zoom Lens

The typical zoom lens on a DV camera covers a range from telephoto to wide angle. In addition to letting you choose an appropriate focal length when you frame a shot, zoom lenses allow you to change focal length *during* a shot, using either a mechanical control button or by manually turning the zoom ring on the lens itself. Unless you're trying for that "caught on tape" look, a

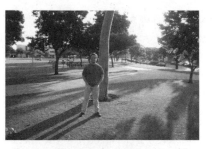

A. Very wide angle

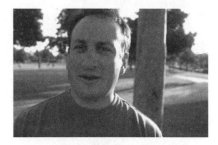

E. Very wide angle

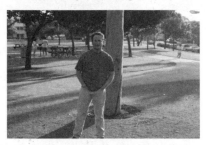

B. Wide angle

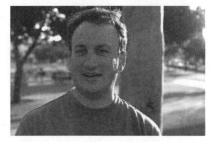

F. Wide angle

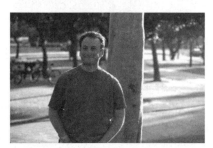

C. Normal angle

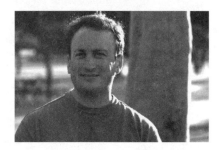

G. Normal angle

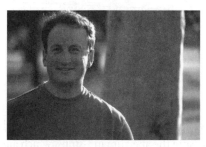

D. Telephoto

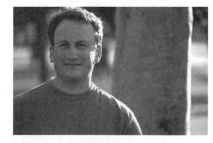

H. Telephoto

FIGURE
9.6
The left four (a–d) images show the same subject at the same distance from the camera shot with four different focal length lenses. The right four images (e–h) show the same subject shot with the same four lenses, but with the camera distance adjusted to keep the subject the same size within the frame. Notice how the size of the tree in the background changes even though the subject stays the same. Courtesy of Gregg Rossen.

good zoom needs to start out slowly, ramp up to the desired speed, then gradually slow to a halt. You can also conceal a zoom by combining it with a pan or tilt.

The mechanical zooms found on most prosumer DV cameras can be difficult to control—they tend to start awkwardly, go too fast, and respond jerkily to any fluctuations in pressure on the button. Unfortunately, many DV cameras have lenses that do not have a manual zoom ring. In either case, practice makes perfect—give your camera operator (or yourself!) time with the camera before the shoot to get a feel for how the camera's zoom works. Most DV cameras also have digital zooms, which are accessed through a menu display. Digital zooms are best avoided, since they work by blowing up the image, rather than moving the optics of the lens, resulting in a low-resolution, pixelated image.

Get to Know Your Camera

Professional D.P.s know their cameras inside and out. Many of them will only work with certain types of cameras, and some will only work with equipment from specific rental houses. The advantage of most digital video cameras is that you can point and shoot and still get a good image. But if you want to get the most from your camera, you should follow the example of the pros and take the time to learn how your camera works. Experiment to discover what it's capable of, and how it reacts in different lighting situations like low-light, night exteriors, and backlight situations. Try to learn where the camera's controls are by feel. While shooting, you may want to switch a feature on or off without taking your eye from the viewfinder. It's better to learn about your camera during test shoots, rather than during your production.

Aperture

Aperture refers to the opening at the rear of the lens. The camera's lens focuses light through the aperture, and onto the *focal plane*. In the case of a digital video camera, the focal plane is a CCD. The size of the aperture is controlled by the *iris,* a series of metal leaves that can expand and contract like the iris in your eye. High-end cameras measure the aperture in f-stops, which are marked on the exterior of the lens itself (Figure 9.5). Higher-numbered f-stop values stop more light. That is, a higher-numbered value represents a *smaller* aperture, which results in less light passing through the lens. Smaller numbers stop less light (Figure 9.7).

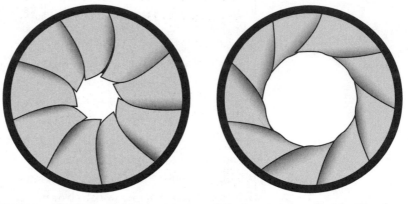

FIGURE **9.7** *The iris on the left is stopping more light than the iris on the right. Therefore, it has a higher f-stop value, and makes a smaller aperture.*

Mid-range cameras do not have f-stops on their lenses, but provide control of the lens aperture with special dials, and with f-stop settings shown in the digital menu display. Lower-end cameras do not display f-stops, but allow for manual iris adjustment and iris locking. Bottom-line cameras do not allow for any manual control of the lens aperture, and rely solely on automated iris settings.

Having control of the iris gives you the freedom to select faster or slower shutter speeds (for stopping or blurring fast-moving action), and to control *depth of field,* which we'll discuss later. While the auto iris function may work fine in "normal" lighting situations, it's usually the wrong choice in more complicated scenes. Leaving the auto-iris on may result in changes in the exposure in the middle of a shot—even the movement of your subjects within the frame can change the exposure. As they pass in front of light sources, the iris will fluctuate. If your camera allows it, you should always work with the auto iris function turned off.

FOCUS

Before you can focus your camera, you need to make sure the viewfinder is adjusted to match your vision. Most cameras, like the ones in Figure 9.4 and 9.12, have an adjustment ring, or *diopter,* on the viewfinder. (Refer to your camera documentation for specifics.) Set the camera lens out of focus, then look through the viewfinder and move the viewfinder focus adjustment until you can see the grains of glass or the display information in the viewfinder itself

Separating the Subject from the Background

By separating the subject from the background, the cinematographer helps the audience decide where to focus their attention within the frame. Separating the subject from the background is particularly useful in video since there tends to be greater *depth of field* than in film. Depth of field refers to how "deep" the range of focus is in an image. In Figure 9.8a, the depth of field is shallow and only the subject is in focus. It is easy to focus your attention on the actor because he is completely separated from the background. In Figure 9.8b, the depth of field is larger, and more detail shows in the background.

Both of these images were shot under the same lighting conditions with the same lens. In a, the depth of field is shallow because the lens aperture is wide open. In b, the lens aperture is closed down all the way, resulting in a less shallow depth of field. To get deeper depth of field, you'll need to open your iris as far as possible (that is, choose a lower f-stop). This will let in a lot more light, which means you'll need to go to a faster shutter speed. (A faster shutter speed will result in more stuttery motion, so you may want to use special neutral density filters to reduce the amount of light entering the camera. This will let you keep your shutter speed down.)

In addition, you'll want to use a longer focal length. To shoot deep depth of field using a DV camera with a zoom lens, you'll want to stand farther away and zoom in closer to frame your shot. Then, make your aperture and shutter adjustments. However, different focal lengths will result in very different-looking images, as we'll explain next.

Beware of judging depth of field in a very small monitor, however, especially your camera's viewfinder or LCD screen. Ideally, you'll want to use a larger field monitor.

If your camera allows, turn off the autofocus mechanism. Autofocus will always focus on the middle of the frame. Since you may want to be more creative than this, stick with manual focus.

To focus a zoom lens manually, zoom all the way in to the image on which you wish to focus and focus the image. Now you can zoom back to compose the shot at the focal length you desire. As long as your subject doesn't move forward or backward, your image will be in focus at any focal length available.

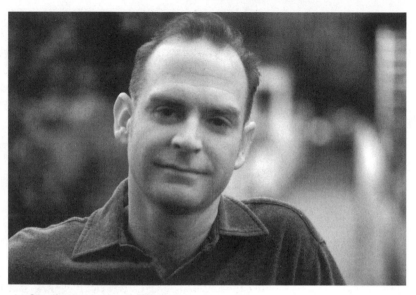

A. Shallow depth of field

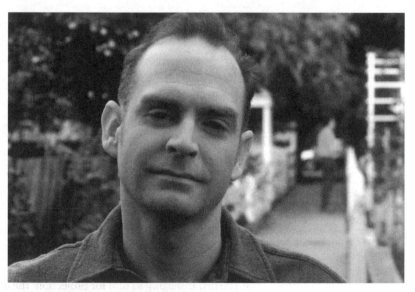

B. Less shallow depth of field

FIGURE
9.8   *In this set of images, the top image has a much shallower depth of field than does the bottom image. That is, the area that is in focus is not as deep as in the bottom image. The top image was shot using a larger aperture (lower f-stop).*

Focusing a Canon XL1

Some DV camera lenses, notably the zoom lens that comes with the Canon XL1, do not hold focus if you use the manual zoom ring on the lens to recompose your shot. Instead, use the mechanical zoom button on the lens. You can also focus by composing your shot first and then adjusting the focus ring on the lens, the same way you would with a prime lens. The only problem with this method is that the wider your shot, the harder it will be to tell if your subject is truly in focus. You can also center your subject, press the autofocus button until it finds the right focus, then turn off the autofocus feature to lock the focus in place. Then recompose your shot as desired. The XL1 has a Find Focus button that allows you to set the focus without using the auto-focus features.

Measuring Focus

If your camera lens has a focus ring with distance measurements marked on it, like the lens in Figure 9.5, you can measure the distance between your subject and the lens to ensure perfect focus. (Of course, you can't be sure of the focus markings on your lens unless you've tested them and found the marks to be accurate.)

If you plan to eventually transfer your video image to film, proper focus is critical. When the image is projected and blown up to 25+ times its normal size, what looked in focus on a small video monitor may appear out of focus. Luckily, most images have a *depth of field* that exceeds the depth of focus. In Figure 9.9, the depth of focus is eight feet from the camera, but the depth of field—the part of the image that *appears* in focus—starts a couple feet in front of the subject and extends to infinity. The woman seated behind the subject will appear in focus, even though she's not on the plane of focus.

If you're having trouble focusing, use your manual iris control to iris down (go to a higher f-stop number). This will increase your depth of field and improve your chances of shooting focused. If you're shooting in a low light situation with the lens aperture wide open, don't count on a lot of depth of field. Compose your shot with the knowledge that only your subject may be in focus.

If you're transferring to film for projection, the only way to be certain about depth of field is to calculate it mathematically. Unfortunately, depth of field calculations for DV cameras are complicated by the fact that DV cameras often lack f-stop or distance markings on their lenses, digital lenses use different optics than 35mm lenses, and DV lens sizes in millimeters do not corre-

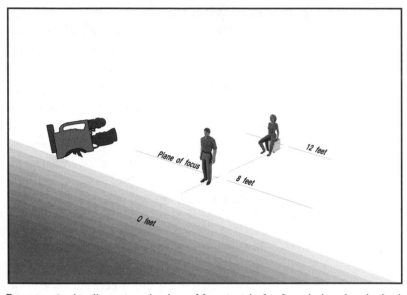

FIGURE
9.9   *In this illustration, the plane of focus is eight feet from the lens, but the depth of field, represented by the white area, is much bigger. Everything in this area appears in focus, including the woman and the background.*

spond to 35mm lens sizes. Standard depth of field charts, such as those found in the American Cinematographer's Manual, do not apply to your DV camera.

Pulling Focus

Film camera operators compensate for shallow depth of field by having the camera assistant *pull focus*. As the camera moves on a dolly, for example, the camera assistant manually moves the focus using the focus ring on the lens. Some lenses have a place to attach a knob that makes pulling focus easier, but either way, it requires a steady hand. You need to be able to pull focus in order to do a *rack focus* shot. Unless you have a camera with high-end features like the one in Figure 9.12, pulling focus on a DV camera is almost impossible.

Faking Focus Pulls
Puffin Designs' Image Lounge includes a Rack Focus filter that you can use to fake some rack focus shots in post-production. Obviously, you'll need to do some experimentation and planning before you rely on such post-production effects.

LENS FILTERS

If your camera has threads on the end of its lens, you can attach special filters that will help you better control color and composition, as well as create special effects. Filters are simply specially prepared pieces of glass housed in a screw-on attachment. Most filters are threaded so that you can screw filters onto filters to stack up effects. Filters come in different sizes, so the selection of filters available for your lens size may vary. Many filters come in different "strengths" whose values are usually measured with a simple number scheme. The higher the number, the more the filter will affect your image.

UV Filters

As we mentioned earlier, you should get at least one UV filter to protect your lens. In addition, UV filters will filter out ultraviolet light and help reduce haze. There are a number of variations of UV filters, including stronger haze filters and warm UV filters, that will add warmth to your image.

Polarizing Filters

Polarizers are used to deepen saturation and are must-haves for shooting outdoors. A circular polarizer attaches like any other filter, but can be rotated to achieve different polarizing effects, such as making an image more or less saturated, or to shift an image more toward warm or red. Shooting with a polarizer is just about the only way to get decent images of cloudy skies.

Polarizers can also be used to eliminate reflections when shooting through glass or windows (see Figure 9.10) and to eliminate hot spots on a reflective surface created by a light source.

Neutral Density Filters

Used for controlling the amount of light coming through your lens, the most common light balancing filter is the neutral density filter. ND filters reduce the amount of light entering the lens in 1 f-stop increments. So, if you're shooting in bright sunlight (which normally requires a small aperture), but you want to shoot with a very shallow depth of field (which requires a large aperture), you can use ND filters to cut out enough light to facilitate a smaller f-stop value.

Your camera may have a built-in electronic ND filter. Check your manual to see how many stops this feature provides.

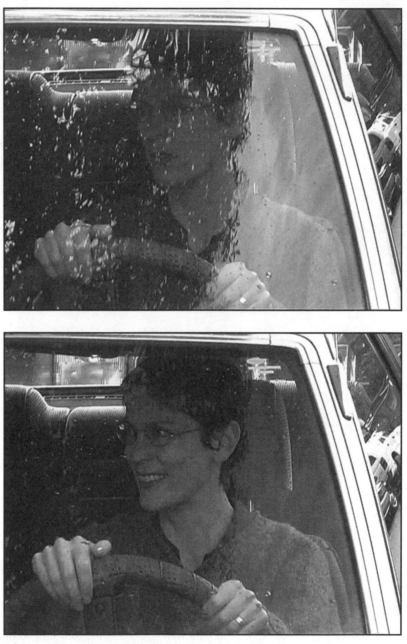

FIGURE   *The window reflections in the first image can be easily eliminated with a po-*
9.10   *larizing filter.*

Color Correction and Light Balancing Filters

There are a number of filters that can correct for tungsten or daylight. In addition, special colored filters can be used to tint your image, or strengthen particular colors.

Contrast Adjustment

High-Contrast filters can be used to improve the contrast ratio (and therefore, apparent sharpness) in an image, while filters such as Tiffen's ProMist and Black ProMist can be used to reduce contrast to achieve more of a film look (Figure 9.11).

Gradiated Filters

Gradiated filters feature a grade from dark to light that can be useful if you need to take down a bright sky but want to keep the area below the horizon line unfiltered.

Special Effects Filters

Special effects filters can be used to make lights flare in starburst patterns, to tone an image sepia, to create extreme fog effects, and much, much more. Before you commit to any of these filters, though, see if you can achieve the same look in your post-production software. Shooting clean, unfiltered video and processing it digitally later will give you more flexibility.

In addition to filters, a *sun shade* attached to the end of your lens will prevent the sun from shining directly on the lens and creating lens flares.

Film Look

There's a lot of advice floating around about how to create a "film look" using diffusion filters. The only way to decide if they work is to do some experimenting with them. If you're planning to eventually transfer to film, this may be unnecessary since the film process itself will result in a "film look." One of the challenges of a successful video-to-film transfer is delivering an image that looks sharp on film. Consult with your film recordist before using lots of filtration or diffusion. We recommend that you avoid using diffusion materials, like softening effects filters or stockings and other fabrics over or behind the lens itself. Use diffusion spray, fog machines, and diffusion on the lights to soften the image, but avoid overusing these items as well.

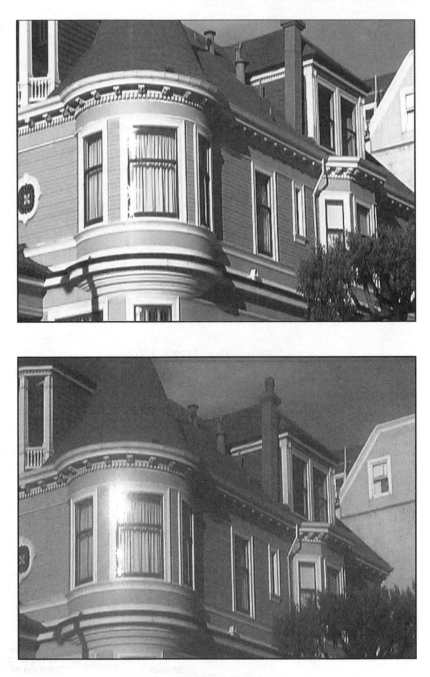

FIGURE
9.11
   Tiffen's ProMist Filter can be used to reduce the contrast in an image and make light flares bloom, creating a more film-like image.

Film typically has a shallower depth of field than does video. One way to get more of a film-like image, then, is to shoot with less depth of field.

We'll discuss film look more in Chapter 18.

OTHER CAMERA FEATURES

If your camera allows it, you should opt for a slow *shutter speed* when shooting for a film look. Usually the slowest speed available on a DV camera is 1/60th of a second, which corresponds with the fastest shutter speed available on most film cameras. In Figure 6.8a and b, you can see the difference between a fast shutter speed and a slower shutter speed. The resulting motion blur of the slow shutter speed will help make your video look more like film. (Refer to your camera manual for instructions on manually adjusting the shutter speed.)

Most DV cameras will allow you to choose between *progressive* and *interlaced scanning*. (See Chapter 4 for an explanation of progressive and interlaced scanning.) Progressive scanning will also make your video look more film-like, as—depending on your camera—the slower shutter speed might be closer to film. However, when shooting with progressive scan, you'll need to be very careful to avoid fast camera moves and fast action on-screen. Unless you are

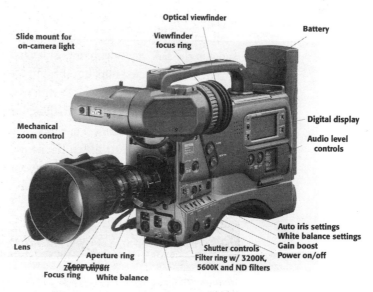

Slide mount for
on-camera light

Optical viewfinder

Viewfinder
focus ring

Battery

Digital display

Audio level
controls

Mechanical
zoom control

Lens

Aperture ring

Zebra on/off

Focus ring

White balance

Shutter controls
Filter ring w/ 3200K,
5600K and ND filters

Auto iris settings
White balance settings
Gain boost
Power on/off

FIGURE
9.12   *The JVC GY-D500 miniDV camera has manual override for everything and lots of high-end features.*

going for a special effect, or plan on pulling lots of stills from your video, interlaced scanning is a better choice.

All newer video cameras come with a *gain boost* feature for low light situations. Gain boost makes everything in your image brighter, including the black areas of your image. A good video image should aim for dark, solid blacks, and bright, clear whites. If the gain is boosted, the blacks tend toward gray. In addition, video *noise* is introduced. Noise is the video equivalent of film grain, except it is a lot more noticeable and distracting. If you are planning to go to film later, you should avoid any gain boosting. Instead, use proper lighting to get a good exposure on your videotape and turn off the gain boost feature.

ASPECT RATIOS

Choosing an aspect ratio is an artistic choice. Needless to say, composing a shot for 1.33 video (or 4:3) is very different from projected film at 1.85 or high-definition television at 1.77 (or 16:9). (See the aspect ratio table in Chapter 4.) Be sure to keep this in mind when you shoot. The DV format's 1.33 aspect ratio is perfectly suited to the current broadcast standard, although the number of TV productions shot in the HDTV 1.77 format will continue to grow. If you're planning to transfer to film, 16mm film shares the same 1.33 aspect ratio as DV, but to get the 1.85 aspect ratio of North American theatrical release format for 35mm film, the top and bottom of the 1.33 image will be cropped out (refer back to Figure 6.12).

If you want to take advantage of the 35mm film format, you'll need to shoot in the 1.77 high-definition widescreen aspect ratio. 1.77 is still slightly smaller than projected film, but the difference is negligible. Most 35mm film cameras have lenses that can be fit with removeable ground glass attachments for viewing crop marks that indicate various aspect ratios through the viewfinder. This helps camera operators compose the shot for the aspect ratio desired (even if it doesn't match the native aspect ratio of the format they're shooting with). Unfortunately, the concept of removeable ground glass attachments hasn't quite trickled down to the DV camera world yet.

TIP

Buyer Beware

Just because a camera is 16:9/4:3 switchable, doesn't mean that the camera records a true native 16:9 image. The change in aspect ratio may simply mean that the image is being re-shaped to fit that ratio (Figure 6.12). If your camera doesn't shoot native 16:9, you can add an anamorphic lens attachment to it that will squeeze the image (Figure 6.13).

TV Title Safe and Action Safe

The portion of the video image that is visible varies from one TV set to another. To ensure that all viewers can see the action and read the titles, SMPTE came up with guidelines for the *action safe* and *title safe* areas of the image. Professional lenses have visual guides visible in the viewfinder that show where the title safe and action safe boundaries lie, much like the guides shown in Figure 16.1. Unfortunately, not all DV camera manufacturers have included these guides in their viewfinders. If your viewfinder doesn't have action safe and title safe guides, be sure to remember that the outer edges of the image may not be visible, and compose your shots accordingly.

CONTROLLING THE CAMERA

There are a mind-boggling number of gadgets available today for controlling the movement of a camera. You can buy anything from giant cranes to special remote control helicopters to heavy-duty underwater gear. In Chapter 6, we discussed tripods, steadicams, and on-board image stabilizing systems. Here are a few more ways to control the camera:

- **Dollies.** There are a number of cheap options for getting that fancy dolly shot. You can make your own skateboard dollies with four rotating skateboard wheels attached to a piece of plywood. Wheelchairs also work well, allowing the operator to sit in the chair and hold the camera while someone else pushes, and you can always try using your car. Shooting out of a convertible or the back of a pick-up truck works best, but take care not to endanger yourself and others.
- **Handholding.** Handholding a lightweight video camera can be a challenge. Some prefer to hold the camera at waist level, balanced against their torso, others at eye level. Using the shoulder strap sometimes steadies the camera, and standing with your legs shoulder-width apart can help steady your stance. As with most camera-operating skills, practice makes perfect.
- **Car camera mounts.** To get good footage inside a moving car, car camera mounts—special vacuum suction devices that attach the camera to the body of the car—are essential.

During the Shoot   Hopefully, you've come to the shoot fully prepared with a shot list, story-boards, and careful blocking of your scenes. Here's a list of odds and ends to remember with during the shoot:

- **Prevent Timecode breaks.** Your post-production will go much easier if you avoid breaks in timecode when shooting. A break in timecode occurs any time there is a blank spot on the tape. Such breaks might prevent your NLE from being able to capture or digitize your footage. Most DV cameras include special controls (usually in the form of buttons on the camera) that will search forward or backward for the last piece of stable timecode. The camera will then cue the tape to the last frame of stable timecode and begin recording from there.

    If your camera doesn't have such a feature, you can protect your tape from timecode breaks by always letting the tape run for a few seconds after the end of your shot. Then, before you begin taping again, back the tape up so that recording begins on top of your extra footage.

- **Calling "Action!"** Believe it or not, there is a very specific protocol to follow when calling "Action" on a film shoot. The assistant director yells "Roll sound" and the sound recordist replies "Speed" once his equipment is running at full speed. Next, the assistant director calls "Roll camera" and the camera person answers "Speed" once the camera is running at full speed. Finally, the director calls "Action!" Even if you're not using a sound recordist, assistant director, or a camera operator, it's still good practice to warn everyone on the set vocally that you're about to start shooting, and give your camera and audio equipment a few seconds to run before you call "Action."

- **Heads and tails.** Allowing a few seconds to roll before the action starts and a few seconds to roll after the director calls "cut" can be crucial during the editing process later on.

- **Crossing the stage line.** Crossing the 180° axis, also known as the *stage line,* is jarring. If you think of your set as a theatrical stage, the 180° axis falls along the proscenium (the front of the stage). Once you've set up your camera on one side of the axis, avoid moving it to the other side (see Figure 9.13). Be aware that this primarily concerns action and dialogue shots. Cut-aways and establishing shots can often get away with crossing the stage line.

- **Eye lines.** If you're shooting a conversation between two or more actors, you need to make sure the eyelines in each close-up match the others, so

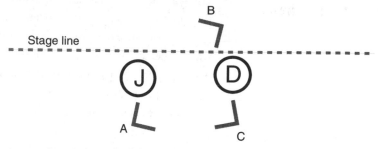

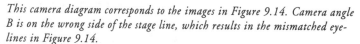

FIGURE
9.13
This camera diagram corresponds to the images in Figure 9.14. Camera angle B is on the wrong side of the stage line, which results in the mismatched eyelines in Figure 9.14.

that when the shots are edited together, they look like they're looking at each other (see Figure 9.14). It's also usually a good idea to shoot dialogue within a scene with the same focal length lens and from the same distance.

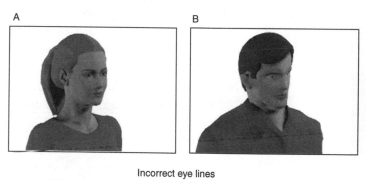

Incorrect eye lines

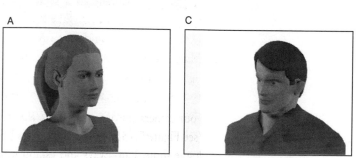

Correct eye lines

FIGURE
9.14
A and B have eyelines that are shot incorrectly, while A and C have eyelines that match.

- **Using a field monitor.** Feature film directors use "video assist" monitors that connect to 35mm film cameras so that they can see what is being seen by the camera operator. A field monitor lets you do the same thing with a video camera. Even if you'll be operating the camera yourself, a field monitor can be an asset, making it much easier to focus and frame your shots, and, of course, it lets others see what the operator is seeing.

- **Camera logs.** Have someone on the camera crew keep camera logs: a list of shots, lens focal lengths, and technical notes with timecode references. If you have trouble later, camera logs can help you decipher the problem.

- **Logging your shots on the set.** You can log shots on paper or using special logging software like Avid's Media Log on a laptop computer or Production Magic's Shot Logger on an Apple Message Pad. Shot Logger comes at a hefty $2250 price tag, but allows for wireless transmission of timecode information directly from the camera into the handheld computer.

TIP

12 bit or 16 bit? 32 or 48 KHz?

As we stated earlier, when editing it's important to be sure you use the same frequency for all of your audio. So, if you've decided to use 48 KHz audio in one part of your project, you need to use 48 KHz audio in all of it. Most cameras, however, don't let you select 32 or 48 KHz audio. Instead they measure audio by its bit-depth, either 12 or 16-bit. In simplest terms, 12-bit audio is simply another way of saying 32 KHz audio, while 16-bit audio is synonymous with 48 KHz audio.

- **Avoid over-coverage of a scene.** You may think you're just burning videotape as you call for Take 23, but you're also burning the energy of your cast and crew and expensive editing time later on.

- **Make-up.** Video isn't known for flattering the human face, and bright lights can make even the most minor skin flaws stand out. We're not advocating the "news anchorwoman" look, but you should always use subtle makeup on all your subjects to cover blemishes, even out skin tones, enhance facial features, and, most importantly, take the shine off hot spots.

- **Room Tone.** At some point during your shoot, your sound recordist will need to record 30 seconds to a minute of *room tone*. Room tone is nothing more than the sound of the room when no one is talking or making sound. This "empty" sound will be used by the sound editor to patch gaps in the soundtrack and to cover rough sound edits.

Because you are trying to record the natural ambient sound of your location, be sure to record your room tone after your set has been fully dressed. Recording it before may produce a different quality tone as there will be fewer sound-absorbing set pieces and props. The end of your shooting day is usually the best time to record room tone. Simply ask everyone on the set to be quiet, and start your recorder.

COMPOSING THE SHOT

Though we don't really have space for an in-depth discussion of the aesthetics and theory behind composition and framing, we can point out some technical concerns to keep an eye on, as well as remind you of some simple compositional guidelines.

Composition

When looking through a camera, it's very easy to pay attention to what you *know* rather than what you *see*. While you may think it's obvious that the focus of the shot is on the tiny figure in the back of the scene, the audience might focus on the big empty room in the foreground. One way to "short-circuit" your brain and pay attention to your eyes, is to methodically check the following:

- **Headroom.** Don't leave a lot of headroom at the top of the shot (unless it's for some stylistic reason). In other words, pay attention to the *entire* frame, not just the area of the frame where your subject is.
- **Cropping.** There are no rules to how you should crop a shot. While you might be tempted to have a subject's entire head in a shot, you can often get more dramatic power by moving in closer and cropping them. The same holds true for scenes or actions. A close-up shot of a hand flexing and tensing as it wields an ax can be more dramatic than a long shot of an entire lumberjack.
- **Leading.** In dialog scenes, if a character is speaking to someone off-frame, you'll want to *lead* the speaker by putting some empty space in front of him or her. Leading is also a good way to create tension. Con-

sider the last scene in *Aliens* when the little girl has fallen down a venti-lator shaft into a water-filled room on an alien-infested planet. When the director cuts to the first shot of the girl standing waist deep in water, he leaves a tremendous amount of headroom. The audience knows that this is just enough space to fit a big, slavering alien, thus heightening the suspense of the scene.

Focal Length

In addition to the framing of your shot, it's very important to pay attention to your choice of focal length. As we discussed earlier, the longer the focal length, the more compressed the sense of depth will be in the shot.

Consider the two images shown in Figure 9.15.

In the top image, we wanted a shallow depth of field, so we stood back, and zoomed in. In the bottom image, we wanted to see more of the background (not just a focused background, but a wider angle) so we zoomed out and moved the camera closer to the actress.

Notice how different her face looks in the two shots. In particular, note the relationship of the size of her nose to her ear in each shot. In the bottom image, her ear has shrunk while her nose has stayed about the same size. Also, her face looks taller and skinnier in the second image. In general, the second image is distorted.

When a telephoto lens magnifies an image, it magnifies everything in the image by an equal amount. So, when we stood back and zoomed in on the ac-tress, everything in the image was enlarged (including the background, which is how telephoto images compress depth). When we zoomed out to a wider angle, the parts of her face that were closer to the camera were magnified more than the parts that were farther away.

Usually, a slightly telephoto lens will be the most flattering focal length you can choose for shooting people. In addition, the compression of depth creates a more intimate sense of space.

When shooting landscapes or sets, consider what kind of sense of scale you want to create. If you're going for a huge space and sense of immensity, go with a shorter focal length to separate the background from the foreground. For in-timate shots, a longer focal length will bring everything closer.

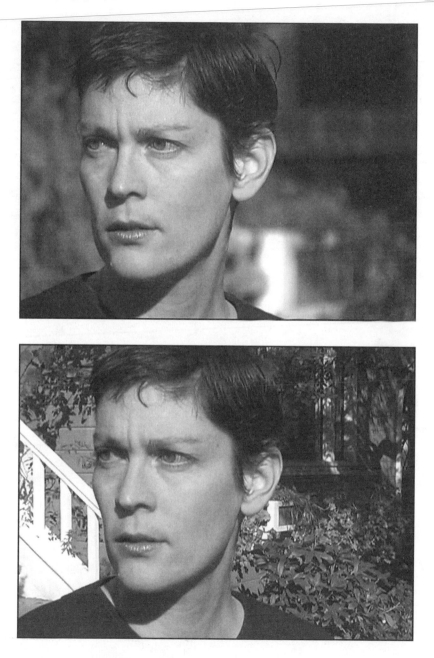

 FIGURE
9.15   *Different focal lengths distort images in different ways. In the bottom image (shot with a shorter focal length) the woman's face looks longer than in the top image (shot with a longer focal length). Also, in the bottom image her ears look smaller and her nose looks bigger than in the top image.*

Respect for Acting

In the sea of technical details, you may forget the most important thing on your set: your talent. Here are a few quick tips on how to help them give a great performance:

- Try to maintain some sort of story continuity as you shoot. It's often necessary to shoot out of sequence, but at least try to stay continuous within each scene.
- Have a closed set if you're doing a scene that involves highly emotional performances or nudity.
- Respect your actors' opinions about the characters they're playing. Even if you wrote the script yourself, you may find that they have new ideas that make your script even better. Remember, they've probably spent the last week or two thinking a lot about that character, and they may have come to a deeper understanding than you have.
- Try to remain sensitive to the mood and material of the scene. If the actor must play a sad scene when everyone is joking around on the set, he or she may have a hard time concentrating or getting in the right mood.

Special Shooting Situations

Almost every project involves some special shooting circumstances, but if you're shooting for a highly compressed delivery format, such as the Web, you'll have a special set of issues to tackle.

SHOOTING FOR THE WEB

Delivering video on the Web requires a huge amount of compression. If you plan your shoot with this in mind, the outcome will be much more successful. Here are some things that compress poorly:

- **Motion.** This means both motion of the subject and motion of the camera. Use a tripod to lock down your shots, and keep the movement of the actors to a minimum.
- **Visually complex images.** Keep the images simple and iconic—close-ups work best.

- **High contrast lighting.** Compression algorithms for the Web don't seem to handle high contrast lighting very well, resulting in clipping of darks and lights. Try for a brightly and evenly lit look.
- **Fine lines, stripes, and other patterns.** Again, simplicity is the key.

Quiet on the Set, Please

Recording the image is only part of the battle—you can't overestimate the importance of good sound. The next chapter covers how to record production audio.

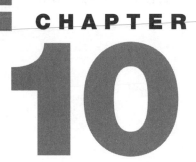

CHAPTER

10

Production Sound

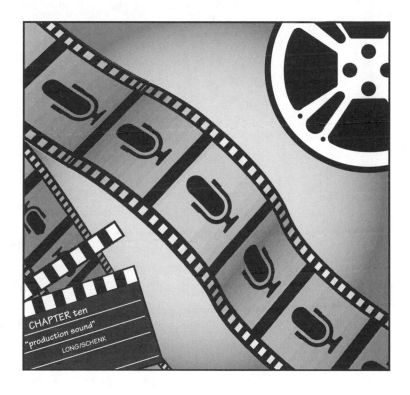

IN THIS CHAPTER

- What You Want to Record
- Microphones
- Setting Up
- Recording Your Sound
- A Good Approach

With all this talk about storyboarding, cameras, and image quality, it's pretty easy to become something of a "video chauvinist" and end up scrimping on your project's sound. So, at this point, it's important to be reminded that *sound is one of the most powerful tools in your creative palette*. With the right music and sound effects, you can do everything from evoking locations to defining moods and building tension. In fact, in many ways, good sound is more important than good video.

As an example, there are plenty of movies that adopt a grungy, low-quality image as a stylistic choice. The makers of *Three Kings* and *π* went to great lengths to create a very rough-looking, grainy, noisy, image style. But did they choose an equivalent low-fidelity for their audio? No way! Audiences are very forgiving of low-quality video—they even find it visually appealing, but if they can't understand the audio, they won't be engaged in the story. Just close your eyes in the theater some time and you'll find that you have no trouble following the story with your ears. Closing off your ears and trying to follow with just your eyes will probably prove more difficult.

Editing, mixing, adding music, and creating sound effects are each a crucial part of your post-production process, but to be successful in those tasks, you have to have clean, high-quality audio recordings. In this chapter, we'll cover the basics of good production sound recording, including how to choose and use microphones, as well as what the best recording options are for different types of projects. Finally, at the end of this chapter we'll detail simple recording set-ups for common shooting situations.

What You Want to Record

Though it is possible to edit the quality of your audio in post-production, don't expect to be able to make the kind of content changes that you can make when editing video or still images. If you've got extra sound, or low recording levels, correcting your audio will be extremely difficult. Your goal when recording audio is to get high-quality recordings of just the sounds you want. Though you will usually record voices, there are times when you'll want to record other things, such as actions that are critical to your story. A hand turning the clicking dial of a safe, for example. Or the philandering husband trying, unsuccessfully, to quietly creep into his house late at night.

It's difficult or impossible to correct a sound, or remove an unwanted sound from a recording, but it's easy to mix sounds *in*. So, if you've recorded high-quality, isolated sound from your primary *foreground* elements, you can always add *background* sound later.

For example, say you're recording two people talking in a crowded restaurant, but one character is difficult to hear because she has laryngitis. You can spend a long time shooting multiple takes, trying to get a version where you can hear every word over the din of other diners. Or, you can ask everyone else in the restaurant to be silent—but continue to pantomime talking—while you record your actors. Then, let your restaurant patrons go back to speaking and record a few minutes of their sound (in the business, crowd noise is referred to as *walla*). In post-production, you can mix together the sounds of your characters with your separately recorded background walla, and have full control over the loudness of the background, letting you mix the background to more easily hear your foreground characters.

Recording good audio requires a lot of preparation, and begins with selecting the right microphone.

Microphones

Though your video camera has a built-in microphone, you won't be able to use it for most feature and documentary work. On-camera mics are typically low quality, and produce tinny sound recorded from all directions. In addition, because of their location on the camera, they frequently pick up camera noise such as motors and hand movements (Figures 10.1 and 10.2). Consequently, to record good audio, you'll want to buy or rent one or more high-quality microphones, which you will connect to your camera or to a separate audio recorder such as a DAT or MiniDisc recorder.

Different types of microphones are designed for different recording situations, so your choice of microphone will be based on matching microphone characteristics to your shooting needs.

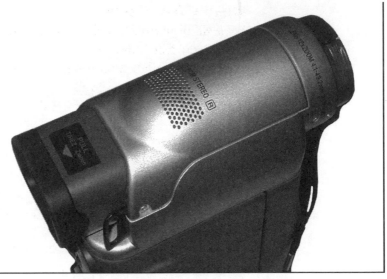

FIGURE   *On-camera mics are frequently housed inside the camera's body, where they are susceptible to picking up camera noise.*

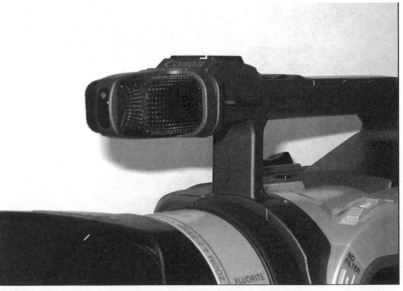

FIGURE   *Even if your camera has an external, shotgun mic, you'll still want to get a higher-quality, better-sounding mic for your shoot.*

WHAT A MIC HEARS

Just as different lenses have different angles of view—some wider, some narrower—that define what they will see, microphones have different "directional" characteristics that define what they will hear. The directional "coverage" of the mic that you choose will have a lot to do with both the content and quality of your recorded sound.

Omnidirectional Mics

As their name implies, onnidirectional mics pick up sounds from all directions. While this may seem like a good idea for recording the sound of an entire room, omnidirectional mics are often not practical for many situations. With their wide coverage, omni mics can pick up far more sound than you may want, including camera noise (and camera operator noise!), as well as ambient sounds like passing cars or people.

Omnidirectional mics work well if they are held close to the subject of the sound—within 12 inches or so—because the subject tends to overpower any background sound. But keeping a mic in this position can be very difficult, particularly if you want it hidden, and especially if your subject is moving.

On the positive side, omnidirectional mics have a low sensitivity to wind and breath sounds, and many provide a "shaped" response that boosts higher-frequency sounds while dampening lower, rumbling sounds. Shaped-response mics are good for preserving the sound of a voice that is being recorded against loud sounds such as traffic or construction.

Unidirectional Mics

Unidirectional (or just "directional") mics, as you might expect, pick up sound from one direction. Because you can point a unidirectional mic at a particular subject, they are well-suited to feature and documentary production, as they allow you to selectively record a particular person or event. Also, because a directional mic can be farther from the recording subject than an omnidirectional mic, they are better-suited to some feature production sets, where keeping a mic close to the subject is difficult. Some directional mics are more directional than others, and which type to choose depends on your shooting task.

Most directional mics are sensitive to sound in a *cardioid* pattern (so named because it looks vaguely heart shaped, see Figure 10.3). A cardioid microphone is more sensitive to sound coming from the front of the mic, and typi-

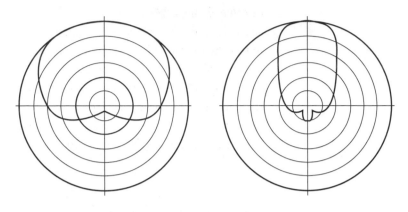

FIGURE   *The cardioid patterns for an omnidirectional and a supercardioid mic.*

10.3

cally *attenuates,* or drops off, sounds around the sides of the mic. Typically, a cardioid pattern is wide enough that a cardioid mic placed more then seven or eight feet from its subject will pick up unwanted sounds.

A *supercardioid* mic has a tighter pickup pattern than a cardioid and is similar to the pickup pattern of the human ear. Supercardioid mics provide good results when used at a distance of 6–15 feet from the subject.

Finally, *hypercardioid* mics have an even narrower pickup pattern that rejects most sounds that are "off-axis" from the direction the mic is pointed. Hypercardioids are, in fact, so directional that they can be somewhat difficult to use. If they stray even a little from their subject, they will not pick up the desired sound. You'll need a diligent mic operator to use a hypercardioid mic.

Contrary to common sense, it's the holes on a microphone that make it more or less directional. Take a look at a typical handheld or clip-on omnidirectional mic. You'll see that most of the holes in the microphone's case are in the very top of the mic, with just a few holes around the sides. Now take a look at a typical hypercardioid mic and you'll see a very long tube riddled with holes along its entire length. What's the deal?

The holes in a directional mic cause the sounds coming in from the sides of the mic to cancel each other out, leaving only the sounds from the front (and sometimes, back). In fact, you can turn a hypercardioid mic into an omnidirectional mic simply by covering up the holes along the sides.

If you can't afford multiple mics or arrange for a *boom operator* (more on this later) on your shoot and you need to shoot dialog scenes, then an omnidirectional mic will be the best choice. Ideally, though, you'll want a mic with a supercardioid pattern and the personnel and equipment to use it right. Later in this chapter, we'll discuss how to mic your scene.

Most microphones come with a coverage chart that indicates the directional pattern of the microphone, and how different parts of the field of coverage respond to different frequencies (Figure 10.4). Though interesting, don't lose any sleep over trying to understand these charts. Most mics are clearly rated as cardioid, supercardioid, or hypercardioid.

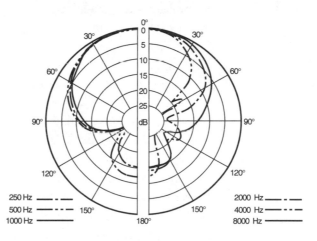

FIGURE
10.4   *Most microphones include a polar chart that diagrams their directionality and sensitivity. The polar chart shows a cross-section of the mic's pickup-pattern, with the mic laying in the middle of the chart, pointed toward the top. This chart diagrams a supercardioid mic.*

TIP

Hands Off That Mic!
Because a mic's directional characteristics can be affected by the way you handle the mic, be very careful when attaching a mic to a stand or pole with a clamp or tape (or when holding a mic in your hand). Be certain you don't cover up any of the holes in the mic's case. Similarly, don't think that you can make a mic more directional by cupping your hands around the front of the mic.

Finally, *parabolic* mics are extremely directional mics that use a large parabolic dish to gather and focus sound onto the head of a unidirectional microphone. Parabolic mics are sensitive to sounds over 200 feet away and are not practical for most feature shoots. However, for difficult shooting situations where a subject is extremely far away (climbing the side of a mountain, for example), a parabolic mic might be the most reasonable way to record sound.

HOW A MIC HEARS

All microphones work by converting sound waves into electrical impulses. There are different mechanisms for performing this conversion, and each has its own advantages and limitations. Typically, different mechanisms are used for different types of microphones.

A *dynamic* microphone is the most basic mechanism, consisting of a simple diaphragm attached to a coil of wire that is surrounded by a magnet (it is, literally, the exact opposite of a speaker). When the pressure of a sound wave hits the diaphragm, it moves the coil of wire within the magnetic field of the magnet. This generates a small electrical current that is fed out of the microphone.

Because of their simple design, dynamic microphones are incredibly rugged and require no external power or batteries. The dynamic mechanism has a very short range, and so is typically only used in handheld mics. Their short range makes dynamic mics well-suited to narration and voice-over recording (they tend to pick up only the voice of the speaker), but frequently impractical for on-set recording.

In a *condensor* mic, a metal plate and a metal diaphragm are separated by a thin gap of air. Both plates are electrically polarized by an external power supply. Because of a property called "capacitance," an electric charge is created between the plates. As incoming sound waves move the metal diaphragm, the amount of charge between the plates changes. The electrical charges produced by this mechanism are tiny and must be amplified using power from either a battery or a *phantom power supply* housed externally. Because the diaphragm in a condensor mic is so small, it requires very little acoustic pressure to make it move. Consequently, condensor mics are much more sensitive than dynamic mics.

An *electret condensor* is a somewhat cheaper, lower-quality version of the condensor mechanism. Electret condensor mics don't require an external polarizing voltage, but do usually include a small battery and pre-amplifier.

Because their pickup mechanisms are so tiny, condensor mics can be made very small—most clip-on mics use electret condenser mechanisms.

Ideally, you'll want to choose a condenser mic simply because they deliver the best quality. However, for recording voice-overs or narration, or for doing interviews in more harsh conditions (bad weather, extreme humidity, etc.), a handheld, dynamic mic might be a better choice.

The Sound of Silence

Deciding not to record "live" audio (also called sync sound) during your shoot can save you a lot of money. For his $7225 film "El Mariachi," Robert Rodriguez decided to forgo sync sound and dub all of his dialog and sound effects later. This not only saved him the cost of sound equipment, but allowed him to shoot in fewer takes, as there were no flubbed lines or interruptions from outside noises. Doing a good dub job can be difficult, of course, but with the aid of digital audio software such as CuBase or Peak, dubbing is much easier than it used to be. European audiences are typically more accustomed to dubbed audio, so much so that even Fellini shot all of his movies this way.

Types of Mics

No matter what type of pickup element is used, mics typically fall into three categories: handheld, lavalier (clip-on), and shotgun. Which to choose depends on your set, and you might find yourself using multiple mics of different types. Obviously, for a dramatic production, keeping the mic hidden is your primary concern (after getting good audio!). But even documentary producers may want more less-obtrusive mics, both for aesthetics and to record their subjects more clandestinely. (Note that we're not advocating illegal wiretapping! Rather, we're simply trying to remind you that a microphone can be a very intimidating object to someone who hasn't spent a lot of time "on-camera." To keep an interview or documentary subject calm and more spontaneous, a less-intrusive type of mic might be preferable.)

We've all seen the handheld mics used by talk show hosts, rock stars, and karaoke singers. Usually omnidirectional dynamic mics, these are the least useful mics for on-set use. Because they typically operate at short range, they have to be held close to the speaker's mouth, making it nearly impossible to keep them hidden (Figure 10.5).

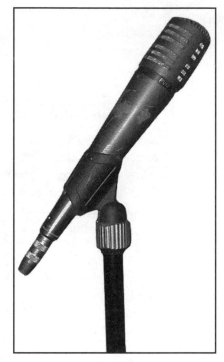

FIGURE   *A handheld mic on a microphone stand.*
10.5

Lavaliers

Lavalier, or clip-on mics, are the small condenser mics that you see clipped to the front of newscasters. Lavaliers are usually omnidirectional mics, but because they are kept so close to the speaker's mouth, they rarely pick up extraneous sound, making them well-suited to recording individual performers. And, because of their small size, they can easily be hidden under clothing (Figure 10.6).

However, note that though omnidirectional, some lavaliers might still have directional characteristics. A somewhat directional lavalier will produce a very clear recording, but might lack some ambient sound that makes for a full, realistic sound (these lavs are typically used for newscasting where the sound of an authoritarian voice is all you're interested in recording). A more omnidirectional lav can record a more natural sound, but you'll have to worry about controlling extra ambient noises on your set.

For scenes involving lots of actors, you'll probably need a separate lav for each performer, which means that you'll have to deal with the requisite logis-

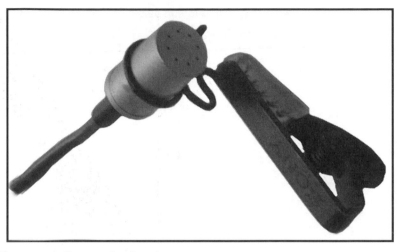

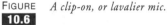

FIGURE   *A clip-on, or lavalier mic.*
10.6

tical troubles such as wiring multiple performers, and managing lots of mic cables. (You'll also need a mixer, which we'll discuss later in this chapter.) Cables can be a problem with any type of microphone. Keeping actors and crew from tripping on them, while also trying to keep them out of your shots, can be a hassle.

Wireless lavaliers are a good solution for complex shoots involving lots of mics. A wireless lav system consists of a normal lav microphone attached to a small transmitter worn by the actor. A receiver picks up the audio and routes it on to your recording device.

Though a great solution to the "obtrusive cable" problem, wireless lavaliers have complications of their own. First, you'll want to be sure you get a system that uses an FM transmitter, for higher quality. Such set-ups are typically somewhat expensive. In addition, you'll have to worry about radio interference from other devices, cell phones, overhead power lines, and so on. Though these problems can be easy to solve, they can take time.

Shotgun Mics

Those long skinny microphones that you often see sticking off of video cameras are referred to as *shotgun* mics. Though varied in pickup mechanism and directional characteristics, shotgun mics provide the greatest flexibility for miking. Most shotgun mics record stereo audio, usually by having two pickups inside, one each for left and right channels (Figure 10.7).

If your camera already has a shotgun mic attached, odds are it's not very high quality. Whatever its quality, the front of your camera is not the best location for a mic. Ideally, you'll want a supercarioid or hypercartioid shotgun mic attached to a boom. We'll discuss using a boom later in this chapter.

A Little of Each

The ideal audio set-up involves several microphones, frequently of different types. If you can only afford one mic, then you'll want to get a directional shotgun mic and attach it to a boom. However, for better sound and greater postproduction audio editing flexibility, wiring actors with lavaliers while simultaneously miking them with a boom mic provides your sound editor with more options for mixing and correcting difficult-to-understand audio.

No matter what types of mics you choose, you'll ideally want to listen to them before you buy. Just like loudspeakers, different mics provide different sounds. Some will boost low frequencies to help create authoritative, booming voices. Others will have more of a "flat," realistic response. Though you can look at frequency response charts for a mic, such stats don't reveal everything about how a mic will sound. Your ear is the best judge of whether or not a mic is right for you.

MIXING

As you may have noticed, most cameras and tape decks only have one place to plug in a microphone. So, if you're using multiple microphones, you'll have to

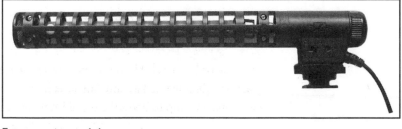

FIGURE   *A typical shotgun mic.*

plug them into a *mixer* to mix their signals down to a single stereo signal that can be plugged into the microphone input on your camera or deck.

When choosing a mixer, you'll need to pick a unit with enough inputs (four is usually plenty) for the number of mics you'll be using. You might also want to select a unit that has a built-in *graphic equalizer*. As we'll discuss later, an *equalizer* will let you slightly modify the sound coming through a mic to add more bass or treble. Equalizers are a great way of improving the sound of a weak voice, or removing certain problems like "shushing" S sounds or hisses.

TIP

Headphones

Headphones are the audio equivalent of a field monitor—you need them to hear (or "monitor") the audio as it's being recorded. Headphones serve a dual purpose as they block out ambient noise from the set and allow the sound recordist to monitor the audio directly. Because the sound recordist wearing headphones is listening to what the mic records, as opposed to what the human ear would hear on the set, he or she will often notice extra noises like crackling mics and distracting background sounds. Even though you can use small "walkman" type headphones, it's best to use the big, professional padded ones that block out as much ambient noise as possible.

CONNECTING IT ALL UP

Unfortunately, connecting your mics to your camera, mixer, or deck involves a little more than just matching connectors. Though you may have the right-shaped plug on your microphone, it may not be wired properly for the jack on your deck or mixer.

There are two different kinds of inputs on a recording device, *line-level* inputs and *mic-level* inputs. Mic-level inputs are designed to receive weak, quieter audio signals. A *pre-amplifier* inside the mic input boosts the incoming signal to increase its level. Line-level inputs are designed for more powerful signals. Most video cameras provide a mic-level input, while most mixers or tape decks provide both mic and line. Note that you can't tell the level of an input by its connector—RCA, Mini, or 1/4″ phono connectors can all be either mic or line level. However, most jacks are clearly labelled *mic* or *line*. If your recording device has only line-level inputs, then you'll need to buy a microphone pre-amp to boost the signal from your mic up to line level. The pre-amp will sit between your microphone and your recorder.

There are two types of microphone connectors, *balanced* and *unbalanced*. You can generally tell whether a mic is balanced or not by looking at the type of plug it uses. RCA, 1/4″ photo, and mini plugs are all unbalanced connectors, while three-prong XLR plugs are usually balanced. One is not better than the other as far as audio quality goes, but if you want to use cables longer than about 25 feet, you'll have to have balanced connectors (Figure 10.8).

Most likely, your camcorder has some type of unbalanced connector, usually a mini plug. If you're using a mic with a balanced connector (usually a mic with an XLR plug), then you'll need to get a special adapter that not only provides an XLR jack, but that also alters the mic's signal. Studio 1 Productions' XLR-Pro provides balanced XLR and mini jacks that are switchable between mic and line levels. The XLR-Pro also provides separate level controls for each input. With its small size, the XLR-Pro can easily be attached to the tripod mount on the underside of your camera, or sit between your camera and your tripod.

With a product like the XLR-Pro, you're free to use higher-end, professional quality mics—at any cable length—with no concern for distortion or incompatible connectors (Figures 10.9 and 10.10).

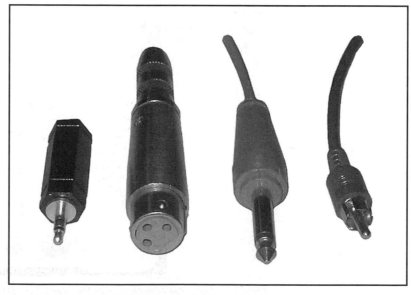

FIGURE
10.8   *Mini, XLR, 1/4″ Phono, and RCA plugs.*

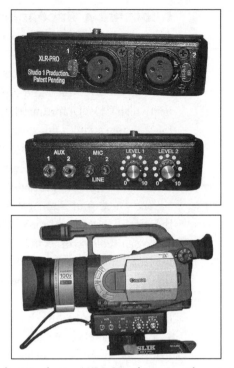

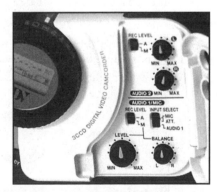

 FIGURE **10.9**   *The Studio 1 Productions' XLR-Pro adapter provides a simple mic mixer on the front, and XLR jacks on the back. A single mini-jack attaches the device to your camera's external mic jack. The XLR-Pro can be easily mounted between your camera and tripod.*

 FIGURE **10.10**   *Higher-end cameras such as the Canon XL-1 provide manual mic level adjustments. However, they might still need an XLR adapter to connect balanced, professional mics.*

CHOOSING A RECORDING DEVICE

After selecting your microphones (and any requisite cables, adapters, and mixers), your next big choice will be to decide where to record your audio. Ideally, you'll hope to record most, if not all, of your audio using your video camera. With 48 KHz, 16-bit audio capabilities, DV cameras boast better audio fidelity than CDs. Unfortunately, attaching microphone cables to your camera for recording audio is not always possible.

For example, if you've got a very small video camera and are planning on doing a lot of handheld camera movements, it may not be practical to have an external microphone or mixer plugged into the camera. Or, perhaps you've got a scene where your actors are inside a car having a conversation, but you're shooting the exterior of the car from a chase vehicle. In this case, you'll need to have an audio recorder inside the car with the actors. Or, perhaps your shoot is over and in reviewing your tapes you've realized that there was an air conditioner running throughout the dramatic climax scene, and you can't understand a word any of the actors were saying. You'll have to bring them in and have them re-record their dialog.

Each of these scenarios is an example of recording *manually-synched sound;* that is, the sound is not being recorded with the same device as the video. As mentioned in the sidebar earlier, recording manually-synched sound can be a great money saver as you won't have the expense of renting or buying expensive microphones. However, you will have the post-production expense of bringing in actors to record, or *loop,* their dialog after your shoot. Fellini used this technique throughout his career, both because it was a money-saver and because it enabled him to direct his actors while the camera was rolling.

But these days, you'll usually rely on manually-synched sound for practical reasons such as those described earlier. If you find yourself in such a situation, then you'll need to choose an audio recording device, either high-quality analog cassette, DAT, or MiniDV. The feed from your mic or mixer will be patched into this device, and your audio will be recorded there. In post-production, you'll have to sync your audio with your video together using your editing software.

Shooting Manually-Synched

Shooting manually-synched sound is, obviously, more involved than shooting automatically synched audio, and requires the careful cooperation of a number of people. First, you'll want to have an operator for your audio recorder. He or she will monitor the recording levels and take care of starting and stopping the tape. You'll also want a person to handle the *slate*.

We've all seen the classic shot of the black and white chalkboard with the clapper bar that is held before a camera. "Scene 1, take 1" says a voice, and then the top of the board is clapped down to make a loud cracking sound. This *slating* is used both to label the shot and to provide an audio/visual cue that can be used to synchronize the video and audio.

Once in the editing room, the editor looks for the frame where the clapper bar is down, and lines this up with the sharp crack of the audio. If all has gone well, the rest of the scene will be in sync.

You can use this same method for shooting DV, but you'll have things a little easier than a film editor. Because most editing programs provide a visual depiction of your audio sound wave, identifying the crack of the slate is very simple.

There is another option, which is to use a special time-code slate. These are electronic devices that, in addition to displaying scene, shot, and take numbers, also display an electronic timecode readout. The electronic slate is connected to a timecode-capable audio deck through a special cable. So, rather than having to look for a visual reference of the slate when synching your audio in the editing room, you can simply read the timecode display on the slate to see how much of an offset you need between your audio and video.

Timecode audio recorders are expensive to buy or rent, and a timecode slate adds even more money. Because it's easy enough to sync audio the old-fashioned way, there's little reason to spend the extra money on special timecode audio equipment.

Instead, buy or build yourself a clapping slate board and be sure to enlist a responsible person to handle the job of filling out and clapping the slate. When slating, make sure the slate fills the frame clearly so that you can read what it says, and make sure the clap is quick and loud, so that it will appear as a sharp spike in your audio track. Also, don't forget that if you missed slating the head of the shot, you can always *tail slate* at the end, as long as camera and sound are still rolling.

The Sound of Two Hands Clapping
As long as you can see it clearly through your viewfinder and hear it from your recording device, clapping your hands together can be a sufficient slate. While not ideal, it's better than nothing.

Setting Up

Getting good sound requires much more than just clipping a mic on an actor and hitting the record button. Good sound recording also involves choosing appropriate mic set-ups for the type of image you're shooting, and careful management of your set or location.

PLACING YOUR MICS

As we've seen, different types of mics have very different characteristics, both in terms of sound quality, and in terms of what they can "hear." To get the most from your mic, you need to place it correctly.

Handheld Mics

Because they're usually omnidirectional, handheld mics need to be placed close to your subject to ensure that they record more of your subject than anything else. Handheld mics can be placed in a microphone stand, whether a tall, floor-standing device, or a small desktop stand. Your talent should not speak directly into the top of the mic. Rather, tilt the mic at about a 30° angle.

TIP

Windscreens

No matter what type of mic you're using, you might need a windscreen—*a foam covering that slips over your mic—to cut out the sound of wind, or particularly breathy voices. Some camcorders, such as the Canon GL-1, include an electronic windscreen, which automatically cuts out certain frequencies to reduce wind sounds. Though these features can work well, they can also cut out more frequencies than you may want. You'll need to test the feature in your particular situation to ensure that it's not degrading the quality of your audio.*

Lavalier Mics

For feature production, you'll usually do more than simply clip a lavalier onto someone's collar or tie. To keep the microphone invisible, you'll most likely want to hide it under the talent's clothing, or somewhere on-set—in a plant, on the dashboard of a car, on a prop. In these cases, try to choose a location that's roughly at mouth-level to the actor, and in the direction that the actor will be speaking. For close-ups, the easiest way to hide a mic is simply to place it out-of-frame. Wherever you attach a lavalier, consider the following:

- Try to position the mic so that it sits about 8 to 12 inches from the performer's mouth.

- As the speaker turns her head back and forth, she might tend to speak more or less into the microphone, making her voice get louder or softer. When attaching her mic, try to predict which direction she will favor, and place the mic on that side. For example, if the actor will be "cheating out" a bit to stay open to the camera when talking to someone on her right, then her head will probably be turned a little to the right side. Place the mic more to that side of her body. The clip on most lavaliers is reversible, making it easier to clip the mic in one direction or another.

- If you're trying to hide the mic inside of clothing, you'll need to make sure that it doesn't rub against skin or clothing when the actors move, as this will create extremely loud noise. With some cleverly placed gaffer's tape, you can usually secure the mic and any surrounding clothing. If the talent is moving a lot, or wearing tight clothes, a lav mic may not be the best choice.

- After clipping the mic to a shirt, arrange the cable as shown in Figure 10.11 (obviously, we're not concerned about hiding the mic in this shot, but you'll want the same cable arrangement, even if it's inside someone's

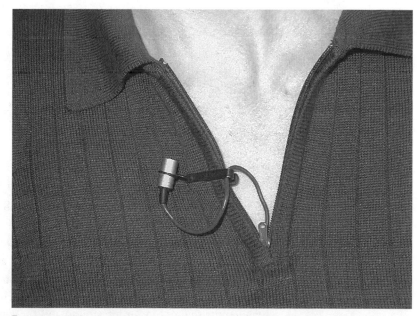

FIGURE
10.11 *When placing a lavalier mic, make sure the mic cable is secure to prevent cable noise and bumps.*

shirt). With the cable looped as shown in the figure, the sound of cable bumps or movements will not be conducted up the cable to the microphone.

- Run the rest of the cable down the inside front of the talent's shirt, and around the waist to the back.
- For most work, you'll need to attach the connection end of the mic cable to a cable extension. These couplers are usually large, and just a little bit heavy. Place the connector in the subject's back pocket or attach it to his waistband using gaffer's tape, clothespins, or binder clips. If clipping the cable, be careful that the clip is not so strong that it damages the cable.
- Once you've wired the talent, let them move around to test their freedom of movement. Make certain that your rigging holds. When you test the level of the mic (more on this later), make sure that you've positioned the mic well to get the best recording of their voice. You may need to move it.
- If you're using a wireless lavalier, then you'll need to test the reception of your system. Make sure you're getting a clean signal on your receiver. Noise or other interference might be caused by cell phones, other pieces of equipment, or any large transmitters that might be in the area. In addition to the difficulty in keeping the transmitter hidden, wireless lavs are also prone to picking up static when the actor's clothes move across the antenna.

Wireless lavaliers can also be confused by transmitter reflections, wherein the transmitter's signal, and reflections of that signal, are both picked up by the receiver. Moving the receiver can often alleviate these troubles.

Shotgun Mics

Because they're usually very directional, it's crucial that you pay attention to what a shotgun mic is pointed at. This means taking note of not just your foreground elements, but your background as well.

For example, if there is a shotgun mic attached to your camera, it will be pointed at your subject when you've framed him or her with the camera. Unfortunately, it will also be pointed at everything *behind* your subject. Whether it's other sounds, or an echo-producing wall, there will be little differentiation between the sounds of your foreground and the sounds of your background. Because you can always add background sound in post-production, your primary concern when recording is to get good audio from your foreground elements. Consequently, a shotgun mic mounted on your camera is not the ideal shotgun set-up. Though fine for stand-up interviews where the subject is directly in front of your camera, a camera-mounted shotgun is a bad choice for recording dialog.

A better choice is to mic your scene from above with the microphone pointed down toward the ground. The easiest way to do this is to attach the mic to a *fishpole* or *boom* and have it held in position by a *boom operator*. A fishpole is a long, telescoping pole with a super- or Hypercardioid mic attached to one end. The pole is usually held above the performer by the boom operator, who tries to keep the mic as close to the performers as possible, without letting it dip into the shot. Because the mic is above the performers and pointed down toward the ground, there is little or no background noise for it to pick up. Consequently, you'll get a very clean recording of just your performers. In addition, this type of miking affords your actors much more freedom to move around without worrying about hitting a microphone or tripping over a cable. Because it's overhead, the mic will also pick up a good mix of footsteps, prop sounds, and other environmental noises that will make for a richer soundtrack. For almost all situations, a fishpole or boom mic will be the best miking option.

(Though people will use the terms *boom* and *fishpole* interchangably, technically a *boom* is a beefed-up version of a fishpole and is usually only used in a studio situation. Booms are typically much larger than a fishpole, with a capacity to extend a mic over 100 feet. Frequently hydraulically controlled, they're not the sort of apparatus the independent filmmaker will take on location.)

Operating a mic fishpole can be difficult work. In addition to the physical strain of holding a long pole overhead for hours at a time, the boom operator must be very focused and diligent to ensure that the best sound is recorded. Remember, because the microphone that is used is typically very directional, even a little mic movement can change the quality of the sound. And, if your subjects are moving, boom operation gets even more difficult.

The boom operator must wear a set of headphones to monitor the audio that is being recorded!

In addition, consider the following:

- **Properly rig the pole.** Though you can try to get away with a makeshift pole, a commercial boom has a number of advantages. First, a shock-resistant mount attaches the mic to the pole and reduces noise from the boom itself. Also, in a professional boom pole, the inside of the pole will often be insulated to reduce sound conduction along the length of the pole. To keep the cable from slapping against the pole, you'll want to hold it taut against the pole when in use, and you'll need to secure any cable slack at the end of the pole to ensure that the cable doesn't slide or move. Professional boom poles come with clips to hold the mic cable against the pole.

- **Mounting the mic.** Though the mic will be pointed at the actors, don't forget that directional mics pick up sounds from the side and back as well as the front. So, be aware of where other parts of the microphone are pointing. In some situations, you might need to angle the mic to ensure that it's not picking up sounds from other directions.

- **Directional mics are more susceptible to wind noise than other types of mics.** You may need a special "blimp" or "zeppelin" style windscreen (Figure 10.12).

- **Choose the right amount of extension for the shot.** How long your pole will need to be depends on how wide the shot will be. For most feature work, a pole between 8 and 15 feet will be adequate. Experiment with the mic and pole before shooting to learn where its center of gravity is, and what is most comfortable. To be able to grip the pole more toward its center, you may want to extend the pole farther than you actually need for the shot. This will provide a more balanced grip. Many poles have locking mechanisms at each extension. Extending to a point just short of these locks will usually make for a stronger pole.

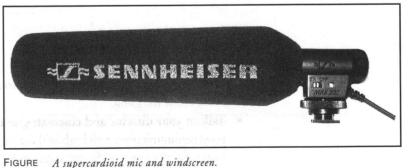

FIGURE   *A supercardioid mic and windscreen.*
10.12

- **Choose your position.** Make sure you choose a position that affords you access to the entire shot, allows you to get the mic as close to the subject as possible, and isn't so uncomfortable that you'll be unable to do your job.

- **Watch your grip.** Remember, noise from your hands—scraping, drumming, etc.—can be transmitted up the pole to the mic, so you want to get a good grip on the mic before you start shooting, and then hold it for the duration of the shot. Gloves are often a good idea in extreme temperatures, both for comfort, and to eliminate the sound of your skin sticking to the metal pole.

- **Holding the pole.** The pole should be held parallel to the ground with your arms straight up, close to your head, and your elbows locked. Microphone poles aren't too heavy, and you should be able to hold this position for a while. Your lead arm will act as a fulcrum for the mic, while your trailing arm can be used to steer. From this position, you can quickly get the mic into the right position. In addition to tilting the pole around, you may need to spin the pole to point the microphone in the right direction. Make sure your grip and stance allow for all the motions you'll need.

- **Positioning the mic.** Remember: if you're a boom operator, your job is to get the best audio possible, and this means getting the microphone *close to your subject!* Don't be shy, get the mic in as low and close as you can. Depending on the framing of the shot, your mic can be a few inches to a few feet above the talent's head. Though you may screw up some takes by dipping the mic into the shot, this is better than discovering later that the audio is lousy because the mic was too far away. To make the mic easier to see in the frame, use a brightly colored windscreen or place a bright-colored label on the front of the windscreen.

- **Adjusting for echo.** If the surface that you're standing on is hard tile or stone, there is a chance that it will reflect sound back up toward the microphone. In your mic tests, if your sound is a little too echoey, consider putting cardboard, carpet, or some other sound-absorbing surface on the floor, below the frame.

- **Talk to your director and cinematographer!** You'll need to maintain good communication with both of these people to ensure that you're not letting the mic enter the frame, and to remind them that you're only trying to get the best audio that you can. With all the troubles present on a shoot, it's easy for nerves to get a little frayed. Stay in communication with the rest of your crew to ensure that everyone stays calm.

Finally, for some situations, you might use your mic pole to mic a subject from below. For close-in shots, low-angle camera shots, and other instances where it might be too difficult to keep an overhead mic out of frame, don't hesitate to hold the boom low, and point it upward. As with overhead miking, you'll still be avoiding background sound and other unwanted noises.

Hanging Mics

Mics can be hung to record large groups of people, or presentations. Typically, an omnidirectional or cardioid mic is best, and you may need more than one if you're covering a large area. You usually need a lot of cable when hanging a mic, so you'll need balanced mics and connectors.

Multiple Mics

If your subjects are too far apart to reach with one boom, consider using multiple mics. Some sound people like to use multiple mics as backups. For example, you can feed a lavalier mic into the left channel and a boom mic covering the same actor into the right channel. When mixing and editing, you can select between channels to get the best sound.

TIP

Think Batteries

Accept it right now: A mic battery will die in the middle of the best take you've ever shot. Your sound will be useless. Though frustrating, the situation will be more frustrating if you don't have any extra batteries! Always pack several extra batteries for each type of mic you plan on using, and be sure to test your mics throughout the day to make sure their batteries haven't died. For shots where you only get one take— pyrotechnic or other special effects shots—consider using more than one mic so that if a battery dies in one mic, you'll still get sound from the other.

GETTING THE RIGHT SOUND FOR THE PICTURE

No matter which type of microphone you use, it's important to consider what the tone of the shot should be. An extreme wide shot, for example, should sound far away, while a close-up should have a more intimate sound. Consider this when selecting the type of mic to use for a shot.

When using an overhead mic, you'll tend to automatically compensate for these kinds of shot changes. Since the mic will have to be farther away from its subject during wider shots, but can afford to be brought in closer during close-ups, your audio recording will have a natural shift of audio "space."

The bass response of any microphone drops off over distance. Consequently, handheld mics and lavalier mics often have a richer, bassier tone—sometimes too rich and bassy—than an overhead mic. This difference in bass tone is called the *proximity effect,* and some microphones have special filters to reduce the amount of bass response in the mic. It's important to be aware of the proximity effect while miking so that you don't create mixing hassles in post-production. If a bass-heavy lavalier is used in a close-up, but a less-bassy overhead mic is used in a cut-away, the actor's voice will sound distractingly different from shot to shot. A good pair of headphones and careful attention to EQ while shooting will help you prevent such problems.

TESTING SOUND

After connecting your mics, you'll want to do a *mic check* to ensure that the microphones are working and that their *input levels* are set properly. Your camera may not have manual control of input levels; in which case, there's little you can do in the way of testing and preparing to record. Simply connect the mic to your camera, attach headphones to your camera, ask the subject to speak, and make sure you can hear her in your headphones. If her voice is obviously too quiet, consider moving the microphone closer to her mouth, and then test again.

TIP

Choosing Headphones

You can use any type of headphones for testing audio, even those little, flimsy Walkman-type headphones. For better fidelity, though, you might want to invest in a larger pair of headphones with better-quality sound, and cups that completely surround your ears. In addition to blocking out noise on a busy set or location, these headphones will allow you to more easily separate what you're hearing through the microphone from what you're hearing "live."

Hopefully, you're running your audio through a mixer. A mixer will not only allow you to use multiple microphones, but will also provide you with level controls for adjusting the volume of each microphone and VU meters. Level adjustment is crucial to getting good audio. If the record levels for a mic are too low, then the resulting sound will be too quiet. If they're too high, however, then distortion and noise can be introduced, and the resulting sound will be ugly and unintelligible.

Sound is measured in *decibels,* though there are two types of decibel scales. *dBSPL* (or *decibel sound pressure loudness*) is a measure of the actual acoustic power of a sound. This is the sound that we hear with our ears. A faint whisper from a few feet away might register at about 30 decibels, while a jackhammer usually meters at about 85 decibels. 135 dB is considered painful, and is the point at which permanent hearing damage can occur.

dBm (or *decibel milliwatt*) measures sound as units of electrical power and is measured using a VU meter that is displayed on your camera, record deck, or mixer. Through careful use of a VU meter, you can ensure that your audio level is set properly (Figure 10.13).

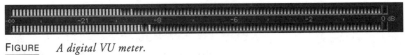

FIGURE   *A digital VU meter.*
10.13

VU meters can seem a little strange at first, because they seem to function backwards. On a VU meter, the zero point does not mean no sound, but rather, ideal sound. Your goal in setting a level is to keep the VU meter readout as close to the ideal as possible. Using your mixer controls, you'll set the level when you test the mic, and then *ride the level* during your production (but not too much!), adjusting the level control to compensate for changes in the loudness of your subject.

With digital audio, the ideal level is somewhere between –12 and –20 dBm. This is the point where you'll want your audio level to *peak* on your VU meter. Try to set the level so that any spikes in the audio level don't go beyond this point. When digital audio peaks, the parts of the signal that go *into the red* are clipped out of the signal altogether. (If you're recording on an analog recording device such as an analog video camera or tape deck, then you'll want the audio to peak a bit higher, at 0 dBm.)

It is during the mic test that you'll also perform any *sweetening* of the subject using a graphic equalizer (if your mixer has one). We'll discuss this type of EQ in detail in Chapter 14, Sound Editing.

MANAGING YOUR SET

As we said earlier, you can perform some amazing editing with modern digital audio applications, but you can't work miracles. It's simply not going to be possible to remove the sound of a passing semi truck, or of that obnoxious couple that was having an argument across the street from your shoot. Consequently, you're going to have to pay close attention to what your set sounds like.

This involves more than just yelling "quiet on the set!" and then waiting for everyone to stop talking. Your ears have an incredible ability to adjust to—and eventually tune out—sounds that might ruin an otherwise good shoot. You'll need to stop and listen to—as well as look at—the set to pick out any potential audio troubles. Once you start paying attention, you might be surprised at all the "white noise" you didn't hear before: air conditioners, refrigerators, fans from computers and equipment. Any one of these things can render a soundtrack muddy and useless.

SELECTING AN AUDIO MODE ON YOUR CAMERA

Different tape formats have different options for audio recording. While most formats are capable of recording stereo sound, DV provides a couple of other options.

With DV cameras, you can choose to record two channels of 16-bit audio or four channels of 12-bit audio. 16-bit audio sounds better than 12-bit audio, and you really only need four audio channels if you're planning on performing video or audio editing in your camera. Since you've already gone to all the trouble of buying a computer, it's silly to do this sort of editing in camera. So, set your camera to 16-bit and mix in other channels in post-production.

Some analog formats let you activate Dolby noise reduction, or switch between stereo and mono recording. Consult your manual for details.

Recording Your Sound

With all your preparations complete (not just of sound, but of lighting, blocking, camera movement, cast preparation, costuming, set dressing, and so on), you're finally ready to start shooting. First, you'll need to get everything quiet on your set or location. When recording, "quiet" doesn't mean "no sound," but rather means to reduce the sound of your set to the natural ambience that belongs there. For example, if you're on a busy street, quiet will mean the sounds of car and foot traffic.

Tell your tape operator to start rolling. If you're recording sound onto your camera, then the camera is all that will roll, but if you're recording non-sync sound on a separate recording deck, then that deck will have to be started as well. For non-sync sound, you'll next need to slate, as described earlier.

Tell your performers and crew to get ready. At this point, if you have a boom person, he or she will need to position the mic and double-check with the director of photography to ensure that the mic isn't in the frame.

After the call to *action,* your boom operator will begin following the sound, while your sound person will monitor your audio levels (if you have such hardware) and adjust them to ensure proper recording.

Finally, with your take completed, *all* your decks will need to be stopped. Next, you do it all again, and again, and again . . .

If there is a pause between takes, your sound person should take the opportunity to ensure that sound was properly recorded. He or she should rewind the tape and play back a little bit of both the beginning and ending, and listen to the sound on headphones. This will help to ensure that good sound was recorded throughout the take. If sound was not recorded, it's the sound person's job to fix the problem and break the bad news that another take will be required.

Documentary filmmakers frequently don't have the downtime between multiple takes that feature filmmakers have. Consequently, whenever they can get a break, the sound engineer should listen to ensure that the recorded audio sounds good. If there's no break during the day, then he or she should double-check different sections of the entire tape to make sure it's all usable. If not, then another day at the location might be required.

A Good Approach

We recommend taking the same approach to audio that you should take to video: Record the cleanest, least-modified sound you can. Then, in post-production, add whatever modifications, effects, grunge, and extra sound that you want. In addition to more flexibility (if you decide you don't want a particular sound, you'll be able to move it), this approach will probably yield higher-quality results. We'll cover sound editing in Chapter 14.

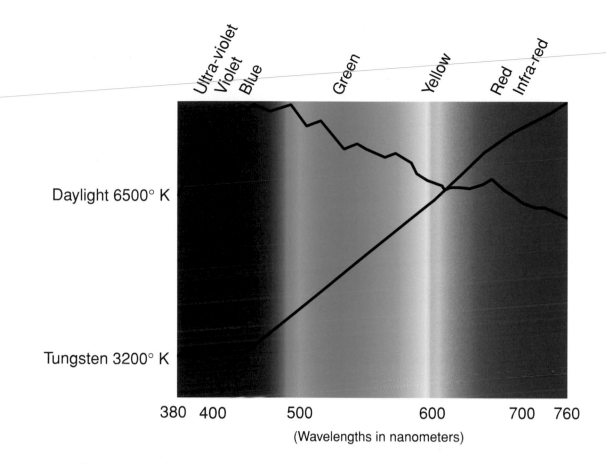

Ultra-violet
Violet
Blue
Green
Yellow
Red
Infra-red

Daylight 6500° K

Tungsten 3200° K

380 400   500   600   700   760

(Wavelengths in nanometers)

Color Plate 1 This chart shows the visible color spectrum and the spectral energy distributions of sunlight and tungsten light. Both cover the entire range of color, but sunlight has much more blue and tungsten has more red.

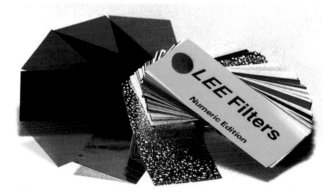

Color Plate 2 This swatch book from Lee Filters shows a selection of lighting gels and reflective materials.

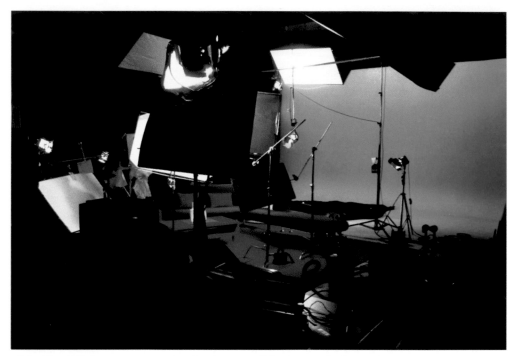

Color Plate 3 Lighting crews use a lot of equipment to light the green background on green screen sets.

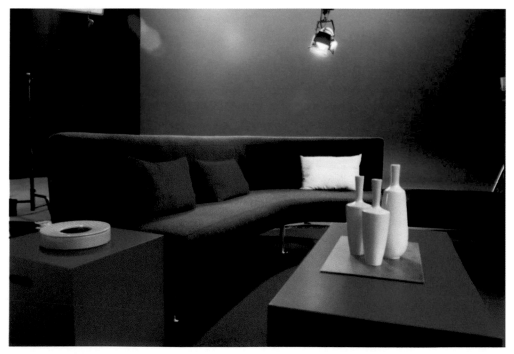

Color Plate 4 This green-screen set was lit and art directed to match a CGI environment.

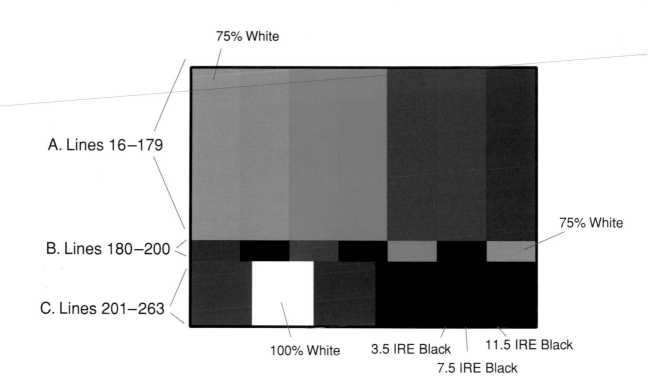

75% White

A. Lines 16–179

B. Lines 180–200

C. Lines 201–263

75% White

100% White 3.5 IRE Black 11.5 IRE Black

7.5 IRE Black

Color Plate 5 Standard NTSC color bars contain three separate test patterns— A, B, and C.

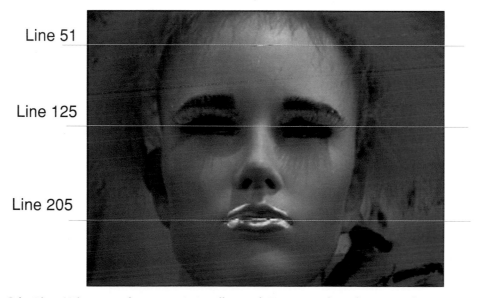

Line 51

Line 125

Line 205

Color Plate 6 This image of a mannequin is well-exposed. Figure 12.9 shows the corresponding waveform images and vectorscope.

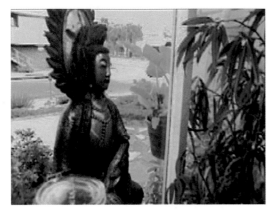

A. This image of a statue was over-exposed during the shoot. This problem can be reduced using the gain controls in your capture utility or hardware "scopes.

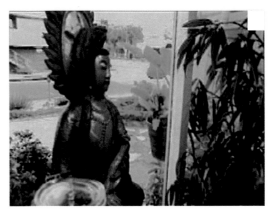

B. As you can see in figure 12.10, the white levels are clipped in some areas, so "pulling down" the whites won't help much. But you can pull down the blacks, giving the image a better contrast ratio.

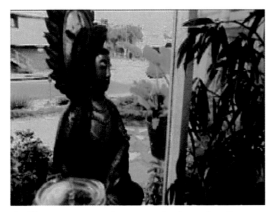

C. The vectorscope in Figure 12.10 shows that the image consists mainly of cyan. Increasing the red gain helps make the hue more balanced.

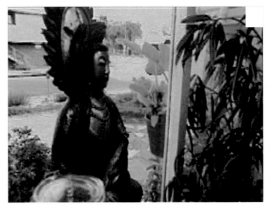

D. Finally, decreasing the blue gain helps bring out more of the warm tones of the statue that are lacking in the original image. Note that the greens in the plant look more natural now. The image is still over-exposed, but it looks much better.

Color Plate 7 This image of a statue is over-exposed.

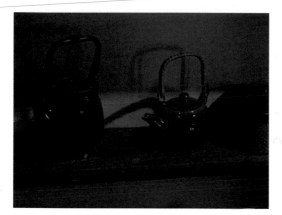

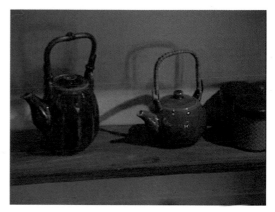

A. This image of two teapots is dull and muddy. The waveform in 12.11 shows a lack of brightness and contrast.

B. Often the first reflex when trying to fix an image that seems too dark is to raise the black levels. But as this figure reveals, raising the blacks only results in an even more washed-out image.

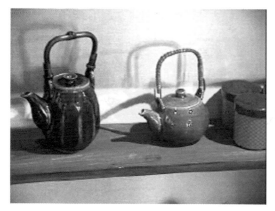

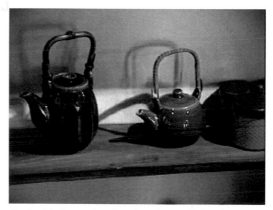

C. By raising the white levels, the brightness of the entire image is pulled up. This appears to be on the right track but if you pull the whites up this much, you'll most likely see artifacting in the image when it plays.

D. In this figure, the whites have been pulled up but not quite as high as in C. To compensate for this, the blacks have been pulled down, resulting in an image with better contrast. Now that the white and black levels are good, it's clear that the color balance doesn't need any adjusting.

Color Plate 8 This image of two teapots is correctly exposed but underlit.

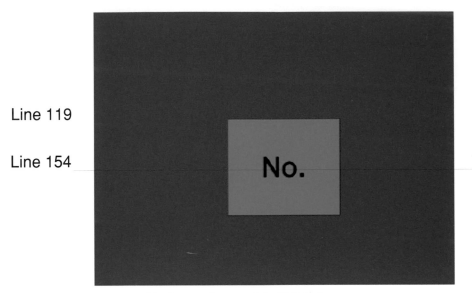

Line 119

Line 154

Color Plate 9 Graphic images like this one often exceed the NTSC color space.

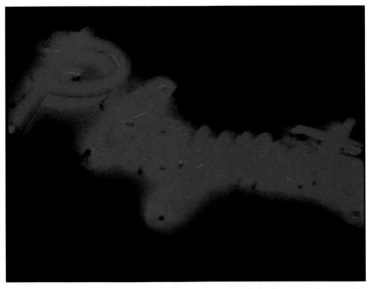

Color Plate 10 Neon lights tend to oversaturate even if they're exposed correctly.

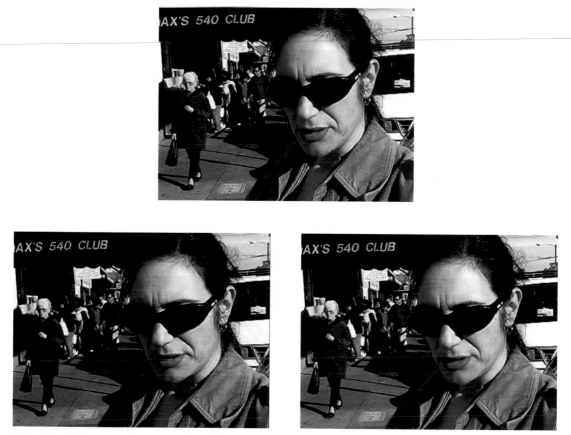

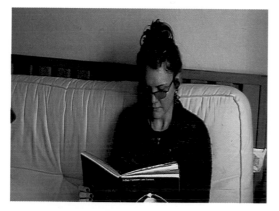

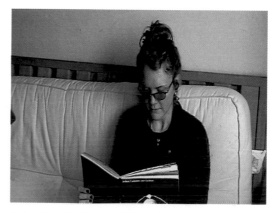

Color Plate 11 Recompressing your video with DV compressor can result in severe quality loss. Our original image was compressed three times (lower left) and then six times (lower right) to show the effects of over-compression.

Color Plate 12 Bad White Balance

Color Plate 13 Corrected White Balance

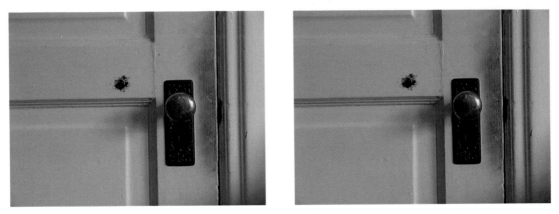

Color Plate 14 When compositing, you'll frequently need to apply color correction techniques to blend one layer into another. Here, we used color balance and blur filters to better integrate the bullet hole into the door.

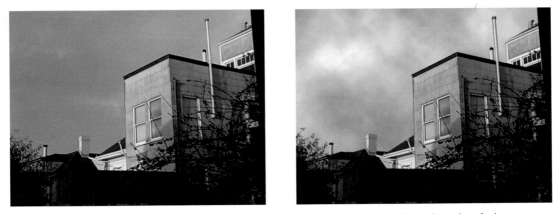

Color Plate 15 Through the use of a hand-cut matte, we can easily replace the sky in this video of a house.

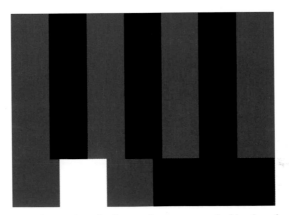

Color Plate 16 If your monitor has a Blue Check control, you can use the blue bars for additional calibration.

CHAPTER

11 Editing Hardware

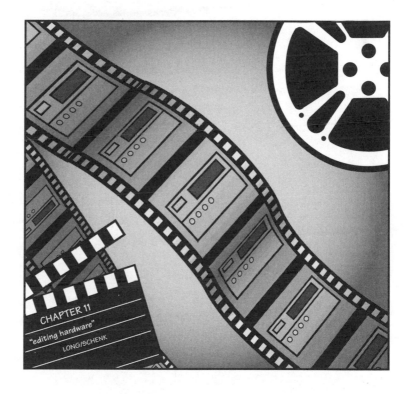

CHAPTER 11
"editing hardware"
LONG/SCHENK

IN THIS CHAPTER

- Hardware and Peripherals
- Digital Video Decks
- Digital Audio Equipment
- Video Monitors
- Hardware Connectors
- Summary

Video decks, audio deck, speakers, NTSC monitors, and more have to be added to any kind of editing setup, even a turnkey system. Unfortunately, you can't just run out and buy any old piece of equipment. In addition to quality and performance differences, you'll also need to sort through some compatibility issues because not every editing package is compatible with every video deck. Fortunately, most vendors publish a list of hardware that has been tested with their software. Though you can use other hardware, there's no guarantee that you won't have technical problems when capturing or laying back to tape.

It's best to choose your software before buying any video hardware. If you haven't read Chapters 5 and 7, you should do so now. If you've already got some video hardware components, make sure anything else you purchase is compatible with what you already own.

Hardware and Peripherals

In a perfectly budgeted world, your editing system would include a lot of specialized video hardware. However, as a low-budget producer, you won't be able to afford most of the items shown in the following list. Don't worry! In many cases you can rent these items, and most productions won't need all of them (Figure 11.1).

- **Video decks (VTRs).** Most editing systems have two video decks: a high quality deck that can play original tapes from your camera, and a VHS deck to make viewing copies.
- **Digital audio decks: DAT, Mini Disc, etc.** Most likely, you'll be recording your audio on your camcorder, but if you record your audio separately, or add music or audio from other sources such as DAT, Mini-Disc, or CD, then you'll need appropriate decks for playback.

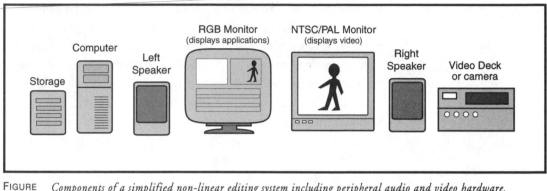

FIGURE
    Components of a simplified non-linear editing system including peripheral audio and video hardware.

- **NTSC/PAL video monitors.** A video monitor is necessary for you to see what your final output will look like. This is the one component that you'll *have* to have throughout the post-production process.
- **Speakers.** All editing systems need a pair of external speakers (or if you're really strapped for cash, headphones) so you can properly hear the sound in your project.
- **Waveform monitors and vectorscopes** (Figure 11.2). Waveform monitors and vectorscopes are used to set proper video levels when capturing video. High-end systems use hardware "scopes," but low-budget productions can usually make do with the software scopes that come with most NLEs. Chapter 12 contains a tutorial on using waveform monitors and vectorscopes to set video levels.

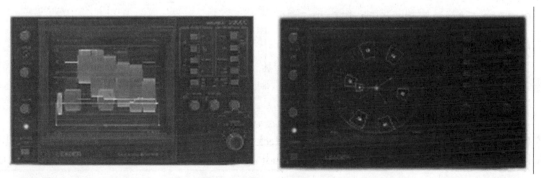

FIGURE
    Hardware waveform monitor and vectorscope by Leader.

- **Switchers, routers, and patch bays** (Figure 11.3). Most filmmakers will be using video from a single source: their camera. But, if you plan on using video from multiple sources—different formats and cameras, for example—then you might consider an inexpensive ($200) router, switcher, or patch bay. These make it easy to quickly switch from one format to another without having to re-wire your system.

- **Audio mixers.** Mixing boards provide on-the-fly adjustment of equalization and gain to control the audio quality of your production and make it easy to manage multiple audio sources.

- **Transcoders.** Transcoders change your video signal from one format into another. Any digital deck that has an analog video output is doing some internal transcoding. External boards like Pinnacle's MADRAS transcode between analog composite video, analog component video, analog Y/C video, Firewire and SDI. Transcoders are a quick but not necessarily ideal fix if your hardware doesn't match your needs.

- **Black burst generator** (Figure 11.4). Professional video equipment should have a video black signal to use as a reference for setting the black level, (more about black levels in Chapter 12) to keep sync, and to use

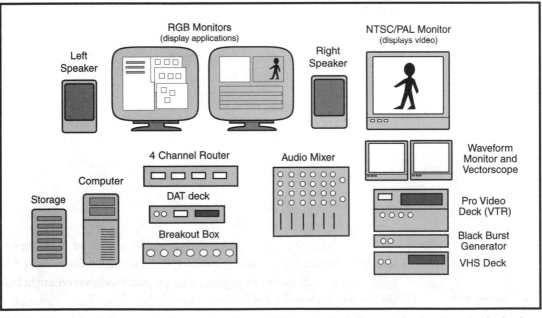

FIGURE
11.3   *Components of a typical professional non-linear editing system, including peripheral audio and video hardware.*

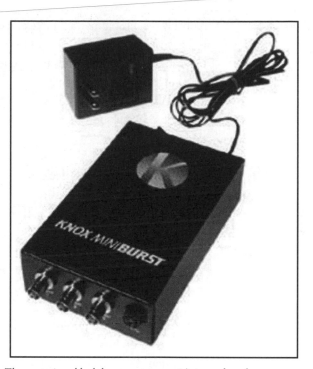

FIGURE   *The mysterious black burst generator—it's just a box that generates a black*
11.4   *video signal, like this* Knox Mini Burst.

blacking tapes (see Chapter 18). (Note: This sync is an electronic pulse
that VTRs need to play properly, and is not related to synchronization
of audio and video.) If your video rolls or is otherwise unstable during
playback, it may be because you need a black burst generator.

Don't Panic!

Despite this daunting list of equipment, most DV producers will be able to get
away with a simplified editing system (Figure 11.1). If you can afford the typical professional editing system (Figure 11.3), then you'll have an easier time
maintaining image quality throughout your project. Producers on a tight budget can rent high-end video hardware as needed, such as when they're capturing and outputting their final master (see Chapter 18 for more about capturing
masters).

Digital Video Decks

Probably the most important piece of hardware in a non-linear editing system is the video deck. Though you can use your DV camcorder as a deck for editing, camcorder tape mechanisms are not necessarily designed for the repeated searching and winding that editing requires. A MiniDV walkman such as the Sony GVD-900 (Figure 11.5) will save a lot of wear and tear on your camera. Here are some questions to ask yourself before you start shopping for a video deck:

- **Will I be using this deck to create my final master?** If so, you'll want the best quality you can afford. If you shot miniDV, this means a DVCAM or DVCPro deck. If you shot Betacam, this means a high-end PVW model deck. These decks offer very stable playback and recording architecture, which results in higher picture quality.
- **Will I be making lots of edits onto tape, or simply outputting my projects as one single edit?** If you chose the former, you'll need a deck that's frame accurate.
- **What existing equipment do I need to be able to work with?** Do you need a deck with a Firewire connection for use with a program like Adobe Premiere, or do you need a deck with SDI connectors to interface with a package such as Avid Media Composer?
- **Do I need an upgrade path to high-end equipment?** Some Firewire-equipped decks offer an upgrade path to SDI, others don't. If you think this is where your production is headed, don't lock yourself in to low-end equipment that you'll later have to replace. Similarly, don't waste money on high-end equipment that might be overkill for your project (Figure 11.6).

Whatever your answers to the preceding questions, the purchase of a video deck always involves weighing price versus performance. The following sections list the features to consider when looking at decks.

Tape Format

This may seem like an obvious one. You shot MiniDV, for example, so you should buy a MiniDV deck. However, some decks are able to play a few different formats. See Table 11.1 for details.

If you shot on miniDV, you can choose between MiniDV, DVCAM, or DVCPro decks for editing and final mastering. A miniDV deck will be signif-

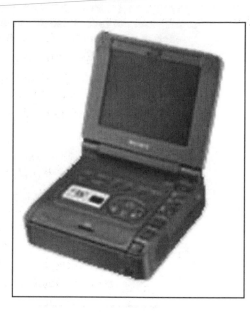

FIGURE
11.5   *The Sony GVD-900 MiniDV walkman can save wear and tear on your camcorder.*

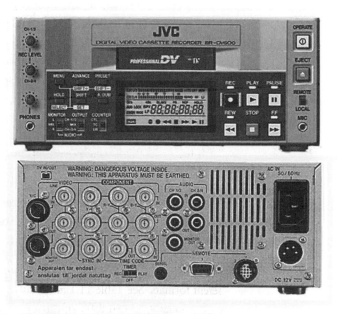

FIGURE
11.6   *The JVC BR-DV600 DVCAM format VTR.*

TABLE 11.1   VTRs compatibility chart. Many digital video decks can play (but not record usually) multiple tape formats. Be sure to check each manufacturer's specifications if you need a VTR that plays back multiple formats.

Tape Format	Can Also Play
Digital-8	Hi8
Sony DV	DVCAM
Panasonic DVCPro	DV* and DVCAM
Sony DVCAM	DV*
JVC Digital-S	S-VHS
Digital Betacam	Beta SP
Betacam SX	Beta SP
DVCPro50	DV, DVCAM and DVCPro
DV	DVCAM**
D5	D3
D9 –HD	Digital-S

*DV tapes must be recorded in SP mode to play back on DVCAM and DVCPro equipment.
**Except the Sony VX700 and VX1000.

icantly cheaper (starting around $1000) but will lack professional features and high-quality internal components that will save you time and trouble. DVCAM and DVCPro decks will allow you to master to the larger and somewhat more stable DVCAM or DVCPro tapes, and will provide advanced features like RS-422 device control and XLR audio I/O.

SDI, Firewire, or Analog I/O

The deck you choose will have to have the right type of interface for your computer. So, if your computer has a digital interface such as Firewire or SDI, you'll need a deck with the appropriate interface. Similarly, if you'll be using an analog digitizing card, you'll need to get a deck with outputs that are compatible with your analog digitizing system. Whether you need composite, S-Video, or component connectors will depend on your analog card. See Chapter 5 for more details on digital and analog video interfaces.

Not all companies are fully compliant in their implementation of the Firewire interface. If you're considering a particular Firewire-equipped deck, *don't* purchase it until you've checked with the makers of your editing software.

They should be able to confirm whether a deck will be fully compatible with their software. Sometimes, one or two features of an editing package will not work with particular decks (or cameras). If you aren't dependent on these features, then go ahead and buy the deck.

TIP

Buyer Beware

Just because a deck uses a digital video format does not mean that it necessarily offers digital I/O. Some professional decks, like the Panasonic AJ-D450 (Figure 11.8) come with analog I/O only -you have to add an optional SDI board for digital I/O. This is also true of some Firewire-compatible decks.

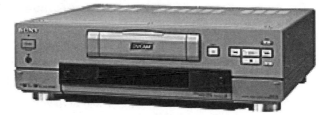

FIGURE   *The Sony DSR30 DVCAM deck with Firewire I/O is capable of reading en-*
11.7   *coded Cassette Memory information off Sony DV tapes, a feature that allows*
          for automatic handling of footage shot in the 16:9 aspect ratio.

Device Control

Your digitizing hardware needs to be able to control your video deck to search through a tape, and to start and stop the playback and record processes. This is accomplished through a serial connection between your computer and deck. If you're connecting your deck to your computer via Firewire, then your software will most likely perform deck control through the Firewire cable.

If you're using an analog or SDI editing system, you'll need to string a serial cable between a serial port on your computer and a serial port on your deck. There are three popular serial device control protocols: RS-422, RS-232, and LANC (also called Control-L).

- **RS-422** is the professional industry standard and carries the SMPTE timecode signal, which, combined with the right VTR, allows for frame accuracy. RS-422 allows the longest cable lengths—up to 1,000 feet.

- **RS-232** and **LANC** are not capable of frame accuracy. You can, however, buy an external serial protocol converter to change your RS-232 or LANC into RS-422. But if you already know you need RS-422, it's best to start with a VTR that offers it.

Frame Accuracy

Frame accuracy means that when you tell your video deck to make an edit at 1:02:10:30, it will make the edit on that exact frame—it won't miss its mark by one or more frames. If you plan to lay your final edited project off to tape in a single pass, then you don't need to worry about frame accuracy.

But, if you want to lay out your finished project in pieces—as you run out of disk space, for example—then you'll need a frame accurate deck; in other words, one with RS-422 device control and SMPTE timecode. Most VTRs are rated by their manufacturers as to their projected frame accuracy, and many DV format VTRs are rated at +/–5 frames, meaning your edit could miss its mark by as many as five frames in either direction. If this isn't something you can live with, be sure to buy a VTR that is frame accurate, and uses RS-422 serial device control rather than Firewire-based device control.

Play-Only Decks

Many professional video decks are available in a much cheaper, "play-only" format—you can use them to play tapes (i.e., for viewing, logging, and capturing), but not to record. For example, Panasonic offers the DVCPro AJ-440 is a play-only counterpart to the AJ-450 (Figure 11.8). These decks are a great option for lowering your costs if you need to rent a deck to do some capturing for a day or two. Or, you can buy a less-expensive play-only deck for digitizing, and then use your camera for your final output.

Video Deck Rentals
Remember that to rent expensive equipment, you'll need to establish credit at a rental facility 7–10 days prior to renting it.

VTR Cleaning and Maintenance

The smaller your recording format, the more destructive particles of dust and debris inside your VTR can be to your video signal. Most VTR manufacturers make head cleaning products specifically designed for their VTRs. Cleaning the heads of your VTR should be done no more frequently than every 50

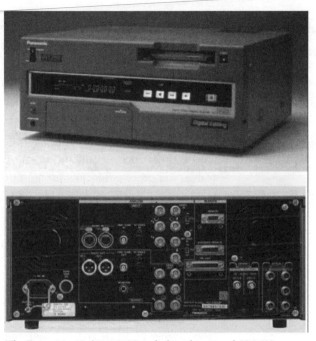

FIGURE
11.8
The Panasonic AJ-450 DVCPro deck with optional SDI I/O.

hours of use. A head cleaning cassette works by running an abrasive material across the playback and record heads in your VTR. Overuse of head cleaning cassettes can result in unnecessary wear and tear on the heads. After inserting the head-cleaning cassette, press play or record, depending on which head you want to clean. Be sure to stop the cleaning cassette after five seconds—the abrasiveness of the cleaning cassette generates heat and can actually damage the innards of your VTR. Never re-use the cleaning cassette once it reaches the end—it's the equivalent of washing with a dirty sponge. Always refer to your owner's manual for specific cleaning instructions before any attempt to clean your VTR. Also, remember that prevention is the best medicine and keep your workspace free from smoke and dust.

TIP

Power and Security

Many editing systems include a battery back-up, in case of a power failure. These batteries act as a central power switch for the system and, in the case of a power failure, keep the system running long enough for you to save your work and shut down properly.

Digital Audio Equipment

As with video, using the analog audio inputs or outputs on any of your digital decks, cameras, or your computer will result in a digital to analog (D/A) conversion that might lower your audio quality. Unfortunately, true digital audio connections using professional digital AES/EBU connectors can cost a small fortune. If you've invested in a high-end video deck with digital audio I/O, sticking with digital audio I/O in your audio equipment may be worth the expense. However, for most independent filmmakers, digital audio is a luxury that is both expensive and unnecessary. Good analog I/O using balanced XLR cables will prove satisfactory for most producers.

Audio CDs

An external audio CD deck is unnecessary these days because your computer most likely has a CD-ROM or DVD-ROM drive in it that you can use to import audio tracks from a CD. You'll end up with something close to timecode if you import audio this way—the imported audio track will always start at 00:00:00:00, and the duration of the track should remain the same every time you import it. So, if you lose your audio media you can reconstruct your tracks using this "bogus" timecode. If you digitize your audio CDs from a CD player, you won't get the CD's timecode, and you may be subjecting your audio to at least one digital-to-analog conversion.

DAT and MiniDisc

You'll need a DAT or MiniDisc player if your production audio was recorded on either of those formats. As with VTRs, just because DAT and MiniDisc are digital formats does not mean that all DAT and MiniDisc decks have digital I/O, in fact many of them don't.

TIP

Grounding Your Electronic Equipment
Heavy-duty electronic equipment, such as video editing system hardware, should always be grounded. This means using three-prong AC cables plugged into a grounded (three-prong) outlet. Some video decks also have an extra ground wiring input.

Audio Mixing Boards

Audio mixers can save you the hassle of having to constantly re-cable your system every time you change audio sources. For as little as $40 you can buy a simple four-channel mixer such as the DOD 240, which is ideal for field use and simple editing systems. The next step up runs from $200–$500 and adds more channels, equalization, and gain control, like the Mackie MS1202-VLZ (Figure 11.9). And finally, an eight-channel digital mixer, like the Tascam TCM-D1000 (Figure 11.9), will run upwards of $1,000.

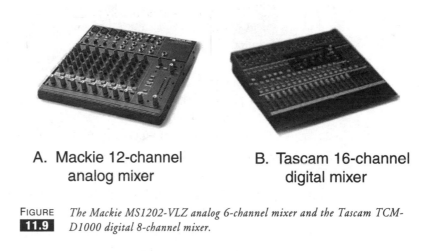

A. Mackie 12-channel
   analog mixer

B. Tascam 16-channel
   digital mixer

FIGURE   *The Mackie MS1202-VLZ analog 6-channel mixer and the Tascam TCM-*
11.9   *D1000 digital 8-channel mixer.*

Video Monitors

A video monitor is a crucial component of every editing system. If you're using a Firewire/DV editing system, you must have a video monitor to see full-motion, full-res video (don't rely on the LCD screen on your camera, it's simply not good enough). If you're using an analog digitizing system, you'll need a video monitor to see a more accurate, interlaced output of your video.

NTSC video is particularly notorious for its poor ability to handle saturated colors. Using bright colors that aren't "NTSC legal" is a common mistake—the saturated reds that look great on a computer screen will bleed, flicker, and generally look awful on an NTSC monitor. (PAL shares these problems, but to a lesser degree.) Having an NTSC/PAL playback monitor next to your computer monitor lets you keep track of how well your video is holding up, and is essential when creating graphics, special effects, or animations that will be output to tape.

Hot Air

The equipment described in this chapter, along with your computer processor and storage drives, can add up to a lot of hot air in the editing room. Invest in air-conditioning if you live in a warmer climate—your equipment will perform better, your computer will be less prone to crashing, and you'll be more comfortable.

Professional Video Monitor Features

Like all video equipment, professional video monitors—$300 to $6,000— offer extra controls and features that go beyond the typical consumer television monitor. Here's what you can get for the extra dough:

- **Better video quality.** We're not just being snobs here, even a lower-end professional monitor will usually deliver much better quality than the average television.
- **Horizontal line resolution.** Professional NTSC/PAL monitors have a horizontal line resolution ranging from 400 to 800 lines, which (simply put) means they are better than most consumer-grade monitors.
- **High-end I/O.** Just like professional VTRs, pro monitors can have analog Y/C, analog component, and SDI I/O
- **Switchable aspect ratios.** Many pro monitors can switch between 4:3 and 16:9—a boon for projects shot with anamorphic lenses or destined for HDTV, although the image will be letterboxed. If you want a bigger image size, you'll have to spring for a true widescreen HD monitor like the one in Figure 4.12.
- **NTSC/PAL switchable.** Many pro monitors can switch between NTSC and PAL. This is a great asset if you shoot your DV film in PAL but need to create NTSC video supporting materials such as trailers, press kits, etc.
- **A/B input switching.** Most pro monitors allow for more than one input source, and you can switch from the "A" source, usually your NLE, to the "B" source, usually your primary VTR. (Note: This doesn't work for DV-format editing systems, since all your video will be coming through your VTR.) This can be useful if you output your project to tape and want to compare what your computer is sending out to what your video deck is actually recording.

DV Decompression

A hardware transcoder such as the Sony DVMC-DA1 will let you capture analog formats through your Firewire port, and will also help you save wear and tear

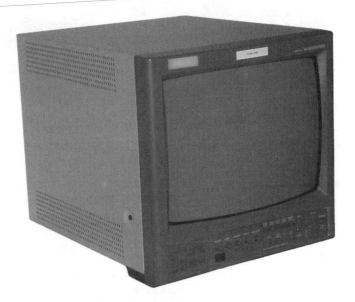

FIGURE
11.10   *A Sony Trinitron professional NTSC/PAL monitor with analog component and S-video I/O.*

on your digital camera or deck when editing. Because the transcoder can convert the digital information coming out of your computer into an analog signal for your NTSC monitor, you won't have to use your camera or deck to preview your edits. The unit will set you back about $500.

- **Underscan, horizontal delay, and vertical delay.** These features let you troubleshoot any video signal problems you may be having. If you want to learn more about video signals and how to diagnose them, check out www.dvhandbook.com/monitors.

Calibrating Your NTSC/PAL Monitor
Just like computer monitors, NTSC/PAL video monitors need to be calibrated. See Appendix A for instructions on calibrating your NTSC/PAL video monitors.

TIP

Cheap Trick
If you can't afford to spend the money on a professional video monitor, you can settle for a cheap consumer television set. Just make sure it has the right inputs to work with your system. If you can afford it, at least spend the money for a TV with S-Video input. The improvement in quality is worth the money.

TIP

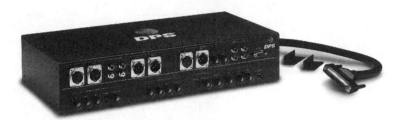

FIGURE   *This break-out box from a DPS Reality system has every sort of connector*
11.11   *you'll ever need.*

Hardware Connectors

The cables that connect the various parts of your editing system together serve to transport the video and/or audio signals from component to component and are the key to maintaining signal integrity. Below are illustrations of the most common cables you'll encounter. (Figure 11.12) Varying configurations of *BNC* cables are used to carry SDI video, analog component video, analog composite video, AES/EBU digital audio, black burst and VITC timecode signals. *RCA* cables are used to carry analog composite video, SP-DIF digital audio, analog audio signals and LTC timecode signals. *XLR* cables are used to carry analog audio and AES/EBU digital audio signals. *Mini* cables carry consumer analog audio signals. *1/4"* or *phono* cables are used to carry analog audio signals, particularly to and from headphones. *RS-422, RS-232* (not shown), and *LANC* (not shown) cables are used for serial device control. Proprietary *S-video* (not shown) cables carry the Y/C video signal. And last, but not least, 4 and 6 pin *IE1394* cables are used to carry DV video, DV timecode and DV device control signals.

TIP

Back to Front
The best way to see if a piece of equipment is right for your needs is to look at the rear panel. Usually this is where all the hardware connectors reside. If the connector you need isn't there, the deck might not support it. A look at the rear panel of the JVC BR-DV600 in Figure 11.6 shows that it has Firewire I/O, analog component I/O, analog composite I/O, analog Y/C I/O, RS-422 deck control, BNC sync input for connecting to a black burst generator, two 1/4" phono audio channels I/O, BNC timecode I/O for dubbing, a single BNC analog composite video monitor out, a single 1/4" phono audio monitor out, an AC power connector and a DC power connector for battery run operation.

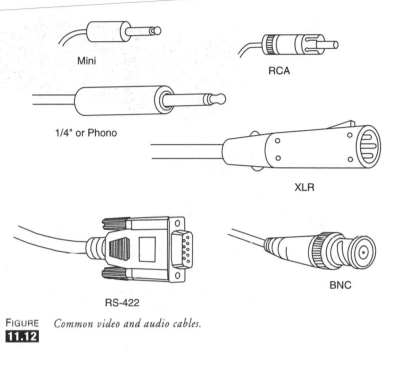

FIGURE
11.12
Common video and audio cables.

Summary

If you've been shooting on DV and plan to edit on your computer using a Firewire interface, then your video hardware needs are fairly simple. At the very least, you'll need a good NTSC monitor, a set of speakers, preferably a deck for playback (rather than your camera), hardware or software scopes for calibrating, and all the right cables to connect it together.

If you want to go higher-end to ensure the best quality, you're going to have to spend a lot more money. Purchasing audio and video hardware is a lot like buying a car and often more expensive. You should research your options and the market thoroughly before you dive in. Consider rental equipment the equivalent of a test drive. You may save yourself the trauma of a dozen little nasty surprises later.

CHAPTER

12 Preparing to Edit

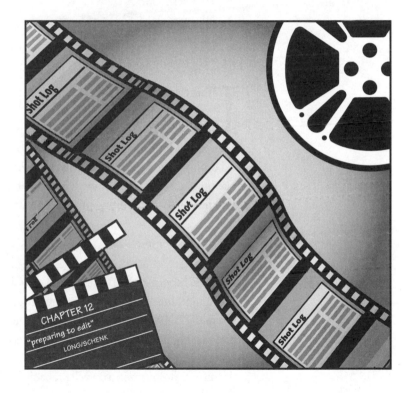

IN THIS CHAPTER

- Worst-Case Scenario
- How to Organize Your Project
- Logging
- Tutorial: Setting Your Video Levels
- Tutorial: Logging and Capturing
- Tips for Better Logging
- Capturing On-Line Quality Video
- Troubleshooting
- Advanced Media Management
- Summary

This chapter covers the traditional domain of the assistant editor: editing room setup and maintenance, organization, logging, and digitizing. Because NLE software is, at heart, an extremely sophisticated way of keeping track of timecode and tape numbers, you've got to stay very organized during your editing. If you don't provide the software with access to accurate timecode and tape numbers, it won't be able to do its job. Therefore, the crucial first step in the editing process is to set up a cataloging system for your media.

Worst-Case Scenario

Imagine this scenario: You've just finished whittling 30 hours of dailies into a 90-minute feature film. You're about to output a master onto a rented digital betacam deck ($900/day) when your computer crashes. After you restart, you realize that about 30 percent of your media is corrupted or missing. What do you do?

If you're well-organized, you will probably be able to reconstruct your project in a few hours, possibly even using batch operations. If not, you'll have to reconstruct from memory. Depending on the degree of disorganization, you may have to scroll through several tapes to find the correct shots, re-capture your footage, and so on. The resulting clean-up job could take days or even weeks.

The longer and more complex your project, the more likely it is that you'll encounter problems such as corrupted or lost media, the need to re-digitize or work on a different NLE system, and the possibility of needing to conform your footage to multiple mastering formats such as broadcast television, theatrical projection, or streaming Web media.

Even without these more extreme troubles, staying organized will make your editing go faster, and make it easier to make changes later.

How to Organize Your Project

Because a typical editing project can contain hundreds of separate pieces of media—video clips, audio clips, still images, computer-generated imagery—spread among dozens of tapes, disks, and hard drives, it's crucial to have a cataloging system that lets you find any piece quickly and easily.

1. Create a Numbering System

As you import files into your project—or capture or digitize video—your NLE will ask you for a label corresponding to the tape, disk, or drive on which the file is stored. If you ever need to re-capture or link to that media, the NLE will be able to ask for the specific tape or disk by name. So, you should label all your media with a unique ID number.

Because there's always a chance that you might need to move your project to a high-end, linear on-line suite, we recommend following the labeling conventions used by those high-end systems. It's best to use tape numbers of six characters or less, since there's a good chance that some piece of software down the line will cut off part of the name, or change the spaces into underscores.

Keep your names simple: AA0001 for your first tape, where AA is your code for the project. If you want to call your first tape "1," do yourself a favor and call it 000001. Write this number on the tape itself, not just the tape box. From that point on, label and number every piece of media that comes into your project—whether it's a MiniDV tape, an audio CD, or a still photograph—*before* you start working with it.

2. Make Sure All Your Videotape Has Timecode

Every piece of videotape that goes into your editing system should have timecode. Without timecode, your computer will have no way of keeping track of where a particular clip is on a particular videotape.

TIP

Setting Up Timecode in Final Cut Pro
If you're using Apple's Final Cut Pro, you'll need to "calibrate" your timecode before you start logging, and every time you change to a different video deck. Refer to your user manual for more information.

3. Keep a Database of All Your Media

Your NLE software will keep track of the tape number, timecode indices, and comments for every clip in your project. At times, other people in your production may need access to this information—perhaps your cinematographer needs to know which take of a shot you're using. If so, you can usually print out a report from your logging software or NLE, or you can keep a separate, simpler database on another computer.

Before you start editing you should also develop some keywords that will be assigned to clips. Keywords allow you to easily sift and filter your media bins to find categories of clips. Keywords can be an invaluable tool for organizing, logging, and finding shots later in the editing process. Consider using the names of characters, topics in a documentary, or locations.

TIP

Storing Your Media
Remember, most digital media is magnetic, and as such it should be treated with care. Keep it away from monitors, CPUs, carpeting, and video decks. Store your tapes in the plastic boxes they came in, not uncovered on top of the tape deck.

Logging

Before you ever start editing your footage, you will have to *log* your tapes. Logging is the process of looking through each tape to determine which scenes, takes, and shots you will capture. When logging, you will note which tape the footage is on, as well as the timecode indicating the beginning and end of the clip. This information will eventually be entered into your NLE.

Though much maligned as tedious and time-consuming, logging your tapes is really the first step in editing. Whoever logs the camera-original tapes is, to some extent, deciding what will end up in the final project. There are a number of products on the market created specifically to log videotape, and of course, you can log from within your NLE itself.

Standalone Logging Software

There are a number of standalone logging programs such as The Executive Producer and Avid's Media Log. Standalone logging software allows you to set up a cheap secondary workstation for logging. The technophobic writer or producer can use these simplified programs to log tapes on their own workstation.

Good Tape Logs
Thorough tape logs can be an invaluable resource if you later need to re-edit the
same sources into a trailer, press kit, or broadcast version.

LOGGING AND DIGITIZING

There are three steps to follow when capturing or digitizing media. For each
tape, you'll need to set the proper video levels, log the clips on the tape to build
a batch list, and, finally, capture the media. Following are tutorials covering all
three processes. Before you begin these tutorials, you'll need to launch your
editing software and create a project. Within your project, create a bin or
folder for your logged clips. Some editors like to make a separate bin for each
tape, others like to group their shots by scene or subject.

These tutorials do not assume you are using a particular NLE, so you might
need to consult your software's manual for details on performing specific tasks.

Tutorial:

SETTING YOUR VIDEO LEVELS

Before you begin digitizing and capturing, you need to adjust your NLE to
correctly read the color from your videotape. To do this, you'll use your software's waveform monitor to set the correct *white level* and *black level*, and the
vectorscope to adjust *hue*.

STEP 1

Enter capture mode in your NLE and open your software waveform and vectorscope. Refer to your software documentation if you don't know how to do
this (Figures 12.1 and 12.2).

STEP 2

Insert a tape into your video deck. Your software should prompt you to enter
the name of the tape. If you're not prompted, enter this information yourself.

STEP 3

Rewind to the head of the tape and play. When you get to the bars and tone
on the tape, you're ready to start calibrating. First, take a look at your waveform

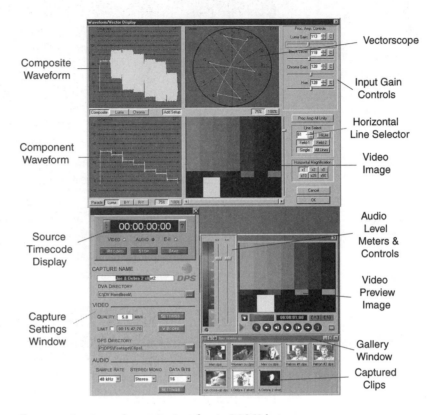

Composite Waveform

Vectorscope

Input Gain Controls

Horizontal Line Selector

Component Waveform

Video Image

Source Timecode Display

Audio Level Meters & Controls

Video Preview Image

Capture Settings Window

Gallery Window

Captured Clips

FIGURE
12.1   *Logging and capturing interface in DPS Velocity.*

monitor—if there's a box that indicates which horizontal line of video you are viewing, make sure the number in this box is between 16 and 179 (Figures 12.3 and 12.4).

STEP 4

As the color bars play on your tape, watch the waveform monitor (it is very important that you do this while your deck is playing, not paused). Each stair-stepping pattern (Figure 12.4a) represents a separate field of video; the wave-form monitor may display either one or two. Look at one of the fields (it doesn't matter which one)—the lowest step on the left corresponds to the black color bar. If you are setting the black level for North American NTSC,

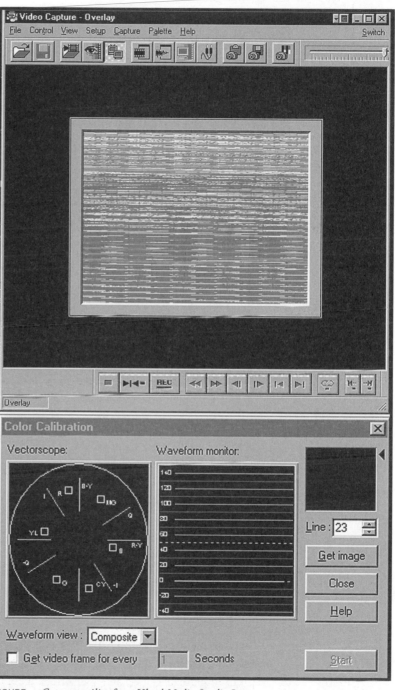

FIGURE
12.2   *Capture utility from Ulead Media Studio Pro.*

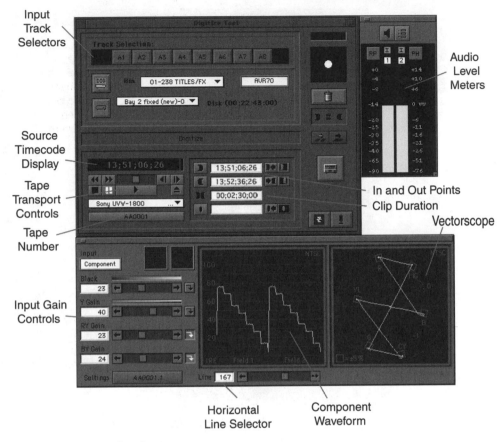

Input Track Selectors

Audio Level Meters

Source Timecode Display

Tape Transport Controls

Tape Number

In and Out Points

Clip Duration

Vectorscope

Input Gain Controls

Horizontal Line Selector

Component Waveform

FIGURE **12.3**   *Capture tools in Avid Media Composer*

use the sliders on your waveform monitor to adjust the black step until it sits at 7.5 IRE. If you are setting the black level for Japanese NTSC for PAL, the black level should be set at 0 IRE. (If you're using hardware monitors, follow these same settings.)

STEP 5

Set the white level by adjusting the rightmost step on the waveform monitor to 75%. Figure 12.4 (a) shows 75% bars with the black and white levels set appropriately. If your software allows to select a different horizontal line, try setting the line between 180–200 and checking your image against Figure 12.4 (b). Select a line between 201–263 and check Figure 12.4 (c).

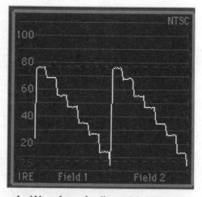

The white level
is set at 75% and
each color bar is
represented by a
"step " on the
stair-like pattern

A. Waveform for lines 16-179

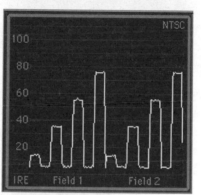

Note that the white
level is set at 75%
and the blacks are
at 7.5 IRE

B. Waveform for lines 180-200

Note that the white
level is at 100% and
the three small black
areas are set to 0 IRE,
7.5 IRE and 10 IRE

These small steps
correspond to the
three small black bars
in the bottomtest
pattern

C. Waveform for lines 201-263

FIGURE

12.4

*These two-field waveform images show how the proper video levels for the
three standard NTSC test patterns should be set. The waveform shows the
brightness of a particular image.*

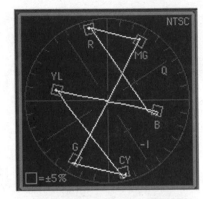

A. Vectorscope for lines 16-179

The top test pattern has a bar for each key color: yellow, cyan, green, magenta, red and blue, resulting in the zig-zag image shown here

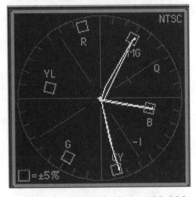

B. Vectorscope for lines 180-200

The middle test pattern only has three bars of color: blue, magenta, and cyan

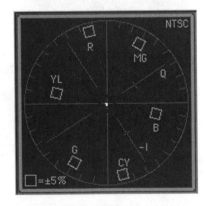

Because there is no color information in the bottom test pattern, the vectorscope is empty

FIGURE
12.5   *These are the corresponding vectorscope images for the three standard NTSC test patterns. The vectorscope records only color, or hue, information.*

TIP

Hardware Waveform Monitors and Vectorscopes
Hardware waveform monitors and vectorscopes are more accurate and easier to
control. If you are serious about your video levels, and especially if your software
'scopes don't allow you to select different horizontal lines, you may want to rent
hardware 'scopes on the days you want to capture high-quality material.

STEP 6

Now that you've defined black and white, the colors in between should fall correctly into place. To make sure, take a look at your vectorscope. The six little
boxes each represent a different color, or hue: R for red, G for green, B for blue,
M for magenta, Y for yellow, and C for cyan. Figure 12.5 (a) shows the ideal
pattern that color bars should show on your vectorscope. Adjust the scope to
get as close to this pattern as possible. Select a line between 180–200 and double-check your colors against the image in 12.5 (b).

STEP 7

If your software allows you to save your video level settings, now is the time to
do so. It's best to name these saved settings to correspond with the tape number. If your NLE does not allow you to save these settings, you may want to
write them down for future reference.

STEP 8

Next you need to set your audio levels using the 60 cycle (60 Hz) tone that ac-
companies the color bars. Open the audio level meters and move the sliders
until the tone peaks at 0. Now you're ready to start logging your tape.

Remember: You should perform these steps *any time you change tapes!* With
practice, the process will only take seconds to complete.

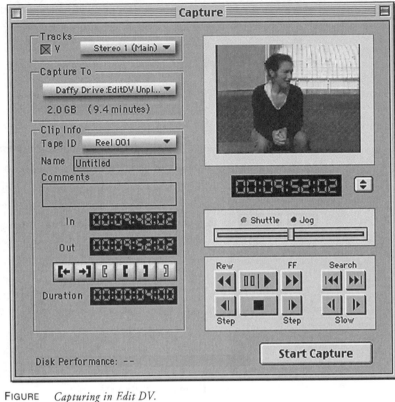

Capturing in Edit DV.
12.6

Tutorial

LOGGING AND CAPTURING

With your video levels set, you're ready to begin working your way through the tape, selecting clips for capture. In this step, you won't do any capturing, you'll simply log the selections that you want.

STEP 1

Use the tape transport controls to find the first shot you want to log. The tape transport controls are a set of buttons that look just like those on a VCR: play, pause, record, fast forward, and rewind (see Figure 12.7).

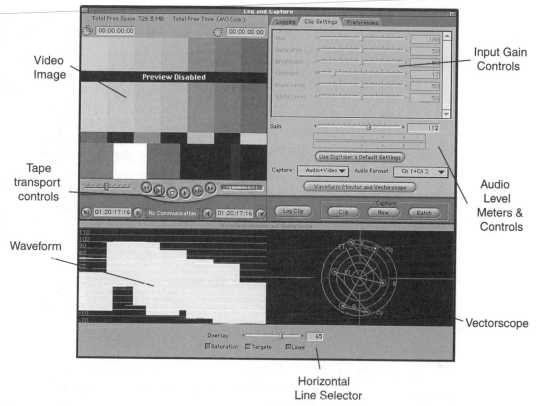

Video Image

Tape transport controls

Waveform

Input Gain Controls

Audio Level Meters & Controls

Vectorscope

Horizontal Line Selector

FIGURE 12.7   *Capture controls in Apple's Final Cut Pro.*

STEP 2

Find the *in-point* of your shot. The in-point is the first frame you want to capture. Set the in-point using your software's controls. Most NLEs let you press "I" on your keyboard to set an in-point. You should see the timecode from your tape appear in the window next to the "In." Compare this timecode to the timecode reading on your deck or camera to ensure they match. Be sure to give a few seconds of *handles* if possible. You also need to be careful to leave enough *pre-roll* for your video deck. (See "Tips for Better Logging" if you don't know what handles and pre-roll are.) Now find the out-point and set it by typing "O" or clicking the "Out" button on your interface. Again, check your timecode. Don't forget to leave a couple of seconds of handles at the tail.

STEP 3

Now you need to enter a name for your shot. Most NLEs also allow you to add other information: the shot number, the take number, whether the take is good (g) or not good (ng), and comments. If you have keywords for your project, you can also add them here. Click on the button that says "log" to log the clip and add it to the bin. Note, however, that the clip has *not* been digitized. It is an *off-line* clip, but the computer knows exactly where it is located if it needs to be captured (Figure 12.8).

STEP 4

Repeat this process until you've logged all of the desired shots on this tape. As you go through the tape, make a note of any quality changes or problems:

FIGURE
12.8
Folder with logged shots in DPS Velocity.

drastic changes in lighting, changes in audio levels, etc. You may need to capture those shots separately so that you can adjust their audio and video levels independently.

STEP 5

Once you get to the end of the tape, you can tell the software to "batch digitize." It will then work its way through your log and capture each clip. If you're using an analog digitizer, you'll need to specify the resolution at which you want to capture. For analog or digital captures, you need to pick an audio sampling rate—44.1 KHz is fine for most projects. Whatever you choose, make sure you stick with it throughout your project. Many NLEs let you save these preferences.

STEP 6

Before you press the Capture button, you should quit any background applications and turn off any networking functions. Once you start capturing, you can take a coffee break while your machines work. It's a good idea to not go too far away, however—NLEs tend to be fussy about capturing, and you may find an error message upon your return, instead of a bin full of media. If so, read on for tips on how to avoid logging/capturing errors.

Tips for Better Logging

Following these simple tips can save time and frustration in the editing room, both now and later:

- **Log first, then digitize.** Logging your tapes lets you skip unusable takes that would waste disk space if captured. If you shot at a 5:1 ratio, you'll probably be trying to log at a 2:1 or 3:1 ratio. Usually, it's best to log all the takes, whether good or bad, during a first pass. Then, you can capture only the good takes during a second pass. This way, you have a complete log of your tapes and can later easily grab additional takes.
- **Calculate available disk space in advance.** There's nothing more frustrating than running out of room on your hard drive before you've captured all your material. Advance calculation of how much media will fit on your drives will save you from such hassles.

- **Avoid logging across timecode breaks.** The biggest troublemakers, when it comes to logging and capturing, are timecode breaks. Any section on the tape that displays no timecode in your deck's counter is a break (we discuss how to avoid these in Chapter 9). The only problem here is that they often go by so fast you can't see them—some pro VTR models have "timecode indicator" lights that flash off when there's no timecode. Most NLEs cannot digitize or capture across timecode breaks.

  When you capture a clip, your deck will rewind to a few seconds *before* your in-point to allow for a pre-roll that will ensure that the tape is up to speed. If these few seconds roll over a timecode break, then your deck will have wandered into unknown timecode, and your NLE will become confused. Hopefully, you've got enough pre-roll on your tape; if not, adjust the pre-roll setting in your NLE. If there's a timecode break after your out-point, set your out-point to the last useable frame of the shot (usually the second-to-last frame or earlier.)

- **Log with "handles."** It's best to log each shot with a few seconds of padding at the head and tail. These *handles* give you flexibility to extend a shot or add dissolves. Some programs like Apple's Final Cut Pro allow you to set up a predetermined handle length for your shots. In most cases, this is a bad idea unless you are positive your tape is free from timecode breaks.

- **Avoid logging extremely long takes.** As you log your tapes you may find yourself faced with a seemingly endless series of uninterrupted multiple takes. Rather than logging this as one giant shot, it's better to pick the best useable sections and log them separately. After you or your editor decides which take to use, you can delete, or take "off-line," the media that you're not using. You don't want to log a shot that's 10 minutes long if you only use five seconds of it. Remember, the goal of logging is to make some initial decisions about the content of your project. While it's nice to give the editor lots of choices, too many choices will make editing take longer.

HOW TO LOG A SCENE FOR CONTENT

When logging, you need to think about the footage the editor and director will need to properly cut the scene. At first glance, many shots might seem unnecessary. To have the most flexibility when editing:

- **Log the dialogue first.** Dialog is the framework of any scene, whether scripted or documentary. If the camera work is bad but the audio is good, it may be worth logging as a back-up.
- **Log cutaways for the dialogue.** Usually reaction shots of the other characters in the scene. Sometimes cutaways will be on the tape before or after the scene itself.
- **Log all the "action."** If a scene involves two people going out to dinner, make sure you get all the "action" or movement in the scene. Entering the restaurant, sitting, ordering, etc. Make sure you have all the moments that set up the scene and that define where the characters are physically.
- **Log the establishing and/or wide shots that set up the scene.** Also, log all the "b-roll" or scenery shots of the location.
- **Log any particularly nice or interesting looking shots.** The camera operator may have shot something that's not in the script but will prove useful later.
- **Log some "room tone."** Room tone is the background sound at a location—whether it's party chatter or what sounds like "silence." You might need it for audio editing.
- **Log the blue-screen correction shot.** If you're logging blue screen footage, log the empty blue screen shots that either proceed or follow each shot. These are important for compositing. (more about these later in Chapter 16).

Capturing On-Line Quality Video

Many people think of *on-line editing* as an output process, but to get "on-line" quality, you have to be very diligent in how you capture your media. If you are eager to start editing, you can go ahead and batch capture according to the procedure described earlier, and start cutting. But at some point before your final output, you'll want to go back and re-capture your video at the highest-quality. This means you'll probably need to forgo the convenience of batch capturing, and capture each clip with custom settings. If you're using a system with multiple resolutions, you'll need to switch to a higher quality setting. Because you've already logged each scene, the computer knows where each clip is on each tape. You'll simply need to adjust the settings and re-capture.

CAREFUL CAPTURING

To get the best quality, you must carefully set the video levels for every scene and/or lighting change (unlike before where you applied uniform levels to the entire tape). If the color bars on your tape were recorded by the same camera that you used for shooting, then they're probably an accurate reference for setting video levels. If the tapes were "striped" with bars and tone using another deck or camera, you'll be able to achieve a ballpark estimation of correct video and audio. See the following sidebar for details.

Doing the work to capture at "on-line" quality can be tedious and boring. You'll need to very closely watch your video as it goes into your computer to make sure there aren't any glitches, drop-outs, or other problems. You'll also want to listen for glitches and distortion in your audio. See Chapter 10 for more on audio levels. Your diligence will pay off in your final output.

Setting Video Levels without Bars

If you set the video levels using the color bars at the head of your tape, as explained earlier, you've probably got your video levels into the right ballpark. For greater accuracy, you'll want to set them using the footage itself. To do this, go to the scene you are logging and look for a shot with good black areas. Use these black areas to set your black level. Unfortunately, your waveform will not show the neat stair-stepping of the color bars test pattern, and not all images will have true black and white areas. Deciphering the image on the waveform may take some getting used to at first. Color Plate 6 shows a frame of video, and Figure 12.9 shows its corresponding waveform images and vectorscope. Next, repeat this process with the white levels.

Now take a look at the vectorscope. It will look something like the squiggly mess in Figure 12.9 (d). If your scene involves people, your goal here is usually to adjust the hues to enhance skin tones. Find a close-up of one of your actors and adjust the red and yellow color gain sliders until you think their skin tone looks its best. You may also want to correct any overall color imbalance in the video signal—if you think the whole image looks green, you can adjust it here. Color Plate 7 and Figure 12.10 show an overexposed image. Color Plate 8 and Figure 12.11 show an underlit image. One word of warning: Although you can use the vectorscope sliders to create color effects, you'll have more control and flexibility if you use your NLE's bright-

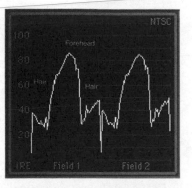

A. 2-field waveform of line 51, the mannequin's forehead is indicated by the bright curve in the middle of the waveform

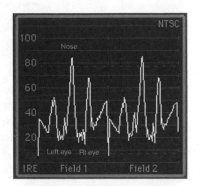

B. 2-field waveform of line 125, the dark areas in the mannequin's eyes are almost black, her nose is quite bright.

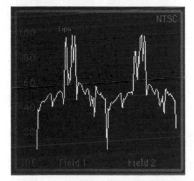

C. 2-field waveform of line 205, the white spots on her lips are almost 100% white but note that the levels aren't clipping above the 100 IRE line.

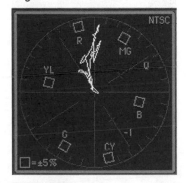

D. This vectorscope of the mannequin shows that the image consist almost entirely of reds, yellows and magentas, reflecting the skin tones and pink wig.

FIGURE
12.9   *The waveform images and vectorscope of the mannequin in Color Plate 6.*

ness, contrast, saturation, hue, and color gain effects filters to create these effects. It's always better to grab clean footage.

If part of the squiggly line extends beyond the circle boundary, this indicates an oversaturated color that will probably be too much for NTSC video to handle, and will result in bleeding. In Color Plate 9 and Figure 12.12, the line extends beyond the circular boundary near the red vector, which indicates that there is oversaturated red in the image. Certain types of colored lights, like neon, often go beyond the legal NTSC color spectrum (Color

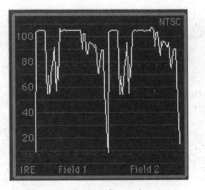
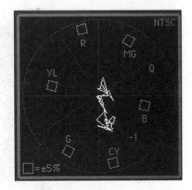

A. This waveform reflects the area near the top of the image where the sky and building are extremely over-exposed. Pulling the whites down will make them "NTSC legal" but they'll still be clipped.

B. The vectorscope reveals that this image is mostly cyan and magenta, by increasing the red the cyan is decreased and by decreasing the blue slightly, the yellow tones are enhanced.

FIGURE **12.10**   *Waveforms and vectorscope of statue in Color Plate 7.*

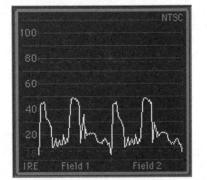
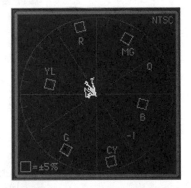

A. This waveform reflects the area near the top of the lower third of the teapots in Color plate 8. Though not necessarily underexposed, the image is dull, with nothing coming anywhere near even 75% white.

B. The vectorscope shows that the colors are dull and desaturated. Most of what is being reflected here is the back-ground, which appears grey but has lots of yellow and red in it, as revealed in Color plate 8D.

FIGURE **12.11**   *Waveforms and vectorscope of teapots in Color Plate 8.*

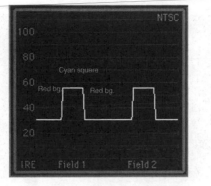

A. 2-field waveform of line 119
shows the cyan square in the middle
and the red background at to the
left and right of it.

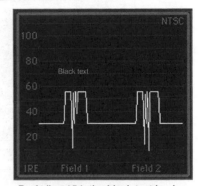

B. At line 154, the black text is also
visible. Because of aliasing, only a
small portion of the text is close to
a true video black (7.5 IRE).

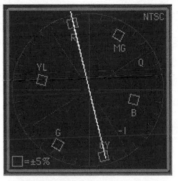

C. A vectorscope of the image
shows that the cyan levels are
good but the red is oversaturated.
This happens often with computer-
generated graphics like this one.

FIGURE
12.12   *Waveforms and vectorscope of graphic in Color Plate 9. The cyan levels are
fine, but the red is oversaturated.*

Plate 10 and Figure 12.13). While you can try to take the edge off by adjusting gain, it's not likely that you'll have much success—if you shot it that
way, it's there to stay. Trying to adjust the levels will just result in making the
rest of the reds in the image look desaturated.

Once you're happy with skin tones and the overall hue of the footage,
you're ready to capture the scene. You will need to repeat this process
every time the scene and/or lighting changes.

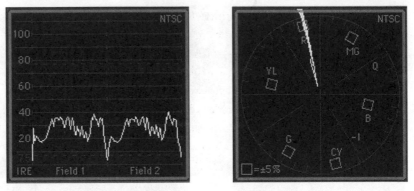

FIGURE   *The waveform of Color Plate 10 shows that the image is not overexposed but*
12.13   *the vectorscope reveals that the red is off-the-scale.*

Troubleshooting   Capturing audio and video is probably the most problem-fraught part of the
non-linear post-production process. It's also the most difficult to troubleshoot
because there are so many things that can go wrong. Here's a checklist of what
to look for when you're having problems:

- **Check your software settings.** Make sure all preferences are set properly. Re-launch. Refer to your software documentation.
- **Check your computer.** Is there enough RAM dedicated to your editing
software? Are other applications running? Are your drives full or fragmented? Mac users should try rebuilding the desktop, zapping the
PRAM, and restarting the computer. Remember, when you shut down
your computer, count to 10 before restarting.
- **Check your cables.** With your computer shut down, check all your cables, connections, and routers (if you have any), and make sure everything is secure. Check that cable lengths are within the approved limits.
If you're using SCSI drives, check your SCSI IDs and termination.
- **Check your hardware.** Check all the settings on your VTR and other
peripheral hardware. Refer to your equipment documentation. If you're
unable to record to tape, check for record inhibit tabs on your videotapes. Make sure all your components are receiving power.

Most technical problems can be solved by thoroughly working your way
through the preceding list, but that can take some time. Here's a list of common problems and probable solutions:

Problem #1: Dropped frames. Frame-dropping is often due to a hardware compatibility problem. Make sure all your hardware conforms to your software manufacturers' specs and recommendations. Dropped frames can also stem from performance bottlenecks: fragmented disk drives, an overtaxed processor, or lack of RAM.

Problem #2: No video coming in. This is either due to a settings problem in your software, or a cabling problem. Check your software settings and preferences, especially video format and device control. Finally, check your NTSC/PAL monitor to make sure video is playing from your VTR—it may be that you are looking at a black portion of the tape. Try another videotape that you know has an image on it to make sure the problem isn't the videotape itself.

Problem #3: No audio coming in. Look at the audio level meters on your VTR, audio deck, and in your software to determine where the audio signal might be stopping. If there are no levels on your deck, make sure that you haven't accidentally muted the deck or changed other audio settings. Try another tape that you know has audio on it to make sure the problem isn't the tape itself. Make sure your audio sampling rate in your software setting matches the audio sampling rate you recorded.

Problem #4: Audio is distorted. Compare the levels on your deck to the levels in your software—are they both overmodulating? If so the problem is on the deck or the tape itself. If your deck has level controls, try to lower them so that they aren't peaking. Use a pair of headphones, or set your mixer to monitor the deck only. If the audio still sounds distorted, it was probably recorded that way, so there's little you can do. If the audio is fine on your deck but overmodulating in your software, check the level controls in your software—are they up too high? Does turning down the gain remove the distortion? If not, check the path your audio signal follows from the deck to the computer—is it getting amped more than once? Is there something wrong with your settings on your mixer? Are you using cables of the wrong impedance level?

Problem #5: Inaccurate timecode. If the timecode on your deck does not match the timecode in your software, you're going to have some serious problems. Final Cut users need to calibrate their timecode; see your user documentation for more on this. If the timecode in your software always starts at 00:00:00:00, your software is probably creating a default timecode for the media, also known as "bogus" timecode, since it is effectively meaningless. This means your NLE is not reading your tape's timecode. Check your capture settings, device control settings, and your device control cabling. Make sure the timecode from your deck is compatible with your software. Some software does not recognize SMPTE timecode, and some software doesn't recognize DV timecode. See your documentation for workarounds, or consider having your tapes "striped" with the compatible form of timecode.

Problem #6: Your software refuses to batch digitize a previously logged shot. This is almost always due to timecode breaks in your source footage. See "Tips for Better Logging" earlier in this chapter.

Problem #7: Audio and video are out of sync. This is usually a playback problem. Older versions of Adobe Premiere are known to be unable to maintain sync in longer edits. If you're using a Canon camera with Final Cut, check the Preferences dialog to ensure that you have the Autosync Compensator option checked. Also, low-resolution codecs, like the one offered in ProMax' DVToolkit, often aren't capable of maintaining true sync. If your answer is "none of the above," pick a frame in your clip or sequence that appears out of sync and check the timecode of the video and the audio—it may be that your tracks in your timeline have accidentally gotten out of sync.

Problem #8: Audio plays too fast. Make sure the audio settings in your software match the audio settings at which you recorded.

Problem #9: Video glitches and drop outs. Check your camera original tape—is the glitch on your tape as well? If the dropout is only on your captured clip and not the tape itself, simply delete the damaged media and recapture the clip. If you've been using your VTR a lot it could need cleaning—refer to the section on VTR maintenance in Chapter 11 and then recapture the clip. If the problem is on your tape and you're using a digital video format there are a couple ways to try to fix digital drop outs. Try cloning the tape (see page 288 for more about clones, dubs and transfers). If this doesn't work try dubbing the tape. If this doesn't work, try dubbing the tape while feeding the record deck an audio signal from another source—a CD player or other VCR. You can then record the audio separately and re-sync by hand in your NLE. All of these processes can help create a more stable video signal and possibly remove the dropout. If it still won't go away, you're probably stuck with it. You'll have to try to fix it using your effects tools in your editing software - more about this in Chapter 15, Color Correction.

Problem #10: My clip looks lousy on my computer screen. Remember, if you're capturing DV through a Firewire interface, your video *will* look lousy on your computer (see Chapter 6 for details on why). Check your software settings and be sure that your NLE is echoing your video clips to your Firewire port. This will allow you to see full-quality video on an NTSC monitor attached to your deck (Figure 12.14).

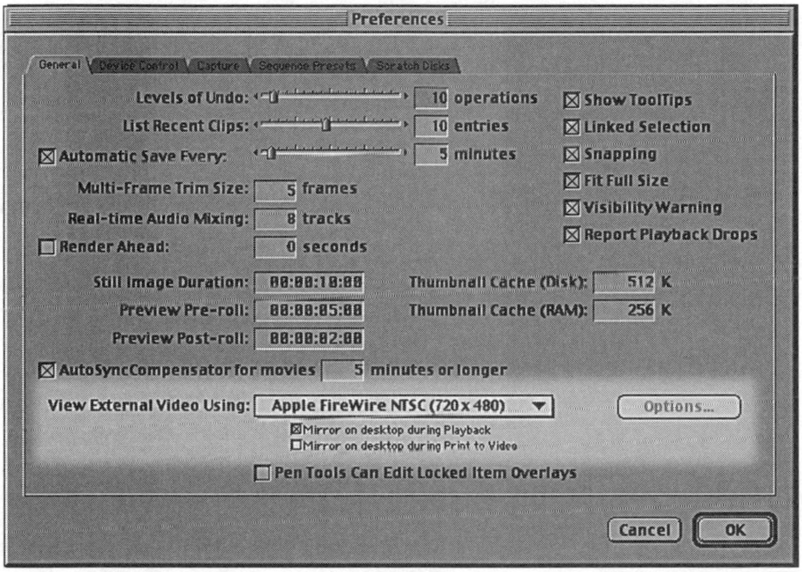

FIGURE **12.14**   *If you're using Final Cut Pro, be sure to set your preferences properly. To see your video on your external monitor (where it can be displayed at full quality), set the "View External Video Using" pop-up menu to Apple Firewire.*

Advanced Media Management

Many top assistant editors do a lot of their media management at the "Windows" or "Finder" level of their computers. Getting to know what the files your NLE creates are called, what they do, and how they're stored can be a huge asset in troubleshooting and computer maintenance. Most NLEs create a *project file* for each project, a *shot log file* for each bin or folder, several types of *settings* or *preferences* files, and *media* files for audio and video. Refer to your software documentation for more information specific to your software.

LOG FILE FORMATS

Most NLEs use proprietary file formats for shot logs, and Flexfiles for film telecine logs. But all NLEs can use text files as shot logs as well. These files consist of a header specific to the editing software you're using, and tab-delimited data that corresponds to the tape name, timecode in and out, shot name, and comments. (Refer to your software documentation for file header specifics.) This means that you can log tapes using any word processor as long as you're good at typing lots of numbers. It also means that if you have trouble importing a shot log file from one application to another, you can open it up in a text editor and troubleshoot it. Refer to your software documentation for the specific file format header your application requires.

BACK-UPS

No editing system should be without some form of back-up procedure.

- **The bare minimum.** Back up your project files and shot logs to a zip disk or floppy. If you lose anything, you'll have to redigitize, but at least you won't have to start from scratch.
- **Optical tape back-up systems.** Optical tape back-up systems like Exabyte, DTS, and DLT are expensive to purchase but relatively cheap to rent for a day (around $200). For around $100 a tape, you'll be able to back up 20 gigs of uncompressed video and audio. If you're going to put your project on the shelf for awhile, this will save you the time of redigitizing. It's also a good safety net if you have lots of special effects footage that you created on your computer.
- **Backing up to digital videotape.** If you shot on a digital video format, you can output your footage back to that format without losing any quality. Be careful though, if any extra compression or transcoding is involved, you may see some artifacts in your image. Backing up to tape is also a good idea if you're creating composites and other special effects shots on your computer.
- **EDLs.** An EDL (Edit Decision List) is a very efficient way of backing up a project. Since an EDL represents your final edit, you can use it later to recapture and reconstruct if necessary. Saving the final EDL is *always* a good idea at the end of a project.
- **Dubs and clones.** If you need to back up your tapes themselves, you'll need to make *dubs,* or duplicates, of your tapes. If your tapes are analog,

you will lose a generation in the process. If you have digital source tapes, you can have them *cloned,* which avoids any risk of generation loss.

TIP

Dubbing Down
You can't dub DVCPRO to DV or DVCAM via 1394. You can't dub DV or DVCAM to DVCPRO via 1394. But you can dub DV to and from DVCAM via 1394.

Weekly Workstation Maintenance

Logging, capturing and editing are processor-intensive tasks for your computer. If you're using your computer to edit for several hours a day, you should follow a weekly maintenance program to keep things running smoothly. You should throw away old render files on a regular basis and run Norton *Disk Doctor* and *Speed Disk*. (Note: Always refer to your user documentation before using any third-party utilities like *Disk Doctor.*) Take the time to make sure none of your drives are filled to the brim—overfilling your drives can lead to lots of crashes.

Summary

Preparing to edit can be a huge undertaking, but if you start out with a well-organized project and log carefully, you'll have the building blocks for editing success. Capturing high-quality video can be a difficult and highly technical process, but if you're concerned about image quality, the pay-off is worth it. Now that your project is ready to go, it's time to move onto the next step: Editing and Locking Picture.

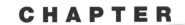
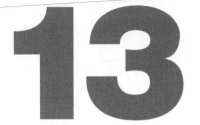

Editing

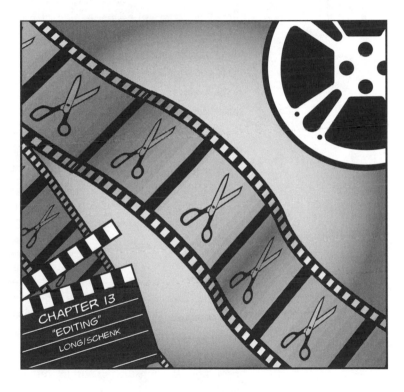

IN THIS CHAPTER

- The Invisible Art
- Building Blocks
- Fine Cutting
- Locking Picture

The Invisible Art

By the time you get to this stage, you've probably been working on your feature for a long time: writing, researching, planning, and shooting. Now it's time to play with it. The history of filmmaking is rife with examples of films that have been rebuilt, restructured, and sometimes resurrected in the editing room.

If the script is weak, it is the editor's job to try to find a way to make it work. If the director was tired one day and forgot to get the cutaways, it's the editor's job to cut the scene regardless. The notorious "cutting room floor" has saved many actors the embarrassment of a weak performance and many cinematographers the embarrassment of poorly shot footage. There's a saying that editing is a no-win situation—if the editor saves the film, the director gets the credit, but if the editor fails to save the film, the editor takes the blame. While it's true that for many people, editing is an invisible art, it's also well-appreciated by those who know better.

Building Blocks

Motion picture film was invented in the late nineteenth century, but editing as we know it today developed slowly over the next 40 years as new technologies were introduced, and more sophisticated ways to tell stories became the norm. The earliest films, like the Lumière Brothers' *Workers Leaving the Lumière Factory* (1895), consisted of nothing more than *shots,* the most basic building blocks for an edited sequence. Turn of the century French filmmaker George Meliès introduced the use of in-camera special effects like *slow-motion, dissolves, fade-outs,* and *super-impositions.* These "magic tricks" developed into the rudiments of a filmic language: fade-ins to signify the beginning, dissolves to transition between one shot and another, and fades-out to signify the ending.

Around the same time, Edwin S. Porter made *The Great Train Robbery* (1903), a film considered to be the beginning of modern editing. Porter developed the technique of jumping to different points of view and different locations, something we now take for granted. In the controversial *Birth of a Nation* (1915), D.W. Griffith took the concept of editing a step further, introducing the use of the *close-up,* the *long shot* (long as in length of time, not as in camera angle), and *panning* to develop story and intensify emotion. He also innovated the *intercutting* of scenes and parallel plot lines.

Russian filmmaker Sergei Eisenstein took Griffith's techniques even further and invented the *montage,* as exemplified by the famous Odessa steps scene in *The Battleship Potemkin* (1925). In 1929 another Russian, Dziga Vertov, made the early cinema verité film, *Man with a Movie Camera,* documenting daily life in Russia with fast-cutting to create intensity and energy.

The invention of sync sound added an entire new level of sophistication in filmmaking, and this turning point is exemplified by Orson Welles' *Citizen Kane* (1941), which used off-screen dialogue, voice-over, overlapping dialogue, and music to enhance the mood and power of the story. Editing styles and techniques have continued to grow and change since *Citizen Kane,* but the early history of film and editing is repeated on a small scale in every editing room as films are cut together using dissolves, close-ups, cutaways, intercutting, montages, and sound to build the final cut (Figure 13.1).

The Language of Film

Whether you prefer the quick-cutting MTV look, a more traditional film-cutting style, or something you come up with all by yourself, the goal of editing is to successfully tell a story. In this regard, editing can be considered a continuation of the writing process: now that the film is shot, the editor needs to do a "rewrite" of the script using the footage that exists. Because the footage has already been shot, this rewrite, or *cut,* will be limited to what was recorded on film or tape. The editor may find that he or she can't always remain true to the original story—the dialogue that looked great on paper seems long and tedious, the "montage scene" that was supposed to play for several minutes ended up consisting of a mere three shots, and so on. The editor's job is to use the screenplay as a blueprint for the final story that will emerge.

Applied Three-Act Structure

If you've studied screenwriting (or read Chapter 2), you've probably heard the phrase *three-act structure* tossed about. Three-act structure originated with the

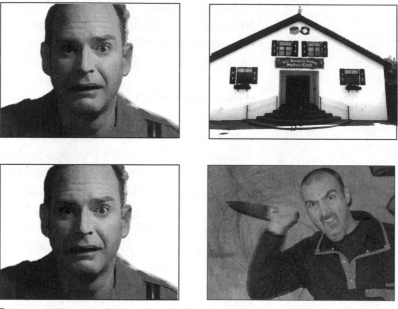

FIGURE
13.1   *The power of editing is easily illustrated when the shot of the San Joaquin Valley Swiss Club is replaced with a close-up of a knife-wielding maniac. We now interpret the actor's expression as terror, rather than dismay.*

plays of ancient Greece and is the basis for most western visual storytelling forms. Three-act structure, put simply, means that every story has a beginning, a middle, and an end. In a typical feature film, the first act, or beginning, ends about 30 minutes into the story, the second act, or middle, ends 45–60 minutes later, and the third act, or ending, comprises the last 30 minutes.

When editing, three-act structure can be applied to each scene and each sequence of scenes as well as the film as a whole. The beginning, middle, and end of a scene are referred to as *beats* rather than acts. Another way to think of these three beats is the *set-up,* the *action,* and the *pay-off.* A typical chase sequence might start with a burglar breaking into a convenience store and setting off the alarm (the set-up), he flees and is chased by the police (the action), but he escapes by gunning his car across a rising drawbridge (the pay-off). Sometimes there is an additional half beat at the end for comic effect—a shot of the frustrated cops sitting in their car on the wrong side of the bridge. If a scene is missing one of these elements, it may seem odd, nonsensical, or boring. Keeping the idea of three story beats in mind can help if a scene or sequence you're cutting seems awkward or unwieldly.

BUILDING A ROUGH CUT

There are several ways to build the first cut of a scene using a non-linear editing system. The simplest method is known as *drag-and-drop editing*. If your shots are named by scene number, shot number, and take number, sort them in that order. Select the good takes of each shot, and drag and drop them into the timeline in your NLE. The result will be a rough string-up of all the good takes of your scene in the order you selected them. If your software offers *storyboard editing*, switch to a thumbnail view in your bin and visually arrange the shots in an order you think will work, then select them and drag-and-drop them into the timeline (Figure 7.2). If your scene is a complicated montage or action sequence, you may want to use *three-point editing* to create a more refined first cut of your scene. Figure 7.3 shows a sequence created using drag-and-drop editing, and a sequence created using three-point editing.

If the scene you're cutting is based on dialogue, a good way to build the first cut is to create a *radio cut*. The idea of a radio cut is to create an edit that sounds good first, without worrying about how it looks. Using three-point editing, you can watch your footage, select the in and out points for each actor's line of dialogue, and then press the Edit button to add each line, in order, to your sequence in the timeline. Once you've created a rough string-up of all the dialogue, go through the scene and make sure all the dialogue edits sound good and that you're happy with the overall flow of the dialogue. Now is the time to trim out extra lines, or add a pause where you think the content of the scene calls for it—such as after a particularly emotional, funny, or shocking line. If you find working with the choppy picture too distracting, you can just turn off the video track monitor in your timeline.

Autosave and Auto Back-Up
Remember to save lots of copies of your sequences as you work. Use the autosave and auto back-up features if your NLE offers them.

TIP

If your scene was shot master shot-style (that is, a wide establishing shot and series of cut-aways), you'll want to set up a series of multiple tracks. Start by editing the entire master shot into your sequence as a guide track. Your scene probably has a selection of camera angles that can then be worked into your master shot. By adding extra video and audio tracks to your sequence, you can edit other shots into the sequence by laying them in higher tracks, and not have to cut up the master shot.

In Chapter 9, we showed an example of master shot-style coverage of a scene (Figures 9.1–9.3). Using that scene as an example, there are seven shots to cut into the master shot: the close-up of Debra, the close-up of Joe, the close-up of Max, the two-shot of Debra and Joe, an extreme close-up (E.C.U.) of the gun, and two reaction shots of patrons at the bar. Figure 13.2A shows an edited sequence in the timeline with the master shot on video track one (V1) and audio tracks one and two (A1 and A2), the close-up of Debra on V2, the close-up of Joe on V3, and the close-up of Max on V4, the two shot of Joe and Debra on V5, and cutaways on V6, V7, and V8.

Now you can work through each shot and remove the parts you don't need (Figure 13.2B). You can then drag-and-drop *within* the timeline to adjust the timing of each shot. Remember that your NLE will play your sequence from the top down, so the video on V8 will cover up any video on the tracks below it, and so on. Once you're happy with the layout and sequence of shots, you can collapse them into a single track of video (Figure 13.2C).

After you build the rough cut of your scene, you're ready to take another pass: refining cuts, extending shots, adding reactions and cutaways, and making sure the whole scene plays smoothly.

Don't Be Afraid to Try Different Versions
Non-linear editing is non-destructive. As long as you save copies of your sequences, you can always go back to an older version if you don't like the changes you made.

TIP

REFINING YOUR ROUGH CUT

There's a saying that if you notice the editing, the film was poorly edited. Traditional Hollywood feature film editors strive for *seamless* edits—edits that don't call attention to themselves and that flow naturally with the action, dialogue, and tone of the scene. The key to creating seamless edits is to make sure each edit is *motivated*. A motivated edit is cued by a line of dialogue, a look or gesture from one of the actors, a sound effect, a music cue, or some other element in the film.

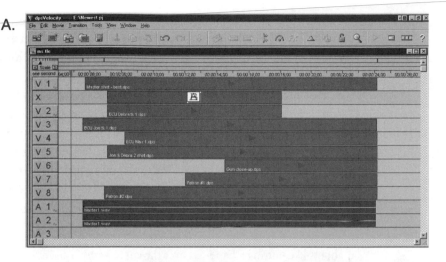

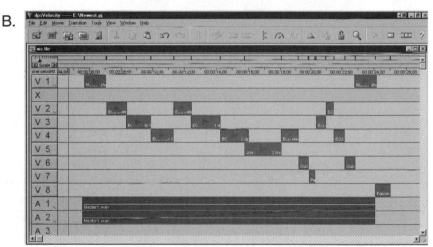

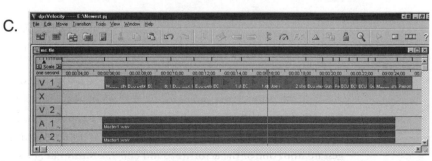

 FIGURE
13.2   *If your scene has a master shot and coverage, you can use multiple tracks in the timeline to help you build a rough cut (A). Once you've whittled down the shots (B), you can drag them down to V1 to create a single track edit (C).*

The opposite of a seamless edit is the jump cut. Jump cuts not only lack motivation, but break up the basic continuity and linear progression of time. It used to be that jump cuts were to be avoided at all costs. Nowadays, even Hollywood films feature carefully placed jump cuts to jar the viewer, add energy, or create a special effect. In *American Beauty*, jump cuts were used to accentuate the dream sequences, while the rest of the movie was edited seamlessly.

Below are different editing techniques you can use to smooth over a rough edit. All of them will work better if they are motivated in some way.

Cutaways and Reaction Shots

The easiest way to smooth a rough edit is to cover it up with another shot. It's almost like putting a band-aid over the cut. *Cutaways* are shots of other things in the scene, outside of the main area of action and dialogue: a fly on the wall, a hand moving to the handle of a gun, a foot tapping on the floor.

Reactions are shots of people reacting to the dialogue and action of the scene: a passerby looking on as the main characters yell at each other, a crowd cheering at a baseball game, a woman ducking as a gunshot rings out. Used properly, they not only cover rough edits, but enhance the story. Conversely, there's nothing worse than a random cutaway. In the example scene we described in the beginning of Chapter 9, a cutaway to one of the bar patrons reacting when the gun is revealed works well, while a cutaway to a static shot of a picture on the wall or a glass on the bar is unintentionally humorous. However, a cutaway to the glass right before the gunman puts a bullet through it can work well. Good directors understand how to shoot a useful cutaway, but often the selection of cutaways for a scene will be of the "picture on the wall" variety.

Avoid Overcutting
Too many unmotivated cutaways can result in the scene looking "cutty." Fast-cutting, like in El Mariachi, *is not the same as overcutting.*

TIP

Overlapping Edits

A common way to refine a dialogue scene is to use *overlapping edits,* also called *split edits* or *L-cuts*. If you cut from one actor to the other at the start of each line of dialogue, the scene can start to feel like a ping-pong match. Overlapping edits help break up this rhythm by extending or shortening the picture but leaving the dialogue the same, allowing you to see the reaction of the one character as the other talks and so on. *Trim mode* and *rolling edits* are useful NLE tools for creating overlapping edits (Figure 7.6).

Matching Action

If your scene involves movement, you may need to *match action* across an edit. Cutting from a wide shot of a man reaching for his gun to a close-up of the gun, from a hand turning a doorknob to the door opening, and from a shot of a man leading a woman dancing the tango to the reverse shot of her as she is dipped, are all examples of edits that need matching action.

Often if you edit two action shots together as they play out in real time, the cut won't work, especially if you are cutting from a wide shot to a close-up, or vice versa. Because the movement across the screen is small in a wide shot and big in a close-up (Figure 13.3), you may need to show more of the action in the wide shot than in the close-up. Matching action becomes second nature after awhile, but it may require some playing around to get the hang of it.

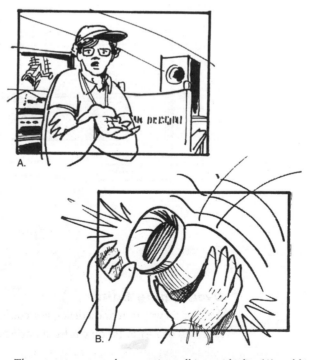

FIGURE **13.3**   *The movement across the screen is small in a wide shot (A) and big in a close-up (B).*

Matching Screen Position

In a well-composed shot, it's pretty easy to figure out where the viewer's eye will be directed. In a close-up, the eye will be directed at the face of the actor; in an action shot, it will follow the line of action, and if there are no people in the shot, it will be directed at the biggest, most colorful or dynamic thing in the frame. Once you determine where the screen position of the viewer's eye is on your outgoing shot, you can pick a similar screen position on your incoming shot (Figure 13.4). This is especially helpful when you're trying to match action. You can also intentionally jar and disorient the viewer by mismatching the screen position (Figure 13.5).

Matching Emotion and Tone

It's pretty obvious that you need to match emotion and tone in terms of the actors' performances when you cut from one shot to another. What's a little less obvious is that emotion and tone are carried in other things besides performance—the amount of camera movement in a shot, the amount of movement

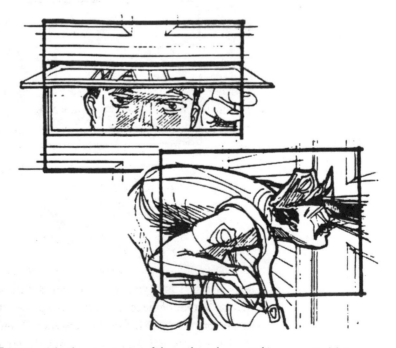

 Figure
13.4
The these two images of the mailman have matching screen positions.

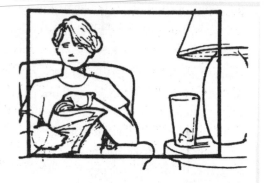

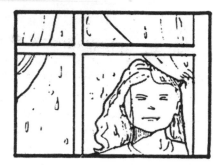

FIGURE
13.5   *The these two images do not have matching screen positions.*

of the actors in the shot, the composition of the shot (wide, tight, etc.), the lighting and overall look of the shot, and the energy of the background elements are all elements that are capable of implying emotion and tone. If your scene consists of an argument between the two main characters, it may work well to start out using wide shots and then get tighter and tighter as the scene heats up. But cutting to a wide shot during the most intense part of the scene will most likely deflate the energy.

Pauses and Pull-Ups

Adding a few seconds of silence can intensify a moment. If one scene shows a man saying "I love you" to a woman, a well-placed pause can completely change the tone of the scene. Putting the pause before he speaks will imply hesitation; put the pause before she answers and you'll have suspense.

Just as pauses in a scene can intensify the moment, shortening, or *pulling-up* the pauses in a scene can help pick up the pace. Whether you're cutting out the "ums" or trimming entire lines of dialogue, you can usually find a lot of "fat" in a scene once you start looking for it.

Hard Sound Effects and Music

A hard sound effect is something short, precise, and fairly loud—a knock on a door, a burst of applause, a screech of tires. These sorts of sound effects startle the viewer a little bit and make it easy to hide a rough edit or smooth a jump cut. If your scene has music, it's a good idea to add it early on as you refine the edit. Music can change the pacing, add emotion, intensify action, and tell the viewers how they should be feeling. Many editors have a supply of CDs that they bring to a project as temporary soundtrack elements.

TRANSITIONS BETWEEN SCENES

There are a number of things that happen "between scenes" in a feature. A change in location, for example, or a jump forward or backward in time, or a jump to an imagined sequence or dream scene. In the early days of filmmaking, each scene began with a fade in and ended with a fade out. Later, title cards were added to establish the scene. Both served the function of establishing a new location and a new point in time. Though filmmakers like Jim Jarmusch still use this technique (in films such as *Dead Man*), the modern filmmaker relies more on the techniques discussed next.

Hard Cuts

The phrase *hard cut* refers to an edit between two very different shots, without a dissolve or other effect to soften the transition. Hard cuts *within* a scene work best if they are smoothed out with matching action, screen position, and other cues. However, hard cuts can often be used to good comic effect, or to force the audience's imagination in a particular direction. Consider the scene in *Raiders of the Lost Ark* when Indiana Jones and Marion are finally on-board the freighter ship. While he suffers with his bruises, she looks at herself in a mirror. As she flips the mirror over to the clean side, we see the other end swinging up toward Jones' jaw. Hard cut to an extreme long shot of the entire ship, and an extremely loud but muffled scream.

Hard cuts *between* scenes work best when they are surprising and jarring: a scene of two lovers kissing ends with a hard cut to an extreme close-up of the woman's hand on a gun as she plots to kill her lover. Or, a close-up of a goalie missing the ball hard cuts to a wide shot of the goalie hanging up his uniform, and so on.

Dissolves, Fades, and Wipes

Using a dissolve to transition between scenes can add a feeling of smoothness, and serve to slow down the pacing of your story. Dissolves usually imply a period of "reflection" or "introspection" and give the audience a moment to chew on what has just transpired. Dissolves can also indicate the start of a dream sequence or flashback.

Fades and wipes are looking pretty out of date these days, but you never know when a fresh eye can make something old look new. The *Austin Powers* films employed a liberal use of wipes for comic effect, and the hard cuts to black between scenes in *Stranger Than Paradise* added a modern feel to a century-old technique.

Establishing Shots

Carefully placed establishing shots announce that a new scene is about to start, help orient the audience, and serve to set the location. Without establishing shots, the audience can feel "lost." Often the establishing shot is built into the first shot of the scene—a crane shot that starts high overhead and ends in a close-up on the main character, a *slow reveal* that pans across a series of objects on a desk and ends on the main character talking on the phone, and so on. If the director didn't shoot a good establishing shot, then you'll have to find something to "cheat," such as the last few seconds of a wide shot after the cast has cleared frame. You don't need an establishing shot for every single scene in the film, just whenever a significant change in location takes place.

Spending more or less time on your establishing shots is an easy way to change the pacing of your project. A long establishing shot with supporting cut-aways will slow things down and give your audience time to "settle in."

To speed things up you can use a short establishing shot, or economize by combining an establishing shot with a split-audio voiceover. For example, cut to a wide crane-shot of a riverboat while playing audio of your main character saying something like, "The way your mother was driving, I never thought we'd get here." This simple split edit serves to establish the location of your new scene, identify which characters are participating, and provide a little exposition about what they have just done.

Clearing Frame and Natural "Wipes"

An easy way to create a smooth transition between two scenes is the to out of a shot as the actor clears the frame and cut into the next shot as the actor enters the frame in another location. This method can become repetitive very quickly if it is overused. When a large object passes through the frame, such as a passing car, a person in the foreground, and so on, it can be used as a natural "wipe," to easily transition to the next scene. In *Rope,* Alfred Hitchcock concealed his few edits in the film by hiding them under natural wipes.

SOLVING TECHNICAL PROBLEMS

Every film has a set of unique technical challenges that often fail to become evident until the editing process actually begins. Here are some of the most common technical issues that get resolved in the editing room.

Missing Elements

The problem you will face most frequently when editing is not having enough material. Whether it's because an actor's mic recorded static, the pick-ups don't match the original performance, or there just aren't enough cutaways to allow you to edit the scene the way you want. Most of these sorts of problems require the sort of on-your-feet, creative thinking that good editors are known for—restructuring the scene so that the bad mic or the pick-ups aren't necessary, or finding an inventive way to recut the scene using jump cuts to make up for the lack of cutaways.

Working with Temporary Elements

It's rare to end up with a film that has every single element you need when you start editing. Whether it's music, pick-ups, or special effects shots, if you don't have all your materials, you'll need some temporary elements in order to create a solid rough cut. Creating a temporary score is a necessity to help "sell" your rough cut, but be sure it's a score that is representative of what you'll be able to use in the final edit.

If you are missing shots because they haven't been shot yet, you can use a placeholder such as a title that describes the missing shot. If you have lots of effects shots and composites, you can use low-resolution proxies imported from your effects software (more about effects in Chapters 15, 16, and 17), or you can create a temporary effects shot or composite in your NLE to use until you get the real thing. Managing lots of temp footage, proxies, and other elements can be an organizational nightmare if you let it get out of control. Be sure to develop some sort of naming convention to indicate what's temporary and what's final.

Working with Low-Res Footage

If you're planning to eventually conform your project in an on-line session, you'll be using low-res footage to create your rough cuts. Be aware that some low-res codecs save space by only compressing one of the two fields in a frame of video. *Single-field resolutions* are fine for rough cuts, but remember that you're only seeing *half* of your footage. If there's a drop-out or other problem in the second field, you may not become aware of it until you do the full-resolution on-line edit. Also, if you edit up to the last frame of a shot, you have no way of knowing what the other field contains—the end of that shot or the head of the next shot or a field of unstable video. Play it safe by not using the first and last frames of a shot unless your video is uncompressed.

Another way codecs save space is by compressing the video into a smaller screen size or by cutting the frame rate. You should probably avoid the latter at all costs—if your codec drops every third or fourth frame, it limits where you can make an edit. Some low-res codecs, such as the DV format low-res codec offered in ProMax' DV Toolkit, do not support sync audio. You'll have to wait until you recapture a high-res version to do anything beyond the most rudimentary sound editing. All of these compression techniques make it harder to see your image clearly and you may find some ugly surprises waiting for you when you see your footage at full resolution.

Working with Widescreen Footage

Widescreen projects offer an additional set of technical challenges for the editor. If you've got a full-resolution, native 16:9 video, the resulting 1080i high-definition files will be at least six times larger than an NTSC file of the same length. You should probably work with low-resolution footage to create your rough cuts, and on-line after you've locked picture. True HD NLEs cost around $100,000.

If you have footage shot using the 16:9 feature of your camera, you'll have to make sure that your hardware and software can display widescreen images. When a DV camera records in 16:9 mode, it notates this on the tape by setting a special 16:9 flag that is stored alongside each frame. To see the true widescreen image when editing, two things must happen. First, your DV codec must recognize and support the 16:9 flag. If it doesn't, it won't be able to tell your editing software that you are editing widescreen footage. Depending on how your software works, you could end up losing the widescreen info.

Second, your NLE must interpret the flag and stretch the video to its correct width. If it doesn't do this, you can still output 16:9 footage (assuming your codec supports it), but you'll have to look at 4:3 squished footage while editing. Though it's possible to edit this way, several months of staring at squished footage can grow tiresome.

3:2 Pulldown

We explained the basics of 3:2 pulldown in Chapter 4, but editing film original material that has been transferred to video presents some special technical issues. Remember that when you're editing video, you're editing in a 30 fps environment. But film only has 24 frames per second. Through the 3:2 pulldown process, extra frames have been added. If you're going back to film, you need to be sure every cut you make will fall on a film frame. If it falls on one of the 3:2 pulldown, "made up" frames, then the negative cutter won't be able to make your edit.

This means you can only make a film edit on every fifth frame of video (see Figure 4.4). Software designed to work with film, like Lightworks, Avid Film Composer, and Filmlogic, use a reverse telecine process to make sure that all your edits occur in the right places. High-end products, like those by Quantel, do heavy calculating get rid of the every fifth frame of video/fourth frame of film limitation. But if you're using a lower-end system, you'll need to do this frame bookkeeping yourself—a chore we do not recommend.

If your project has telecine transfers from film but you do not intend to go back to film, you'll have to deal with an entirely different problem. When film is transferred to video, in addition to the 3:2 pulldown process, it is also slowed down by .1% in order to achieve the 29.97 frame rate of NTSC video. If you have synched audio transferred with your film to videotape, the audio will also be slowed down .1%, but if you have your film transferred to video without sound and capture the sound separately, you'll have to slow it down by .1% in order for it to sync up with your telecined film.

Fixing audio problems is covered in Chapter 14.

Fine-Cutting   Now that you've got a decent rough cut, it's time to take a harsher look at it: Is it working? Does the story work, does the dialogue make sense, does it flow naturally, does it convey the desired mood? Fine-cutting is when you will try to make the story and presentation work.

Usually at this point there's an important editing cliche to remember: the cutting room floor. If your film isn't working, you may need to cut it down. Maybe it's that montage sequence that you love but which comes out of nowhere and destroys the natural build of a love story between the main characters. Or maybe it's part of a secondary storyline that just doesn't fit anymore. Whether it's a scene, a shot, or just a line or two of dialogue, cutting out the things that don't work can do wonders for your film.

Woody Allen routinely makes drastic changes between his rough cuts and his fine cuts, often rewriting and reshooting *half* of the movie! This is true for films including *Interiors, The Purple Rose of Cairo, Hannah and Her Sisters, September,* and *Crimes and Misdemeanors.* Such massive re-working is often necessitated because Allen relies on very long master shots. If one line of a 5-minute scene is wrong, no amount of editing can save it. In the case of *September,* several actors were no longer available and were replaced (Sam Shepherd with Sam Watterston, and Maureen O'Sullivan with Elaine Stritch).

After Allen saw the rough cut of *Crimes and Misdemeanors,* he threw out a third of the original story, rewrote it from scratch, and started reshooting. In the process, Mia Farrow's character changed from a geriatric social worker to a television producer, the documentary that Woody Allen's character was shooting changed from a film about retired vaudeville performers to a film about Allen's TV-producing brother-in-law, and a character played by Sean Young was cut completely.

Though not everyone has the luxury to reshoot as thoroughly as Woody Allen, it's important to recognize that even a director as skilled and experienced as he still has to feel his way through a project, and make massive changes to reach his goal.

EDITING FOR STYLE

The editing of feature films today has been strongly influenced by music videos, documentaries, and commercials. Fast cutting, visual effects and jump cuts are the hallmark of "cool." Movies that fit this model include *Trainspotting, The Matrix,* and *Run Lola Run.* But there's also a countertrend in independent cinema that involves a no-frills style and lots of long shots where the action plays out with very little manipulation, such as the French documentary film *Trop Tot, Trop Tard* (Too Early, Too Late), or recent movies by Olivier Assayas (*Irma Vep, Late August, Early September*). Also popular is the handheld look borrowed from cinema verité and reality television, as seen in *The Celebration*. The choice is up to you, but a strong editing style can save an otherwise weak film.

DURATION

Though it may sound trivial, one of the biggest jobs in editing is arriving at the proper duration for the project. Some projects have built-in durations: commercials are usually 10, 30, or 60 seconds long, and TV shows are 28 minutes or 52 minutes. Trailers vary from short commercial spots to several minutes long (don't make the mistake of boring viewers with a trailer that tells the whole story). Press kits usually include the full-length trailer(s) from the film, the 30- or 60-second teaser trailer(s), possibly a longer scene or featurette, and some selected takes, such as I.D. shots for each key cast member.

If your project doesn't fit neatly into a predetermined slot, it may by more challenging to arrive at the right duration. If you're editing a short film, keep in mind that it's rare for festivals to accept shorts that are longer than 10 minutes. The average length of the old Warner Brothers cartoons was six minutes, and most people seem to expect a short film to be about that length. If yours is a feature film, it will have to be at least 80 minutes long to qualify in most festivals. It used to be that a typical feature film was 90 minutes long, but lately, "serious" films tend to be at least 120 minutes and can often be as long as 180 minutes. Remember, your story should dictate the duration of your film, not an arbitrary number that is the trend of the day.

THE BIG PICTURE

Russian filmmaker Andrei Tarkovsky aptly described filmmaking as "sculpting in time," and the longer your film, the more complex the "sculpture." As you try to get a final cut, here are some things to look at in terms of the structure of your film as a whole:

- **Rhythm and pacing** If you start with a high-energy action scene and try to keep up that level of energy until the end, you'll probably fail. Action seems more intense when it follows a period of calm, and calmness seems more profound when it follows intense action or emotion. Good rhythm and pacing allow intensity to build over time, creating suspense and engaging the audience in the story.

- **Set-ups and pay-offs** Earlier, we talked about the concepts of set-ups and pay-offs within a scene or sequence of scenes. But in a long film, there are also lots of set-ups that occur in the early part of the film and don't pay off until much later on. Make sure all the set-ups that play out over time are paid off later on.

- **Emotion** Emotion is built into the script and the actors' performances, but editing plays a role as well. If scenes aren't allowed to develop or build, the emotion, whether happy, funny, angry, sad, etc., will fall flat. When you look at the film as a whole, make sure all the emotional beats that you intended are there.

- **Compressing and expanding time** How long is the period of time covered in your story—a day, two weeks, five years? Does the structure of the film seem appropriate for the film's length? Would it benefit from re-arranging the order and playing with the time frame?

Locking Picture

Last, but not least, you need to *lock picture*. Locking picture means that you have finished editing for story and will not make any further changes to the content of the film. You may still have some outstanding effects shots that need to be dropped in, but you won't be making any changes that affect the duration. Once picture is locked, it's time to take a more serious pass at editing the sound.

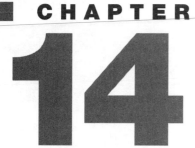

CHAPTER

14 Sound Editing

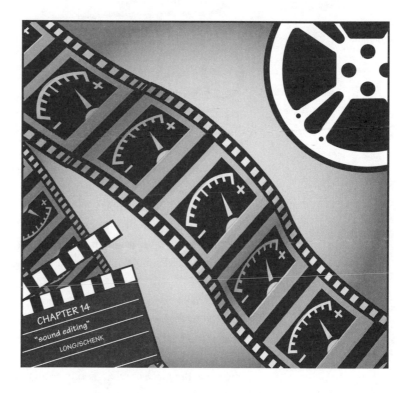

CHAPTER 14
"sound editing"
LONG/SCHENK

IN THIS CHAPTER

- Sounding Off
- Setting Up
- Dedicated Sound Editing Apps
- Editing Sound
- Equalizing Is Your Friend
- Choosing Sound Effects
- Music
- Fix It in the Mix?

Once you've finished your editing and have *locked picture,* you're ready to start editing your sound. Obviously, as you've been editing, you've been cutting the dialog and natural sound in your footage to fit together, but as you probably discovered, things don't always go as planned when shooting. You may have encountered problem areas such as inaudible dialog, unwanted extra sounds, dropouts, or discontinuities in audio quality. And, of course, you probably didn't edit in any sound effects or music, unless they were essential to your picture editing (matching action to a particular piece of music or sound effect, for example).

Sound editing is the process of cleaning up all the mistakes and problems in your sound track, adding music, sound effects, and any re-recorded dialog, and mixing and equalizing the whole thing so that it sounds as good as it possibly can.

Like most production processes, post-production sound has been greatly changed by desktop, digital editing tools. Your NLE probably has basic sound editing tools, multitrack mixing capabilities, equalization, and a selection of special effects filters for altering the sound of your audio. These features can often take the place of what used to require huge rooms full of equipment and engineers. However, as with video editing, there are times when you still might need to go to a professional audio suite to get higher fidelity sound, or to enlist the services of a trained professional.

Sounding Off

As we discussed in Chapter 10, sound often has more of an effect on your final product than does video. While your image can get away with being greatly degraded, bad audio will quickly result in a frustrated, bored audience that most likely won't be able to follow your story.

In addition, good sound editing can help strengthen the effect of a video edit, or cover up bad recording artifacts. A few simple sound effects can ease the transition between pieces of audio shot at different times or on different locations.

But most of all, sound—whether sound effects, music, or sometimes *silence*—can add to, or completely create, the emotional impact in a scene. Can you imagine the shower scene in *Psycho* without the screeching violins? Or the shark in *Jaws* without the rumbling bass notes? And, of course, just try to imagine a sad scene of emotional confession without a sweet, heart-tugging swell of strings beneath it.

Music is often the most obvious sound effect, and we're all familiar with the experience of music providing important pieces of information. For example: A car drives up, a person we've never seen gets out, and the music suddenly becomes very ominous. Cut circus music into the same scene, and the audience will have a very different reaction.

Music is also used to set tone or atmosphere. If you were fortunate enough to see one of the early director's cuts of *Blade Runner*, you saw a movie with an orchestral score, rather than Vangelis' synthesized score. As compelling as the visuals in *Blade Runner* are, laying orchestral music beneath them created a very different atmosphere.

Sometimes, it is the musical score that carries all of the dramatic pacing in a scene. Try watching the last few minutes of *Jurassic Park* with the sound turned down (this works especially well if you've never seen the movie). You may be very surprised to realize how the movie doesn't really have a strong ending. Instead, you're simply led to the ending by the musical score.

When you think of sound effects, you often think of special effect kinds of sounds like laser blasts or explosions. But most of the time, your sound effects will be incredibly normal, everyday sounds. As with music, sound effects can often be used to increase the emotional intensity of a scene. Imagine a scene you've probably watched dozens of times: our hero is distracted as a villain sneaks into the room, slowly raises a gun, cocks the trigger, and prepares to fire. Next time you watch such a scene, pay attention to just how loud that trigger-cocking sound is. Would the scene carry as much impact without the help of this sound effect?

These types of augmented sounds can add a tremendous amount of drama to a scene, and they're a great way to help the audience along through a quieter, dialog-free scene.

Finally, good sound editing can often be used to "dress" a set to make it more believable. If you cut to a shot like the one shown in Figure 3.4 and throw in echoing ambient sounds of Arabic crowd noise, a faraway steamship horn, and some middle-eastern music, your audience will believe that your location really is somewhere in the Middle East.

Like picture editing, the full importance of sound editing can be something that's very easy to overlook. In the rest of this chapter, we'll cover the types of equipment and software you'll need for good sound editing, as well as provide tips for what types of edits you should be making.

Setting Up

Before you begin any sound editing, you need to determine what types of sounds you'll need. Your sound editing process should begin with a screening of the finished edit of your feature. Ideally, you'll want to have your director, editor, sound editor, and music supervisor present at the screening. Your goal is to determine just what sound edits and effects will need to be created.

For each and every scene, you'll need to identify problems, needed sound effects, and how and where your musical track (if any) will be edited into the scene. This process of watching, assessing, and listing your sound requirements is called *spotting*.

Next your editor or sound editor will need to prepare your project file in your NLE. Presumably, you already have at least two tracks: a stereo left and stereo right track from your original camera audio. You may have some additional tracks if you performed any preliminary audio editing or special effects work when you were editing picture. You'll want an additional stereo pair for your music, and another track for special effects. Finally, you might want still another track for ambient *rumble* tracks that will be used to smooth the transitions between different sounds and locations.

By the time you're finished, you may have created many, many more tracks. Depending on how you will output your final project, these tracks will be mixed down to just a few tracks, a process we will detail in Chapter 18.

After the spotting session, you should have a better idea of what sort of work lies ahead of you. Now you can start thinking about what type of equipment and software you'll need to perform your edit.

EDITING SOUND IN YOUR NLE

You will probably be able to perform most edits—audio cuts as well as cross-fades and simple effects—using the sound editing features of your NLE. Most editing packages provide a waveform display that makes it simple to zoom in on a sound to trim and cut, or to eliminate or replace problem areas (Figure 14.1). As we said earlier, editing packages also usually include most of the audio filters you'll need for creating simple effects, and for sweetening audio.

To determine if you'll need any additional sound editing software, you'll want to evaluate your NLE to see if it has certain audio editing essentials. Consult your manual and do some tests with your software to determine if your NLE provides the following:

- **Support for the number of tracks that you'll need.** Most editing packages provide support for dozens of audio tracks. Though your final master may only have four to eight tracks, being able to create extra tracks makes it easier to keep your project organized. If you are using a lower-end editing package that only provides 2 or 4 tracks, then you may need to take your audio elsewhere.

- **Level control for each track.** Any respectable, high-end editing package will have this feature, usually in the form of a simple line across the audio track that can be dragged up and down, and edited with control points. Play with your software's controls to see if you feel comfortable with this interface. You may decide you want to take your audio out to a program that provides a more traditional mixing interface. You may even want to take your audio out to a real mixing console.

- **Can your NLE *scrub* audio?** For some edits, you absolutely have to be able to scrub through your audio very slowly. Scrubbing means that your audio plays at variable speeds as you drag your mouse through the clip. Ideally, you want an audio scrubber that slows the audio down

FIGURE   *Waveform editing in Premiere.*
14.1

when scrubbing, just like you'd hear if you played an analog tape at slow speed, as opposed to a scrubber that plays sampled bits at normal speed (the way a CD player does when you search forward or backward). Good scrubbing capabilities can be essential for making precise cuts, or identifying individual words, sounds, and syllables.

- **Sweetening and correcting filters.** There are a number of filters that you'll want to have to improve the quality of your audio, and to correct problem areas. At the very least, you'll want an equalizer filter to adjust the various frequencies in your sound (Figure 14.2). Ideally, you'll want to have a *Notch* filter of some kind, a good selection of *gates* and *compressors,* specialized filters such as *de-essers,* and click and hum removers.

- **Special effect filters.** For added control, special effects filters such as echoes, reverbs, delays, and flangers can be used for everything from creating special sounds to faking ambience in a recording. Most higher-end NLEs will include a full complement of effects filters (Figure 14.3).

More Is More
If your editor supports Adobe Premiere-compatible plug-ins (or provides support for another plug-in architecture such as AudioSuite or TDM), then you can

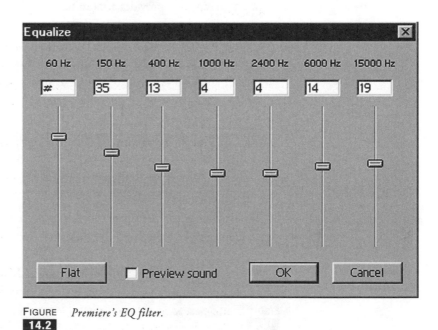

FIGURE   *Premiere's EQ filter.*
14.2

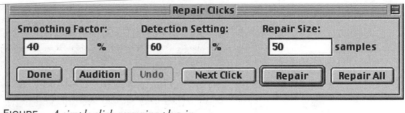

FIGURE
14.3   *A simple click-removing plug-in.*

easily add additional sound effects filters. For many specialized effects, plug-in support can be invaluable. Check out www.dvhandbook.com/audioplugs for a detailed listing of audio plug-ins for different architectures.

Dedicated Sound Editing Apps

If, after looking at your NLE, you decide that you need more audio editing power, then you'll want to consider a dedicated audio editing application. Most NLEs only let you edit between individual frames, so if you need to make *very* precise edits, such as an edit at an interval that's smaller than a single frame, or 1/30th of a second, you'll need to move your audio out of your NLE and into a dedicated app.

Like picture editing, audio editing can be a very tactile process. Feeling where a cut should fall, or "riding" a level or EQ adjustment, are processes where you often want a fine level of hands-on control. If you prefer such controls to a mouse-driven audio editing interface, then you should consider moving your audio to an application that provides better on-screen controls (Figures 14.4 and 14.5), or even hardware consoles that can be attached to your computer .

Dedicated audio editors provide a number of other powerful features, such as the ability to define and label *regions* in an audio track. This makes it very simple to label what each part of an audio waveform is, making it easier to spot locations for additional edits.

To select a digital audio application, you'll want to consider many of the same questions introduced earlier. In addition, look for the following:

- **Can the app open a QuickTime movie?** Many audio editors let you open a QuickTime movie and perform edits directly onto their audio tracks. In addition, being able to watch your video while editing your audio makes many audio processes much simpler.

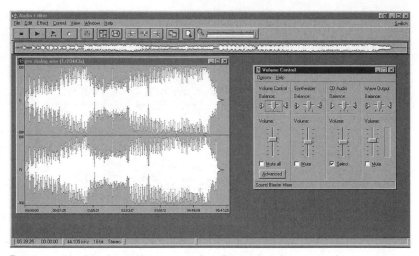

FIGURE
14.4   *Ulead Media Studio Pro provides robust audio editing controls.*

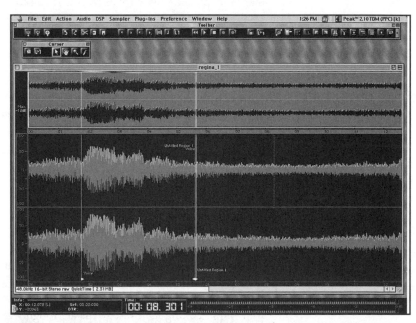

FIGURE
14.5   *While Bias' Peak provides a full-featured, stand-alone audio editing environment.*

- **Does the app support the timecode you are using?** Though timecode is not essential for performing outboard edits on small pieces of your audio, you'll need it if you want to edit all your sound on a different software app or system (see the "Moving Your Audio" sidebar).
- **Destructive or non-destructive?** Many higher-end audio applications can perform *non-destructive editing*. These programs are able to perform edits and effects without altering your original data, making it easy and safe to try many complex edits without having to work on space-wasting copies of your audio.
- **Editing in real-time.** For easier editing, you'll want an application that can apply effects in real-time. When applying subtle EQ changes, for example, it's preferable to have your audio editor continuously loop and play the sound so that you can hear changes as you make adjustments. Many applications can perform simple stereo effects in real-time. For other effects, and for real-time processing of additional tracks, you'll need a system with special hardware.
- **Do you have room for more hardware?** If you do opt for a system with special hardware, make sure you have enough slots in your computer to support more expansion cards.

Obviously, if you're not going to be performing your audio edits yourself, then software may not be a concern. If you will be using a professional audio house to perform your final audio edit, or if your sound editor has his or her own audio hardware, then you will need to find out how you need to deliver your audio. You should also plan on delivering *all* of your original audio material. That is, all of your videotapes if you shot sync sound, and all of your original audio tapes if you shot non-sync sound (actually, you'll want to deliver clones of your tapes). There's no telling what your sound editor may need in the way of audio. Whether it's re-recording a sound, or building an entirely new sound from other material on your tapes, to do his or her job well, he or she will need all of your source material.

AUDIO HARDWARE

Your sound editing hardware needs are roughly akin to your regular editing needs, though typically at a smaller scale. Though you can get away with performing all of your edits in software, you may want special hardware to augment the process.

Moving Your Audio

Obviously, if you're going to edit your audio outside of your NLE, you'll need to move your audio.

If you need to perform a quick fix on a short, isolated piece of sound, then you can simply export your audio from your NLE in whatever format your sound app requires (AIFF, .wav, QuickTime, etc.). Be sure to export at full-quality so that the sound editor has a high-quality sound signal to work with. Also, no matter how you manipulate the piece of audio, you must take care to maintain the *frame rate* (usually 29.97 fps) and the *audio sampling rate* (44.1 or 48 kHz). This ensures that you'll be able to import the new treated audio back into your NLE without losing sync.

If you want to re-edit all of the sound in your entire project, the easiest way to take it out is by outputting *split audio tracks* to digital tape (DAT, DV, Digibeta, DA88, etc.). Assuming you've got a locked cut of your picture, you'll have some tracks of sound that you edited along with the picture. By outputting each track to a distinct channel on digital tape, and then capturing each track separately in your sound editing app, you'll be able to start polishing the sound with a decent rough cut of the sound already in place. You may need to use more than one tape to get all of your tracks moved, and those tapes will need timecode that matches the timecode in your NLE. If the digital tape format you're using isn't capable of recording timecode, then each track will need to have sync marks, or *2-pops* that match the countdown on your locked picture. 2-pops are a single frame of 60Hz audio reference tone cut into the countdown at the same frame that the two second counter appears on screen. Timecode and 2-pops are absolute necessities for this kind of work—losing sync for an entire project is *one of the worst things that can happen in post*.

If you didn't capture high-quality audio in your NLE, or if you just want to start over with clean audio, you can use EDLs to reconstruct your sequence. You'll need a high-end sound editing software and hardware that supports timecode and EDLs. Creating an EDL is covered in detail in Chapter 18—if you're creating an EDL for audio only, be sure to talk to your sound editor to make sure you include all the necessary information in the EDL.

High-end sound editing apps like ProTools are designed to work with either a low-res capture or a hardware-synched videotape version of the locked picture cut. Whether you choose split track outputs or an EDL, you'll also need to output a viewing copy of your locked picture sequence with a countdown, including a 2-pop, and preferably with visible timecode. When you're done editing the sound, you can reunite the polished audio with the final video master on tape or in your NLE. (More about final mixes and audio outputs in Chapter 18.) As we mentioned earlier, it's crucial that you maintain the same frame rate and audio sampling ratio that you used in your NLE if you want your project to stay in sync.

Audio Deck

If you want to take your audio out of your computer for editing in a studio, then you'll need some place to put it. Your best option is to record to a DAT or DA88, as most studios will be set up for those formats. You could also, however, dump your audio out to a DV tape, and take your deck and tape to a studio. There, your audio could be bumped to DAT or DA88 for editing.

Mixers

If you're more comfortable with sliders and knobs than with a mouse, then you may want a mixing board for mixing and balancing your tracks. Though you might have used a simple mic mixer or 4-track mixing board during your shoot, you'll probably want a beefier mixing board for your post-production editing.

Microphones

Obviously, if you end up needing to re-record dialog, or to record sound effects on location, you'll need microphones. For voice-overs and other dialog recording, your best option will be a good handheld mic. Whether you're choosing to record directly into your computer, or recording into a tape deck, be sure you have the necessary cables and connectors to hook up your mic.

SOUND EFFECT SOURCES

Once you start editing, you'll need a number of different audio sources at your disposal. In addition to your original audio tapes, you'll probably end up recording extra sounds on your own (called *wild sounds*). You may also want to invest in a sound effects library. Companies like Sound Ideas provide vast, detailed collections of high-quality pre-recorded sounds. These can be essential tools for adding effects and ambience to your audio tracks. (See www.dvhandbook.com/audio.) If you're editing in a studio or post-production facility, they may have a sound effects library you can use.

Foley is the process of recording special ambient effects in real-time while watching your picture. Door slams, footsteps, pouring water, clinking dinnerware, and all sorts of other "everyday" sounds that may not have been recorded during your shoot can be added by a *foley artist*. Foley work is usually done on a special stage equipped with props, cars, surfaces, and materials.

Your mic may have picked up many ambient sounds while you were recording. Depending on the nature of your mic, though, these sounds may have varying degrees of quality, tone, and presence. If you used a very directional mic to shoot footage of a woman getting out of a car, dropping her keys, picking them up, and closing the card door, some of the sounds may sound too far away or muffled since they were out of the primary field of the microphone. Foley sounds are an easy way to bring these sounds forward to increase the audience's involvement in the scene.

The advantage of adding sound effects with foley work (rather than editing sounds from a sound effects library) is that a good foley artist can often do all of the sounds for one shot in a single take. In addition to being faster than editing sounds separately, foley sounds will use fewer tracks in your mix.

With a good mic and a lot of care, you can do simple foley work on your own, though if a scene is very dependent on good foley sounds, you'll probably want to go to a professional foley studio.

Editing Sound

Once your equipment is in place, it's time to start working your way through the list of sound edits that you created during your spotting session. In addition to the obvious sound effects—gunshots, screams, footsteps, howling wind, etc.—and the questions of mood, atmosphere, and drama that we discussed earlier, there are a number of other sound edits that might be on your list. Following are all things you should look for when spotting and editing:

Unintelligible Dialog

This may seem an obvious concern, but we're going to state it anyway. Remember that *you* already know what your actors are saying. Whether you wrote, directed, or edited (or did all three jobs), you've probably heard each line hundreds of times. Consequently, you might be more forgiving of a mumbled or quiet line of dialog. Pay close attention to your character's speech and make sure that it is clear and intelligible. If it's not, consider using EQ (more on this later), boosting the level, or using a different take (either audio, or both audio and video). As a last resort, you can always bring the actor in to re-record or "loop" his or her dialog (more on this later, also).

Changes in Tone

Does the overall audio quality change from one edit to another? Changes in tone can result from changes in microphone placement, changes in location, changes in ambient sound, or just weird "acts of God" that you may not be able to explain. Hopefully, you recorded some room tone at your locations.

A change in tone can often be masked by fading from one audio source to the next to mask the change in sound quality. A bed of room tone, ambient sound, or music can further conceal this "edit" (Figure 14.6).

Is There Extraneous Noise in the Shot?

When shooting on location, it can often be difficult to keep a quiet, controlled set. If there's extra, distracting noise—a loud conversation or music playing, for example—see if you can mask these sounds by placing sound or music effects that will keep your audience focused on your action.

Remember: The audience will pay attention to the things you lead them to. Just as you can brighten the foreground of your video to draw attention to your subject, you can "brighten" the foreground of your audio to ensure your audience listens in the right "direction."

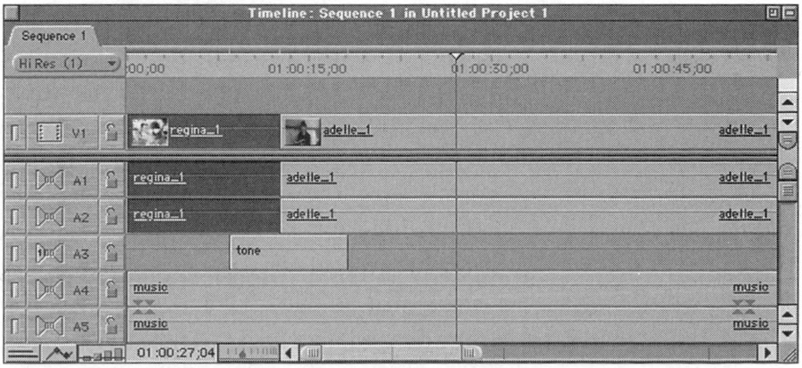

FIGURE 14.6   *To improve sounds with mismatched tone, we can apply a bed of room tone. A cross-dissolve between the two bad tracks might further improve things.*

Are There Bad Video Edits That Can Be Reinforced with Audio?

Sometimes, a video edit with weak motivation can be reinforced with a good strong sound. The easiest way to reinforce an edit is to place a beat of music at that location. The rhythm of your music track will carry through to the audience's visual sense. If you're using pre-recorded, or "canned," music, consider adjusting the start of the music so that a strong beat falls on your weak edit. If you're working with an original score, perhaps your composer can suggest a change in music.

In addition to music, weak edits can be reinforced with an off-camera sound effect. A breaking window, for example, will provide plenty of motivation for a cut to another shot.

Is There Bad Audio?

There are any number of technical problems that can lead to corrupted audio, from a boom operator bumping the mic, to a short in a cable, to interference with electrical fields. For some thumps and bumps on the microphone, you can usually just bring the level of the audio down or cut it out. Hopefully, there's no dialog or other important sounds during those scenes. If there are, you may need to re-record those audio elements. As we'll see later, other troubles can be corrected through EQ adjustments.

The clicks and pops that can result from a short in a cable are usually easy to fix because they're brief. Even if a click falls over dialog, removing it usually won't affect the quality of your subject. Remember that, as with bumps, when you remove a click or pop you don't want to delete it, or use a "close gap" command, as this will shorten your sound and throw your sound and video out of sync. Instead, use a "lift" command if your NLE allows, or select the area and use a silence command to reduce the selected area to nothing, or copy an appropriate length of room tone into the selected area.

If you have a hum in your audio, then your life might have just gotten very complicated. Some hums are fairly easy to fix and can be removed with a simple notch filter. Fluorescent lights and some electrical sources can sometimes create a 60 Hz hum in your audio. Setting a notch filter to remove all the sounds at 60 Hz can frequently eliminate or reduce a hum. Note that hums sometimes produce harmonic hums that also need to be removed. You can remove these with separate notch filters, or use a special hum remover that automatically notches harmonics.

Some hums may be too "dirty" (that is, they fall over too much of the audio spectrum) to be removed. In most cases, looping your audio and rebuilding your sound track is your only option.

If your hum is slight, you can often reduce or eliminate it with a simple EQ filter.

Are There Vocal Problems You Need to Correct?

While flubbed lines can often be fixed by re-recording or pulling audio from alternate takes, other vocal problems may require special filtering. For example, if an actor's dialog has loud, shushing "s" sounds, you can often correct these with a "de-essing" filter or with an EQ adjustment.

DIALOG EDITING

When you edited your picture you, obviously, cut together your dialog as well. However, you'll need to do a fair amount of editing to get your dialog organized so that it can be easily adjusted and corrected, and to prepare it for the final mix.

Checkerboarding is the process of arranging your dialog tracks so that one voice can be easily adjusted and corrected. Your goal is to separate different speakers onto different tracks so that you can manipulate and correct their dialog with as few separate actions as possible. For example, if you've decided that all of your lead actor's dialog needs a slight EQ adjustment, having checkerboarded audio will make it simple to apply a single EQ filter to all of your actor's speech.

It's called checkerboarding (or *splitting tracks*) because, as you begin to separate different speakers, your audio tracks will begin to have a "checkerboard" appearance as can be seen in Figure 14.7.

You won't necessarily separate out every single voice or even every occurrence of a particular speaker. Though you might be trying to split out a particular actor, splitting tracks during short lines or overlapping dialog may not be worth the trouble. In addition to splitting up your dialog, you'll also need to move all of the sound effects recorded during your production onto their own track.

In an NLE, the easiest way to split tracks is simply to select the relevant portions of the sound track and copy and paste them to a new track. Remember not to cut, or you'll throw the remaining audio out of sync. Remember also

FIGURE
14.7 *Checkerboarded dialog editing.*

that you'll be copying stereo information—two tracks—for each actor. When you've copied all of your data into the appropriate tracks, you can delete your original audio tracks.

This is where the 30 to 60 seconds of *room tone* that you recorded during production will come into play. You'll use room tone to smooth the differences between different speakers, to fill silent areas and to improve the sense of ambient space in your audio. If you didn't record room tone, then you can try to build up a sample of room tone by cutting and pasting together quiet moments from your original audio track.

ADR

Automatic dialog replacement is used to replace badly recorded sound, fix a muffed line, or insert dialog that could not be recorded on location. If you didn't record dialog during your shoot, ADR is where you will "dub" your film.

In a professional ADR facility, a projector or deck shows the scene to be re-recorded, then immediately re-winds and plays the scene again (without audio) and the new dialog is recorded. Sometimes, a continuous "loop" of the scene is shown; hence the term "looping."

The actor is usually cued with a series of regular beeps that count down to the start of recording. Their goal is to match their vocal performance to what they just saw on-screen.

Though you might be tempted to rely on re-recording—you may think it easier than trying to get things correct on-set—be warned that getting good ADR is hard work. First, you'll need to try to match the tone and quality of the original recording. Everything from mic selection and mic placement to the qualities of the recording room will affect the tone of your recording. As if getting the actor to match his voice to the lip movements recorded on-screen isn't difficult enough, consider also that the actor's performance will probably be at a somewhat different energy and emotional level than what was originally shot. Outside of the scene, with no actors, build-up, or motivation, it can be difficult for an actor to achieve the same performance quality that he or she delivered on-set.

ADR works best on long shots because it's easier to see sync problems on close-ups. An example of a scene that could benefit from ADR is a long shot of two people having a conversation near a freeway. The production sound will be very bad due to the noise from the freeway. Since the actors are far away, the dialogue can be easily replaced, and perfect sync isn't necessary.

If you have a product that supports TDM or AudioSuite plug-ins, then you can use Synchro Arts VocAlign to automatically stretch or compress a re-recorded piece of dialog to match the original production recording. If this sounds impossibly amazing, it is. But it works! If your feature requires a lot of accurate ADR, VocAlign is worth the money.

Non-Dialog ADR

Other looping jobs will be simpler. Voice-overs (such as those used in a documentary, or in a flashback scene in a dramatic feature) as well as other vocal sound effects will be recorded during your ADR sessions.

For example, if you shot a restaurant scene with a silent background (to better record the voices of your actors), ADR is the time when you will bring in people to fill in the sounds of the other restaurant patrons. (*Walla* is the term for the mumbling, unrecognizable din of a crowd of people.) But remember, if you can, try to get away with cheating wild audio instead of paying for an ADR session.

Equalizing Is Your Friend

If your home stereo has controls for adjusting bass and treble, then you're already familiar with a very simple form of equalizing (or *eq*). An equalizer lets you control the loudness of different parts of the sound spectrum, called frequencies. For example, if you want to add some resonance to a voice, you might choose to use an EQ adjustment to boost the bass frequencies in the sound. In a sense, an equalizer is just a very refined volume control that allows you to make certain frequencies of sound louder or softer.

A *graphic equalizer* provides sliders for adjusting the volume of specific frequencies, as measured in Hertz (Hz). Move a slider up and the sounds within that frequency will get louder; move it down and they will get softer. It's important to remember that each slider represents a point on a curve. By moving the sliders, you are re-shaping the curve. In other words, frequencies *around* the slider will be affected also (Figure 14.8).

The best way to learn how to use EQ is to just experiment, ideally with an editor or NLE that provides real-time filtering. Consider using an EQ filter in the following situations:

- **Sweetening or adding richness.** With a simple boost to the low or lower mid-range, you can add presence and richness to a voice. Don't add too much, though, or you'll end up with a muffled sound.
- **Making speech more intelligible.** Raising the mid-range frequencies (2000 Hz, or 2 *kHz*) and reducing frequencies below 100 Hz will frequently make for clearer dialog.
- **Wind and mic bumps.** Wind and microphone noise (such as the low rumble noises caused by poor mic handling) can be minimized by reducing the low frequencies (60–120 Hz)

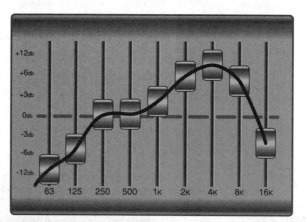

 FIGURE
14.8   *The frequencies between the slider controls on your equalizer are connected by a curve. So, adjusting one frequency will shift the frequencies in between. Don't expect to be able to adjust* only *the frequencies on each slider.*

- **Reducing hiss, and other high-frequency sounds.** Just as you can eliminate low-frequency rumbles, you can also eliminate tape hiss and other high-frequency sounds by lowering frequencies above 5 kHz.
- **Simulating audio sources.** You can use EQ to simulate the sound of a voice on a telephone, or music from a car radio by rolling off the appropriate frequencies. For telephone voice, boost everything between 400 and 2000 Hz and lower everything else. The same effect can be used to simulate a low-quality car radio, by using less extreme values. In other words, keep more of the high and low end than you would for a telephone effect (Figure 14.9 and 14.10).

Note that to perform good EQ adjustments, you need to be sure you're listening to your audio on speakers with a wide dynamic range. If you're using speakers with a poor response at one end of the audio spectrum, you'll neither be able to hear or correct troubles.

Mixing Boards
If you're going to do a lot of equalizing, it may be faster to EQ your audio as you capture it by running it through a hardware mixing board, like the ones shown in Figure 11.9. Similarly, if you want to add an overall EQ to your project when you output, a mixing board is the fastest way to do this.

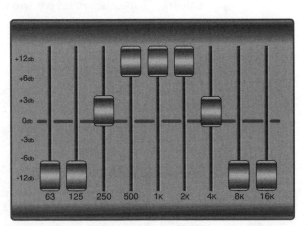

 FIGURE
14.9   *With some simple EQ adjustments, you can easily simulate the sound of a voice coming through a telephone . . .*

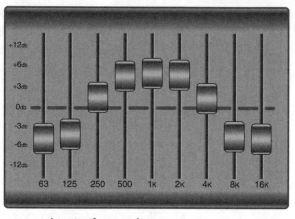

FIGURE   *. . . or sound coming from a radio or car stereo.*
14.10

SPECIAL FILTERS

As with video, audio editing has been greatly changed by the advent of digital editing tools. There are a number of specialized applications and plug-ins that can help you fix any number of problems.

Digidesign's DINR

The Digidesign Intelligent Noise Reduction plug-in for TDM or AudioSuite systems can be used for removing any kind of noise from a recording. Tape hiss, rumbling air conditioners, or gnarly hums can all be automatically eliminated. If a bad noise artifact has wrecked some or all of your sound, DINR may be able to save your footage, or prevent an expensive ADR session.

Digidesign's Aural Exciter

Aural Exciter is an excellent tool for increasing the intelligibility of voices in your audio tracks. In addition, Aural Exciter provides powerful features for bringing muddled sounds into the foreground.

Digidesign Sound Replacer

Sound Replacer does just what it says, it replaces sounds already in a mix. For example, if you mix down your audio and then decide that the doorknob foley isn't quite right, you might be able to use Sound Replacer to reach into your mix and replace the doorknob sound with something else.

Arboretum Ionizer

Similar to DINR, another excellent noise reduction plug-in with extra special effects and pre-set functions for cleaning field recordings and telephone interviews.

Special Effects

For creating new sounds, embellishing old sounds, and creating special effects, there is a huge assortment of plug-ins that do everything from simulating doppler effect to changing pitch and tone, to simulating the sounds of instruments and machinery. For an up-to-the-minute list of hot audio plug-in vendors and cool new effects, check out www.dvhandbook.com/audio.

Choosing Sound Effects

Your choice of what to use for a particular sound effect will weigh greatly on the effect of the scene. For example, if a scene needs the sound of a dog barking in the distance, you'll get a very different effect if you choose to use a Chihuahua or a Doberman. Depending on the tone of the scene, one may be a much better choice.

Going with the choice that is less obvious can often have very serendipitous results. Don't hesitate to try a number of different ideas, including ones that might initially sound strange. For example, consider the sound of the tornadoes in the movie *Twister*. Rather than stick with simple sounds of storm and flying debris, the editors added guttural, snarling, sucking sounds that give the twisters an almost conscious, animal-like menace.

Don't hesitate to create your own sound effects. A good mic and some simple field recording equipment can help you get good source material. In addition to getting sounds that exactly match the pacing and length of your video, you may come up with very original sounds. Consider the laser blasts from *Star Wars*. Originally created by banging on the tail ends of power lines, these sources were masterfully manipulated into high-tech, futuristic effects.

When adding any type of effect, don't expect it to be perfect as soon as you drop it in. Most likely, you'll have to go through a lot of trial and error. There are no rules or numbers you can follow for these processes. Instead, follow your ear. It's the best judge of what sounds good.

To improve and blend in a sound effect, remember that you have all of the following to work with:

- **Levels** Make sure the level of the sound matches the intensity of what's on the screen. A small handgun shouldn't sound like a cannon, after all.
- **EQ and effects** You can use EQ to improve the quality of your sound effect and to try to separate it from other sounds in your mix. Other effects can be added to match the sound effect to its surroundings. The sound of dropping a bowling ball in a cathedral, for example, will require a sound with a lot more reverb and echo, than the sound of dropping a bowling ball in a 7-11.
- **The mix** You might be able to improve your sound effect by adjusting other tracks in your mix. Maybe it's not that your airplane sound effect is too quiet; perhaps your dialog is too loud. Play with your entire mix when editing in a sound effect.

Music

As we discussed earlier, music can be used for everything from helping to establish a sense of location, to setting a mood, to embellishing an atmosphere. You'll probably spend a lot of time considering and tweaking the music in your production, and the nature of the tweaking will depend largely on the source of your music.

Typically, there are two types of music used in a feature: the music that *underscores* the action, and the *source* music that is meant to sound like it's coming from a source in your scene (radio, television, singer, etc.).

Most movies use a combination of original music composed specifically for the project, and pre-recorded music that is licensed from an artist and publisher. Determining how much of each to use will depend on your project and the nature of the mood you are trying to create.

An original score can serve to bind themes and characters together throughout your feature. Through the use of repeating motifs and recurring melodies, a well-written score can provide a lot of narrative structure and continuity.

There are a number of reasons why you might choose to use pre-recorded material. Your characters might be listening to a piece of music, for example, or perhaps you've found a song that simply serves the scene better than your original score. Finally, certain songs, particularly music from a particular period, can do a great job of enhancing the authenticity of your scene.

Such pre-recorded material can also be mixed and layered on *top of* your original score. In addition to creating an interesting "soundscape," pulling a song out of the scene and into the score can be an effective way to move a scene forward, and join one character's action to something else in the movie.

License to Play

When licensing music for use in a film, you'll most likely have to pay a hefty fee. You'll also need to secure the rights, both to the music and to the particular recording that you want to use. Often the cheapest solution is to acquire the "performing rights," which means you can hire a band to replicate the song. Whatever your needs, it's really best to consult an entertainment lawyer for these sorts of things, and be sure to do so early on in your production. Otherwise, you could very easily end up with a movie that can't be distributed.

Most movies have two people involved in selecting and arranging music. A *composer* writes the original music, while the *music supervisor* selects any pre-recorded material. Often, it is the music supervisor who will select a composer and help guide him or her through the creation of the music.

When you've finished editing your picture, you'll want to sit down and have a screening with your music supervisor or composer and discuss any ideas that you might have about appropriate music. In some cases, you might simply discuss what sort of feeling or emotion you're hoping to convey.

You may have already chosen some music to use as "scratch audio" during your editing process. You can use this to suggest music that you feel is appropriate. However, it's often better to simply give your music supervisor some direction and see what he or she can come up with. He or she may arrive at ideas that you had never considered, but that works perfectly. One problem with using scratch audio is that it's very easy to get attached to it. Be careful not to get too enamoured of a piece of music that you can't afford to license!

Also, don't use scratch music that you would never be able to afford to produce. In other words, if you can't afford to pay for a full orchestra (or to license an orchestral recording), don't use any orchestral music in your scratch audio.

Music Libraries

Just as there are tons of stock footage houses and sound effects CDs out there, there are lots of companies that specialize in selling music libraries on CD. With some, you pay a largish sum for the CD itself ($200 or so), and that purchase includes the license to use the tracks on the CD. Others charge per track and per minute. The quality and variety of music available on library collections has improved greatly over the last 10 years.

In addition to ideas about mood and tone, you may need to give your music supervisor or composer a *cue list* showing exactly what pieces of music are needed, and whether or not they have specific timings. If there are musical events that need to happen at particular times (a dramatic organ sting when the villain enters, for example), then these will be listed on your cue sheet.

TIP

The Sound of Silence

Don't forget about the power of silence. Not only is silence sometimes more effective than music, it often makes the preceding and following music more powerful. Don't feel pressured to fill every moment with sound and music. Do as much experimenting with no music as with music.

Your music supervisor and composer will usually present you with a number of options for each section of music in your project. You can take these to your editor and see how they work. At this point, your editor or sound designer may have suggestions of how to mix different pieces of music together, or how to mix music with natural sound, or how to apply reverb or other atmospheric effects to better fit the music to the action and mood.

Finding a Composer

There are a number of resources for contacting and auditioning composers and music supervisors. You can see a list of these resources at `www.dvhand-book.com/music`.

Whoever does the work of choosing a composer may be tempted to select someone simply on the basis of the composer's music. This may not be the best criterion. Certainly you want to consider a composer's musical tastes and skill, but simply listening to a demo reel gives you no idea of how well the music served as a score. You will also get no idea of how well you can communicate with the composer, or how tuned in he or she might be to the themes and ideas within your piece.

Before you make any decisions, you'll need to show your picture to the composer, discuss ideas, and see how well you can work together.

Today, composers are typically given about six weeks to write a score. While most big-budget films devote 1.5 to 2.5 percent of their budget to a score, low-budget films can often come in much lower. If the composer likes your work, he or she may be willing to work for much less.

In addition to paying your composer, you may need to pay the musicians required to record the piece. If you were imagining a full orchestral score, remember that you'll have to pay all the people in said orchestra. Many composers can cut production costs by using synthesized instruments, or synthe-sizers augmented with a few acoustic instruments. You'll need to discuss pro-duction costs with your composer, and try to determine what sort of music you can afford to record.

Do It Yourself

If you're thinking that you might like to try your hand at composing your own score—or maybe you have some friends who you think could do a good job—remember that composing for the screen is not as simple as just sitting down and writing a song. Not only do you have to compose to achieve a particular narrative or emotional goal, but also, depending on the edits of your scene, you may need to compose with the intent of having certain movements, motifs, or beats occur at a particular time.

In addition, you'll need to compose with the understanding that your music will be competing with other sounds. Remember, your score is meant to complement and assist in the storytelling process. When composing, make sure that you are supporting the other audio in the scene. For example, a scene with a lot of young children talking on a busy playground would not be well-served by lyrical, high-pitched violin music, as the violins might be too close to the timbre of children's voices. When mixed with the natural sound, your music would only serve to muddle the sound and make the scene less intelligible.

Fix It in the Mix?

As we'll discuss in Chapter 18, when you perform your final output to tape or film, you will also perform a final, finished mix. Though your final mix will give you the chance to balance your audio levels, and equalize your tracks, don't think that you can just wait and fix any audio problems then. It's best to try to get your audio as well-mixed as possible during your sound editing. This will make it easier to identify any problems with your audio, and will make for a shorter (and possibly less-expensive) mixing session when you create your final output.

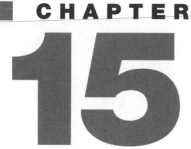

CHAPTER
15

Color Correction

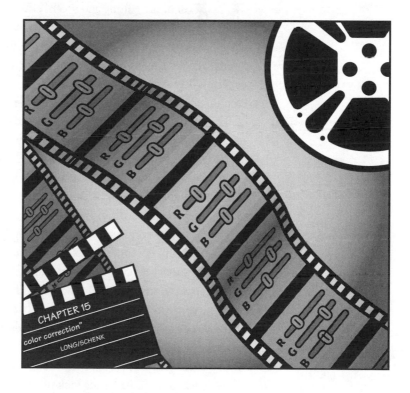

CHAPTER 15
color correction"
LONG/SCHENK

337

IN THIS CHAPTER

- To Compress, or Not to Conpress
- Color Correction
- Tutorial: Correcting White Balance
- Put a Clamp on It!
- Correcting Color for Film

Most of the editing and special effects packages that we've mentioned so far provide powerful tools for correcting and changing the color in your video. Whether you use these tools for artistic reasons—adding more blue to an image to strike a tone—or for more practical concerns—correcting bad white balance—an understanding of the color correction features of your software is invaluable.

Though we've chosen to discuss this topic *after* the chapters on editing, it's important to understand that color correction—as well as the special effects covered in the next two chapters—will usually be performed *during* your editing process. When working on a digital project, most special effects are not something that you apply to a finished, edited project. Rather, they are created and added during the editing cycle.

For most color correction tasks, you'll simply use filters and controls inside your editing app. For more complex corrections, and also for the type of composites and special effects we'll introduce in Chapters 16 and 17, you'll use specialized applications such as Adobe After Effects. Consequently, you'll often find yourself switching back and forth between programs as you process and alter a clip in an effects package, and then edit that clip into a sequence using your editing program.

In this chapter, we'll tell you how to use the color correction tools in your editing package to improve the look of your video, as well as to fix problems that may have occurred during shooting.

To Compress, Or Not to Compress

Before we start talking about manipulating the image, it's important to consider some workflow issues that will help you both preserve the highest-quality image and ensure that you make the most efficient use of your disk space.

Think about the following scenario: You're editing a low-budget sci-fi epic about extra-terrestrial book authors who invade the Earth and begin boring everyone to death by reading detailed digital video specifications at them. You have a 45-second long edited sequence of the Grand Canyon. At 10 seconds into this segment, you want to composite an animation of a flying saucer over the edited footage of the Grand Canyon. The saucer will take about 10 seconds to majestically descend into the Grand Canyon and will be out of site by 20 seconds into the clip (Figure 15.1).

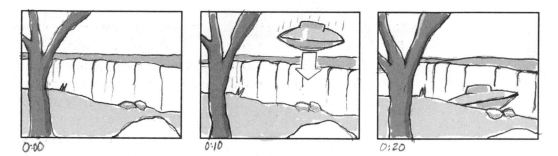

FIGURE
15.1   *With good storyboards, we can better determine which parts of a clip are required for an effect.*

Though you're editing in Adobe Premiere, you plan on performing the composite of the spaceship using Adobe After Effects. So, you'll need to export footage from Premiere, import it into After Effects, perform the composite, and then bring the composited final footage back into Premiere. Simple, right?

Not necessarily. Though people often tout digital video's "generation-less" editing, the fact is that if you're not careful when moving video files back and forth between programs, you *will* see a loss of quality. Remember that when it comes out of your camera, digital video has already been compressed by the camera. Like the JPEG compression that is used in graphics files on the Web, DV compression is *lossy;* that is, image quality is lost when the video is compressed. Compressing it again results in more loss of quality.

(See Color Plate 11 for examples of overcompression.)

Every time you import a DV clip into an editing or effects program, the clip is decompressed and displayed on your screen. If you perform any functions that alter the image—cropping, applying filters, correcting color, compositing, etc.—then the computer must calculate new pixels and recompress the footage when you go back out to tape or write a DV file to your hard drive. If you're performing cuts-only editing with no effects, then the computer simply copies the original footage back to tape in the new order that you've specified. No re-compression occurs (Figure 15.2).

So, when moving your files between programs, you want to be sure that you don't expose the footage to another round of lossy compression. However, to save disk space, you will want to perform some kind of *lossless* compression on

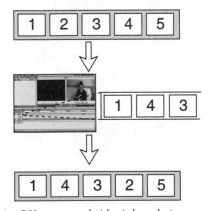

FIGURE
15.2a   *When editing DV, compressed video is brought into your computer. With your editing software, you might reorder the scenes in your video. When you output to a file or tape, the computer simply rearranges the compressed video into your specified order.*

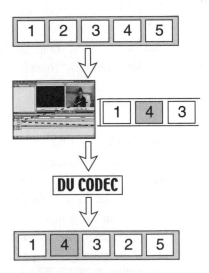

FIGURE
15.2b   *But, if you perform an operation that alters the contents of the video image, then the computer will have to recompress that footage before outputting. To much recompression, and your image quality will noticably degrade.*

clips that you move between programs. In the interest of storage and processor efficiency, it's important to do a little planning.

Though our Grand Canyon sequence in the preceding example lasts 45 seconds, the section where the spaceship will be seen is only 10 seconds long. Therefore, rather than move the whole 45 seconds into our compositing program, it's better to move only the 10 seconds that matter. In general, most effects shots are very short—a few seconds here, a few frames there—so you'll be able to get away with moving very short clips between your effects and editing packages.

In the preceding example, our compositing work will proceed as follows:

1. First, we find the 10 seconds of footage that we need for our composite.
2. This footage is marked for output. In most editing programs, you do this by setting special In and Out points in your timeline that denote which section of a sequence will be rendered and output.
3. Next, we output the selected video. In our output settings we'll select the QuickTime *Animation* codec as our compressor. The Animation codec is lossless, but creates substantially larger files than the DV codec. Because the Animation codec doesn't compress as much as the DV codec, being selective about the footage you work with will save you a lot of disk space (Figure 15.3).

FIGURE
15.3   *No matter what application you're exporting video from, at some point you will be given a choice of which QuickTime codec to use for compression. When moving between applications, use a lossless codec like Animation.*

4. The resulting 10-second clip will be imported into After Effects. There, we will perform our composite.

5. In After Effects, we'll render our finished composite. Again, we'll choose the Animation codec when saving, to ensure the highest quality.

6. Now we'll import the new, composited, animation-compressed clip into Premiere and edit it into our sequence, replacing the footage that was there before. When we create our final output, this new clip will be compressed with our DV codec, but as this is just one extra level of compression, we probably won't see a difference.

In the interest of staying organized, when naming new files—such as composites and other effect clips—use the same naming conventions that you used when you digitized your footage

Be aware that even if you are creating effects within your editing package, there is a chance that you could expose the clip to more than one level of compression. Say you have applied a color correction to some video in a sequence. Later, you decide to nest that sequence inside *another* sequence, and apply a sharpening filter to the whole thing. Depending on how your editing software works, there's a chance that this will cause your nested piece of video to be compressed twice. Study your software's manual for a better understanding to determine the order in which filters are applied. Ideally, you want to be sure that you only pass your video through one round of filter application (and, consequently, one round of compression).

Note that if you're using an analog compression system to import your video, you still need to worry about recompression. Remember, the only difference is that your digitizing card is performing the initial compression rather than your camera. As with DV, make certain you don't recompress more than you have to before going back out to tape.

When moving files between apps, you'll also want to be sure that you *always* use the same frame size and frame rate. Note that some applications will default to 30 fps rather than 29.97. The only time you should render to a different size or time base is when you are intentionally trying to shrink your movie for output to the Web or other low-bandwidth medium.

Making Space

If disk space is of critical concern, then it may not be practical to have huge, Animation-compressed files laying around your hard drive. If you find yourself in

this situation and need to free up some space, consider converting your Anima-tion-compressed files to DV-compressed files by simply printing the Animation-compressed footage out to tape. You can then reimport the footage and treat it like any other captured DV footage. However, depending on what you have planned for the rest of your post-production, such a process may not be advisable as it will introduce an extra round of compression.

Color Correction

At its best, a DV camera can shoot beautiful images with nicely saturated, ac-curate colors. At its worst, a DV camera can shoot horribly ugly images with unflattering casts of green or red. Fortunately, most DV cameras err more to ward the beautiful side but, through operator error or plain old bad shooting conditions, at some point you're probably going to need to adjust the color in your footage.

It might not always be bad news that sends you to the color controls of your editing application. Often, you'll want to perform color adjustments for more artistic reasons. Perhaps you want to amp up the reds or blues in an image to strike a certain emotional tone. Or maybe you simply like certain colors more than others. Whatever the reason, color correction tools will be some of the most-used functions in your editing program.

Though all editing packages include some type of color correction, the controls for these features vary widely. In this section, we're going to discuss when and how to use color correction to solve certain problems. Though some tutorials and examples may center around certain products, we have presented our steps in a generic, conceptual fashion that should make it easy to translate the steps to other products.

TIP

Use That NTSC Monitor!
Video (whether NTSC or PAL) can't display as many colors as your computer can so the image on your computer is not a very good reference to use when correct-ing or adjusting color. Be sure you have an NTSC monitor connected to your sys-tem, and use that as a reference when making any change that alters the video image. Unfortunately, no two monitors are the same, but by calibrating your NTSC monitor with standard color bars, you can at least get it close to an ac-cepted standard. www.dvhandbook.com/calibration.

CORRECTING BAD WHITE BALANCE

As we discussed in Chapter 9, properly white-balancing your camera before shooting is essential to getting good color. Unfortunately, there are a number of reasons that a camera's white balance can go wrong. A bad auto white balance function can often perform inaccurate—or outright bad—white balancing, and can sometimes change white balance in the middle of a shot. Even if you're manually white balancing, mixed lighting situations—tungsten lights in a sun-filled room, for example—can yield troublesome results.

Bad white balance can lead to everything from a simple green tinge in highlight areas, to an extreme blue cast throughout the entire image. Color Plate 12 shows a *very* poorly white-balanced shot of a woman sitting on a couch. Before we shot this scene, we had been shooting outside on a very cloudy day. Though we had white-balanced the camera outside, after quickly moving inside, we forgot to re-white balance for the new lighting conditions. As you can see, the bad white balance resulted in an extreme blue cast throughout the image. Color Plate 13 shows the image after it was corrected.

Most NLEs and many effects packages include filters for adjusting the color balance, saturation, and hue of an image (Figure 15.4). In the following tuto-

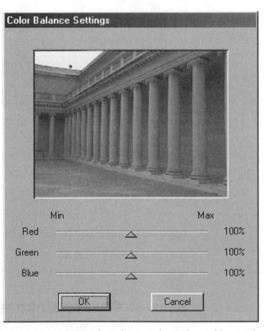

FIGURE   *Adobe Premiere 5.1 provides a basic Color Balance filter with sliders for ad-*
15.4   *justing the red, green, and blue values in a layer.*

rial, we will use combinations of these filters to correct our image. In many programs, you might need to apply multiple copies of the same filter, each with different settings. It's important to note that your program will process these filters in the order they are applied. So, if you apply a filter to change the amount of blue in an image, and then apply *another* filter to change the amount of red, the second filter will operate on the already processed, less-blue image that resulted from the first filter.

When correcting color in any application, follow these general steps:

- Identify the main color problem, (e.g., it's too blue) and apply a filter to correct it.
- Examine the results and use additional filters to "touch up" the image.

Tutorial

CORRECTING WHITE BALANCE

In this tutorial, we are going to use color correction filters inside our editing package to correct the bad white balance shown in Color Plate 12. Our goal will be the color balance shown in Color Plate 13. Though the resulting color is not ideal (look at the strange magenta and green tones in the shadows of the adjusted image), it is certainly better than the original. And, since we can't afford a re-shoot, saving the footage through color correction is our only hope of salvaging the scene!

The colors in an image can be divided into three categories: highlights, midtones, and shadows. When trying to decide how to color correct an image, start by identifying problems within these categories. As you adjust the first category, it will become more apparent what corrections need to be made to the other categories. For example, you may find that only highlight colors are out of balance. Adjust these, and then see if the midtones or shadows need adjustment.

For this tutorial, we will be correcting the footage using Apple's Final Cut Pro version 1.2. Final Cut's Color Balance filter lets you specify which range of colors you want to adjust.

STEP 1: CREATE A PROJECT.

Create a new project, import the clip *adelle_1,* and place it on the timeline.

STEP 2: ADD THE FIRST FILTER.

Though at first glance it may look like this footage is completely blue, closer examination reveals that the woman's skin tones, and the wood frame behind her, are fairly accurate. It's the white wall, and the white cushion that are particularly blue. Since these fall under the Highlight category of color, adjusting the highlights will be our first step.

Add a *Color Balance* filter to the clip.

In Final Cut, the Color Balance filter provides three radio buttons for targeting the color temperature you want to adjust. Click the Highlights button to target highlights. Because we want to remove the blue cast, begin by sliding the blue slider to the left until it reads approximately –70. If your program doesn't allow you to target a particular range of colors, that's okay, you just might need to make additional adjustments later (Figure 15.5).

Now look at your image. Much less blue, but now the highlights are a little too green. No problem, drag the green slider to the left until it reads roughly –50. Better, but still not quite right.

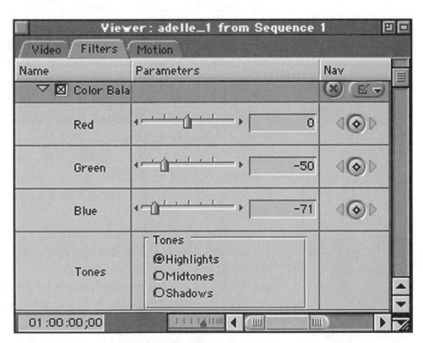

 FIGURE   *Adding the first color balance filter. Your goal is to address the biggest prob-*
15.5   *lem in your image. Don't expect to fix everything all at once.*

STEP 3: ADD ANOTHER FILTER.

Though most of the blue cast was in the highlight areas, there's still a good amount of it in the midtones. Add another Color Balance filter to the clip, but set it to target the midtones.

Again, our first step is to reduce the blue. Drag the blue slider to around –60. Look at your image and you'll see that, like before, we now have too much green. Drag the green slider to around –40.

Much better, but now there's a very slight pink tinge. This can be removed by putting the red slider at –10.

STEP 4: ADD YET ANOTHER FILTER.

We're almost there, but take a look at the highlights in the corner of the couch. They're a little green. We could go back and lower the green slider in our first filter to further reduce the green highlights, but this will create other problems. Because the filters are calculated in a certain order, if we go back and change an earlier parameter, the filters and parameters that are calculated later will no longer serve the function we intended. So, add a third Color Balance filter.

Click the Highlights button in the new filter and drag the green slider down to about –30. This should remove most of the green highlight.

STEP 5: NOW, ADD A FILTER.

Though the color now looks much better, the image has ended up a tad darker because of our adjustments. Add a *Levels* filter to the clip. Drag the Gamma slider to the left to increase the brightness of the mid-tones (Figure 15.6).

TIP

Always Avoid Brightness and Contract

If your NLE provides Levels *or* Curves *filters, always use these for adjusting the brightness and contrast of an image. Never use* Brightness *and* Contrast *filters, as these controls tend to wash out your image. With a Levels or Curves filter, you can control the contrast and brightness, while preserving the white and black tones in your image. (Brightness and Contrast filters tend to change black tones to gray.)*

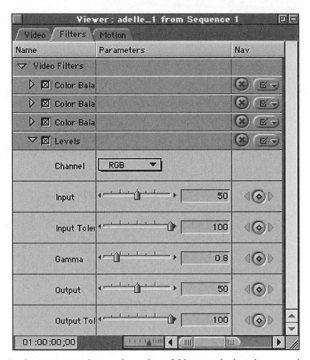

FIGURE **15.6** *In this case, it took a good number of filters to deal with every color problem in our shot. Sure, these will slow render times, but they're cheaper and faster than re-shooting!*

That's it! You've successfully removed the color cast and saved the footage. Now, however, it's important to scrub through the clip and make sure that your settings are accurate for all the sections of your video. In this clip they work fine throughout, but if we had moved the camera or done some other activity that changed the lighting of the scene, then we might need to change the settings for different parts of the clip. If your NLE allows you to animate filters using keyframes, then, with some patience, you can usually get smooth changes in adjustment from point to point within your clip.

This stack of filters will all be calculated and applied when you render and compress your final video. So, by applying all of these filters at once, you'll only have to compress your video once (at final render time).

MATCHING FOOTAGE FROM DIFFERENT CAMERAS AND SHOOTS

Though tape formats are standardized, there's still a lot of latitude for camera manufacturers to tweak and customize. Consequently, cameras from different vendors can shoot images with different colors and qualities. If you end up shooting with multiple cameras—either simultaneously, or at different times during your shoot—you could very easily end up with different shots in the same scene that don't have quite the same color quality or sharpness.

Low-budget filmmakers who are borrowing equipment are especially susceptible to this problem, as they may not always be able to borrow the same gear. If your principal shoot is over and you're now trying to get some "pick-up" shots, you may find yourself shooting with a different brand or model of camera, or with the same camera but during a different time of year when the light is slightly different.

Matching footage from different cameras can be difficult because it's often a combination of factors that make footage from one camera look different from another. When performing such adjustments, consider the following:

- Use the same approach that we used earlier: identify the main problem, correct it with a filter, then use additional filters to remove lingering color troubles.

- Note that some cameras have different levels of sharpness and detail. Differences in detail can often be perceived as slight differences in tone or color. Just as a pattern of black and white dots in a newspaper photo can appear gray to the eye, more or less detail in an image can make color appear different. Experiment with using lightly applied Unsharp Mask filters to sharpen details from softer cameras. Be very careful, though! When sharpening, you run the risk of increasing aliasing and other artifacts in your image.

- If you determine that there's an easy fix for the color from one camera—maybe it just needs less red, for example—then consider applying this effect by adjusting the chroma levels when you capture. Not all programs provide such a feature, and such tools don't offer fine controls, but if this approach works, it will save you a lot of rendering time.

- Be careful of flesh tones. In the previous example, the blue cast in the image appears mainly in the bright whites of the walls and couch. It's easy to focus on these areas when applying correction. However, it's important to ensure that, while correcting the background of the image, you don't corrupt any skin tones in the foreground. The human eye is very discerning about skin tones and can easily recognize incorrect, or "bad" color.

Correcting Part of an Image
Through the use of masks, stencils, alpha channels, or layers, you can selectively apply color corrections to part of an image, rather than to the whole thing. You can even apply different color corrections—one to the foreground, another to the background. We'll discuss this more in Chapter 16.

USING TRACKS AND LAYERS TO ADJUST COLOR

If your NLE or effects program provides control over *transfer modes,* then you can perform color adjustments by layering different video tracks on top of each other. Though not so useful for color correction, stacking tracks (or layers in a compositing program) is an easy way to increase contrast, pump up color, and create unique color effects.

Usually, when two video tracks occupy the same space in the timeline, the track that is higher in the stacking order is the only one that's visible. Lower tracks are simply covered up. However, if your NLE provides control over the transfer mode of a layer, then you can set upper tracks to mix and blend with lower tracks. (If you've ever changed the transfer mode of a layer in Photoshop, then you've seen such effects in action.)

If you change the transfer mode of a layer, then the pixels in that layer will be mathematically combined with pixels in the lower layer (that layer, in turn, can be combined with the layer below it, and so on and so forth). The pixels that result from the combination can often be very different from either of the original pixels (Figure 15.7).

You Say Track, I Say Layer
When we speak of putting a video clip on a layer, *this is synonymous with putting a video clip on a* track. *No matter what terminology your editing or effects package uses, the concept is the same.*

LUMINANCE CLAMPING

Now the bad news: If you're editing DV footage using a Firewire system, there's a good chance that the DV CODEC your system uses might be screwing up

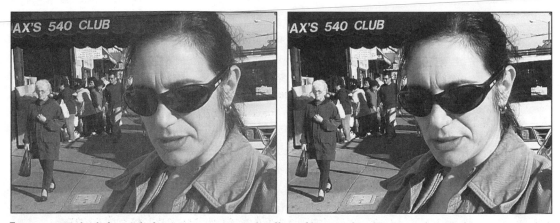

FIGURE
15.7   *In this before and after series, you can see the effects of layer stacking. To create the second image, we stacked three copies of the same footage. The bottom copy was left normal. The copy above that uses a Lighten transfer mode, while the layer above that uses a Hard Light transfer mode.*

your color. To understand why (and what you can do about it), you need to understand how digital video handles the *luminance*—or brightness—information in a video signal.

As we discussed in Chapter 4, video signals contain luminance information and *chrominance,* or color, information. With these two pieces of data—what color something is, and how bright that color is—your video monitor can recreate an image. Luminance is measured using a scale called IRE, where white is 100 IRE (or 100%) and black is 7.5 IRE (or 7.5%). Remember, though, 100 IRE is simply the value of *white,* and is not necessarily the brightest color that can be displayed. Your camera, whether DV or analog, is capable of shooting colors that are brighter than 100 IRE, and you'll see these areas as bright highlights and "hot" spots.

When a video signal is digitized, the luminance of each pixel is assigned a numeric value between 1 and 254. Black is defined as 16, and white is defined as 235. By putting white at 235, rather than 254, the digital luminance scale has enough "headroom" for the areas of your image that are brighter than white.

Unfortunately, your computer uses a slightly different measure of luminance. On your computer screen, black is represented by 0, while white is represented by 255. In trying to reconcile these two different systems, your DV CODEC runs into some problems.

For example, some DV CODECs will scale the black in a video signal from 16 down to 0, and the white from 235 up to 255. The values in between will be scaled accordingly. The problem with this approach is that all of that headroom above 235 gets clipped off, or *clamped*. So, highlight areas of your image that normally appear as a *range* of whites will get reduced to flat blotches of white (Figure 15.8).

However, if your DV CODEC leaves the white and black values alone, then you run into another problem. Because your computer uses different standards for black and white, video with black and white values of 16 and 235 will appear less contrasty on your computer screen. Whites will appear slightly gray, rather than white. In addition, any graphics you've created on the computer will have "illegal" blacks and whites (since they'll be using the computer's measures of black and white) and will have more or less contrast than your digital video.

So what's a DV filmmaker to do? That depends largely on which CODEC you are using and what type of editing and effects you are creating. First, you need to decide if your CODEC performs luminance clamping (sometimes referred to as *luminance scaling*).

- **Apple DV** The Apple DV CODEC that's built-in to QuickTime 4 clamps luminance and, unfortunately, there's no option to make it do otherwise. In addition, the QuickTime CODEC performs a slight adjustment to the midtones (or *gamma*) to darken DV images so that they'll appear better on your computer screen. (You can undo Apple's

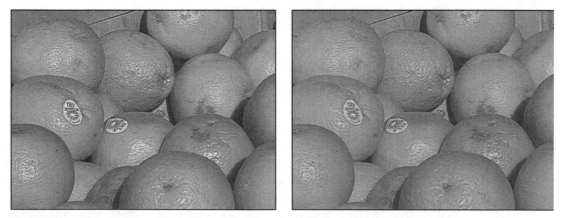

FIGURE
15.8   *Two adjacent frames. The image on the left is unclamped, the image on the right is clamped.*

automatic gamma correction by applying a Levels filter to your footage. Use a gamma setting of about 1.2. If you later want to undo this correction, apply a Levels filter with a gamma of around .84.)

- **Digital Origin DV** The DV CODEC that ships with DigitalOrigin's EditDV and MotoDV products provides an option for deactivating luma clamping. Selecting *SoftDV On* prevents the CODEC from scaling luminance, while *SoftDV Off* activates luminance scaling. The Windows version of the CODEC also lets you alter the black point of an incoming clip, and provides separate controls for compressing and decompressing.

- **ProMax DV Toolkit** The DVSoft CODEC that ships as part of ProMax's DV Toolkit provides several options. *Clamped Luma* does just what it says and scales luminance values. DVSoft also lets you control the clamping of *chroma,* which is an ideal solution for times when you overlight a scene and end up capturing illegal colors (for example, reds that are so bright that they bleed) (Figure 15.9).

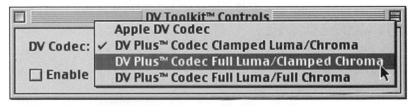

FIGURE   *ProMax's DV Toolkit provides several options for compressing video with or*
15.9   *without luminance clamping, as well as chrominance clamping.*

No matter how your CODEC handles luminance, you'll be safest if you simply try to avoid illegal hot spots when shooting (that is, keep from shooting with values over 100 IRE). This is fairly simple if your camera has a zebra feature, (see Chapter 6), as the zebra display will show you over-exposed areas of an image. You can then iris or shutter down to control them.

If your camera doesn't have a zebra feature, your next best option is to take a good field-monitor to your shoot. If you calibrate the monitor with standard color bars, and keep tabs on your footage while you shoot (or better yet, use the monitor as your viewfinder), you can do a good job of controlling hot spots. If you really want to get picky, you could even take a scope with you and monitor your signals to look for illegal color.

If you don't have a monitor, or your shoot precludes using one, then spend some time before you shoot learning to recognize hot spots in your camera's viewfinder. Connect your camera to a monitor and pay attention to how images in the viewfinder compare to images on the monitor.

There will be times, though, when you can't avoid illegal luminance. Perhaps you can't avoid a harsh backlight and decide to over-expose your background to be able to see the foreground. Or maybe you're choosing to over-expose part of your image for stylistic reasons. In these instances, you'll be much better off working with a CODEC that allows you to use the full, rather than scaled, range of luminance. Such a CODEC will keep your over-exposed areas from turning into blobby areas of white. If you're using the Apple CODEC, and are shooting a lot of over-exposed footage, you may find it worth investing in the ProMax DV Toolkit.

If your production involves a lot of computer-generated images or graphics, you'll need to give some additional thought to your luma options. Because your computer-generated imagery (CGI) will use values of 0 and 255 for black and white, respectively, using scaled luminance will result in better composites since your CGI elements will have a contrast range that's more in line with your video.

IRE, It's the Law
An F.C.C. law, to be exact. If your project is ultimately destined for broadcast, you'll need to be particularly careful about keeping your color and luminance values within the legal limit. Most broadcasters will not accept video with signals that go beyond the legal NTSC limits.

PUT A CLAMP ON IT!

MANUAL ADJUSTMENT OF LUMINANCE

No matter how careful you are when shooting, there's always a chance that you'll have video with blown-out whites that don't respond well to luminance clamping. In these instances, you may want to try manually clamping the luminance. For this to work, you'll need a CODEC that allows you to deactivate luminance clamping.

Using a program like After Effects, apply a Curves filter to the offending clip and set the black point at 0. However, rather than cut off the whites at 235 (the way a luma clamping CODEC will), create a curve that will slowly roll off the whites. This will keep your hot spots from turning into a solid mass of white. Note that this will change the contrast in your image, but altered contrast will probably be better than flat, solid highlights. And, your highlights will now be legal for broadcast (Figure 15.10).

Remember to reactivate the clamping in your CODEC before you continue.

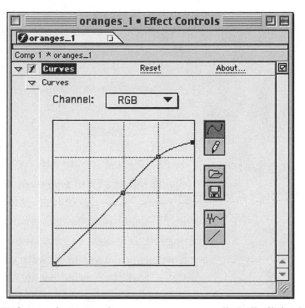

FIGURE
15.10   *With a simple Curves adjustment, you can manually "roll off" bright spots rather than clamping them.*

Luma Clamping Troubles

If you are using a CODEC that clamps luminance, you face another problem besides having your highlights reduced to flat blobs of white. Say you have a 4-second clip and you need to crop the frame to a smaller size during the last 2 seconds. The easiest way to do this would be to make a cut in the clip at the 2-second mark, and then apply a crop filter to the second part of the clip.

This cropping will cause your NLE to render new pixels for that clip, which of course, will require recompression using your chosen CODEC. Unfortunately, if your CODEC performs luma clamping, the second clip will now have very different luminance values than the first clip. Because the two clips are butted against each other, this change in luminance will be very obvious, and quite distracting.

What can you do? The best choice is to find a CODEC that lets you render unclamped video. If this is not an option (either due to cost or availability), then you need to get the computer to re-render both clips (and possibly your entire movie) so that every clip will be subject to the same clamping. If you apply a 1-pixel crop to each clip, then the computer will be forced to re-render everything. Because your video is overscanned, you'll never see this 1-pixel loss.

Correcting Color for Film

If your project will eventually be transferred to film, color correction in the computer will be a bit of a problem. If you've ever tried to print images on a color printer, you've probably discovered that what's on your screen doesn't always correspond to what comes out of your printer. The same is true for transferring images to film. The reasons for the disparity are many, and range from differences in color gamut between video and film, to differences in transfer processes, to differences in how the film is exposed during the transfer.

Professional editing and effects houses try to deal with this problem through expensive, complicated procedures for calibrating monitors and other digital equipment. In the end, such systems still give little assurance of what the final color will look like. If your final destination is film and you want to do a lot of color correction and color effects, it's a good idea to talk to your film transfer house. Tell them you're concerned about color control and ask their advice on how to proceed.

ONE MORE THING

Finally, we recommend color-correcting your footage before you composite any other elements on top of it. Your composited layers may have color issues of their own, so it's better to separate the color troubles that your layers might have. Once you've corrected each layer, you can composite them together and then apply touch-up corrections to smooth the "seams" of your composites. If you're not sure what we mean about composites, don't worry, a thorough discussion of compositing is coming up next.

16 Titling and Simple Compositing

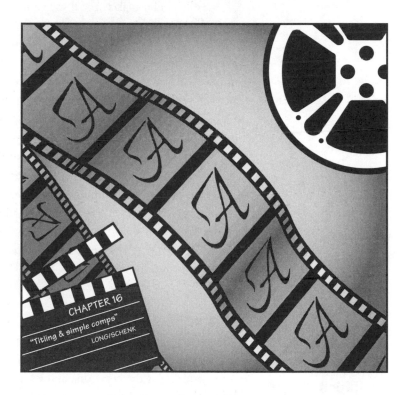

CHAPTER 16
"Titling & simple comps"
LONG/SCHENK

IN THIS CHAPTER

- Making Titles in Your NLE
- Compositing with Keys
- What Is an Alpha Channel?
- Compositing with Mattes

Compositing is one of the most powerful effects tools available to the digital film-maker. You'll use compositing techniques for everything from repairing drop-outs, to creating video collages and special effects.

When we say "compositing," we're referring to the process of layering multiple images to create a final "composite" image. The layers can be QuickTime movies or still images but, if you do your compositing work well, your audience will simply see a single, well-integrated shot. Your biggest concern when compositing will be to craft the mechanisms of *transparency* that will allow one image to be superimposed onto another. Once your composite is built, you'll need all of the color correction techniques we introduced in the last chapter to blend the layers into a seamless, cohesive image.

The simplest, most common compositing task is the creation of titles and credits. Every movie needs opening titles and a final credit roll, and some movies—particularly documentaries—will probably need titles throughout. The creation of titles marks the start of our compositing and special effects discussions, which will continue into Chapter 17.

Titles and Simple Graphics

Though your production may not need fancy special effects such as 3D-rendered dinosaurs, or complicated composites and morphs, it probably will need a title sequence at the beginning and a credit roll at the end. If you're shooting a documentary, you might also need to use titles to identify interviewees and locations. Though your editing software probably includes some titling functions, they might not be up to creating a cool, animated title sequence, or even a simple list of rolling credits.

In this section we'll cover the basics of titling and graphics and, along the way, introduce most of the concepts that you'll need to understand to pull off the more complex, sophisticated effects that we'll cover in the next chapter.

MAKING TITLES IN YOUR NLE

Most editing packages include titling functions that let you superimpose simple text titles over your images. Some packages include more advanced functions such as rolls and animated text. Your editing package's manual should cover everything you need to know to use the built-in titler. But, no matter what software you use, there are several things to keep in mind when building your titles.

Note that it is absolutely essential that you have an NTSC monitor hooked up to your system when you are creating titles! The only way to determine the legibility of your titles and graphics is to see them on an NTSC screen.

Titles for Film Projects

If you're finishing your project on film, the resolution of titles created in the internal title tool of your NLE will be too low for projection. You'll need to create high-resolution titles using Photoshop or After Effects and have them transferred directly to film. You can also have titles created with an optical printer, which is how all film titles were created until recently. The independent feature Boys Don't Cry *used optical printing for their titles and effects.*

Safe Titles

In Chapter 9, we discussed the *action safe* area of a shot. As you'll recall, to compensate for the possible differences between different television sets, a video signal actually contains more picture than can be displayed. Your TV or video monitor will crop off a good amount of this *overscanned* area.

Because it's impossible to determine how much a particular TV or monitor will overscan, some lowest-common-denominator averages have been determined. If you stay inside these averages, the odds are pretty good that your video will not be cropped outside the edge of the monitor. The *action safe* area is the larger of the two regions, while the *title safe* area is a little smaller. Keep your titles within this area and they should be viewable on any screen.

Most titling functions allow you to display both action and title safe guides. If your editing package doesn't provide guides, then try to avoid placing text in the outer 5% or so of your screen (Figure 16.1).

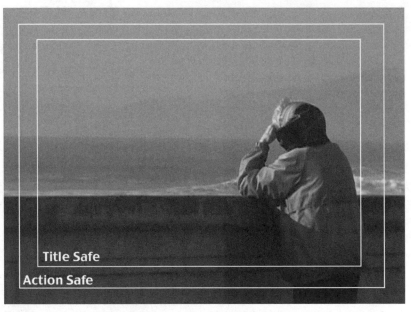

FIGURE **16.1**   *If you want to be sure your titles aren't cropped by the viewer's monitor, be sure to keep them within the "Title Safe" area.*

Safe Colors

NTSC and PAL video have much smaller color gamuts than your computer monitor. This means that colors that look fine on your computer screen may not display correctly—in fact, they might look plain awful—when displayed on an NTSC monitor. Very saturated colors will tend to bleed and fringe, with reds suffering the most. (Color Plate 9 and Figure 12.12 show good examples of oversaturated red created in an internal titler.)

Unfortunately, the titling functions of most editing programs will let you choose colors that are not NTSC "legal." This means you may have to do some experimentation to find colors that are safe for NTSC display. The easiest way to determine if a color is safe is to simply look at it on an NTSC monitor or a vectorscope.

Both After Effects and Photoshop provide a *Broadcast Colors* filter that will convert your graphics to NTSC-safe colors. These tools make it easier to reduce a color to something legal.

When choosing colors, also pay attention to what will be behind your titles. If you're superimposing titles over video, be sure that the colors you pick are visible throughout the entire clip. Though a blue title might look great at the beginning of a clip, make sure there are no blue, title-obscuring objects moving through the frame later in the clip. For better visibility, consider adding a slight drop-shadow or outline to your text (Figure 16.2).

Title Titles

Like everything else related to filmmaking, there's a whole mess of terms related to titling. Whether you use these terms or not is up to you.

Title Card A non-moving title.

Head Credits The typical series of title cards that fade in and out at the beginning of a movie. Typically, head credits follow (roughly) this order: studio, sometimes a producer, title, lead actors, casting, music, music supervisor, costumes and makeup, designer, director of photography, executive producer, producer, writer, director.

Tail Credits (or End Credits) The credits at the end of a movie.

Title Roll A long list of titles that scrolls from the bottom of the screen to the top. Usually used for End Credits. A very efficient way of presenting titles, as every name is on-screen for the same duration.

Title Crawl A line of titles that moves horizontally across the screen, usually at the bottom.

Supered Titles that are superimposed over other video.

Lower Thirds Titles that fit into the lower-third of the frame. Usually credits identifying a speaker, such as you might use in a documentary.

Pad A colored background or stripe behind a lower third title. Pads improve a title's legibility.

Textless version A print of your feature with no titles. Sometimes necessary for foreign distribution.

Choosing Your Typeface and Size

Remember that NTSC video is lower resolution and much less sharp than the video on your computer screen. Typefaces with fine lines and swirly details may not read very well on-screen.

When superimposing titles over video, make sure that the typeface you choose is readable throughout the clip. Fast-moving images with lots of clutter will make smaller, finer-lined typefaces more difficult to read.

When choosing a type size, legibility should be your first concern. At small sizes, some typefaces will be more legible than others, but in general, anything below 20 points will be too small (Figure 16.2).

Ordering Your Titles

If you're working with union actors, their contract may specify where their name must appear in the title sequence. Similarly, credit position may have been stipulated from a "producer" when you talked him or her out of some funding. Be sure to consider all of these agreements and obligations when ordering and creating your titles.

TIP

Start with a Word Processor

If you have a long list of titles, such as lower thirds for a feature-length documentary, subtitles for an entire film (or even just a scene or two), or a long credit list, use a word processing program to create the list of titles and be sure they are proofread and error-free before you start creating graphic titles. You can easily cut and paste them into your cg titler and save hours spent typing and fixing mistakes.

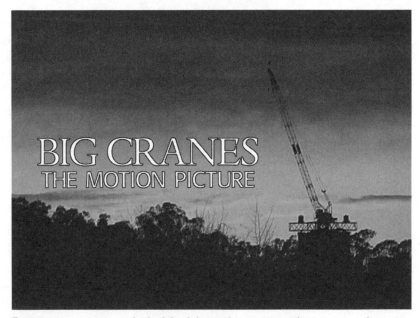

FIGURE   *Be sure to consider both legibility and composition when creating titles.*
16.2

Placing Your Titles

If you're planning on superimposing your titles over video, you'll want to give some thought to their placement, not just for the sake of readability, but for good composition as well. Hopefully, you shot the underlying videos with titles in mind. Though titles may sit on top of an image, they should not be thought of as separate. Be sure to consider the composition of the whole image—titles and video—when placing your graphics. If your titles are going to move about the screen, make sure they are readable across any and all action over which they are superimposed.

Legible titles don't really do any good if the viewer doesn't have time to read them. A good rule of thumb is to leave the title up long enough for you to read it two times aloud. Usually this means at least four seconds for a fairly short title, not including fades in or out. Even if you read fast, the title will probably be up long enough for most people to read it.

In general, pay close attention to the pacing of your head title sequence. Remember: This is the beginning of your presentation and is a chance for you to set an initial tone for your story. If you have already presented a "prelude" before the credits, your title sequence can function as a dramatic beat to prolong what has come before. Though you don't want to bore the audience with a long title sequence, if the beginning of your story is somewhat slow and somber, a slower title sequence might be just the thing to slow your audience down to a more receptive pace. Titles can serve as another beat in your storytelling process, so give them some thought.

Learning from Other People's Titles

Next time you're at the movies, consider how the director has used the title sequence. Many action movies, for example, skip titles all together and cut right "to the chase," so to speak. James Bond movies are famous for their elaborate title sequences that occur *after* an initial high-energy sequence. These sequences serve to bring the audience down from the chase-scene high to the typically more sedate "first" scene.

Some movies choose to superimpose their titles over initial, expository action. Be careful with this technique, though. You don't want to distract the audience from your exposition, and you don't want to give short shrift to your titles.

At the opposite extreme from these approaches are the title sequences used by Woody Allen in most of his movies. Simple slates on a black back-

> ground, these titles sequences are completely separate from the "main" presentation.
>
> Though you may think we're making rather a big deal out of something that can be very simple, don't forget that every frame that you show the audience can—and usually does—carry some sort of information about your story. Consequently, it's worth the time to make sure you're using your title sequence as well as you can.

CREATING TITLES IN PHOTOSHOP

If your editing package doesn't include a titler, or if you want to create fancier titles than what your editing app can create, you can always craft titles in a paint program or image editor. After you've created your title images, you can take them into your editing or special effects package and composite them with your video or other graphics. In the next section, we'll cover everything you need to know to perform simple composites.

Compositing 101

In theory, compositing sounds like a very basic effect: put one layer of video on top of another to create a composite. In practice, though, compositing is one of the most powerful tools at your disposal. At the simplest level, you can use compositing tools to superimpose custom titles and graphics over your video, or stack clips on top of each other to create a video collage. More sophisticated compositing tools allow you to do everything from mixing computer-generated elements with live video, to placing your actors inside virtual sets. Though good compositing tools are the foundation of all special effects work, they can also be used for more everyday concerns such as fixing dropouts and altering the color of an image.

In most non-linear editing packages, you can create a simple composite by creating multiple video tracks, each with a different clip, and all stacked on top of each other (Figure 16.3). Dedicated compositing programs such as Adobe After Effects provide more compositing power by letting you stack many layers of video and stills. In addition, After Effects lets you nest one composition inside another to ease project management. After Effects also lets you animate the properties of layers to create sophisticated, animated effects.

No matter which program you use, the process of compositing is fairly simple. First, you import your video clips and stack them up in the appropriate

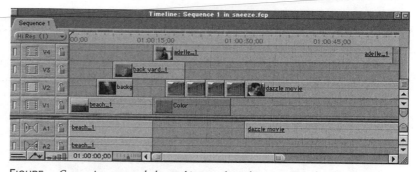

FIGURE
16.3
Composites are made by stacking tracks or layers on top of each other, and then specifying how those layers will combine.

order. Obviously, if you put one piece of video on top of another, the upper clip will simply obscure the lower clip. So, after creating your stack of video, you must define the method by which each layer will reveal the contents of the underlying layers. The method you choose will depend on the type of footage with which you are working.

Compositing methods fall into two categories: *keys* and *mattes*.

KEYS

If you've ever seen a local TV weatherman standing in front of a weather-filled map of the country, then you've seen an example of *keying*. The weatherman, of course, is not really standing in front of a map. Rather, he's standing in front of a blue or green screen that is electronically *keyed* out and replaced with the image of the map (Figure 16.4a, b).

Most NLEs provide keying functions that let you superimpose footage shot in front of a colored screen over another video clip, animation, or still image. In these programs you import both your blue-screen footage and your underlying layers, stack them up, and then tell the program to apply a *chroma key* (sometimes called a *color key*) to the uppermost layer. The chroma key feature will provide controls to let you select which color you wish to key out.

When the image is rendered, the computer will look for every occurrence of the specified key color, make it transparent, and use the information from underlying layers to fill in the now-empty space.

A *luminance key* functions the same way, but rather than keying out pixels of a certain color, a luma key keys out pixels of a certain brightness. Many pro-

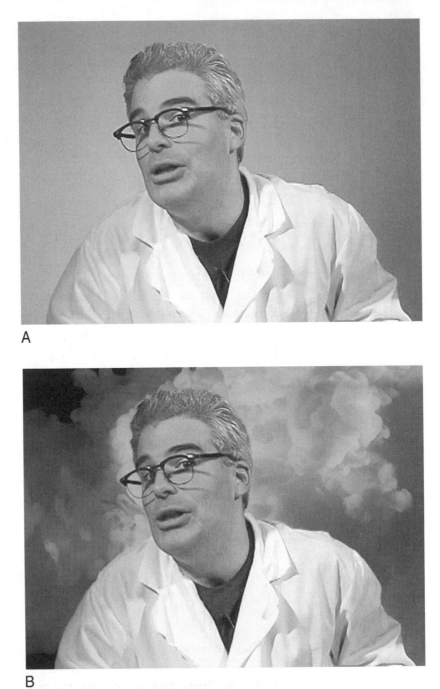

A

B

FIGURE

16.4
The image on the top was shot in front of a blue screen, which can easily be "keyed out" and replaced with another image, such as this billowing smoke.

grams offer variations of these keys, such as screen, multiply, or difference. Consult your manual for details.

Because you must shoot in front of a specially colored screen, and perform very precise lighting, chroma key effects are not ideal for every compositing task. They are usually used for situations where you want to superimpose a person in front of another video clip or still (the screens are blue or green because there is rarely any blue or green in the skin tone of a healthy human). Luminance keys can be used for situations where you can't put a blue-screen behind your foreground element. For example, you could use a luma key to key out a bright sky behind a building. Luminance keys can also be used to touch-up parts of a chroma key composite that have not keyed out properly.

Shooting blue- or green-screen footage requires a great deal of care and expertise.

Tutorial:

CREATING A LUMINANCE KEY

A luminance key lets you superimpose one layer over another by knocking the dark parts out of a layer to expose underlying layers (or, you can knock out bright areas). In this tutorial, we'll use a luminance key to superimpose a flash of gunfire over another video clip (Figure 16.5).

For this tutorial, you'll need an editing or effects package that provides luminance keys (Adobe Premiere, Apple's Final Cut, Adobe After Effects, EditDV, DPS Velocity, Avid Media Composer, etc.).

STEP 1: SET UP YOUR PROJECT.

In your editing package, create a project. Import the files *hand-gun.mov* and *GS125.mov* from the *Luma Key Tutorial* folder. *Hand-gun.mov* is a short clip showing a hand "firing" bullets. It was shot with a Canon GL-1. *GS125.mov* is from the ArtBeats Gun Stock Digital Film Library and is a short movie showing a number of muzzle flashes shot in near darkness.

Place the *hand-gun.mov* clip on the first video track in your timeline. Create a second video track above this one. Place the *GS125.mov* in the upper video track.

STEP 2: FIND THE FIRST MUZZLE FLASH.

Double-click on the *GS125* clip in your timeline to load it into your source monitor. Scrub through the clip to find a muzzle flash that you like. Position

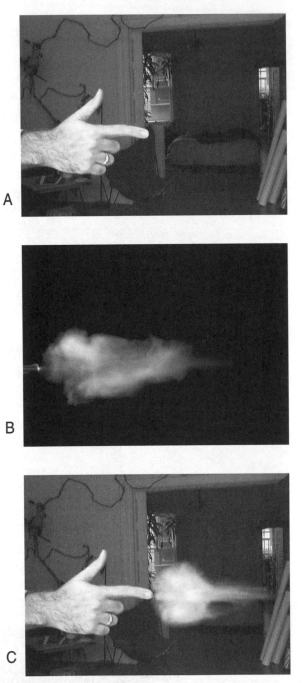

FIGURE
16.5 *In this tutorial, we're going to superimpose the footage of a muzzle flash over footage of a hand to create a final composite that will show a hand firing bullets.*

the playback head on the first frame of one of the muzzle flashes and set an *In* point. Scrub forward one or two frames to be sure the flash has ended, and set an *Out* point.

Note that most of these flashes are only one frame. Depending on your computer's performance, you may not see each frame during playback. Consequently, you'll probably have to scrub to find the single frames. Look for places in the clip where the hand recoils. This is a good way to zero in on the flash.

STEP 3: POSITION THE FLASH IN THE TIMELINE.

In the timeline, scrub through your footage and watch the program monitor to find the frame where the finger seems to fire. This is where you want the muzzle flash to appear (Figure 16.6). Position the *GS125.mov* clip in a higher track so that it begins at the point in time where the finger fires. Note that the program monitor will now be filled with the muzzle flash on black image of the *GS125* clip. Your background will be completely obscured, but not for long . . .

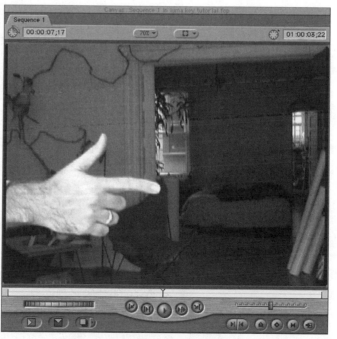

FIGURE 16.6   *Your muzzle flash footage should start right when the finger begins to recoil.*

STEP 4: DEFINE YOUR LUMINANCE KEY.

Add a luminance key to the *GS125* clip. If you're unsure of how to add a key, consult your manual for details. Some luminance keys allow you to choose between keying out light areas or dark areas. Others default to keying out darker areas. If your luma key provides an option, set it to key out darker areas.

Most luminance keys provide at least two sliders for adjusting the key effect, one that specifies which values will be keyed out, and another that controls how transparent those areas will become. Adjust the sliders in your luminance key filter until the black areas are gone and only the flash remains. Your goal is to find a balance of settings that eliminates the background without reducing the luminance of the flash too much. Pay particular attention to the edges of the flash. Even though it's only one frame, a hard edge, or a black fringe will be noticeable to the viewer (Figure 16.7).

STEP 5: POSITION THE FLASH IN THE FRAME.

With your key defined, you can now probably see the background beneath the muzzle flash. Unfortunately, the flash is probably over at the left side of the

FIGURE *Experiment to find luminance key settings that eliminate the background, without dulling the intensity of the flash, and without creating a hard, distinct edge on the flash.*

screen. Obviously, we want it to look like it's coming out of the finger. Using your software's motion controls, reposition the flash so that it sits just off the tip of the finger. You might also want to try scaling it down so that it doesn't overwhelm the composition.

Finally, many of the flashes in the GS125 clip have a visible gun barrel on the left side of the frame. Your motion control facility should allow you to crop the barrel without affecting the flash (Figure 16.8).

STEP 6: NOW DO THE REST.

Render your footage and take a look. Pay close attention to the timing of the flash; it may need to be moved forward or backward a frame or two to match the recoil of the finger. You might also see that you need to adjust the settings of your luminance key. When you're satisfied, choose another four muzzle flashes and edit them into the appropriate locations (Figure 16.9).

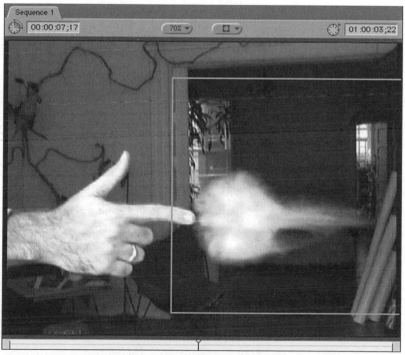

FIGURE

Move the muzzle flash to the end of the "barrel" and scale it down to be more appropriate to the "calibre" of this finger.

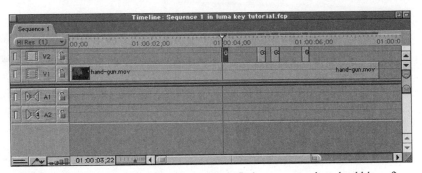

FIGURE   *When you've placed all of your muzzle flashes, your timeline should have five*
16.9   *clips on it.*

TIP

Filtered Footage
If you don't have, or don't want to use, clip footage of a muzzle flash, consider using a computer-generated one. DigiEffects' Delirium collection of After Effects plug-ins includes an excellent Muzzle Flash filter that can generate muzzle flashes for you.

That's it! With the simple application of some stock footage and a luminance key we've created . . . well . . . a kind of silly special effect. But, you can see that, in a more practical situation, such effects would save you the danger and expense of using a real gun. In the next chapter we'll increase the realism of the shot through the use of a little rotoscoping, but first, let's see if we hit anything during our little target practice.

Tutorial:

USING A CHROMA KEY

In the last tutorial we used a luminance key to knock out dark areas of a layer. But, not all footage is suited to luminance keying. With *chroma* keying, we can knock out a specific color to reveal underlying layers.

A chroma key is usually used to knock out a background so as to superimpose an element over other footage. That's what we're going to do here to create footage of gunshots hitting a door. (The results of this footage can be edited onto the end of our previous tutorial to create a finished shot of a hand firing bullets that hit a door.)

For this tutorial, you'll need an editing or compositing package that supports chroma keying.

STEP 1: SET UP YOUR PROJECT.

Create a project and load the following media from the *Chroma Key Tutorial* folder: *door still.psd, bullethole still.psd, bullethole.mov.* Place *door still.psd* in your timeline. (Note that, in the interest of saving space on the CD, we have chosen to use a still of the door, rather than a movie. In practice, it's a better idea to use a video of the door, even though there's no movement in the image. A movie will show changes in noise and grain, while a still will have a slightly different quality that will be recognizable to your viewers.)

STEP 2: ADD A BULLETHOLE.

Add the *bullethole still* to a layer or track above the door's layer (this bullet hole is a still from the same ArtBeats Gun Stock collection that provided the muzzle flashes). The door will be completely obscured by the blue surrounding the bullet hole.

STEP 3: ADD A CHROMA KEY.

Add a chroma key to the bullet hole still. Next, you need to specify the color you want to "key out," or eliminate. Many chroma key functions provide an eyedropper tool that you can use to sample the key color directly from the image in your program monitor. Other programs require you to specify the color numerically, or with a slider.

Don't be surprised if you don't see any changes after selecting the color. Most blue-screens have a degree of variation in them, so selecting one single color isn't going to eliminate a whole field of slightly varying hue. Fortunately, most chroma keys also have some sort of *Tolerance* control that lets you specify a degree of variation from your chosen color. Adjust the tolerance control until your background is removed.

Your chroma key function also probably provides controls for thinning and blurring (or feathering) the edges of the keyed areas. Adjust these to eliminate any remaining blue fringes around the bullet holes, and to soften the edges to better blend them into the door.

STEP 4: POSITION AND SCALE THE BULLET HOLE.

At its normal size, this bullethole is kind of large (after all, it was plainly a small-calibre finger). Scale down the bullet hole to something more appropriate, then position the hole somewhere on the door. In After Effects, we can

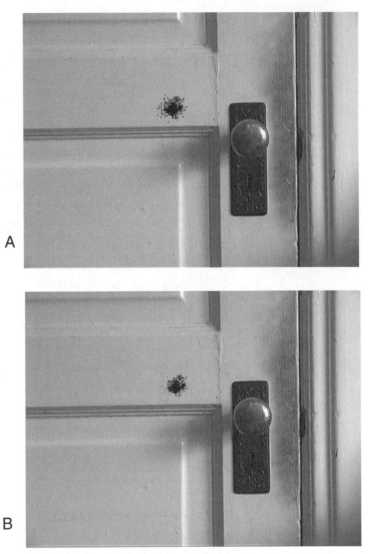

FIGURE
16.10
By feathering the edge of our chroma key, we can blend the bullet hole into the underlying video.

scale the bullet hole layer by simply dragging one of its corners to resize. We can then re-position by simply dragging the image to another location. Other programs might require the use of a dialog box or special motion command.

STEP 5: TINT THE HOLE.

At this point, the bullet hole plainly looks like it's floating over the door layer. But why? What's not quite right? As we've discussed throughout this book, video is composed of luminance and chrominance information (lightness and color). It's good to think in those terms when trying to match two pieces of video, either when editing shots into each other, or compositing them on top of each other. Is there a chrominance difference between the bullet hole and the door? Unfortunately, because the door footage was underlit, it has a very slight greenish hue to it. This is in fairly sharp contrast to the strong reddish tones of the splinters in the bullet hole layer. Using the color correction facilities in your package, apply a slight green tint to the bullet hole.

Next, look at the luminance of the hole. It's a little bright compared to the duller tones of the door. Again, using the color correction tools at your disposal, adjust the luminance to darken it a little bit. Because the bullet hole has few highlights, and because its blacks are very black, you can probably concentrate your luminance adjustments to the midtones. See Color Plate 14 for before and after examples of this color correction.

STEP 6: STILL NOT QUITE RIGHT.

It still looks like a decal, doesn't it? Consider the overall image quality of the two layers. Is there any difference? The bullet hole looks sharper and more detailed than the door. This makes sense since the bullet hole was shot using 35mm film and digitized at high-resolution. Apply a slight blur to the image (Figure 16.11).

STEP 7: ADD THE REST.

When you're satisfied with your first bullet hole, make two more copies of it and stack them on separate layers. Drag each copy to a different location on the door. You should also apply different scale amounts and a little rotation to each bullet hole to hide the fact that they're really all the same image. There were four shots fired from our "hand-gun." For the last one, let's see it actually impact the door.

STEP 8: ADD THE LAST HIT.

Bullethole.mov actually shows a whole bullet hit. Drag it into yet another layer and apply the same chroma key, color balance, and blur filters that

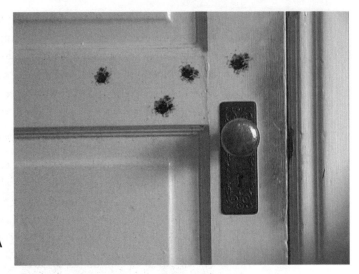

A

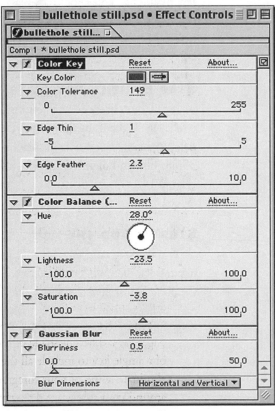

B

FIGURE
16.11   *Our final composite looks good, but as you can see, it takes a good number of filters to get it there.*

you applied to the still images. Position, scale, and rotate the layer appropriately.

That's it! Now, you can render out a final shot and edit it into your footage of the hand-gun firing. If you cut to door shot right before the impact of the last bullet, you'll have a somewhat dynamic little scene.

Non-Special Special Effects

Often, when you think of special effects, you think of giant dinosaurs, or horribly be-weaponed space cruisers. But you will probably find that most of your special effects needs fall into the simple, non-special realm like the muzzle flashes and bullet holes we just created. As special effects hardware has grown less expensive, it has become reasonable to create digital effects for many tasks that used to be achieved practically.

Even relatively "simple" practical effects—such as gunfire—can quickly become expensive, even for a high-budget feature. Paul Verhoeven's *Starship Troopers,* for example, used over 300,000 rounds of blank ammunition! With the effects power of the average desktop computer, it's worth spending some time assessing whether some of your "normal" shots and effects might be cheaper to produce through special effects technology.

Keying Tips

Getting a good key—no matter what type you're using—has more to do with shooting good footage than post-production tinkering. However, there are some things you can do to get better results from key footage. Consider the following when defining your keys:

- **It may take more than one.** It's okay to apply more than one key to an image. Because it can be difficult to evenly light a blue-screen background—particularly a large one—you'll often find that your blue-screen is darker around the edges than in the middle. In other words, the edges are a different shade of blue. Rather than adjusting the tolerance of a single key to include all the blue—a process which will most likely eliminate some of your foreground—use one key for the lighter blue around your subject, and another key to eliminate the darker blue.

- **Try mixing keys.** There are some instances where you can use a chroma key to knock out a background, and a very slight luma key to eliminate some of the leftover fringy weirdness. Because it's easy to overlight the foreground when lighting your blue-screen, an additional luma key can help remove halos around your subject.

- **Use garbage mattes.** Don't worry about trying to key out areas that don't contain a foreground element. Instead, mask those areas with a *garbage matte*. Most editing packages include a cropping tool or masking tool that lets you easily crop out unwanted sections of the frame (Figure 16.12). For more complex garbage mattes, consider using an alpha channel (which we'll get to shortly).

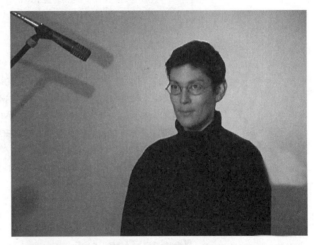

A

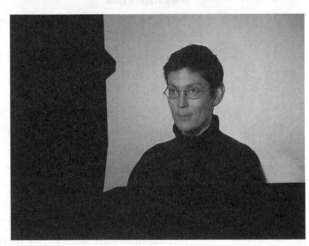

B

FIGURE
16.12   *You'll have an easier time keying out the background in this shot, if you first use a "garbage matte" to cut away the unwanted stuff around the edges of the frame.*

- **Use better software.** If the keying function in your editing or effects package isn't doing a good enough job, or if your production depends on a *lot* of key effects, consider investing in some higher quality keying software such as one of the special plug-ins from Ultimatte. Also take a look at Puffin Designs' *Composite Wizard*, which includes extraordinary filters for improving your composites. In addition to helping you remove fringes around your foreground elements, Composite Wizard can automatically match the overall color tones of your foreground and background. Composite Wizard can also add light to the edges of your foreground to make it look like your foreground element is affected by the lighting in your background plate.

Some chroma keying plug-ins and apps can use *screen correction* to improve the quality of their mattes. For screen correction to work, you'll need to shoot an additional plate of your blue-screen set with full lighting but no foreground elements. The keying package can use this plate as a reference to pull a cleaner matte.

MATTES

Because it's difficult to get a good composite using a key, and because it's not always possible to hang a colored screen behind something, you can also perform composites using a special type of mask called a *matte*. Akin to a stencil, a matte makes it possible for you to cut areas out of one layer of video (or a still) to reveal the layers lying below. For example, say you want to create a composite showing a giant tuna flying behind a building. Because you can't hang a giant blue-screen behind the building, you'll need to use a matte inside your compositing program to knock out the background behind the building layer to reveal the giant flying tuna in the underlying layer.

In the analog film world, mattes used to be drawn by hand. Their purpose was to act as a stencil when inserted into a stack of film. For example, if you wanted to composite a shot of a model spaceship into a background that was shot on location, you would photograph film of the model spaceship against a blue background. Matte cutters would then go in and, by hand, black out the background of *each frame* of the model spaceship footage. Through a photographic process, a negative, or inverse, of the matte would be created. You would place the background and inverse matte into a special machine called an *optical printer*. The optical printer would project the footage of the background onto a new piece of film, but the inverse matte would leave a perfect, space-ship-sized hole in the image. Before developing the piece of film, you would place the spaceship footage and the positive matte into the optical printer and project that onto the new piece of film. The spaceship would project into the hole left from the previous shot, while the matte would keep the background from being over-exposed. Through this sandwich of film clips, you would have your final composite.

If that doesn't sound complicated enough, consider what happens to color when it's diffused through several layers of celluloid. Though that bright red spaceship model might look great on your original film, after projecting light through it *and* several other pieces of film, its color will definitely change.

As a digital film-maker, you don't have to worry about such problems and, in most cases, you can have your software create a matte for you automatically. But best of all, your digital mattes can have varying degrees of opacity, rather than the simple stencil-like opacity of a practical matte.

Most of the time, color is stored in a still image or movie by splitting it into its component red, green, and blue parts, and storing each component in a separate channel (for some print applications, color is stored using four channels: cyan, magenta, yellow, and black). When viewed individually, each channel appears as an 8-bit grayscale image. When combined, the channels mix together to create a full-color, 24-bit image (Figure 16.13a).

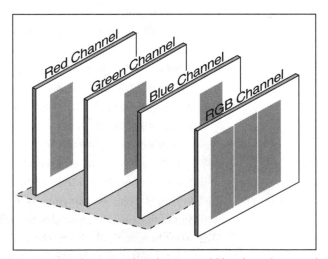

FIGURE **16.13a** *In a normal color image, the red, green, and blue channels are combined to create a full-color image.*

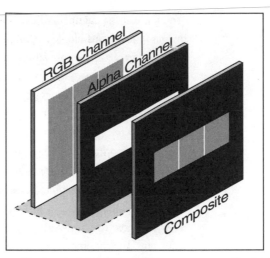

FIGURE
16.13b
If you add a fourth, "alpha" channel, then you can specify which full-color pixels will actually be seen, and how opaque they will be.

A fourth 8-bit grayscale channel, the alpha channel, can be added to an image or movie. If you see a product that claims a 4:2:2:4 color sampling ratio (instead of the usual 4:2:2), the fourth number refers to the alpha channel, which is usually uncompressed. Each pixel in the alpha channel specifies the level of transparency that will be used when compositing the image or video with something else. In other words, the alpha channel is like a stencil, but with the advantage that some areas can be defined as semitransparent.

In Figure 16.20A, you can see how the different channels combine to create an image. The red, green, and blue channels are mixed together to create a full-color image. In Figure 16.20B you can see how the alpha channel is then used to determine which parts of this full-color image will be opaque, and which will be transparent. If an area is transparent, underlying video or image layers will show through.

Because each frame of your video includes its own alpha channel information, you can create animated alpha channels (also known as a *travelling matte*) that correspond to the action in your clip. So, in the preceding example, our alpha channel would be animated to follow the movement of the spaceship.

Most of the time, the alpha channel will be stored in your movie document. You won't have to think about where it is, or go through an extra step to import it into your project. However, there may be times when you want to create a separate alpha channel movie for use in more complicated special effects.

(You'll use alpha channels when creating titles or other superimposed graphic images in programs like Photoshop.)

There are a number of ways to create an alpha channel. Many programs—such as 3D rendering and animation programs—can create alpha channels automatically when they generate an image. Some editing and effects programs let you generate alpha channels from a key. For example, you could use a chroma key to pull an alpha channel matte from blue-screen footage. For certain effects, working with an alpha channel is easier than working with a key, and alpha channel mattes are fully editable—that is, you can go in and reshape them if you need to—unlike key effects.

Finally, alpha channels can be created by hand. In the next tutorial, we'll show you how to hand-craft an alpha channel for superimposing text over a video clip. In Chapter 17, we'll use special tools to create more complicated, animated mattes.

PIXEL ASPECT RATIOS

As we mentioned in Chapter 4, though the pixels on your computer screen are square, many DV formats—including DV, and MiniDV—use rectangular pixels. Unfortunately, this means that images can be stretched and distorted as you move back and forth between different pieces of software.

Because DV-format video uses rectangular pixels, it will appear wide when displayed on your square-pixel computer monitor. Most editing and effects programs compensate for this by squishing the image horizontally to bring it back to a 4:3 aspect ratio on your computer screen. (If your software doesn't do this, you'll just have to get used to working with stretched footage. *Don't* perform horizontal squishing yourself, or your video will be distorted when it goes back to tape.)

Today, most video packages let you specify a pixel aspect ratio—many even let you explicitly configure for DV format—when you create a new project. Consult your software's manual for more info on how to set pixel shape (Figure 16.14).

If you're creating graphics in a paint, image editing, or 3D application, you'll need to do some extra planning if you intend to move those graphics into an editing or effects app for later output to tape.

If you are using a square-pixel videotape format such as VHS or Hi-8, you can go ahead and create your graphics at 640 x 480 pixels and import them normally. If you're using DV video, then you'll need to create your graphics at

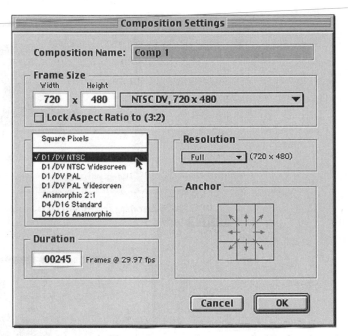

FIGURE
16.14
Most editing and effects packages now let you specify a pixel aspect ratio when creating a project. Shown here is the Composition Setup dialog from Adobe After Effects 4.1.

720 × 480 pixels. After you've moved your graphics into your editing or effects package, you may need to set the horizontal scale of each graphic to 90%. This will reconcile them to a 4:3 aspect ratio.

Note that you could scale the image in your painting or editing app, but if you need to go back and make changes or additions later, you might have a very difficult time working with the squished images. Consequently, it's usually easier to apply the 90% reduction in your effects package. (Note that this only works if your editing or effects package can be set for rectangular pixel aspect ratios.) (Figure 16.15)

In our tutorials, we assume that you are selecting the correct pixel sizes and project settings to compensate for the pixel aspect ratio of you chosen format. For details on settings for particular software applications, see www.dvhandbook.com/pixelshape.

TIP

Modifier Keys
Adobe Systems does a great job of creating identical keyboard commands and interfaces for their separate Mac and Windows products. However, to better un-

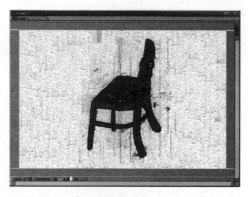

FIGURE
16.15a
When creating images for export to video, start with pixel dimensions of 720 × 480.

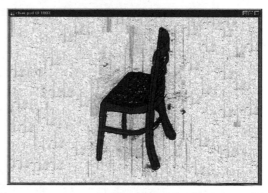

FIGURE
16.15b
The image may appear too wide when imported into your editing or effects programs.

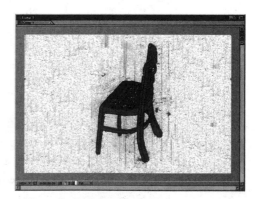

FIGURE
16.15c
By simply applying a 90% horizontal scale, you can return the image to its correct aspect ratio.

derstand the following tutorials, note that Command *on the Mac is synonymous with* CTRL *on a Windows computer, and* Option *on the Mac is synonymous with* ALT *on a Windows computer.*

Tutorial

CREATING A TITLE IN PHOTOSHOP

If your editing package doesn't have a titling function, or if its titler is under-powered, you can use a painting or image editing program to create titles. In your editing program, you can then superimpose your graphics files over your video. (If you don't want to super your graphics, but just want them on a solid background, you can simply import a graphic into your editing package as-is.)

Let's say you want to superimpose a simple title graphic over an establishing shot in your video. Though you could go to your favorite paint program, grab the text tool, type some graphics, and save the file, when you import this graphic into your editing or effects package, the background behind the text will be solid, and thus will obscure any video layered beneath it.

You could try to use a chroma or luminance key like we described earlier, but keys can result in ragged edges around your characters, and require much more time to render. There are some better solutions.

If you will be performing your composite in Adobe Premiere, Apple's Final Cut, or Adobe After Effects, then creating a title with Adobe Photoshop 5.0 or higher will be fairly simple, because these programs provide direct support for files in Photoshop format:

- First, create a new document in Photoshop. If your video is in DV format, you'll need to create a document that is 720 × 480 pixels with a resolution of 72 pixels per inch. Other video formats—and some analog digitizing cards—may require different sizes. (For example, if you're using a Targa 1000 or 2000 board for outputting video, use 720 × 540; if you're outputting for film, you'll use a resolution anywhere from 1728 × 736 to 2020 × 864.) Check your manual for details. In the New Document window, enter the correct dimensions and check *Transparent* to give the document a transparent background.
- Now you can simply pick a color, grab the Type tool, and create your title. Your text will be created on a separate *Text* layer. The layer's title will be the first few words of your text. Depending on your editing application, you may have to choose *Layer>Text>Render Text* before you save.

- Save your document as a Photoshop file and import it into Premiere, Final Cut, or After Effects. Upon importing, you'll be given a choice as to which layer you want to import. Select the text layer, and your text will be imported with full, correct transparency. Place the text in a track that's higher in the stacking order than your video. When previewed, you'll see your text super'ed over your video!

If your editing package doesn't directly support Photoshop files, or if you're using an earlier version of Photoshop, or if you want to perform a more sophisticated composite (such as text that fades from top to bottom), then you'll need to manually create an alpha channel mask for your text.

STEP 1: CREATE A DOCUMENT IN PHOTOSHOP.

Create a new document with the appropriate dimensions (720 × 480 if you're using DV). In the New Document Window, enter your dimensions, and under *Contents*, click *White*. This will create a document with a solid, white background. As an alternative, you can open the document *Safe Guides.psd*, located on the CD-ROM. This Photoshop document measures 720 × 480, has a white background, and includes a separate layer showing action- and title-safe guides. If you choose to use this document, make sure the Background layer is the active layer. You don't want to create content in the Safe Guides layer.

STEP 2: SELECT A COLOR AND CHOOSE YOUR TOOL.

Click on the Foreground color swatch to select a color for your text, and then click and hold on the Text tool in the tool palette to pop-out a submenu of other text tools. Select the Type Mask tool, the second tool in the menu and the one that looks like a "T" composed of dashed lines.

STEP 3: CREATE YOUR TYPE.

Click in your document window in a location close to where you want the center of your text to be. Enter your text in the resulting Type Tool dialog (be sure to click on the Center Justify button) and set the typeface, size, leading and other parameters. You won't be able to correct this text later, so check your work carefully. Click OK when finished.

STEP 4: POSITION YOUR TYPE.

After clicking OK, you won't actually see any text on your screen. Instead, you'll see a selection, or outline, of your text. You can position this outline by dragging it around with the Move tool (Figure 16.16). (As a shortcut, you can hold down the Command key to temporarily change your cursor to the Move tool. When you let go, it will revert to the text tool.)

STEP 5: COLOR THE SELECTION.

To create your type, select *Fill* from the *Edit* menu and choose to fill using the *Foreground* color. This will fill the selection with your chosen color.

STEP 6: CREATE THE ALPHA CHANNEL.

Now, select *Save Selection* from the Select menu. Accept the defaults in the *Save Selection* dialog and hit OK. Open the *Channels* palette. Now, in addition to the normal Red, Green, and Blue channels, you should see an additional channel called *Alpha 1*. Click on this channel in the Channels palette to look at your new alpha channel.

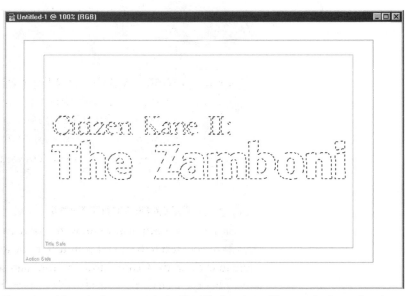

FIGURE   *After creating type with the Type Mask tool, you'll see a selection rather than colored text.*

The black areas of the channel will be completely transparent when rendered in your editor. In other words, any video positioned underneath these areas will show through. The white areas of your alpha channel will be completely opaque. Video beneath these areas will not show through. Instead, the color information in the document—in this case, your colored text—will show (Figure 16.17).

STEP 7: SAVE YOUR DOCUMENT.

If you're using the Safe Guides document, switch back to the Layers palette and discard the Guides layer. Now save your document in a format supported by your editing or effects package. Note that you'll need to select a format that supports alpha channels, such as TIFF, PICT, or Photoshop.

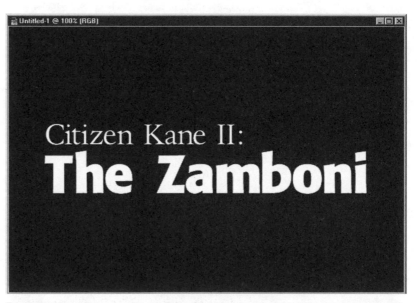

 FIGURE **16.17**   *The white areas in our alpha channel indicate which pixels in the image will be completely opaque; in this case, our text. Black areas indicate areas that will be completely transparent (that is, invisible). In this case, our white background will be invisible.*

STEP 8: IMPORT YOUR TITLE AND VIDEO INTO YOUR EDITOR.

Launch your editing package and import your source video and the title document you just made. Place both documents in your timeline, with your title document in a higher layer.

STEP 9: DEFINE TRANSPARENCY.

Now you need to tell your software to use the alpha channel that is included in your text document. Some applications such as Adobe After Effects automatically treat the alpha channel as a mask and render appropriate transparency. Other applications, such as Avid Media Composer, will ask you to define the alpha channel when you import the image. Still other applications, such as Adobe Premiere, require you to define the alpha channel as transparent, just as you would define a chroma key to knock out a colored background. Consult your manual for details. If your unsure of where to find such information, check the index for terms such as Setting Transparency, or Alpha Channels.

That's it! Remember that if you want to change the text, you not only have to recreate the colored text, but the corresponding alpha channel as well. If you're putting multiple titles on the same screen, you may want to consider creating separate title elements in separate documents, and then arranging them on-screen in your compositing program. This will make it easier to keep your titles discreet and editable.

Sidebar: Text Fringing

Depending on the size of your text and the color of your background, you may see a thin white fringe around your text when it is composited. Photoshop smooths text by slightly blurring the edges of each character into the background, a process known as *anti-aliasing*. Because the background in your document was white, the intermediate hues within the blur contain a lot of white. If the background in your composite is not white, these white pixels may show up.

If your final destination is video, the odds are that this fringe won't be seen. However, if your video is bring prepared for CD, or on-line distribution, or if your titles will be scanned directly to film, then it just may be visible. You have several options for removing it.

- Grab a still from the video over which it will be composited, use this as the background layer in Photoshop, and recreate your text over this layer.
- Before exporting, click on the alpha channel in the Channels palette and apply a Minimize filter (Filter>Other>Minimize). Specify a Radius of 1 pixel. If you're using a very thin-stroked typeface, this may cause some of the type's lines to break apart.

Though this may seem like a lot of work just to get a simple title, remember that there will be times when you'll be using these techniques to create titles that can't be made any other way.

Congratulations! Though this example may seem pretty simple (and somewhat boring), you've actually just learned a fundamental, basic task that you will use over and over again for any type of effects work. Alpha channel masking is an essential concept for all types of visual trickery, from advanced color correction to sophisticated effects. In the next section, we'll take your alpha channel understanding a bit farther.

MORE SOPHISTICATED MATTES

In the previous example, you created a simple alpha channel that defined a transparent area within your title, allowing you to "knock out" the background of your title and reveal some underlying video. Now, we're going to take things a little bit farther and add some cool effects to your title, by creating variations in the transparency of your text.

As you saw earlier, black areas of an alpha channel are completely transparent, while white areas are completely opaque. Alpha channels can also hold gray information, which define areas that are *partially* transparent (or "partially opaque" if you're one of those "glass-half-empty" people). In this tutorial, we'll recreate our alpha channel to create a title that has a smoky transparency that varies in opacity (Figure 16.19).

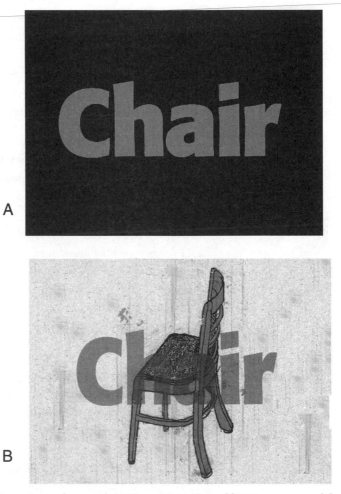

FIGURE
16.18   *Returning to the example in Figure 16.17, if we add 50% gray to our alpha
channel, then the resulting color pixels will be 50% transparent. You will actually be able to see a muted, dulled image of the layers laying below.*

Tutorial: ## VARIABLE TRANSPARENCY

For this tutorial, you'll need the title document that you created in the previous tutorial. If you don't have that document, you can use the *variable title.psd*
document located in the *Variable Transp. Tutorial* folder on the DV Handbook CD-ROM. Before we begin, there's one more thing you need to know
about alpha channels.

In the previous tutorial, you created an alpha channel by defining a selection with the Type Mask tool, and then saving that selection using Photoshop's

Save Selection command. In case you hadn't guessed already, it's called *Save Selection* for a reason. Open the Channels palette and drag the Alpha 1 channel down to the leftmost button at the bottom of the Channels palette. You should now see a dotted-line selection of your text. This is the selection that you saved earlier, and you can use it to re-fill your text if you want to change the text's color. You can also use the selection to change your alpha channel.

STEP 1: LOAD YOUR SELECTION.

If you haven't done it already, open the title document you created earlier. Open the Channels palette and "load" your alpha channel selection by dragging the *Alpha 1* channel down to the leftmost button at the bottom of the Channels palette. (This is the *Load Channels* button, and we'll be using it a lot.) As you probably know, when you've selected an area of a document, any image editing actions—painting, filters, etc.—will be constrained to the selected area.

STEP 2: MODIFY YOUR ALPHA CHANNEL.

Just as you can paint color information into the RGB channels of your document, you can paint transparency information into your alpha channel. For example, if you were to grab the Brush tool, choose a 50% gray foreground color, and paint in your current selection, your text would appear 50% transparent when composited in your editing program. We're going to do something a little more interesting.

Pull down the *Filter* menu, and scroll down to the *Render* submenu. Select *Clouds*. You should now see a smoky, grayscale cloud texture within your selection (Figure 16.19).

STEP 3: LOOK AT YOUR TEXT.

Press Command-D to deselect. Click on the RGB channel in the Channels palette to return to the normal, color view of your document. Your text should look exactly the same, as we've made no changes to the color information; we've only changed the transparency information that sits "beneath" the color.

STEP 4: SAVE YOUR DOCUMENT.

Save your document and return to your editing package. Repeat the compositing steps that were performed in the last tutorial, beginning at Step 8.

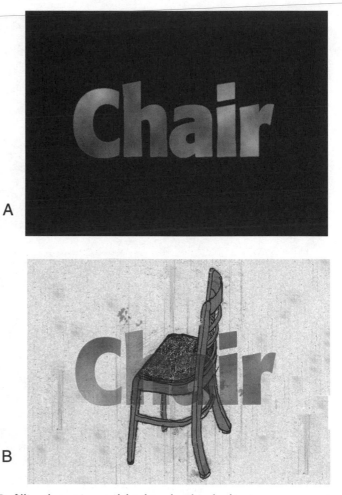

FIGURE
16.19 *By filling the text in our alpha channel with a cloud texture, we can create a turbulent field of varying transparency.*

When you're finished, you should see a title with variable, smoky transparency.

The ability to vary the transparency of an image lets you do things that traditional, analog matte users can't do. We'll get to even more sophisticated alpha channel work in the next chapter, but in the meantime, continue playing with some alpha channel effects to be sure you're comfortable with the concept. For example, try using the Photoshop Gradient tool to create text that fades from full opacity to full transparency (see Figure 16.20).

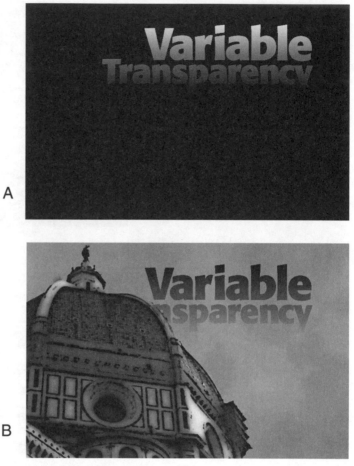

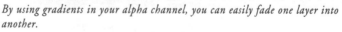

FIGURE
16.20   *By using gradients in your alpha channel, you can easily fade one layer into another.*

Moving Pictures

Today, most editing programs include motion facilities that let you move a still image or video clip around the screen. Though great for creating cool video collages composed of lots of moving images that cascade around the screen, motion features are also ideal for creating animated titles and credit rolls.

Whether or not you think you have a need for such features right now, go ahead and take a look at this section, for in our discussion of motion, we'll introduce several concepts and practices that you'll use to create other types of effects. Because motion features are dependent on a process called *keyframe animation,* reading this section will be a good introduction to the animation effects that we'll create in the next chapter.

BASIC MOVEMENT

When we speak of the motion features in an effects or editing package, we're not talking about features that let you control the motion of objects *within a shot.* In other words, you're not going to be able to take a video clip of a basketball game and control the motion of the ball . Instead, motion control layer is limited to specifying the movement of the entire layer. In addition to position, you can control a layer's other properties such as opacity, scale, and rotation.

By combining motion control features with alpha channel masks and multiple layers, you can create some very sophisticated animations.

Keyframes and Interpolating

In traditional hand-drawn cell animation, a director draws certain frames that indicate where a character should be at a particular time. These *keyframes* might occur every 10 frames, or every 2 minutes, depending on the amount and nature of the action in a scene. Once the keyframes are defined, a group of animators draw all of the intervening frames that are required to get from one keyframe to the next. This process is usually called *inbetweening* or *'tweening.* It can also be referred to as *interpolation,* as the animators must figure out, or interpolate, which frames are required to get from one state to the next.

This same keyframe/inbetweening approach is used in editing and effects packages to animate the properties of a clip or image. By *properties,* we mean the parameters and characteristics that define how a clip looks, such as position, scale, and rotation. Some packages add control over additional properties such as distortion, opacity, or 3D rotation. Many programs also let you animate the parameters of any filters you might have applied to a layer, letting you change the amount of, say, gaussian blur or color balance that you've applied to a video clip. The ability to animate all of the properties of a clip is an easy way to create complex effects (Figure 16.21).

Most keyframe interfaces work roughly the same way:

- Go to a particular point on the timeline
- Adjust the parameter you want to animate
- The computer will either automatically set a keyframe at that point, or you'll have to manually tell it to set a keyframe. During playback, the

FIGURE
16.21   *The Timeline window from Adobe After Effects. Notice the keyframe markers.*
             Also notice that there are many animatable properties ranging from position
             and opacity to parameters of filters that have been applied to the layers. In ad-
             dition, you can also adjust the acceleration and velocity of an animated change.

computer will automatically in-between all of the frames between your
keyframes.

- Repeat the above steps until your whole animation has been defined
- Render and play the video to see the full animation, including all of the
  in-between frames which the computer has interpolated.

Some programs also give you control over the velocity of an animated element. Such controls let you make an object slowly accelerate and decelerate as
it moves, and make it possible to sync the animation of a property to another
element in your composition.

A discussion of the specifics of the animation controls is beyond the scope
of this book. If you are not familiar with the features of your package, consult
your manual. Look for topics such as *Animation, keyframes,* and *velocity.*

Tutorial: ## CREATING A CREDIT ROLL

Credit rolls look much more professional than credit screens that pop up and
down. In addition, a credit roll is a very economical use of screen space and
time. Unfortunately, few editing packages provide a credit roll feature, and
those that do are often very limited, with no support for multiple text sizes,
and little control over color.

In this example, we're going to create a simple end credit roll. A movie with a big cast and crew will require a credit roll with a pretty small type size (since a larger face will require more time to roll the whole credit list). Because legibility is a concern at small sizes, it's best to use slightly off-white text on a black background (using slightly off-white will prevent bleeding text or flickering). Because credit rolls are usually not superimposed over anything, you don't have to worry about creating an alpha channel (Figure 16.22).

STEP 1: CREATE YOUR CREDITS.

In Photoshop (or any other image editing program) create a document that is 720 pixels wide. (If you're using a format besides DV, or a digitizing card that produces video with a different format, you may need to use a different width. See your documentation for details.) Specify a document length of around 2000 pixels. You may need to make the document longer or shorter later. Define a background that is black (Figure 16.23).

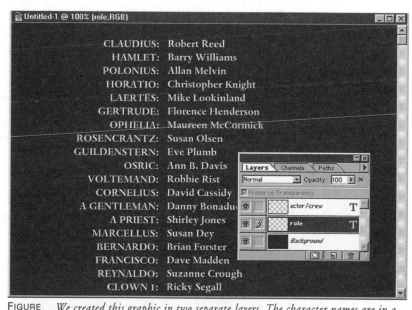

FIGURE

16.22

We created this graphic in two separate layers. The character names are in a right-justified layer, while the actor names are in a left-justified layer. The two layers can be easily positioned to create a typical credit-roll layout. On the downside, changing or re-ordering names can be confusing, as you have to make changes to both layers.

Claudius	Robert Reed
Hamlet	Barry Williams
Polonius	Allan Melvin
Horatio	Christopher Knight
Laertes	Mike Lookinland
Gertrude	Florence Henderson
Ophelia	Maureen McCormick
Rosencrantz	Susan Olsen
Guildenstern	Eve Plumb
Osric	Ann B. Davis
Voltemand	Robbie Rist
Cornelius	David Cassidy
A Gentleman	Danny Bonaduce
A Priest	Shirley Jones
Marcellus	Susan Dey
Bernardo	Brian Forster

FIGURE
16.23 *An easier way to create and maintain layers is to use the text tool in Adobe Il-lustrator. Since Illustrator provides tab stops and other typographical niceties, creating a credit roll is a snap. Some NLEs can import Illustrator files di-rectly. If yours doesn't, just open the file in Photoshop at 72 dpi to turn it into a normal, bitmapped Photoshop document.*

Select a typeface that is easily readable at smaller sizes (around 20 points) and enter your text. If you're using Photoshop 5, your text will be inserted as a Type layer, which means you'll be able to go back and edit it later.

STEP 2: SAVE YOUR DOCUMENT.

Once you've entered your text, crop out any extra length, and save your document in Photoshop format. Next, flatten the image and save it again in a format your editing or compositing program can import. If need be, you can always go back and make changes to your original, layered document, re-flat-ten, and then re-save.

STEP 3: IMPORT YOUR CREDIT ROLL INTO YOUR EDITING OR COMPOSITING PROGRAM.

For this project, we've chosen Adobe Premiere, because that's where we've been editing the rest of our project. After importing the credit roll image, drag it to the timeline and animate it.

CREATING A CREDIT ROLL IN YOUR WORD PROCESSOR

As you can imagine, making revisions to a credit roll in Photoshop can be difficult. If you don't have a copy of Adobe Illustrator or Macromedia Freehand, you can always create a credit roll using your word processor. For this method to work, you'll need a program that can convert Postscript files into PDF format. Adobe's Acrobat Distiller is the most common solution, though there are many other commercial and shareware application. Check out www.dvhandbook.com/pdf for details on specific products.

Creating a credit roll in your word processor is very simple:

1. Set your text using your word processor's formatting controls. Pick your desired typeface and size, and use tab stops and indents to format your text.
2. Be sure that you have a Postscript printer driver selected, and then print your credit roll to a PostScript file. Your print dialog should contain simple controls for printing to a file.
3. Using your PDF-making software, convert the Postscript file into a PDF file.
4. Open the PDF file in Photoshop. Photoshop will *rasterize* (convert to pixels) the image into a single Photoshop layer.
5. Create a new layer and fill it with your desired background color. Put your background layer behind your text layer and flatten the image.

That's it! Note that with this technique you can create a credit roll using any program that can print to a Postscript file (word processors, page layout programs, etc.).

Making Titles for Film

If your final destination will be a film output, then you should have your titles recorded from the digital files directly onto film, rather than transferring them from videotape along with the rest of the project. Avoiding the intermediary step of video will produce much sharper titles (particularly at small sizes) when projected.

You'll need to create your titles at the proper aspect ratio, and at film resolution using your NLE's titler or an image editing package. Typically, film resolution is 2K per frame, or about 2020 × 1092 pixels for 1.85 theatrical

> release format 35mm, although the image size can vary from 1K to 4K, and the pixel dimensions depend on the aspect ratio of your final film.
>
> Be sure to keep your titles within the TV safe guidelines, even though you'll be creating files with a wider aspect ratio. If your images are more complex, such as superimposed titles on video footage, you should create the composite in After Effects, render the file at the proper film resolution, and have it recorded directly to film from the rendered file.
>
> Transfer houses such as EFilm, Digital Filmworks, and Eastman Kodak's Cinesite, all located in Hollywood, can transfer your titles to film for $2–$5/frame, plus set-up fees. Usually there is a minimum order of 50' of film per transfer (about 30 seconds). If you're very particular about color fidelity, talk with your film house about their color needs.

Tutorial:

ADDING CAMERA SHAKE

So first we told you to buy a camera with good optical image stabilization. Then we nagged you and berated you to use a tripod during your shoot. Now we're going to risk sounding hypocritical and show you how to *add* a shaky camera effect to your footage. Why on Earth would we want to do this? Next time you see a big action/adventure movie, pay attention to how much the camera shakes when something explodes or when cars crash into each other. Adding a camera shake can greatly increase the sense of impact in a special effect or stunt shot.

Earlier in this chapter we created a video of a finger firing a gunshot. We're going to return to this clip now and add a tiny bit of camera shake to make the image more compelling. We'll do this by animating the position of the clip to make it jitter up and down.

We recommend using Adobe After Effects for these types of effects, as its motion features are much more simple, as well as more powerful, than any other program. However, though After Effects is the ideal tool, you can use any editor or effects package that allows you to change and animate the position of a layer (Figure 16.24).

STEP 1: CREATE A PROJECT.

In After Effects, create a project, and import the hand-gun.mov file from the Camera Shake Tutorial folder located on the DV Handbook CD-ROM.

Create a new composition with the same size and duration as the movie. Place the movie in the composition.

STEP 2: ENABLE ANIMATION OF MOTION.

In many programs you must specify that you want to animate a particular property before you can set any keyframes for that property. This ensures that you don't accidentally set keyframes for things that you don't want to animate. In the After Effects Time Layout window, open the arrow next to the Hand-Gun.mov file. Now open the Transform arrow. Next to each property is a small stopwatch icon. Click the stopwatch icon next to the Position property to tell After Effects that we will be setting keyframes for the position of this layer.

STEP 3: SET THE FIRST KEYFRAME.

In the Time Layout window, scrub forward until you find the frame where the first muzzle-flash occurs. When we clicked the stopwatch icon in Step 2, After Effects automatically set a position keyframe at frame *one*. The current time marker is now at the first frame of muzzle flash. If we reposition the frame here, After Effects will automatically interpolate between the first frame and the current frame, creating a very slow movement of the image between those two frames. That's not what we want. We want a sharp jolt from the first position to a new position.

Back up one frame and set a new keyframe by clicking in the checkbox at the extreme left of the Time Layout window, in the same row as the Position property. This will set a keyframe at our current position—one frame before the muzzle flash—and serve to "lock down" the position of the image until we want it to move.

STEP 4: SET THE NEXT KEYFRAME.

Now move forward one frame. You should be back on the first frame of the first muzzle-flash. Click on the image in the Comp Window. You should see a bounding box and handles appear over the image. Press the *up* arrow key three times to move the image up three pixels. Now click the *left* arrow key twice to move the image two pixels to the left. Notice that After Effects automatically sets a keyframe for you. Be sure to thank it.

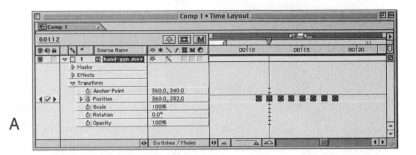

A

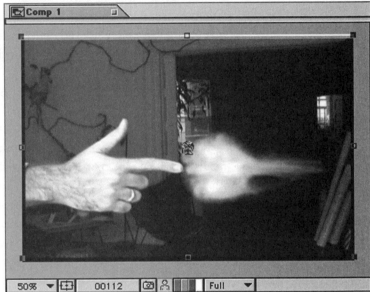

B

FIGURE **16.24** *By setting keyframes for the "hand-gun" layer's position, you can make it jitter up and down, resulting in the appearance of a shaky camera.*

STEP 5: BRING THE IMAGE BACK DOWN.

Think about how you might shake a camera when you are startled. The initial movement will be sharp and extreme. Going back to your original position will be slower. We don't want a huge shake in this case because the gunfire is not a huge event. However, we still want a slower return to our original position.

Move forward one frame. Press the *down* arrow twice and the *right* arrow once. This will move your image most of the way back to its original position.

Now move forward one more frame. Press the *down* arrow once and the *right* arrow once. This will return your image to its original location.

STEP 6: NOW DO THE REST OF THE FLASHES.

Use the same technique to shake the camera during the rest of the flashes. The flashes have different intensities, so not all the shakes need to be the same. Also, move the frame in different directions and in different amounts so that each flash doesn't look identical. You may also find that you want to put a second, smaller movement immediately after your first one. This will create a "bounce" as the camera returns to its original position.

When you're done, render your movie and give it a look. You may find that some shakes are too quick and need to be slowed down. You can click on a particular keyframe and reposition your image to adjust the degree of shake, and slide the keyframes around to adjust the timing of your camera shakes.

You'll probably also notice that when we moved the frame, we exposed the empty black space that's lying beneath it. If your final destination is video, this is not a problem, as we only moved the frame a few pixels. These black areas are at the far extreme of the Action Safe area, so any monitor will crop out these areas.

If you're going out to film, or distributing this movie on the Web or CD, then you'll have a couple of options:

- **Place another copy of the original footage beneath the shaking copy.** When the top copy moves, it will reveal the lower copy. Though the pixels aren't necessarily accurate, they're close enough that no one will notice.
- **Shrink your image size or enlarge your footage.** Instead of the previous option, you can always just crop your frame to eliminate the black areas. If you're going to the Web or to CD, you're probably going to be reducing the size of your image anyway (usually to something like 320 × 240 or smaller). So, even if you crop your image now, you'll have plenty of pixels left to do a good resizing later. We'll discuss resizing for Web output in detail in Chapter 18.

TIP

Automatic Camera Shake

If you can afford to spend some extra money, buy the After Effects Production Bundle, which includes a number of powerful extra plug-ins. In addition to superior keying functions, the Production Bundle includes special motion controls such as motion tracking (which lets you match the position of one layer to the movement of an image inside another layer) and The Wiggler, which can automatically insert random, shaky-camera-like motion (Figure 16.25).

DigiEffects Delirium also includes a special camera shake plug-in that can greatly ease the creation of camera shake effects.

FIGURE
16.25 *DigiEffects Delirium collection of Adobe After Effects plug-ins includes an automatic camera shake plug-in.*

ELIMINATING CAMERA SHAKE

Don't worry, we're not going to tell you to take out all of that camera movement that you just put it. However, you can use similar techniques to stabilize footage shot with a shaky camera. *This process is hard, time-consuming work! Don't use it as a substitute for good shooting!*

Just as we animated the movement of an image to make it shake, we can animate the movement of an image to make it stand still. The easiest way to script such an animation is to pick a reference point on your image, and animate the position of your image so as to keep that reference point in the same place. Here are some guidelines:

- **Work at high magnification.** Remember, you're concerned about tracking an individual pixel. So pick an area of high contrast and zoom in close!

- **Use guides.** If your program allows you to set guides on an image (as in After Effects), set guides along the top and side of the pixel you are going to use as your reference. This will make it easier to tell if your reference point is in the right position.

- **Remember to think backwards.** Zoomed in close, it can be difficult to remember which direction you need to move. You may have to switch back and forth between frames to figure out which direction the camera is moving (you may also have to stop for a moment to figure out which frame you're looking at). Once you've figured that out, move the camera in the opposite direction.

- **Don't expect your reference to always look the same.** Unfortunately, as the camera moves and the light on the object you're tracking changes, the pixel colors and patterns will change slightly. Though your reference point may have been a nice solid black pixel in the first frame, it might be a 60% gray pixel in the second. Depending on your camera, it may even change color as it moves! Consequently, when trying to decide how and where to move the frame, you may need to look at several frames before and after your current location to get an idea of how the pattern you are tracking is changing in appearance.

- **Don't use motion blur!** If your program can blur motion to smooth animation, be sure this feature is off!

- **Watch those sub-pixels.** Some programs actually calculate movement using distances smaller than a pixel. When zoomed in close, if you press the arrow key to move the image, you may not see anything happen.

This is because the program has performed a sub-pixel movement. You may have to zoom out to test your footage, or zoom out a few steps and try again. You can probably find a zoom level that will let you move in single pixels.

- **Aim for a reasonable amount of correction.** If your image is really moving a lot, you'll have to settle for merely calming it down, as opposed to making it completely static.

As in the previous example, as you move the frame, you'll be exposing the empty space around the edge of the layer. You can fix this problem with the same steps described in the last tutorial.

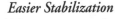

Easier Stabilization

There are two much easier ways to stabilize an image, but they will both cost you some money. The After Effects Production Bundle includes Motion Tracker and Motion Stabilizer features that can stabilize your image.

Puffin Designs' Commotion includes an even better excellent image stabilization feature. In addition, Commotion can stabilize an image and then restore its shakiness later. With this feature, you can stabilize an image to create certain effects that would be difficult to create with shaky footage, and then restore the footage—with its new effect—to its original motion. Note that Commotion DV does not include this feature. We'll deal with Commotion in more detail in Chapter 17.

Summary

You'll most likely find yourself doing some keyframe animation during the course of your project, whether to create animations or simply to create effects that subtly change over time. The most important thing to remember when setting keyframes is that the computer will *always* interpolate between two keyframes. So, as we saw in our last example, there will be times when you'll need to stop the computer from moving something around by setting a keyframe whose value is the same as its predecessor. Tracking down incorrect keyframes can be tricky, so be sure to save often when you're scripting your animation.

Every movie needs a title, and many movies also need effects that can only be created using alpha channels, keys, and keyframe animation. The best effects are those that your audience doesn't notice, that are so real they don't stop to think "how did they do that?" Whether it's simple color correction or complex compositing, honing your skills with these tools and concepts will help you create less intrusive effects. In the next chapter, we'll build on these concepts and practices to create more complex effects.

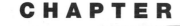

CHAPTER

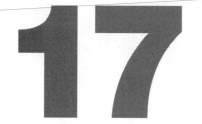

Rotoscoping and More Compositing

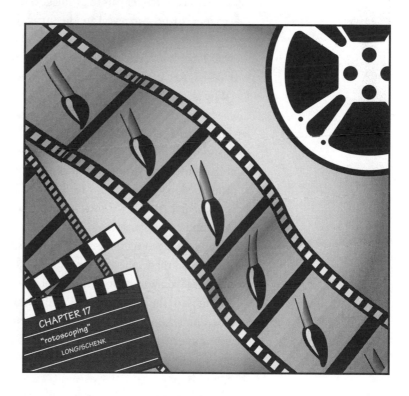

IN THIS CHAPTER

- Rotoscoping
- Special Effects
- Making Your Video Look Like Film
- Rendering

I n Chapter 16 we introduced the concept of compositing, and showed you
how you can render part of an image transparent—using a key or an alpha
channel matte—to reveal another image lying below. In this chapter, we're
going to show you how to create more complex mattes, as well as show you
how to touch up your composites with painting tools, and how to layer your
composites to create more sophisticated effects.

Why all this talk about compositing? Compositing features are the work-
horse functions of any special effects process. Yes, you may have spent weeks
creating maniacally detailed 3D models and animations of a thundering herd
of gerbils, and the results may be incredibly detailed and realistic, but unless
you can convincingly composite that animation onto your location footage of
a plain in Montana, you won't have a shot. No matter where your special effects content is created—painted by hand, shot with a film camera, generated
by a computer—in most cases, it will need to be combined with live footage.

Even if your project doesn't require any such special effects, you will need
to understand these tools if you want to perform more complicated color correction, or if you want to fix technical problems such as dropouts and glitches.

For most of the tutorials in this chapter, we're assuming you own copies of
Adobe Photoshop and Adobe After Effects. Though you might be able to
achieve some of our compositing and rotoscoping goals using your editing program, if you're serious about any kind of effects work, you really need a copy
of After Effects.

Our advanced compositing discussion begins with the digital update of a
technique that is as old as cinema.

Rotoscoping   Put simply, rotoscoping is the process of painting, drawing, or scratching on a
piece of film. If you ever shot super-8 footage as a kid and scratched laser

beams directly onto the film, then you were rotoscoping. A more impressive example, though, is the epic Disney rotoscopes that can be seen in such productions as *Cinderella*. To achieve some of the extraordinarily realistic, fluid movement, animators painted over footage of live actors dancing and moving.

The digital filmmaker has many applications for rotoscoping. At the simplest level, painting directly onto the frames of your video can be a brute force solution for achieving certain types of effects. In fact, if you're patient and talented enough, you could simply paint in all the effects you wanted! More practical examples include removing wires from models or actors, touching up the seams in a composite, adding optical effects such as lighting changes, smoke, fire, or lightning, and performing color correction. In addition, rotoscoping tools let you create complex alpha channels that can be used for fine compositing work.

In the next section, we'll lead you through a number of rotoscoping examples and tutorials and, whenever possible, we'll try to show you these techniques using applications that you already have, such as Adobe Photoshop. However, if your project will require a lot of rotoscoping effects, we heartily recommend that you buy a rotoscoping package such as Puffin Designs' Commotion, either the full version or the more affordable DV version. Though you may be loathe to spend more money on software, a package like Commotion will more than pay for itself in time savings.

PAINTING ON FRAMES

Just as Disney used to paint on celluloid, you can open up the frames of a movie and paint directly onto them using your familiar painting and image editing tools. Some programs like Commotion and MetaCreations' Painter allow you to directly open a QuickTime movie (Figure 17.1). These programs provide a simple interface for painting on a frame, and then moving to the next or previous frame to continue painting. They also offer special *onion-skinning* features that display a semi-opaque copy of one or more previous frames to help you position your paintings on the current frame.

In addition, programs like Commotion provide special tools for painting over several frames at one time (for creating real-time, "painted on" effects) and for cloning from one frame to another—an ideal way to create certain types of effects.

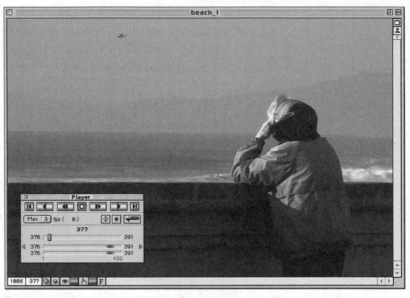

FIGURE
17.1   *Puffin Designs' Commotion lets you open a QuickTime movie for rotoscoping with its full assortment of painting tools. Commotion loads as many frames as it can fit into RAM to provide full-frame, real-time playback.*

Finding Painter

Unfortunately, at the time of this writing MetaCreations, the makers of Painter, have announced that they are selling off their entire graphics line. While Painter will probably still be available by the time you read this, we don't know who the publisher will be, or how the product might have been upgraded. Check www.dvhandbook.com/painter for more information.

If you don't have an app that can open QuickTime files directly, you can always use your favorite image editor or paint program. Obviously, to use one of these programs, you'll need to get your footage into a readable format. Fortunately, most editing and effects programs can export footage in a number of "still" formats. However, you'll need to be careful about managing these images so that you can convert them back into video later.

As we discussed earlier, most effects shots are fairly short, usually just a few seconds, sometimes even just a few frames. Consequently, you usually won't need to move huge amounts of data around. If you'll be rotoscoping in a painting or editing program, you'll need to do the following:

- Isolate the section of video that you want to manipulate.
- Export that section as a series of numbered still images. The file format you choose should be one that can support the full range of color in your video and should, obviously, be one that your painting or image editing app can work with. Most NLEs and effects programs can export PICT, TIFF, or Photoshop format (you don't want to use JPEG, GIF, or any other lossy, compressed format). When exporting, create an empty folder on your drive and point the exported files into that folder. Your editing package will take care of sequentially numbering each image file. As long as you don't change the name of any of these files, you'll be able to easily reimport them later (Figure 17.2).

BMP Sequence
Cineon AE Format Sequence
ElectricImage IMAGE
FLC/FLI
Filmstrip
JPEG Sequence
PCX Sequence
PICT Sequence
PNG Sequence
Photoshop Sequence
Pixar Sequence
✓ QuickTime Movie
SGI Sequence
TIFF Sequence
Targa Sequence

le Settings

Compo:
Format: ☐ Import into project when done

☑ Vide
Format O
Animation   nnels :   RGB
Spatial Qu   Depth :   Millions of Colors
                                                   Color :   Premultiplied (With Black)

☐ Stretch
                    Width   Height
Rendering at: 720   ×   480   ☑ Lock Aspect Ratio to (3:2)
Stretch to: 720   ×   480   Custom
Stretch %:   ×   Stretch Quality   High

☐ Crop
T: 0   L: 0   B: 0   R: 0   Final Size: 720 × 480

☐ Audio Output
Format Options...
44.100 1 Hz   16 Bit   Stereo

                                                        [Cancel]   [OK]

FIGURE **17.2**   *Adobe After Effects will let you save a movie as a numbered series of still images. You can open each of these images in a paint program or image editor for rotoscoping.*

- Using your image editor, open, paint, and resave each file without changing its name.
- Import your numbered images back into your editing or effects application. Most apps have an option for importing a "numbered sequence." This sequence will usually appear in your project window as a normal movie clip.

Notice that by following this procedure, you will preserve your full image quality since you'll never expose the frames to any compression.

Tutorial:

ROTOSCOPING A SIMPLE IMAGE

The easiest way to learn the workflow we just described is simply to try it. For this tutorial, we're going to return to our "hand-gun" movie that we developed in the last chapter. When we left off, we had just added a camera shake to make the firing of the gun more dramatic. Now we're going to use some simple rotoscoping techniques to paint some lighting effects onto the movie.

When the muzzle flashes, it should light up the hand, and possibly some of the shinier objects in the room. We could create a flash effect by applying a Levels filter to brighten the whole image, but this wouldn't look quite right as everything in the shot would be brightened equally. We want to brighten just the objects that are near the flash; that is, the hand.

As with the Camera Shake tutorial, we will be using After Effects and Photoshop for this example.

STEP 1: OPEN YOUR PROJECT AND PREPARE YOUR MEDIA.

Open the Camera Shake project that you created at the end of Chapter 16. Our plan is to rotoscope each frame where there is a muzzle flash. We don't want to use the frame in our current composition, because it has been moved to create our shake effect. Instead, we want to manipulate the original image. So, create a new composition and place the hand-gun.mov file into it.

STEP 2: EXPORT YOUR SINGLE FRAMES.

In your new composition, place the current time marker on the frame containing the first muzzle flash, then select *Composition>Save Frame As>File*.

Enter the name *muzzle flash 1.psd* and save the file. This will save the current image as a Photoshop file.

STEP 3: PAINT IT.

Open *muzzle flash 1.psd* in Photoshop. As we explained earlier, our goal is to add highlights to areas that would be flashed by the muzzle fire. Select the Dodge tool and paint the inside of the thumb, the front of the forefinger, and the tops of the other fingers that would be illuminated by the flash. You might also want to remove the shadow around the ring on the ring finger. You'll need a small brush and you might need to use several strokes.

Now is also a good time to correct any weirdness in the flash itself. When we cropped the image, we ended up cropping a little too much off the left, resulting in a hard edge on the flash. Using the smear and clone tools, we can easily correct and reshape the flash.

There are some dull specular highlights on some of the objects in the background, particularly the molding on the doorway frame, and the bright white rolls of paper. Brighten these highlights using the Dodge tool. When you're done, save the image in Photoshop format (Figure 17.3).

STEP 4: IMPORT THE MODIFIED IMAGE.

Back in After Effects, import your now-modified muzzle flash 1.psd image and place it in your camera shake composition. Place it in a layer above the hand-gun.mov layer and position it so that it begins on the exact frame as the muzzle flash in the original movie. Shorten the layer's duration to one frame (Figure 17.4).

In the previous tutorial you repositioned the movie to make the camera appear to shake. Set the muzzle flash 1.psd layer to the same position as the movie.

After Effects does not perform pixel aspect ration compensation when it imports a Photoshop image. In other words, the imported image will be too wide because of the difference in DVs rectangular pixels, and the Mac's square pixels. You can compensate for this by specifying DV pixel ratio in the comp. settings dialog.

That's it! You've effectively replaced the original frame with the new, modified one. Now you can perform the same procedure with the other muzzle flashes and then export your rendered shot to your editing program.

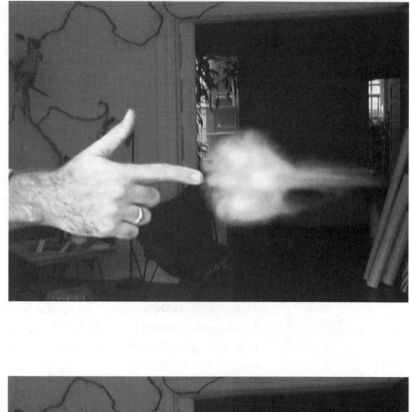

A

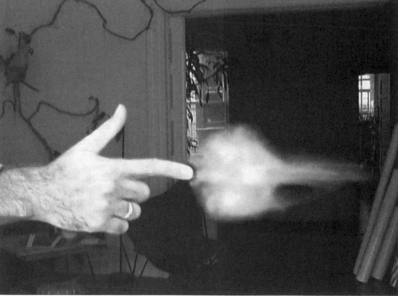

B

 You can use Photoshop's Dodge and Burn tools to paint in a flash on the frame of video where the "gun" fires.

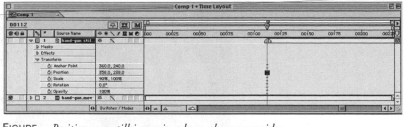

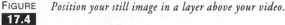

FIGURE   *Position your still image in a layer above your video.*
17.4

Whether working with single or still frames, the process just described is the basic workflow for rotoscoping. In the following tutorials we'll be using these same techniques to move video between compositing, painting, and rotoscoping applications.

BETTER ROTOSCOPING THROUGH FILTERS

As we saw in Chapter 15, most editing programs provide special effects filters such as the Color Balance and Levels filters that we used for color correction. Adobe After Effects-compatible filters have become something of a standard for effects plug-ins, and if your app supports them (or if you're using Adobe After Effects), you can buy filters that do a lot of special effects tasks that have traditionally fallen into the realm of the rotoscoping artist.

Often referred to as *opticals,* there are many effects that, until the advent of computers, were painstakingly rotoscoped by hand. Lightning bolts, sparks and flashes, laser blasts, and special color adjustments are all effects that can now be achieved automatically through filters. Though these filters don't always provide exactly the effect you're looking for, they often serve as an excellent starting point and can sometimes be combined with other filters and effects to get the desired look.

As a reference, here are some of the packages we recommend for creating a variety of "optical" effects:

- **DigiEffects Delirium** The Delirium collection is probably the most useful single collection of plug-ins that we've seen. Providing excellent Fire and Smoke filters, along with very impressive Rain, Snow, and Fairy Dust filters, Delirium provides an excellent balance of practical effects with fun, "trippy" effects (Figure 17.5).

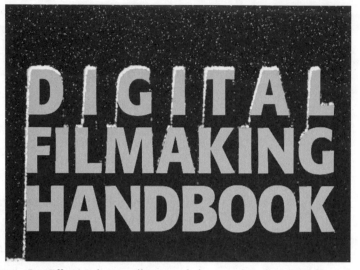

FIGURE
17.5   *DigiEffects' Delirium collection includes a number of excellent After Effects filters, including this very realistic Snowstorm filter.*

- **Cycore Computers' Cult Effects Vol. One** is best-known for its Paint plug-in that lets you paint directly onto frames in After Effects, thus providing a convenient rotoscoping environment. Cult Effects also includes other impressive filters, such as an excellent lightning filter, and a number of seemingly abstract filters that can be used to create very practical, real-world effects such as flowing lava and mud-slides (okay, "practical, real-world" for people who live in a particularly exciting, effects-heavy world).

- **Alien Skin Eyecandy** provides a number of improvements over After Effect's built-in filters, including a Gaussian Blur filter that can extend beyond the boundaries of a layer, and an HSB Noise filter. Eyecandy also provides excellent filters for beveling, chiseling, and carving shapes out of a layer, as well as a nice filter for making a layer glow.

- **Atomic Power Corporation's Evolution** collection is an impressive package of 14 plug-ins, including a Multiplane filter that simulates the multiplane cameras used by Disney animators. For creating animations with a strong sense of depth, this plug-in is one-of-a-kind. Other standouts include the Shatter plug-in, Wave World and Caustics plug-ins for creating water, and Foam, an all-purpose flocking system.

- **Puffin Designs' Image Lounge** packs a variety of plug-ins into this powerful package. In addition to very stylized text, texture, and distortion filters, Image Lounge includes high-quality fire, clouds, and smoke effects, and unique to this package, special camera effects such as focus racks (Figure 17.6).
- **ZaxWerks' EPS Invigorator** For creating cool title sequences and simple 3D effects, EPS Invigorator is indispensable. A full 3D extrusion and rendering tool, EPS Invigorator puts a tremendous amount of 3D power directly into After Effects.
- **Re:Vision Effects' Videogogh** There are a number of filters for creating realistic, natural-media effects such as painting and sketching, but none come close to Videogogh. Utilizing the technology they created for the movie *What Dreams May Come,* Re:Vision has created a package that can turn your video into beautiful, hand-painted masterpieces. Though it only does one thing, if you need a hand-painted look, this is the package to choose.

ROTOSCOPING AN ALPHA CHANNEL

As we saw in the last chapter, an alpha channel matte is essential for compositing elements and layers that don't have a background that can be easily

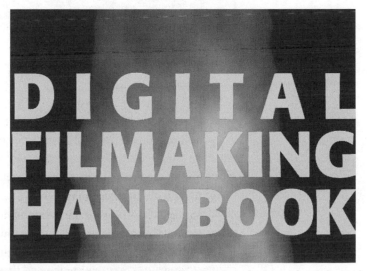

FIGURE
17.6   *Puffin Designs' Image Lounge collection is one of many packages that includes a fire filter.*

Sidebar: Stock Footage or Filters?

As we saw in Chapter 16, there are a number of effects that can be achieved by compositing stock film footage with your video. Fire, smoke, lightning, gunshots, weather, and many other effects can be achieved by purchasing high-quality stock footage from companies like ArtBeats. Or, if you're really resourceful, you can always create your own footage for compositing.

But as you can see from the list of special effects filters, there are a number of plug-ins that will also create fire, smoke, lightning, even rain and snow. So which is the better choice?

If realism is your primary concern, stock footage wins out over current plug-in technology. In addition, compositing stock footage with other video—even when using complex luma and chroma keys—will be faster than rendering effects with plug-in filters.

On the other hand, special effects plug-ins offer a degree of control and scriptability that you'll never get from stock footage. If you need flame, for example, that flickers and flares at precise moments, or lightning that travels between two very specific points, then plug-in effects will be the better choice. In addition, plug-ins don't take up additional storage on your drive the way stock footage can.

Ideally, of course, you want both, frequently mixed together. For good fire effects, for example, several layers of composited fire for realism mixed with plug-in fire effects for more control.

---

cropped or keyed out. If your foreground element is computer generated—a 3D animation, for example—then your 3D animation package will probably render an alpha channel for you. But, if your foreground element was shot on video or film, then you'll need to create an alpha channel by hand.

Just as you can use rotoscoping techniques to paint into the image in a piece of video, you can also use rotoscoping techniques to paint into the alpha channel of a piece of video to create complex, hand-painted mattes. As you'll see in the following tutorials, you'll often use a number of different tools and applications to rotoscope your alpha channel. (See Color Plate 15 for before and after shots of our intended effect.)

Tutorial:

PAINTING AN ALPHA CHANNEL BY HAND

Painting an alpha channel by hand is often the only way to create a matte for a complex foreground. If your foreground plate contains a variably hued background that can't be keyed, or a complex foreground with more detail than you can easily crop, then hand-painting your alpha channel may be your only option. If this sounds tedious, don't worry, there are a number of tips and shortcuts that make hand-cutting an alpha channel matte much simpler.

Open the *Backyard Tutorial* folder on the *DV Handbook* CD-ROM and take a look at the *Backyard raw.mov* file. You should see a 1.5 second establishing shot of a house (sorry, we'd love to have longer, more meaningful clips, but we felt it was more important to deliver full-res DV, than lower-res, smaller clips). Though the shot of the house is nice, we were originally envisioning a more dramatic sky. Our goal in this tutorial is to knock out the existing sky and replace it with something more dramatic. To do this, we'll need to create a custom alpha channel matte to define transparency in our *backyard raw* layer. This layer, along with a more dramatic sky layer, will be placed in After Effects to produce a final composite.

STEP 1: STABILIZE THE FOOTAGE.

Unfortunately, our backyard source plate has a tiny bit of movement to it. We're going to stabilize the image because we want it to be still and because it will ease the creation of an alpha channel that will work throughout the whole movie.

As we discussed in Chapter 16, stabilizing an image by hand is possible, but very difficult. Consequently, we've chosen to use Puffin Designs' Commotion 2.1 to stabilize the image. Commotion has an excellent motion tracking feature that can stabilize an image with the push of a button (well, two buttons) as you can see in Figure 17.7. Note that Commotion DV, the lower-end sibling to Commotion 2.1, lacks the motion tracking feature that is required for image stabilization.

If you don't have a copy of Commotion or the After Effects Production Bundle, don't worry, we've included a copy of the stabilized footage, called *backyard stabilized.mov*.

Commotion Troubles

One downside to Commotion 2.1 is that, upon opening a movie, Commotion will strip out any non-video tracks. Consequently, if you've got audio, timecode, text tracks, or any other non-video information that you want to save, duplicate

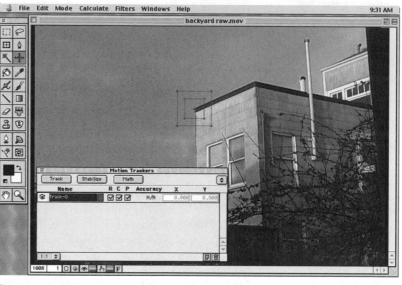

FIGURE
17.7   *Stabilizing footage using Commotion's motion tracker and stabilize feature.*

your file before you import it into Commotion. After you've exported your movie from Commotion, you can always copy back the extra tracks from your duplicate copy.

STEP 2: CREATE YOUR PROJECT.

Load the backyard stabilized.mov file into After Effects and place it in a new composition. Since this footage is a stable, static shot (thanks to Commotion), we don't need to create an alpha channel for each frame in the movie. Remember, our goal is simply to eliminate the sky and the tiny bit of motion that occurs in the frame—the waving tree branches in front of the house don't cross into the sky. So, we can simply create an alpha channel for the first frame and trust that it will work for the whole movie. Save the document as *backyard.ae*.

STEP 3: EXPORT THE FIRST FRAME.

We will be creating our alpha channel in Adobe Photoshop, so our first task is to get the first frame of our movie into a form that will be usable in Photoshop. With the current time marker on the first frame of the movie, select

Composition>Save Frame As>File to export this frame as a Photoshop file (Figure 17.8).

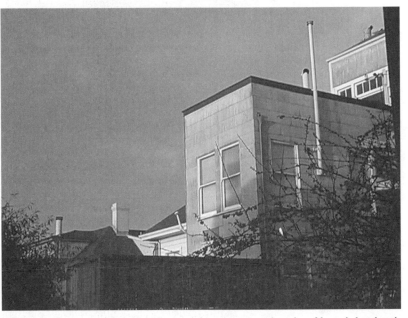

FIGURE
17.8
We can export the first frame of this movie as a Photoshop file and then hand-cut a matte in Photoshop.

STEP 4: OPEN THE IMAGE IN PHOTOSHOP AND START THE MASK.

Take a look at the image and consider what will be required to cut a good mask. Fortunately, this image is pretty simple. The houses and chimneys all have a good, strong border. The only potentially troublesome area is the bush to the left side of the image. As we saw in Chapter 16, you can create an alpha channel in Photoshop by defining a selection, and Photoshop has a number of tools for creating selections.

You could try to use the Magic Wand tool to select the sky, but unfortunately, the sky is slightly cloudy, meaning the magic wand won't be able to zero in on a single color. Similarly, the sky is a little too mottled for Photoshop's Color Range tool. If you're using Photoshop 5.5, you might be wondering why we aren't just using the Magic Erase or the Extract command, both of which were designed to eliminate backgrounds. The problem with these tools is that they simply erase the background, they don't define a selection or provide any way of translating the masking information that they generate into an alpha channel.

No, the only way out of this one is to paint the mask by hand. Fortunately, Photoshop is well-equipped for this sort of work. Click on the Photoshop QuickMask tool located at the bottom of the Tool palette. When in this mode, we can simply paint the areas that we want to mask. Masked areas will appear red. Grab a big brush and fill in the large, empty portions of the sky. Don't worry about getting in close around the houses or foliage, just mask out as much of the sky as you can using a large brush.

Change Your Cursor
The rest of this lesson will go much easier if you go to File>Preferences>Display and Cursors and set Painting Cursors *to* Brush Size.

STEP 5: OUTLINE THE HOUSES.

Now grab a smaller brush and zoom in to the right side of the image. Our goal here is to create a tight mask around the houses. Fortunately, the houses are mostly made of straight lines. Click at the right edge of the image where the doorway meets the top of the frame. Position the edge of your brush against the line of the roof, and click. Follow the roof-line and you'll see that that edge goes for a short distance and then turns 90° to the left. The corner of that angle is the end of the first straight "segment." Hold down the Shift key and click once at this corner. Photoshop will automatically connect your first click to this second click and create a straight line between. Continue outlining the houses using this manner until you reach the shrub.

STEP 6: PREPARE FOR THE SHRUB.

Obviously, trying to paint around the shrub will be a frustrating exercise. Instead of painting around the shrub, Make a couple of broad strokes around it to close it off from the rest of the image. Your painted areas should now look like Figure 17.9. Click on the Selection button at the bottom of the Tool palette (the button to the left of the QuickMask button). This will convert your painted areas into a selection. Save the selection into an alpha channel. We won't be using this channel, but we're going to save it anyway, just in case something goes wrong in the next step.

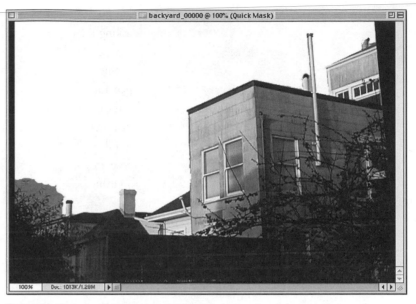

FIGURE
17.9   *With the QuickMask tool, we painted around each house and up to, but not including, the complex shrub. We'll add that selection later using a different tool.*

STEP 7: SELECT THE SHRUB.

With your selection still selected, pick the Magic Wand tool. Hold down the Shift key and click on the sky-filled areas in the bush. With the Shift key held down, each Magic Wand selection will be added to your hand-painted selection (though the alpha channel you saved earlier isn't being altered). Continue Magic-Wand-selecting the areas around the bush until you feel like you've selected all of the most conspicuous areas. Don't expect to get rid of all of the varying hues of sky visible in the bush, and don't worry, we're going to correct for those problems later. If you make a mistake that you can't undo, press command-D to deselect, then reload your selection from your alpha channel and start over with the Magic Wand (Figure 17.10).

STEP 8: SAVE YOUR ALPHA CHANNEL.

When you're satisfied with your bush work, save the selection. Now open up the Channels palette and you'll see you have two alpha channels. You can delete the first one, as it was our safety copy. Click on the second one to view

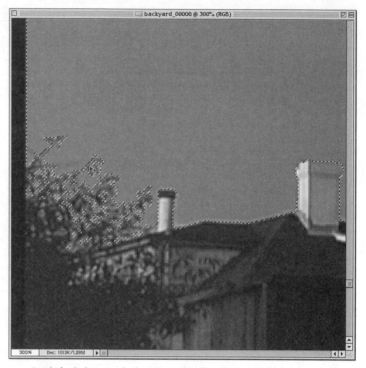

FIGURE   *By shift-clicking with the Magic Wand tool, we can add the shrub to our se-*
17.10   *lection.*

it. The Magic Wand tool does not create the smoothest selections, so select the
Blur tool and paint over the "bush" areas to smooth out, or feather, the Magic
Wand selections that you made in Step 7. Remember, the blurry, gray areas of
the mask will be semi-opaque when composited and will serve to smooth and
blur the fuzzy bush shape into the background (Figure 17.11).

SAVE 9: SAVE YOUR DOCUMENT.

Now we want to do something new. We're going to apply this alpha channel to each frame in our movie. Rather than copying our alpha channel information into our movie file, we're simply going to export the alpha channel
from this document, and attach it to our movie in After Effects.

From the Channels palette menu (the triangle thing in the upper right-
hand corner of the Channels palette), select *Duplicate Channel.* For Destination, select *New.* Hit OK, and a new document will be created. Before you save

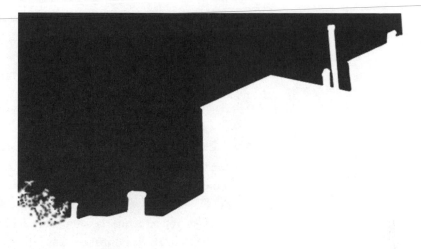

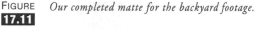

FIGURE   *Our completed matte for the backyard footage.*
17.11

this document, however, you'll need to change its Mode to Grayscale. Select Image>Mode>Grayscale.

Save the document in Photoshop format as *backyard matte.psd*.

STEP 10: CREATE SOME CLOUDS.

Before we leave Photoshop, we're going to create some clouds to place in the background. Though we could use stock footage of clouds, or render ani-mated clouds in a 3D program, we're going to stick with a simple still of some wispy clouds. Create a new RGB document measuring 720 by 640 pixels at 72 dpi. Click the foreground color swatch and select a slightly undersaturated, reddish-orange. Choose Filter>Render>Clouds. Voilà! Instant clouds. Save this document as a Photoshop document and call it clouds.psd.

STEP 11: BACK TO AFTER EFFECTS.

Open the *backyard.ae* file that you created earlier. Import the *backyard matte.psd* document and the clouds.psd document. Place the clouds in your composition *beneath* the backyard stabilized.mov layer. You won't see the clouds at all, since the backyard plate is obscuring them. Place the backyard matte document into your composition, and layer it *above* the *backyard stabilized* file. It should completely obscure the *backyard stabilized* layer. In the Timeline window, click the eyeball icon in the backyard matte layer. This should make the matte layer invisible (Figure 17.12).

STEP 12: DEFINE THE ALPHA CHANNEL.

Now we want to tell After Effects to use the backyard matte layer as the alpha channel of the *backyard stabilized* layer. Click on the *backyard stabilized* layer in the Time Layout window and choose Effect>Channels>Set Channels. Set Channels lets you re-define the source of each channel in the current layer. We want to use our backyard matte document as the alpha channel for the *backyard stabilized* layer. In the Set Channels dialog, change the *Set Alpha to Source* pop-up menu to *Luminance*. In the field above that, set *Source Layer 4*

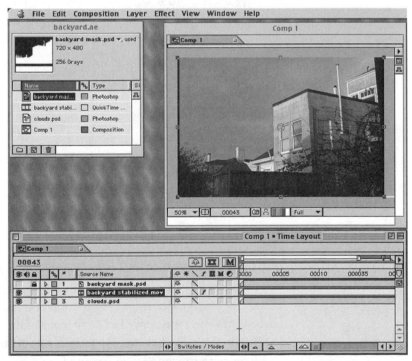

FIGURE *Our AE project before activating our alpha channel. Note that the backyard matte layer has its visibility turned off. We don't need to see it, we just need access to its luminance information.*

to *backyard mask.psd*. This tells After Effects to use the luminance information of the *backyard matte* layer as the alpha channel in the *backyard stabilized* layer. Because the backyard matte layer is all luminance (it's black and white, no chrominance), it will correctly interpret our alpha channel.

You should now see the clouds composited behind the houses!

If there is slight fringing or other artifacts between the foreground and background, you can always go back to Photoshop and try to correct them. Before you go to that much trouble, though, render the file out (using the Animation compressor, of course) and import it into your editing program. Then, take a look at the footage on your NTSC monitor. You may find that any slight fringes aren't visible.

For a little extra drama, consider adding a slight movement to the clouds layer to make it slowly drift behind the houses.

CREATING ANIMATED ALPHA CHANNELS (OR, "YOU TOO CAN MAKE TRAVELLING MATTES")

In the film world, when you cut a separate matte of each frame of film to follow the action of an element, you are creating a *travelling matte*. You can create the same effect in your DV files by creating an animated alpha channel. Using the same techniques that we described in the previous tutorial, you can create a separate matte for each frame of your video. When played back, the matte will "travel" about the frame to follow the action and properly mask the elements in your movie.

If you think hand-cutting a separate mask for each frame of your movie sounds like a tedious chore, you're right! Fortunately, there are some techniques and tools that can greatly simplify the process.

Tutorial:

COLOR CORRECTING PART OF AN IMAGE

In Chapter 15 we showed you how to use color correction filters to change the color in your image. When a color correction filter was attached to a layer, the filter's effect was applied to every frame of the clip. In this tutorial, we're going to show you how to color correct *part* of your image—not just some frames, but a specific element *within* a frame.

Open the Animated Alphas folder and watch the *jose.mov* file. You should see a brief clip of a big green parrot sitting on a perch. To make a more stylized image, and to bring more attention to the bird, we want to convert the background of the image to black and white.

Converting a movie to black and white is easy; we simply use a Saturation filter to desaturate the movie, effectively stripping away all the color information. However, if you desaturate the jose.mov file, everything, including the bird, will be desaturated. We need a way to mask the image so that the effect is only applied to the background. In other words, we need an alpha channel.

However, unlike our previous example, the area we want to mask in this movie (the parrot in the foreground) is moving. If we use a simple, single-frame matte like we used in the previous tutorial, parts of the bird will move outside of the mask and be subject to the same desaturation as the background. So, we must create an animated map.

Again, we assume that you will be using Adobe Photoshop and Adobe After Effects for this tutorial. This particular process is much easier using either Puffin Designs' Commotion or their less expensive Commotion DV.

STEP 1: MOVE YOUR VIDEO INTO PHOTOSHOP.

Photoshop can't open QuickTime movies, so you'll need to convert the jose.mov file into something that Photoshop can open. Create a project in After Effects and import the jose.mov file. Create a composite with the same size, frame rate, and dimensions as the movie. Place the movie into the composite and choose Composition>Make Movie.

Create a new folder on your hard drive called *jose stills*. Title your movie *jose stills* and save it in your new folder. In the Render Queue dialog, click on the *Current Settings* text next to *Render Settings*. Set Quality to Best and hit OK. Now click on the *Current Settings* text next to *Output Module*. Click on the pop-up menu next to Format and select *Photoshop Sequence* (Figure 17.13).

Hit OK, and then press Render. After Effects will write out your movie as a series of Photoshop documents, numbered in sequential order. You will modify each of these documents, and then bring the modified documents back into After Effects.

Don't worry about saving this After Effects project, you don't need it for anything else.

STEP 2: OPEN THE FIRST FRAME IN PHOTOSHOP.

In Photoshop, open the first of your stills. Take a look at the image to assess what will need to be done for this effect to work (Figure 17.14). First, the

FIGURE   *In After Effects, you can render a movie as a series of still images.*
17.13

good news: the background behind the parrot is composed of glass bricks that are mostly shades of gray. This means that our matte doesn't have to be perfect. If there's some extra space around the bird, it probably won't matter, as those areas will look mostly gray anyway.

If you go back and watch the movie again, you'll see that his movements are mostly confined to a horizontal axis and that his overall shape doesn't change too much when he moves. His feet and tail are firmly planted, and even his back and wings stay fairly stationary. His movement is confined to his head, neck, and beak. This makes our job easier.

At this point, there are two ways to proceed. You can paint a mask using the QuickMask tool, as we did in the last tutorial. After painting the mask and sav-

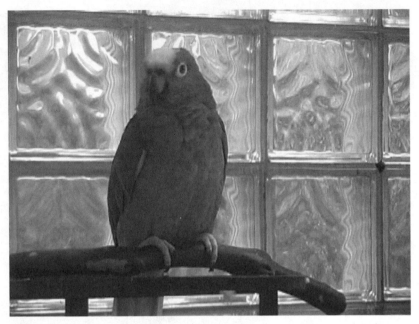

This is the image we'll be masking. We'll need to create a matte that changes
17.14 *with the movement of the parrot.*

ing it as an alpha channel, you can copy that channel into the next frame. If
the mask needs to be altered, you can correct it, and then copy that new mask
to the next frame and so on and so forth.

A more flexible alternative is to use Photoshop's Pen tool to define a path
around the bird. You can use this path to create an alpha channel, then copy
the path to the next frame, adjust it, create an alpha channel, and move on to
the next frame.

Because they are easier to modify, we're going to use paths.

STEP 3: CREATE A PATH.

Open the Paths palette and click on the New Path icon at the bottom of the
palette. Select the Pen tool and begin tracing around the parrot starting on the
left side where his foot touches the perch. Work all the way around, including
his toes (don't worry about the toenails, they're already black) and the section
of green visible between the wood perch and the metal perch support. Finally,
work your way back to where you started and close the path.

After completing your outline of the bird, you'll need to outline the section of tail that hangs below the perch (Figure 17.15).

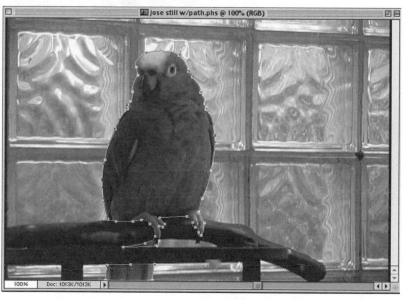

FIGURE
17.15   *We can use Photoshop's Pen tool to outline the bird, and then convert this path to a selection. Because paths are easily modified, it will be easier to change this selection for later frames.*

STEP 4: CONVERT THE PATH TO AN ALPHA CHANNEL.

When you're satisfied with your paths, hold down Command and Shift and click on each path to select them all. From the Paths palette menu, choose *Make Selection*. Make sure *anti-aliased* is checked and set a Feather value of 1. Hit OK and a selection will be made, based on your path.

STEP 5: SAVE YOUR SELECTION AND YOUR DOCUMENT.

Choose Save Selection from the Select menu and accept the defaults. A new alpha channel will be created. Now save your document (Figure 17.16).

STEP 6: MOVE YOUR PATHS.

Press Command-D to deselect your selection. Make sure that all your paths are still selected (if not, Command-Shift click on each one to select them all)

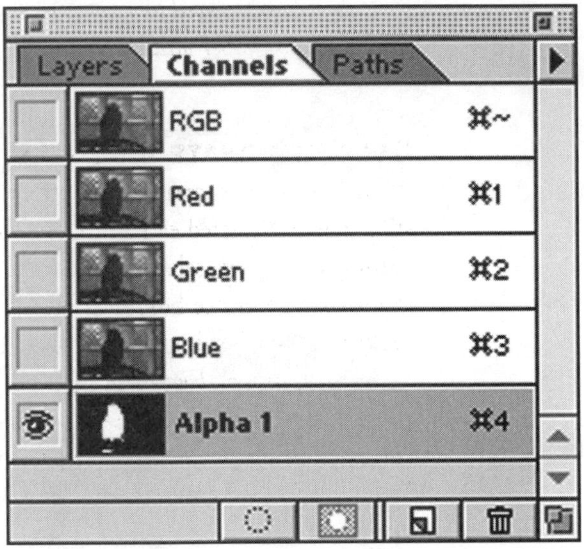

FIGURE **17.16** As in the previous tutorial, your Channels palette will show the red, green, blue, and your new alpha channel.

and hit Command-C to copy them. Open the next still in the sequence and hit Command-V to paste your paths into this document. If your paths need to be moved, you can drag them to the proper position while they're still selected. If they need to be adjusted, drag individual control points until the path fits the bird in the new frame.

STEP 7: NOW REPEAT STEPS 4 THROUGH 6 FOR EACH FRAME.

Now make your selection, save your document, and copy the paths to the next frame. Continue in this manner until all of your frames have been given an alpha channel. Many of the frames will be fine as-is—you won't need to adjust the paths. It's only when he starts moving that you'll have to make a lot of adjustments. When you've processed each frame, quit Photoshop and return to After Effects.

TIP

Let Us Work for You
If you don't want to go to the trouble of cutting each matte, we've included a movie called jose with matte.mov *that already has an alpha channel. You can use it for the remainder of this tutorial. However, to save space on the CD, this*

movie has been reduced to pixel dimensions of 360 × 240. You'll need to adjust the size of your other media accordingly.

STEP 8: CREATE A NEW AE PROJECT.

In After Effects, create a new project. If you are going to use the modified stills that you created earlier, choose *File>Import>Import File Footage.* In the ensuing dialog box, select the first frame of the sequence. Be sure to check the Photoshop Sequence box, then hit OK. If you're going to use the *jose with matte.move* file, just import it as normal.

In the *Interpret Footage* dialog, accept the default of *Treat as Straight.* If you're using the *jose with matte.mov* file, be sure to check the Invert Matte checkbox (when we created the alpha channel we masked out the foreground instead of the background—this is no big deal since After Effects can invert it on import).

Create a new composition with the same size, duration, frame rate, and pixel shape as your imported movie.

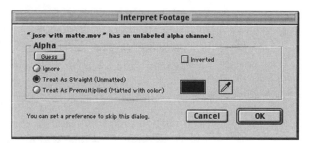

FIGURE   *When you import the* jose with matte.mov, *be sure to select Treat as Straight*
17.17   *in the Interpret Footage dialog. (See your After Effects manual for details.)*

STEP 9: ADD YOUR MEDIA.

Place the movie in the composition. You should immediately see black in place of the background. This is because After Effects is already interpreting the alpha channel in your movie, and rendering those areas transparent. Because there's nothing beneath the movie, the masked areas appear as black.

Now import the original jose.mov file and place it in your composition. In the Timeline window, drag the jose.mov layer down so that it sits below your masked layer.

Now your composition should look normal. Since the masked foreground layer is sitting on top of the original background layer, and the two layers are in perfect sync, you can't tell that any modifications have been made. But, of course, they have, and the result is that you now effectively have one layer for the background, and another layer for the foreground.

STEP 10: ADD YOUR FILERS.

Click once on the lower layer in the Timeline window to select it. From the Effects menu, select *Adjust>Hue/Saturation*. In the Hue Saturation controls, slide the *Master Saturation* slider down to –100. Close the Effects window.

That's it. Your background should now be grayscale, while your foreground is still color! Of course, for added effect, you can also modify the foreground layer or apply additional filters and effects to either layer.

BUILDING EFFECTS WITH MULTIPLE LAYERS

In the last tutorial, you built a complicated effect by stacking slightly modified versions of the same video clip. Though it may seem simple, this is an important concept, and an approach that many beginning compositors often miss. It can be tempting to try to create a lot of effects inside of one layer by applying filters and masks. However, most of the time, you'll need to break an effect down into a number of different processes, and use a separate copy of your video for each process. For many effects, you'll create several duplicates of a video clip and spend a lot of time cutting a different alpha channel for each clip. These clips will be filtered and manipulated separately, and then stacked on top of each other.

In the next tutorial, we will combine layer stacking with rotoscoping to create a complicated effects shot of a person literally sneezing his head off.

Tutorial:

EXPLODING HEADS

In this tutorial we're going to create a complex composite using several instances of the same video clip. By combining several hand-cut mattes, a lot of hand-painting, and a filter from Atomic Power Corporation's Evolution collection, we will create a movie showing a person's head shattering into a million pieces after an over-strenuous sneeze. (In the industry, this type of film is known as "high concept.")

When planning an effect like this, you may not be able to imagine exactly what post-production manipulations the shot will require. Most likely, you'll have to feel your way through the process and add new layers and filters as you see they are necessary. However, you can make some informed decisions about how to begin.

There is a demo copy of the Evolution plug-in package on the *DV Handbook* CD-ROM. Install it into your copy of After Effects before you begin this tutorial.

The Sneeze tutorial folder contains a video clip called *sneeze orig.mov*. This is our source footage which shows a person sneezing, and then stumbling out of frame. To see how the shatter plug-in works, load the sneeze orig.mov footage into After Effects and apply the Evolution Shatter effect. You'll see that the whole image shatters, and in a form that doesn't really look like a shattery explosion (Figure 17.18).

We can easily adjust the plug-ins settings to create a more appropriate type of shatter. But since we want just the head to shatter, we need to mask out the rest of the frame using an alpha channel. This will be our starting point.

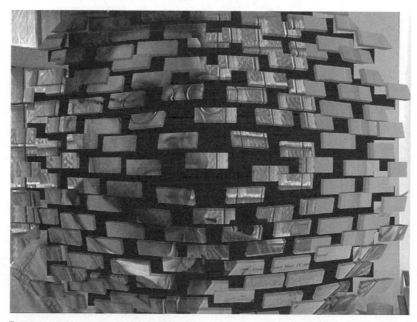

FIGURE
17.18   *The Evolution Shatter filter is nice, but we want to change its shatter settings to create more of an explosion effect, and we want the plug-in to only affect the actor's head.*

STEP 1: CREATE AN ALPHA CHANNEL OF THE HEAD.

First, you need to decide when in the movie you want the shatter to occur. As far as creating an alpha channel goes, the frames after this point won't matter because the head will already be shattered, while the frames before don't matter because we won't be trying to filter them. So, we only have to create an alpha channel for one frame. We chose 00:00:03:10 (or frame 101) since there's a nice, slight head jerk that will add to the feeling of impact.

TIP

Choosing Time Display in After Effects

For some parts of this tutorial, we will be using Puffin Designs' Commotion, which displays frame numbers rather than time code. To make it easier to move back and forth between After Effects and Commotion, you can set After Effects to display frame numbers, by going to File>Preferences>Time, and selecting Frames.

For this tutorial, we will be creating masks as separate files, rather than as alpha channels embedded in our movie files. This will allow for more flexibility to correct and change the mattes. Because we only need an alpha channel of this one frame, you can easily create the mask in Photoshop. In After Effects, export a still of frame 101 from the *sneeze orig.mov* movie. To do this, load the *sneeze orig.mov* movie into a composition, select its layer in the Time Layout window, and then choose Composition>Save Frame As.

Rather than create a selection as we did in previous tutorials, you can simply paint over the background areas with black paint, and the foreground areas with white paint. Because you probably won't need to re-edit this image, go ahead and use Photoshop's Image Size command to perform a 90% horizontal scale. Scaling your image here will save you a tiny bit of rendering time later. Save this image as a Photoshop file called *head matte.psd* (Figure 17.19).

STEP 2: SET UP YOUR PROJECT.

Now go back to After Effects, create a project, and import the *sneeze orig.mov* movie and the head matte.psd file that you just created. Make a new composition with the appropriate size and duration to hold the movie. Name this comp Main.

In a moment, we will use our new matte to confine the effects of the Shatter plug-in to the actor's head. Since this matte will eliminate the rest of the frame, we will see *only* a shattering head. So, as we did in our previous tutor-

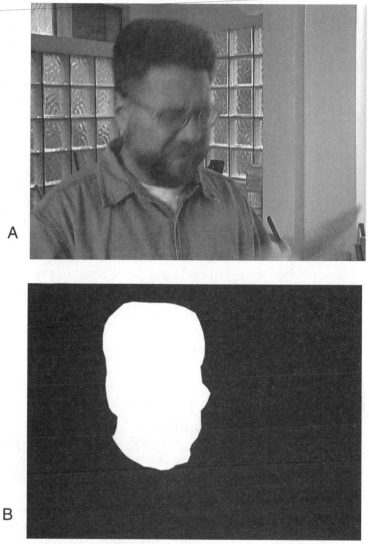

FIGURE
17.19   *Still frame, accompanying matte.*

ial, we will need to layer two copies of the same movie on top of each other. The top one will have the matte and the Shatter effect applied, the bottom will serve to keep our "background" visible.

Place the *sneeze orig.mov* file into your composition. This layer will be our background.

STEP 2: PREPARE THE SECOND LAYER.

At this point, we could start heaping more layers on top of the first one. In the interest of housekeeping, though, we're going to isolate some effects and layers by putting them in their own compositions. These compositions can then be nested inside our main composition to ease organization of our project.

Create another composition with the same settings as the first, but name this one *Exploding head*.

Add the *sneeze orig.mov* clip to the Exploding Head composition and double-click on it in the Time Layout window. This will open the movie in its own layer and allow you to easily set the in-point. Drag the current time maker to frame 100 and click the In-Point button. Close the window.

With the in-point set here, the movie in this comp now starts one frame before we want our explosion to begin (the Evolution Shatter effect doesn't become visible until the second frame of the movie).

Now import the head matte.psd image you created earlier. Add it to you Exploding Head comp and disable the matte's visibility by clicking its eye icon in the Time Layout window. Click on the *sneeze orig.mov* file to select it, and use the Set Channels filter to assign the head matte.psd's luminance values to the *sneeze orig.mov* movies alpha channel (Figure 17.20).

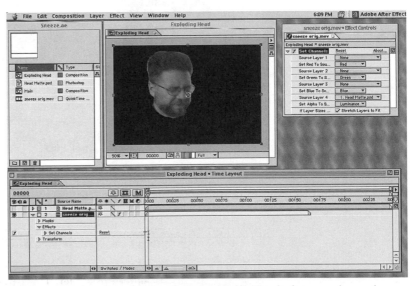

 FIGURE 17.20 *Our second composition, Exploding Head, after the footage and matte layers have been added. Note the Set Channel filter, which is used to activate the matte.*

STEP 3: ADD THE SHATTER.

Now put the Exploding Head comp inside the Main comp. The easiest way to do this is inside the Project window. Just drag the Exploding Head comp on top of the Main comp.

The Main comp should now have two layers, the *sneeze orig.mov* clip and the Exploding Head comp. Notice that the Exploding Head comp acts just like any other layer. You can move it, change its in- and out-points, and re-layer it. If you want to go back and change its contents you can, and those changes will automatically filter up to the Main comp.

Re-position the Exploding Head comp so that it begins on frame 100 (Figure 17.21).

You can also add filters to a nested comp. Do that now by selecting the Exploding Head layer and choosing Effect>Evolution>Shatter. To get the best-looking shatter, you'll need to change some settings in the Shatter filter dialog. Open the Shape property and set Shatter Map to Glass.

Click on the crosshairs next to Shape Origin and click in the comp window, just below the person's nose. Set the Shape Repetitions to 20. Set the shape direction to about 60°, and set the Force 1 position to just above the person's right eye. (Incidentally, there's no science to determining these settings. These are simply parameters that we came up with after a lot of trial and error. As you work through creating the shot, you may want to create a different-looking shatter.)

Close the Effects window and position the current time marker at frame 101 to see the beginning of your explosion. Then render a small test movie so that you can see the entire effect (Figure 17.22).

Something's very wrong, isn't it? The shattering effect looks nice, but there's still a head left behind. Obviously, the shatter effect can't calculate what's be-

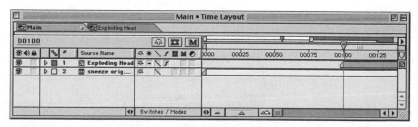

FIGURE
17.21
With the Exploding Head comp properly positioned, the explosion will occur right after the actor has sneezed.

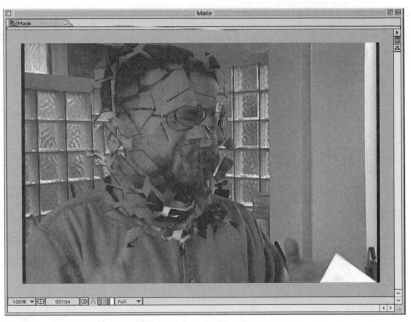

FIGURE
17.22   *The shattering head layer composited on top of our original background footage. At least the shatter is now confined to the actor's head.*

hind the head in our footage, so we're going to need to create that information ourselves through some very tedious rotoscoping.

STEP 4: START ROTOSCOPING.

In our Main comp we have our original video layer, and a shattering copy of that same video layered on top of it. If our bottom layer was footage of a headless body, then when the top layer shattered, it would reveal the underlying headless footage and our effect would work.

Unfortunately, we didn't shoot footage of a headless body (we had cast a headless body, but he turned out to be a real prima donna and so we fired him), but we can create some headless body footage through rotoscoping.

How to rotoscope is up to you. You could export the movie as a set of still files and repaint them in Photoshop. Or, as we chose to do, you could open the movie file in Commotion and rotoscope it.

Your goal is to paint out the head, and build a collar and hole to go where the head used to be. We used Commotion's SuperClone tool to clone from an empty frame at the end of the movie over the head in each frame (Figure 17.23).

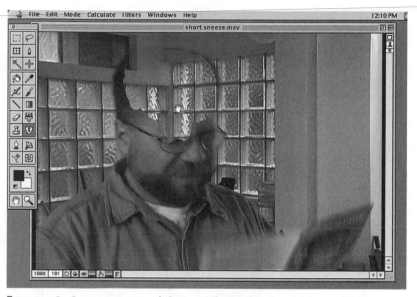

FIGURE   *In Commotion, we used the SuperClone tool to clone background from an*
17.23   *empty frame at the end of the movie.*

After that, we used the Rotospline tools to build and animate a collar shape that follows the action in the clip. We also built an animated rotospline for the hole where the neck used to be. These shapes were filled with special patterns of color and then touched up using the Brush, Blur, and Dodge/Burn tools (Figure 17.24).

However you choose to do it, the process will take you a while. To save you some time, we have included a rough, first pass of our rotoscoped movie, a file called *sneeze roto.mov*. Though a good place to start, this file still needs work to clean up some cloning artifacts, and to retouch and improve the collar and neck. For now, it will work fine.

STEP 5: ADD THE ROTOSCOPED MOVIE.

Back in After Effects, replace the *sneeze orig.mov* movie in your Main comp with your new rotoscoped version. Render the movie (Figure 17.25).

Now things are looking better! When the head explodes, you should see a headless body that staggers off-screen.

However, the effect could still be better. The explosion looks like an animated explosion stuck on the front of a piece of video. It would be more real-

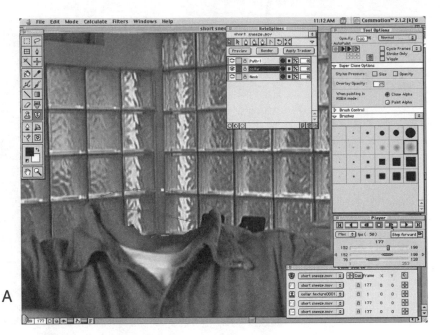

A

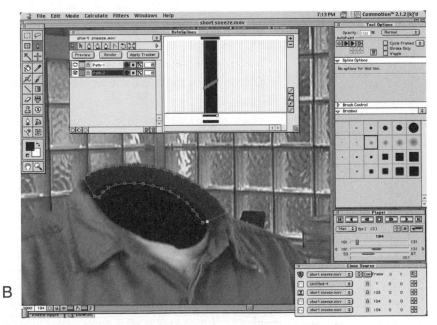

B

FIGURE
17.24
A First we used the Rotospline tools to build an animate a collar shape.
B Then we used the Paintbrush, Blur, and Dodge/Burn tools to fill in the collar and neck.

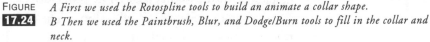

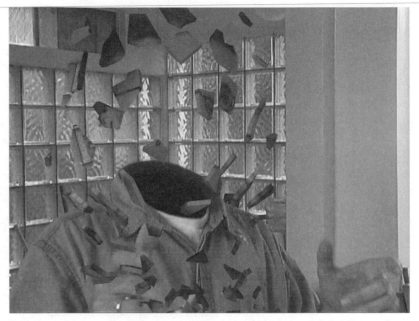

FIGURE   *The same After Effects project, but now with the rotoscoped, headless version*
17.25   *of our original footage.*

istic if the explosion had a sense of depth. Is there a way we could get some of
the explosion parts to fly *behind* the body? Of course!

What if we added another copy of the headless body, but this one with a
matte, so that the explosion pieces were obscured by the matte? Obviously, we
don't want all of the explosion to fall behind the body, so we'll create a second
instance of the exploding head layer. This addition will also add drama to the
shot by adding even more shattering debris.

STEP 6: MASK THE BODY.

Unlike our head matte, the body matte that we'll use to mask our second
shatter effect will actually need to be a travelling matte. Using whatever technique you prefer, create a travelling matte of the relevant frames of the headless body movie. Obviously, you don't need to worry about anything before
frame 101. Take a look at your previously rendered movie to determine how
long the explosion lasts. You don't need to worry about masking any frames
after this point.

Again, we chose to use Commotion and created a simple, animated roto-spline to follow the outlines of the body. We rendered the matte as a separate file, which is stored on the CD-ROM as *body matte.mov*.

STEP 7: ADD THE NEW EXPLOSION.

Back in After Effects, create a new comp called *body w/matte*. Put the sneeze orig.mov and body matte.mov files into the new composition. As before, set up body matte.mov to serve as the matte.

Now add the body w/matte comp to your Main comp. Put the current time marker at frame 106. As you can see, the body w/matte layer now obscures part of the explosion, making it look as if the shattered pieces are falling behind the body (Figure 17.26).

Now we need to get pieces falling in front. In the Time Layout window, duplicate the exploding head comp. Drag the copy so that it is the topmost layer. Now you should see some pieces in front of the body as well. Note that, with the same settings, both copies will produce identical shatter patterns. Change the Shatter settings on one of the Exploding Head layers to create a different-

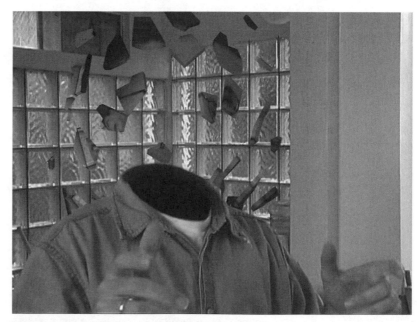

FIGURE   *The shatter fragments now fly behind the body.*
17.26

looking explosion. We chose to change the lower layer to create the effect of pieces flying backwards (Figure 17.27).

Now render the movie.

Looks better, but there's still a problem. The shards of the top explosion fly in front of the actor's right hand. Since the hand serves to indicate a lot of

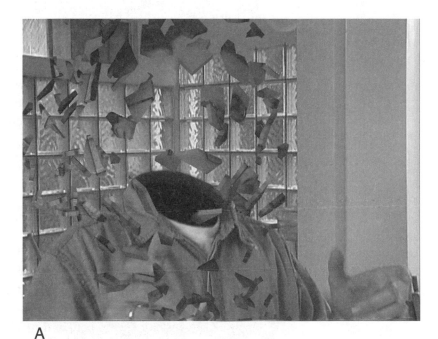

A

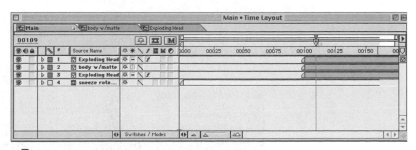

B

FIGURE **17.27**   *We managed to get shattering pieces to fly both in front of, and behind the body, by stacking several copies of the same layer.*

depth in the image, we should create yet another masked layer—this time of the hand—to put in front of everything else.

STEP 8: MATTE THE HAND.

Again, using your method of choice, create a matte for the relevant frames of the hand. As before, watch the original footage to try to determine which frames will interact with head fragments. You don't want to worry about masking frames that don't matter.

STEP 9: ADD THE FINAL LAYER.

Back in After Effects, create another comp called Hand. Add another copy of the sneeze roto.mov as well as a copy of the hand matte. Use Set Channels to set up your alpha channel. Add this comp to the Main comp and put it at the very top.

Render the movie.

Much better! Head parts flying everywhere! In front of the body, behind the body, and behind the hand. However, we want to make one more small adjustment.

The Shatter plug-in renders its fragments with very sharp, defined edges. The amount of sharpness doesn't really match the quality of our original video, so we need to soften the explosion images up a bit to better match our source footage.

Apply a Gaussian Blur filter to both of the Exploding Head layers. Set a Blurriness of 2.0. You can experiment with more blur, but you don't want to blur the images too much, or they'll be blurrier than our source footage.

Render the final movie out using the Animation compressor, put it in your editing package, and take a look at it on your NTSC monitor (Figure 17.28). There, you can better see how to fix the collar and neck rotoscoping, as well as look for any left-over clone artifacts.

Use Field Rendering

If you're outputting for DV, be sure to set "Field Render" to "Lower Field first" in the "Render Settings" dialog. Otherwise, your video will have a weird stutter.

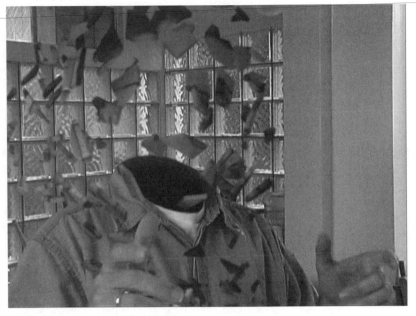

FIGURE   *The completed compositing.*
17.28

To touch-up the movie you can choose to re-paint your final movie, or go back and correct the sneeze roto.mov file, and then re-render your movie. Because we used multiple copies of that same movie, you can simply correct the original file and your changes will filter throughout your whole After Effects project.

Performing your touch-ups on your final rendered movie might be the best choice, as you won't waste time touching up areas that are obscured by falling debris. In addition, you can use the opportunity to smear the falling artifacts so that their motion quality better matches the footage of the actor.

If you perform your touch-up in the original rotoscoped file, then you can always make other changes and improvements in After Effects, and re-render the file.

You might also play with animating the values of the blur filters that you applied to the Exploding Head layers. By setting keyframes for the blurriness, you can make the fragments get more and less blurry as they speed up and slow down throughout the course of the explosion.

As you can see, with just a single clip of video and some clever layering, you can create very complex effects. Ideally, you'll need to do some planning before you shoot your initial footage. For the exploding head shot, for example, you might have been able to ease your rotoscoping work by shooting some additional photographic plates. In the end, you'll want to weigh the time and money spent rotoscoping against the time and money needed to shoot multiple plates.

Special Effects

With the procedures and concepts we've covered in the last three chapters, you now have all of the basic tools that you'll need to create most any effect. Of course, there is a whole bunch of other tools and programs you can learn for creating the content that you will composite into your video, but your compositing process will always involve the concepts we've covered here.

Many complex effects will involve the same techniques we've been using, but at a much higher magnitude—many more layers, composites, and custom-generated mattes, each serving to add a little more to your shot. As we saw in the last tutorial, many effects are simply a process of patient trial and error. It may take you a while to find the right combination of layers, filters, hand-painting, and custom settings to achieve the effect you're looking for.

In the rest of this chapter, we're going to present a number of effects that use and build upon the skills we've already discussed. These effects cover everything from fixing drop-outs to making your video look more like film. Hopefully, these examples will help you better understand the concepts we've already covered, and recognize how these concepts can be combined and altered to create more effects.

We will not be presenting step-by-step tutorials for these discussions. Rather, we'll simply outline the steps required to achieve each effect. We will present no new concepts, so if you find yourself confused, look back over the previous chapters.

FIXING A DROP-OUT

If you've ever worked with analog video footage, you've probably developed a healthy fear of drop-outs, those brief moments of static and jittery footage. Fortunately, with digital video, drop-outs are a little more manageable and there are a number of ways to repair them.

As we discussed in Chapter 4, some tape formats are more resistant to drop-outs, but in the end, all types of DV are susceptible. A drop-out occurs when the magnetic particles in a particular part of the tape get scrambled. This can occur because of magnetic damage to the tape, and can even be caused over time by the effects of gravity.

In digital video, a drop-out appears in your image as a box of gray, usually 32 pixels wide, and varying in height. You can often get rid of a drop-out simply by rewinding the tape and playing it again. If the drop-out was caused by some kind of debris, this will often shake it loose and clear your image (Figure 17.29).

If that doesn't work, try playing the tape on a different deck or camera. Sometimes, you'll find that drop-outs appear on one deck but not on another. If the tape plays properly on another deck, you can try capturing your clip from that deck, or you can try making a digital copy from the good deck to the bad.

If the drop-out persists, your best course of action is to repair the problem digitally. Fortunately, most dropouts only last for one or two frames, so digital fixes are fairly simple. There are several approaches to take.

- **Edit the previous frame over the frame with the dropout.** This is the least favorable alternative as it will create a brief, possibly perceptible

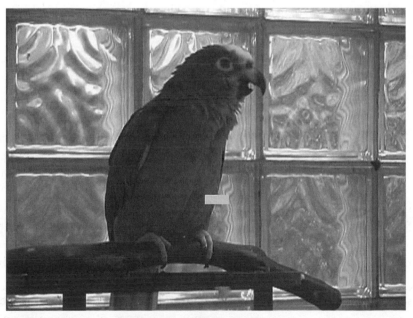

FIGURE 17.29   *Drop-outs in digital video are different from analog drop-outs. Though no less annoying, they can be easier to fix.*

stutter in your motion. If you're in a hurry, though, this will be the quickest fix.

- **Rotoscope the dropout.** Take the individual frames into an image editor and fix the bad areas with a paint brush or clone tool. If you have a copy of Commotion, use the SuperClone tool to clone the same area from a good frame.
- **Mask and composite over the dropout.** Take a still of a frame that isn't bad and composite it over the bad frame. Using cropping or masking tools, matte the upper layer to create a small patch that covers the dropout in the lower layer.

FIXING LOST VIDEO

In a really messed-up analog tape, you may find places where the audio plays fine, but the video loses sync. This is usually a sign of a corrupted control track. If you have dubbed analog footage to DV with the idea of capturing it, your editing program may not be able to handle the break in timecode caused by the corruption. You can sometimes fix this problem by doing an additional dub from your analog tape. Try the following:

- First, do a straight dub from your analog tape to DV (you may have already done this).
- Next, do another dub from your analog tape to DV, but this time, take only the video. For the audio, take the output from *another* source, such as a CD player, another tape deck, or a DVD player. This external audio source may help you get a cleaner copy of your video, with a continuous control track.
- In your NLE, sync up the audio from your first dub with the video from your second dub. There might still be a glitch, but at least your NLE will be able to work with the footage.

COMPOSITING ELEMENTS FROM A 3D ANIMATION PACKAGE

For the ultimate control when creating special effects, you may want to consider rendering some elements using a 3D animation program. This is a whole art and science unto itself, of course, but 3D rendering is how the most complex, most realistic effects are created. Whether you're needing to create rampaging dinosaurs, marauding tornadoes, or even a more pedestrian effect such as adding extra cars to a street scene, 3D animation tools will give you far more control than practical models or photography.

Unless you're very skilled and experienced in 3D modeling, rendering, and animation, you'll probably need to enlist someone else to do your 3D work. As a digital filmmaker, though, you'll want to be sure to consider the following:

- **Storyboard!** Though easier than practical shooting, 3D animation still requires a lot of time and effort. Don't waste your money or your animator's time. Prepare and storyboard everything before you have someone generate animation.
- **Use your whole crew.** Be sure your 3D animators are in contact with your cinematographer and designers. Good communication between your crewmembers will ensure that your computer-generated elements will match your live action.
- **Make sure your 3D animations have what you need to perform your compositing.** Do your animations need alpha channels? Do others need luma key? These concerns have to be considered ahead of time. Also, make sure your animations are created with pixel dimensions that will allow for any necessary resizing. In other words, be sure to plan for differences in rectangular and square pixels.
- **Don't get fancy unless you can afford it.** There are many things that can complicate a 3D effects shot. If you shoot video of a background using a moving camera, for example, you'll have a very difficult time matching the movements of your virtual 3D camera to the motions of your real camera. Unless you can afford a lot of skilled, expensive animators, keep your 3D shots simple.

Making Your Video Look Like Film

No matter how great your video looks, many videographers still envy the look of film. With its softer contrast and focus, different color gamut, grain, and slower frame rate, images shot on film look very different from what you can shoot on video.

Before you get dead set on a "film" look, though, spend some time to look at what you already have. Film may be pretty, and it's certainly what we're all used to watching, but a good three-chip DV camera is nothing to sneeze at either. Rather than trying to force it to be something it's not, consider what DV can do that film can't, and consider playing to those strengths.

If you're dead set on a film look, though, there are a number of things you can do. Some of them (progressive scan, 16:9, special filtering, etc.) involve shooting and were covered in Chapter 9. Others are digital processes that can be applied in post-production.

Before you go filtering all of your video, though, be aware that there are different concerns for different types of output. If your final output will be film, then you don't need to worry about most of what is covered here. The transfer to film will be all you need to make your video look like film. Don't add extra grain, gamut enhancement, temporal changes, or special filters. (We cover film transfers in detail in Chapter 18.)

If your final destination is the Web or CD, then you may not need a thorough "film-look" treatment. Highly compressed video, for example, won't be able to show subtle grain effects, and will probably screw up your carefully tailored color-balance adjustments. In addition, the slower frame rates will make any temporal changes irrelevant. You can go ahead and experiment with some of these techniques, but don't be surprised if a lot of your work ends up invisible, lost in a morass of compression artifacts.

Film-look is really for people who are mastering to video for distribution on video. Your goal is to make your footage look as it if were shot on film and transferred to video. When creating a film look, there are three characteristics that you'll need to modify: texture, color, and temporal quality.

CREATING FILM TEXTURE

A piece of motion picture film consists of a layer of photo-sensitive silver halide particles suspended in an emulsion that is bonded to a strip of celluloid. The texture of these particles results in what's known as *film grain*. The more light sensitive the film stock, the bigger the silver halide particles, the more visible the grain. Instead of grain, video has electronic *noise* that looks very different—it's bigger, moves around more, and is more colorful. To get a film-like texture out of a piece of video, it's a good idea to start with a relatively noise-free signal. Ultimatte's Grain Killer is a plug-in that is used to get rid of video noise when creating blue-screen mattes. Next you need to add grain; the easiest way to do this is to use one of the plug-ins listed later in the chapter, or you can create your own grain using a simple compositing technique in After Effects.

CREATING FILM GRAIN

You can use a simple nested composition in After Effects to add film grain to your final project. Though you can add film grain to your effects on a shot-by-shot basis, it's usually easiest to apply the effect to your finished edit. Note that this will require a *lot* of disk space and a good amount of rendering time.

You'll begin by rendering your finished cut into a QuickTime movie. Ideally, you'll want to use the Animation CODEC to produce a lossless copy of your project. If you're hurting for disk space, you can go ahead and use the DV CODEC, but if you've already exposed your footage to one or two levels of compression, this might not be a very good idea.

Once you've rendered your final output, create an After Effects comp and import your footage. Now you're ready to add grain.

STEP 1: CREATE THE GRAIN COMP.

Create a second comp called *Grain,* using the same dimensions and settings as your footage comp. From the *Layer* menu, choose *New Solid,* and create a 50% gray solid that fills your entire comp.

STEP 2: CREATE THE GRAIN.

Now we want to make this gray solid into a noisy gray solid. We'll then composite this over our footage. With the gray solid selected, choose *Stylize>Noise* from the Effects menu. Choose 100% noise and uncheck the *Color Noise* box.

To keep the effect from being too strong, we want to reduce the contrast of the grain. To do this, we will apply a simple levels adjustment. Choose *Effect>Adjust>Levels.* Drag the *Output Black* slider (the left slider on the lower graph) to the right, until it is about halfway between the left edge and the midpoint. The *Output Black* field will read approximately 74.

Now drag the *Output White* slider to the equivalent position (it will read about 188). Your effects settings should look something like Figure 17.30. Close the Effect Controls window.

STEP 3: BUILD YOUR COMPOSITE.

Place the *Grain* composite inside your main composite and layer it above your video layer. You should see a grainy gray field. Select the *Grain* layer in

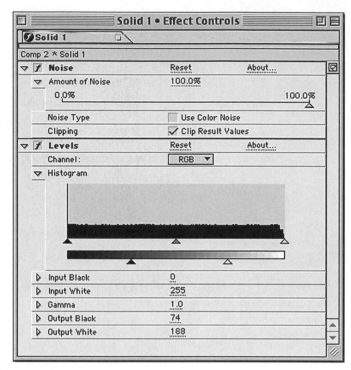

FIGURE *Use these settings to create a layer of film grain.*

your main comp, and choose *Layer>Transfer Mode>Hard Light*. Now you should see your grain superimposed over your image. It's too grainy, isn't it? Set the Opacity of your Grain layer to about 20% and you'll have a much more subtle effect (Figure 17.31).

That's it! Instant grain. What's more, it's instant, adjustable grain. You can alter the opacity of your Grain layer to make the grain more or less pronounced. Try adding a Gaussian Blur filter to your Grain comp to make the granule size larger or smaller. (Use really small Blur amounts—.3 to 1—to make the grain "chunkier.")

CREATING FILM COLOR

Film typically has a very different color quality than video. What's more, different types of film yield very different types of color. We've all seen the bright, Technicolor pastels of 1950s cinema, and we've also seen the hip, over-exposed

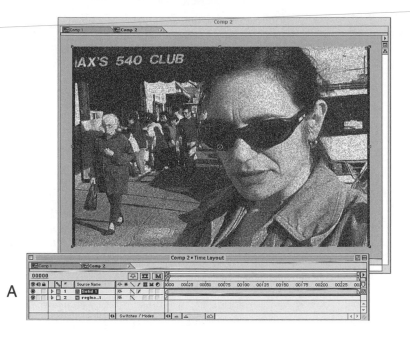

A

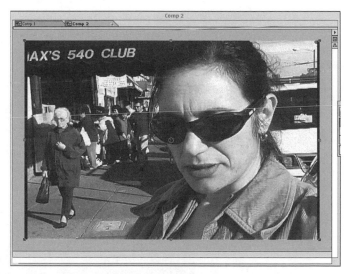

B

FIGURE   *With a slight opacity adjustment, you can reduce the intensity of your virtual*
17.31   *film grain.*

grunge colors of modern music videos. Using the color correction techniques presented in Chapter 15, you can often push or pull the colors in your video to appear more like film color. We say "often" because if your video was underlit, or suffers from other color artifacts, you're going to have less latitude to play with when shifting your color.

Film typically has a lower contrast ratio than video. Keep this in mind when making color adjustments. As we mentioned in Chapter 9, you can shoot with special ProMist filters to reduce the contrast in your video image, to soften colors, and to create blooming highlights.

You can also create a simple ProMist-like effect in After Effects. Just create a new comp and add *two* copies of the comp to which you want to add the ProMist effect. Apply a Gaussian Blur (20–40%) to the upper copy, and set its opacity to around 20% and its transfer mode to Lighten.

You can adjust the amount of the effect by experimenting with the opacity and blur amounts. If you've got a lot of hot spots that you really want to see bloom, try switching to a much smaller blur amount, and using the Luminance transfer mode (Figure 17.32).

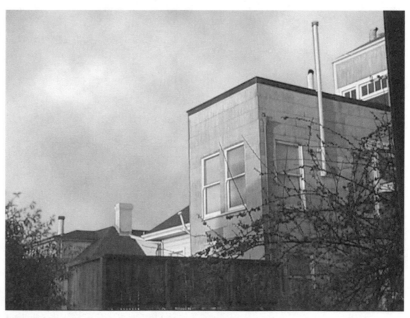

FIGURE   *Applying virtual ProMist filters in After Effects.*
17.32

Higher Contrast

In a similar manner, you can *increase* the contrast of a clip by layering two identical copies and applying an Unsharp Mask filter to the upper one. Set an Unsharp Amount between 50–70, a radius between 25–40, and a Threshold of 0. Keep the upper layer's opacity at 100%, but change its transfer mode to Darken.

CHANGING VIDEO TIME

With its frame rate of 60 fields per second, video effectively has more than twice the frame rate of film's 24 frames per second. While you might think that more frames must be better, in the case of moving images, it seems that less frequently is more. Film's slower frame rate tends to engage the viewer more than video's perfect, higher-frame-rate motion. Since film presents the viewer with less information, it effectively asks them to do more, and thus brings them "into" the scene in a way that video can't do.

As we discussed in Chapter 9, if you shoot progressive scan video, you've got a good head start on a more film-like motion. If you shot normal, interlaced, 60-field motion, you'll need to do some post-production processing to change the temporal quality of your video.

De-Interlacing

The easiest first step is to de-interlace your video. De-interlacing will throw out one field of video, and duplicate the remaining field to fill in the missing lines. This means that every pair of fields (that is, every 60th of a second of displayed video) is identical, effectively reducing your frame rate to 30 fps. This will immediately give your video a more film-like motion. Unfortunately, it will also lower the detail in your image and can worsen any existing aliasing troubles.

You can try to soften the aliasing problems with a localized blur, and improve detail with some strategic sharpening. Obviously, these processes will take time, so you'll want to do some experiments before you commit to de-interlacing. Try some short clips and make sure that the de-interlacing effect gives you results that you like.

Blurring

Film also has a very characteristic motion blur that results in images that are a little softer and blurrier than the sharp contrast of video. Hopefully, when shooting, you kept your shutter speed to something reasonable like 1/60th of a second, so you've already got some motion blur in your image. You can try to create more blur through post-production manipulation, but be warned that less is definitely more when adding such effects.

Blur a single color channel. Though it won't produce the most accurate results, adding just a little blur to a single color channel (red, green, or blue) in your video can serve to soften the image just enough so as to imply a slurry film look. Blurring different channels will yield very different results, so do some experimenting with each channel.

PLUG-INS

There are a number of good plug-ins that can create a film look for you. If you're serious about matching particular film stocks, creating a complicated effect such as old film, or having a high degree of control, the extra expense of these filters might be worth it.

- **DigiEffects Cinelook/Cinemotion** The premiere plug-ins for creating a filmy look, Cinelook provides excellent, exhaustive controls for modifying the color of your video (you can actually pick film stocks by name from a list of standard film types) and its temporal quality. In addition, Cinelook provides excellent control for adding grain, damage, flicker, even burning film! Though Cinelook provides good temporal adjustments, Cinemotion provides more advanced 3:2 pulldown simulation for the exacting producer.

- **DigiEffects Delirium, Aurorix, and AgedFilm** Some of DigiEffects' other plug-in collections include film simulators. Delirium provides a FilmFlash plug-in for simulating the flicker of a film camera, while Aurorix provides an AgedFilm filter for adding debris. Windows users can buy the stand-alone AgedFilm plug-in for adding debris, scratches, and color shift.

- **ArtBeats libraries** ArtBeats, the company that sells the muzzle flashes and impacts that you used in earlier tutorials, also sells a nice collection of Film Clutter. These scratches, countdowns, hairs, and dirt can be luma or chroma keyed over your video to create a very convincing old film look.

Rendering

As you may have already discovered when rendering your projects, creating special effects involves a lot of waiting. Though you can try to reduce the wait time by adding processor cards to your computer (such as the BlueIce After Effects accelerators from Iced, Inc.) or by optimizing your use of effects and filters, in the end there's no getting around waiting for rendering.

Be aware, however, that if you have followed the rendering suggestions we gave in Chapter 15, and are moving your video between applications using the Animation CODEC, then there's a good chance that you'll have *another* shorter rendering step when you get back to your NLE. Remember that before your NLE can send footage back to your camera (for output to tape, or for display on your NTSC monitor), the footage has to be compressed with the NLE's codec. So, after importing your Animation-compressed footage from After Effects, you'll have to let your NLE compress the footage into DV or MJPEG-compressed footage for output to your camera.

Note also, that if you're ultimately going to film, some of the film-look suggestions we presented in this chapter may be irrelevant. We'll cover final output (including film transfer concerns) in detail in the next chapter.

18 Outputs

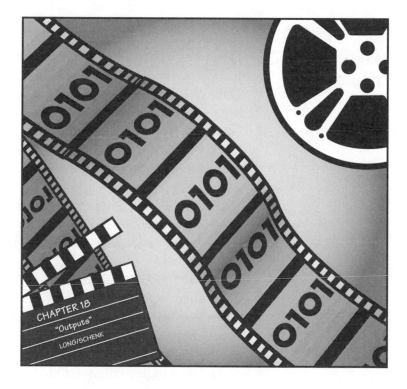

CHAPTER 18
"Outputs"
LONG/SCHENK

IN THIS CHAPTER

- Mastering Your Outputs
- Videotape Masters
- The Final Audio Mix
- Outputting to CD-ROM
- Outputting for the Web
- DVD Authoring
- Getting Your 35mm Release Print

Mastering Your Outputs

There seem to be two attitudes toward the task of outputting final masters: nonchalance or terror. Either people think "it's no big deal—just stick a tape in the deck and hit Record," or they envision their budget spinning out of control while words like "on-line," "streaming media," and "film recording" send them into a panic. Both reactions are based on ignorance—creating a high-quality final output is a process that takes a lot care, research, and attention to detail, but if you're properly prepared you should have no trouble getting the results you want. Whether you're doing it yourself or with the help of professionals at a post-production facility or film laboratory, knowing how the process works will help you master the art of output.

THE BEST-CASE SCENARIO

If your project is a feature film, you will probably create more than one master, as well as many supplemental materials. A film that gets theatrical distribution usually needs all of the types of outputs described in this chapter. You'll need VHS viewing copies to apply to film festivals. You will need streaming media output to post trailers and promos of your film on the Web. (page 492). If your film is accepted to a festival, you'll need a film print for screening. You'll need a videotape on-line to get a good videotape master (page 467). You'll need to have mixed stereo audio tracks on your videotape master (page 478). You'll need a backup of your NLE project files, just in case you need access to them again. You'll back up your uncompressed copies of your video and audio on optical tapes or DV tape (see Chapter 12, "Backing Up"), page 288, and also keep an EDL of your project. In addition, you'll make an 8-track output of your audio so that you can easily remix it at a later date if necessary (page 480), and you'll take your master videotape to a film recordist who will create a negative (page 497). You'll need digital files of your titles and special effects shots and have them transferred to film separately.

Say you screen the resulting release print at Sundance, and find a distributor who wants to release the film in theaters and, later, broadcast the film on the Independent Film Channel and also on European TV. You'll have to decide whether to broadcast from your videotape on-line master or, more likely, create a new master from the film print by having it telecined back to videotape (page 478). You'll take the 8-track audio-only output you created and remix according to the different broadcast specifications of the Independent Film Channel and European broadcasters. For Europe, you'll need a split-track dialogue, music and effect (DM&E) mix in addition to a stereo mix, so that they can dub your film into other languages. (page 480). If you hate dubbed films, you'll probably have to add subtitles yourself, with the help of a post-production facility that specializes in subtitling. Finally, the new telecined videotape master will be used to create the DVD (page 495), the CD-ROM press kit (page 482), and also the VHS dubs for home video distribution (Figure 18.1).

THE BIG DECISION

Most likely, you have no idea what will happen to your film once you've finished post-production. Will you need a film print or simply a videotape master? The most cautious choice is to start small, but keep your options open: create a "do-it-yourself" videotape master and audio mix; put your trailer or clips up on the Web as streaming media; and make some VHS outputs as viewing copies to pass around. Be sure to back up your media and your project in case you want to go back and re-edit or re-master and eventually finish on film. We recommend that you read this entire chapter before proceeding.

Videotape Masters

If you're ready to make a videotape master, you need to decide whether to do it yourself using your NLE, or to go to a post-production facility for a high-end digital on-line master. You'll need to take into consideration the format you shot on, the format you wish to master on, and whether or not you want to eventually make a film print.

If you shot on a digital format, you can save a lot of money by creating a master yourself. The quality of your master is entirely dependent on how much care you took with your video levels when you originally captured your

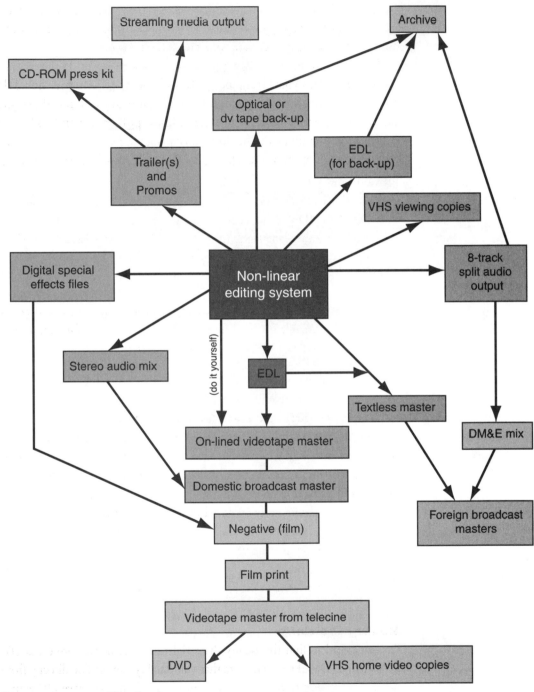

FIGURE
18.1 *Outputs workflow flowchart.*

footage (see "Capturing," Chapter 12). Professional on-line editors will know how to get the highest quality from your original tapes, and will probably create a better-looking master than what you could do yourself.

If you shot on an analog format, like BetaSP, your decision of how to master will depend on your final product. If you're going to film, you should do a professional tape-to-tape on-line session. If your final goal is broadcast, you can create a master yourself. If you can't afford a professional on-line but are bent on going to film, you should recapture your video in an uncompressed format. Even if this means renting extra equipment, it will save money in the long run.

TIP

Counting Down
Any output you make should have a 10-second countdown and a title card before the actual sequence starts at hour 01:00:00:00. To be safe, the countdown should have a 2-pop at the 2-second mark of the countdown to guarantee sync. The title card, also called a head slate, should list the name of the project, the name of the producer/director, the name of the editor, the production company, the date of the output, the type of output (master, rough cut, audio-only, textless, etc.), the total run time (TRT), and, possibly, contact and copyright information. It's also a good idea to put this same title card up as the tail slate at the end.

PREPARING FOR A PROFESSIONAL ON-LINE
Having your project on-line edited by a professional editor adds a level of polish that is hard to replicate yourself, but the high quality comes at a price. Most on-line sessions start at around $500 an hour. Depending on the number of edits in your project, an on-line session for a 90-minute feature could take four or five days, maybe more if you have lots of effects. If you're new to the world of high-end video, the expense and the atmosphere may be a bit daunting. As with any part of the filmmaking process, don't be afraid to ask questions. Remember that only the inexperienced refrain from asking questions. The more experienced you are, the more questions you'll have.

Making the Calls
First you need to find the facility that's right for you. If your project is DV, DVCAM, or DVCPro, make sure that your facility can on-line directly from that format. A surprising number of post houses do not yet have DV equipment. Instead, they will probably offer to "bump up" your DV tapes to BetaSP

(just say no!) or Digital Betacam (expensive and unnecessary). Instead, go with a house that's DV-friendly.

You also want to determine how many source decks are dedicated to your session. The more source decks you have at your disposal (you should have a minimum of two), the faster you can finish. Next, you need to determine what your mastering format will be. If you're spending the money for an on-line session, you should make it worth your while and master to a high-quality, and expensive, format like Digital Betacam or D1. You should also arrange for a clone of your master—also known as a *protection copy*—once it is completed. If something goes wrong with your master, or if you sell your project, you'll still have a high-quality copy for yourself.

Stripping Down Your Sequence

You'll have to take an EDL to your on-line session, and to output a good EDL, you'll need to prepare your edited project. Make a copy of the project and remove all of the elements that don't need to be there for the on-line session—temporary titles and effects, music, voice-over, etc.—from the copy. This is the copy you will use for your on-line session. All that should remain is the video and audio that came from your timecoded source tapes, including special effects shots that you created and mastered onto videotape. You should make sure all of your video is on a single track (Figure 18.2).

TIP

Hour 01:00:00:00
Make sure that the first frame of your edited sequence starts at 1:00:00:00. Although it isn't crucial, it's standard for masters and outputs to start at hour one. Things will go smoother (i.e., faster) at the post facility if you follow the norm.

Your goal in an on-line is to get your video laid down correctly. You'll polish and correct the audio later, when you mix your sound. That said, you don't need to put any audio in your EDL if the DigiBeta or D1 master isn't going to be the source for the sync audio in your mix. (Read the audio outputs section if you're not sure how you'll be mixing your audio, page 478.) If you do want to add the sync audio during your on-line, *checkerboard* it across three tracks (Figure 14.7). The fourth audio track should be left empty to save room for a guide track (see below). Professional videotape formats have four channels of audio, so even if you don't want a guide track, you'll have to make sure your audio is limited to four tracks.

A. This locked sequence would result in a "dirty" list.

B. The same sequence, collapsed onto a single video track and stripped of all effects, non-standard transitions and audio.

FIGURE
18.2
A timeline view of a locked edited sequence (A) and the same edit, stripped of all temporary and/or unnecessary elements (B).

The List

After you've stripped your project down to its on-line essentials, you'll be ready to create an edit decision list, or EDL. You'll create the EDL in your editing software and take it to the on-line facility along with your source tapes. Before you make your EDL, it's important to talk to the post facility to find out exactly how they need the EDL formatted. Here's a list of things to ask about:

- **EDL type.** Different types of linear editing hardware need different EDLs. The most common format is CMX, which is considered the default format. Other popular formats include Sony, GVG, and Axial. Ask your post house what type they need.

- **Disk type.** Most linear editing systems cannot read PC or Mac formatted disks; instead, they use another format, called RT11. To format an RT11 disk on a PC or a Mac, you'll need an *unformatted* 3.5" floppy and a software utility that can format RT11 disks, such as Avid's EDL Manager. If you can't create an RT11 disk on your system, make sure the on-line facility knows you'll be bringing a disk in another format and that you'll need transfer time before your $500+/hr on-line session starts.

- **Sort mode.** The edits in your list can be sorted in several different ways, depending on the needs of your project and the requirements of the on-line facility. *A-mode* is the most common and easiest to understand. A-mode EDLs are sorted in terms of master record-in. In other words, your edits will be performed in a linear manner, from start to finish. This is the simplest and most intuitive way to go, but often *C-mode* is a better choice. C-mode EDLs are sorted by source tape number, then by master record-in. With C-mode, the on-line editor starts with the lowest tape number and sets the video levels for that source tape. Then all the shots from that reel are edited onto the master. The same procedure is followed for the next source tape and so on. Say you have 20 source reels and 650 video edits in your list. With A-mode, the on-line editor will have to set the video levels up to 650 times; with C-mode, they'll need set up as little as 20 times. Other sort modes include B, D, and E modes, which are rarely used for long format projects. Figure 18.3 shows a short EDL sorted in A-mode and C-mode.

- **Number of events.** Depending on your EDL type, you may be limited to 800 or 1000 lines of text per EDL. Since each edit, also known as an *event,* takes up at least one line of text in an EDL, if your project has more than 800 edits, it's best to break it into two EDLs. Make this cut at a hard edit somewhere in the middle of your project.

- **Track selection.** You'll need to decide which tracks to include in your EDL. Usually, this will be one track of video and the sync audio that goes with it. Remember that videotapes can only have four tracks of audio and one track of video.

- **Optimizing your EDL.** Usually this is done by the post-facility. They'll go through your EDL and make sure there aren't any unnecessary edits in the list. This is also known as list cleaning. Unless you thoroughly understand the EDL process and the equipment involved, this is best left to the experts.

- **Comments.** Most NLEs allow you to add comments to your EDL— you can add notes to the on-line editor, tape names, clip names, and other information. Usually the list you give to the post house should not have any more text than absolutely necessary, due to the aforementioned number-of-events limitation. Instead, you should create a secondary EDL with comments that you print out for yourself and other human readers.

- **Pre-reading and b-reels.** If you want to dissolve between two shots on the same source tape, this will be accomplished using pre-read edits or a b-reel. To create a dissolve, linear editing systems need to be able to play the a-side of the dissolve and the b-side of the dissolve simultaneously. A linear editing system with pre-read capability is able to store the frames contained in the b-side of the dissolve in memory. If this option isn't available, you'll need to create a "b-reel"—a new source tape with all the b-sides of dissolves that occur on the same source tapes. You can do this yourself ($) or have the post facility do it for you ($$).

- **Digital Video Effects (DVEs)** Unless you've got very deep pockets, an on-line session is not the place to deal with complicated special effects. But if you do plan on doing anything more than a simple dissolve in your on-line session, you'll need to order special DVE equipment for your session. Kaleidescope, ADO, and Sony DME 3000 are some of the more common hardware-based DVE generators that are typically used in an on-line edit session.

EDLs and DVEs

EDLs can be rather limited when it comes to information about digital video effects. While motion effects, dissolves, color effects, and resizing are commonly included in an EDL, you should check with your post-production facility before assuming that their equipment can *automatically* recreate these effects. Typically, you will be limited to dissolves, 20 standard wipes (all of which you'll probably hate), and one static superimposition track. Anything more complicated will have to be re-created by the on-line editor. In addition, if you have motion effects in your sequence, you need to make sure you've used a frame rate that the linear editing hardware supports. Ask the post house to send you a list of acceptable frame rates and/or percentages.

Event	Tape I.D.	Source In	Source Out	Master In	Master Out
001	005285 V C	17:09:22:20	17:09:23:14	01:05:11:10	01:05:12:04
002	005287 V C	19:22:55:18	19:23:00:29	01:05:12:04	01:05:17:13
003	005286 V C	18:23:50:17	18:23:58:17	01:05:17:13	01:05:25:13
004	005285 V C	17:28:50:16	17:28:51:15	01:05:25:13	01:05:25:12

A-mode EDL   Tracks selected (in this case video only)

001	005285 V C	17:09:22:20	17:09:23:14	01:05:11:10	01:05:12:04
002	005285 V C	17:28:50:16	17:28:51:15	01:05:25:13	01:05:25:12
003	005286 V C	18:23:50:17	18:23:58:17	01:05:17:13	01:05:25:13
004	005287 V C	19:22:55:18	19:23:00:29	01:05:12:04	01:05:17:13

C-mode EDL

FIGURE **18.3**   *A short CMX format A-mode EDL (A), and a C-mode EDL (B) (with callouts).*

Guide Tracks

To avoid confusion during the on-line session, it's a good idea to create an *audio guide track* that will serve as a guide while you are editing. If you place a copy of the audio from your final edit onto one of the audio tracks on the tape you will be on-lining onto, you will have an audible reference that will help you ensure that your edits are correct, and in-sync. Audio guide tracks are especially useful if you're doing a C-mode online, or editing in video only.

Before your on-line session, do an output of your final edit (not the stripped-down version!) with mixed audio onto a timecoded video source, preferably BetaSP or a DV format. Have the post facility record a track from your mixed audio output onto one of the four audio tracks on your DigiBeta or D1 master. Remember that this is usually a real-time process, so you'll want them to do it overnight to have it ready for your session.

Some people also like to have a visual guide, which can be created by recording the video from your output onto the DigiBeta or D1 master. During the on-line session, the guide video is covered up by the high-quality on-line video. Usually the quality difference is large enough that it's easy to determine what's old and what's new. However, tracking down a missed shot or a flash frame is much harder with guide video than with a black master tape. We recommend that you use an audio guide only. Whatever your preference, be sure to let the post facility know what you want in advance—some will automatically create a video and audio guide, others won't.

TIP

Field Dominance

If you're using DV Format, your project will be "field two dominant" as opposed to the usual field one dominance. There's nothing wrong with field two dominance as long as everyone is aware of it. Label all your tapes "Field Two Dominant." Make sure you let the post-facility you're working with know that your EDL is field two dominant.

Supervising the On-Line Session

As a director or editor supervising an on-line session, your goal is to make sure your final master looks as you intended it to look. For example, you might have a scene that was intentionally shot with unnaturally blue levels. Unless you are there to tell them otherwise, the on-line editor will probably try to correct this "problem" by taking down the blue. Every project will include several situations like this, so it's important that you sit in on the session.

You should arrive at the session with a printed version of your EDL containing comments, source names, and clip names. If you find the EDL confusing to read, spend some time at your NLE learning to interpret and understand where each scene begins and ends on the printout. You should also "spot" your film for scenes that have technical problems like bad color or drop-outs. All of these things should be noted on your printed EDL. Make a photocopy of your EDL and notes for the on-line editor.

Your secondary goal when supervising an on-line session is to make sure it doesn't take too long. Two heads may be better than one, but they can also waste a lot of time chatting, discussing the merits of leaving the scene blue or correcting it, and so on. Let the on-line editor stay focused, and avoid talking and interrupting too much. Just because you're sitting there doing nothing doesn't mean they aren't busy setting your video levels and managing your list. On the other hand, you are not expected to pay for "down time." If there are technical problems (that aren't *your* fault), or if the on-line editor makes an error, pay attention to how much time it took and make a note of it. These things are inevitable, and most on-line editors will be taking notes of such things themselves. At the end of each day, they'll have you sign a sort of invoice—be prepared to negotiate over lost time and technical problems.

TIP

Semi-Supervised On-Line Sessions
Save time and money by doing an overnight, unsupervised, C-mode on-line edit. Then spend the next day or two going over your project in a supervised session to fix any errors or drop-outs, and to add special effects.

Color Correction and Titling Sessions

After you've got your on-line master, it's common to spend half a day doing an additional color correction pass, usually on a DaVinci. The DaVinci offers a level of control that isn't available to the on-line editor. Usually the color correctionist aims to make skin tones look their best. Be aware that having your project color corrected can result in a one-frame offset. When you lay back your audio mix to the master tape, you'll want it to start a frame later.

It's always a good idea to have a clone made of your master before you add titles. This *textless master* will be the master for foreign dubbed and sub-titled versions. Also, if you're transferring to 35mm, it's better to transfer the textless master to negative and have film resolution titles added later separately.

Next, you'll spend a few hours creating titles or *chyrons* (so called because they're often created on machines manufactured by Chyron). Typically, you'll only do chyrons of your end credit roll. Be prepared to provide a proof-read text file of your credit list on a floppy. If your film is a documentary, you may need to add some *lower thirds* (see Chapter 16). If you need a sub-titled master, you'll have a clone made of your master and provide a text file with all your sub-titles on it. Usually, you'll want to go to a facility that specializes in sub-titling.

Now you're ready to finish the audio.

THE DO-IT-YOURSELF DIGITAL ON-LINE

We're going to make a big leap of faith and assume you've got computer hardware with enough processing power (Chapter 5) and editing software (Chapter 7) to play back full-size, full-motion video. If you didn't capture your video carefully the first time, you'll need to recapture to get the best quality video into your project (Chapter 12). If your editing software doesn't offer control of video levels, you should rent a hardware waveform monitor and vectorscope for a day to help you recapture your footage.

If your source tapes were analog and you're planning to transfer to film, you should re-digitize them uncompressed. Compressed MJPEG videos, like Avid's AVR77, will not look good on film because their artifacts will be magnified when projected.

Whether you're working on digital or analog video, be sure that all your digital effects shots are in place and rendered at the best quality possible. Lastly, you should rent a DVCAM, DVCPro, or Digital Betacam VTR for a day to record your master videotape. This will set you back about $200–$900. Refer to Chapter 11 if you have more hardware questions, and Chapter 12 for detailed instructions on capturing on-line quality video.

TIP

Presentation Values
If you do your own on-line and dubs, be sure to create professional–looking tape labels for tapes that you are sending out. 3M and Avery create blank laser printable tape labels for all sizes of videotapes. For VHS, get plain cardboard or plastic boxes. Tape labels should include the following information: production company, producer/director's name and contact info, project title, date, total run time (TRT), and format.

Preparing Your Sequence for Output

Before you output your video, you need to prepare your sequence. Make sure you've replaced all temporary footage and proxies with the real thing. If your project is longer than the available master tapes for your videotape format, you'll need to break your sequence into two parts. Be sure to make these breaks at a hard cut, not a dissolve. You also need to determine whether you'll be outputting your audio or doing it as a separate pass.

Head Room

Avoid using the first minute or two of the videotape for your project. This is the part of the tape that is most prone to physical damage. Instead, cover the head of the tape with bars and tone followed by a head slate and a countdown. Most videotapes are a minute or two longer than their stated length, so don't worry about wasting a little tape.

Insert vs. Assemble Edits

There are two different ways to make an edit onto videotape: *assemble* edits and *insert* edits. A typical piece of videotape consists of several tracks: the video track, 2–4 audio tracks, an address track for timecode, and a control track. The control track contains sync pulses that indicate where each frame starts and ends.

An assemble mode edit records over all the tracks on the tape including the control track. When you stop recording in assemble mode, a short break results in the control track (see Figure 18.4). In this break or hole there is no video signal, no audio signal, no timecode, and no control track. The result is an image that we've all come to know as "snow" on our television sets. Assemble edits tend to be frame accurate at the in-point but not at the out-point. If you are planning to lay off your entire sequence to tape in one pass, there's nothing wrong with using an assemble edit. In fact, if you're going out to a DV format, you won't have a choice, as DV decks provide only assemble editing. However, if you need to lay off your project in more than one pass, you need to be certain that you set the in-point of your second edit *before* the hole in the control track.

Black and Coding

Before you output using an insert edit, you should start with a tape that's been "blacked and coded." Set the timecode start at 00:58:30:00 and send a black signal from your black burst generator into your VTR. Hit Record and let the VTR

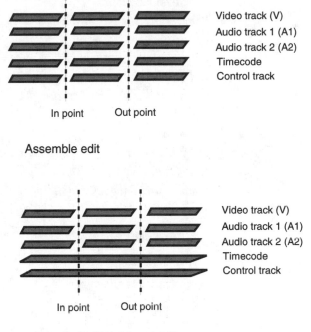

Assemble edit

Insert edit (V1, A1 and A2)

FIGURE
18.4   *Assemble editing vs. insert editing.*

record timecode and black video onto the duration of the tape. This process in-sures a stable video signal and timecode starting at 1:00:00:00 a minute and a half into the tape.

Insert edits offer much more control than assemble edits. With insert edits, you can record over any track except the address track and control track. To make an insert edit, you need to start with a tape that's already striped with a control track and timecode (*black and coded* tape). Make a 3-point edit by set-ting an in and out on your edited sequence and an in-point on the record deck. You can choose to output just the video track, just the audio tracks, or all three. If you plan to make lots of short edits onto tape, insert editing is the way to go. You won't have to worry about breaks in the control track, and you can easily make changes to stuff you've already output to tape. If you think you need to do lots of insert editing, make sure your software *and hardware* are capable of frame accurate device control and insert editing out to tape.

Watch Your Output!
It may sound silly, but lots of people don't watch their output as they're recording. By the time you get to the point of outputting your master, you've probably watched your project hundreds of times. This time, forget about story, pacing, and other concerns, and just watch the video images, looking for drop-outs, glitches, and other inconsistencies.

Protection Copies
In addition to creating a textless master, It's a good idea to make more than one copy of your final master. You can either do two outputs from your computer or, if your master is digital, have it cloned at a post-production facility.

Videotape Masters from Telecine

To make a videotape master from a film print, you need to do a film-to-videotape transfer, or *telecine*. Your film negative will be put on a machine, typically a Rank Cinetel. As it plays, the image will be recorded onto videotape. The telecine operator can do some color correction during this process, but if your film is already color-timed, it's unlikely that it will benefit from any serious tweaking.

If your film was shot on video, then transferred to film, then telecined back to video, you may find that you don't like the results. Wim Wenders' film *The Buena Vista Social Club* was shot on several different videotape formats, primarily Digital Betacam and MiniDV, then transferred to 35mm film. The producers decided that a telecined video master wouldn't look good, so they went back to their original videotape sources and created a new videotape master in a linear on-line bay at Encore Video in Hollywood, using a combination of effects on a Sony DME 3000 to get a "film look" effect.

The Final Audio Mix

Your final cut may have 20 or more tracks of sound if it's a complicated feature. To do an output, you'll need to mix those tracks into a more manageable number, usually two or four tracks. High-end professional videotape formats usually only have four tracks of audio, while low-end professional and consumer videotape formats usually only have two tracks. Mixing the audio consists of setting the levels for each piece of sound in the project and then combining the tracks into a final mix. There are several standard types of mixes:

- **Mono** Mixing all your audio down to one single track is called a mono mix. While mono mixes are sufficient for VHS viewing copies, for any other final output, you should at least do a stereo mix.
- **Stereo left and right** Stereo mixes are what we're all most familiar with. The tracks in your project are mixed down to two channels, left (track 1) and right (track 2). For true stereo, these tracks should be slightly panned to the left and right, respectively, but often only the music is true stereo. Some stereo mixes feature specific sounds that move from the left to the right channel, much like those old Led Zepplin guitar riffs. For broadcast and film, a stereo mix is standard.
- **Dialogue, Music and Effects (DM&E)** In a four-channel DM&E mix, the sync dialogue is mixed down to one channel, while the stereo music is placed on the second and third channels. The fourth channel is used for sound effects. By keeping these three elements separate, a DM&E mix allows you to keep your remixing options open. For example, you can easily replace the dialog for foreign language dubbing.
- **Surround sound** Surround sound may seem out of the league of the independent filmmaker, but with the advent of the "home theater" and HDTV, surround sound may soon become standard. Dolby Digital (or AC-3), DTS (Digital Theater System), and SDDS (Sony Dynamic Digital Sound) are the currently available digital surround sound formats. Dolby Digital and DTS use 5.1 channels: left, center, right speaker in the front of the theater, left and right surround speakers in the rear, and an LFE (Low Frequency Effects) subwoofer channel. (The subwoofer only uses a tenth of the dynamic range of a normal channel; hence you get a total of 5.1 channels.)

  SDDS uses 7.1 channels, adding center-left and center-right speakers in the front. In addition to theatrical support, Dolby Digital is also supported by DVD players and digital televisions using the ATSC DTV format. Surround mixes are generally balanced toward the front channels, with the rear channels used for occasional effects or ambience. Overuse of the rear channels tends to distract the viewers from the screen.

  There are a number of software plug-ins for encoding Dolby surround. See www.dvhandbook.com/surroundsound for details.

PREPARING FOR A PROFESSIONAL AUDIO MIX

The quality of the digital audio in most NLEs (44.1 or 48 kHz) is sufficient enough to merit using the tracks directly from your NLE as sources for your mix. To do this, you'll need to do a split-track output from your NLE. How many tracks you choose to output can vary depending on your project, but it's somewhat impractical to output more than eight tracks. The video decks you're likely to have in your editing room will only be capable of recording two audio channels. If you rented a Digital Betacam or high-end Betacam SP deck, you'll be able to record four channels. If you need to output more channels than that, you'll have to use additional videotape stock with matching time-code. One popular solution is the Tascam DA88, which records eight channels of digital audio plus timecode onto a blacked and coded Hi8 tape (Figure 18.5).

As with video on-lines, it's important to arrive at the audio mix prepared. Before you go to the mix, you should have a sound spotting session to make notes of things you'd like to fix or change. A basic professional mix starts with a short *sweetening*, or sound editing, session. If you know of special effects you want to add, it's a good idea to let the sound effects editor know about them in advance so that he or she will have some options loaded up and ready to work with at the beginning of your sweetening session. Your sound effects editor will probably be working on a ProTools, Fairlight, or other high-end

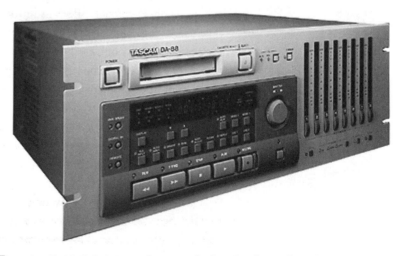

 FIGURE *Tascam's DA88 records up to eight digital audio tracks with SMPTE time-*
18.5 *code using Hi8 tapes.*

sound editing system. Unless you've got lots of time and money, the amount of sound editing you'll do in the sweetening session will be limited to things you couldn't do on your NLE, such as edits smaller than a frame of video.

After you've tweaked your sound, it's time to mix. Your tracks will be sent through a large mixing board and out to a high-quality sound recording format like 24-track tape or DAT. The mixer will set the levels as your video master plays, and the resulting audio will be recorded. Once you've gone all the way through your entire project, the tracks from the 24-track will be recorded back onto to your videotape master, a process known as the *lay back*. If you want more than one type of mix—for example, a stereo mix and a DM&E mix—you'll have to make two videotape masters to lay back onto.

DO-IT-YOURSELF FINAL MIXES

Doing the audio mix yourself using your NLE gives you the luxury of time. Since you won't be paying expensive hourly fees, you'll have the freedom to get your mix exactly right. Most likely, you were mixing your tracks as you worked, so you'll probably only need a final pass to set the levels across the whole project.

When it comes to mixing, dialog is usually king. Watch your VU meters on your video or audio deck as you mix; they're more reliable than the digital meters in your NLE. The dialogue should tend toward a consistent dB range throughout your project. Music and effects should fall at a significantly lower dB except in special circumstances when they need to be intentionally louder. Mixing is a very subjective art, and lots of people think their way of mixing is the only way to do it right. If you're not confident about your "ear," get a professional sound editor to come in for a day and do a mixing pass on your film.

But Will It Play in Peoria?
Lots of sound editors have a secondary set of speakers in their editing rooms. These speakers are designed to sound like a low-quality TV speaker. Silly as it may sound, listening to your mix through lousy speakers can help you determine whether your mix is working under the worst possible conditions.
Conversely, if high fidelity is of primary concern, don't depend on the small "multimedia" speakers hooked up to your computer. Either invest in better-quality speakers, or, if you have a nice stereo system, string a cable from your computer to your stereo and use it to monitor your audio.

No matter how many audio tracks you have, you'll want to start by mixing them down to eight tracks. A typical eight-track configuration includes two tracks of checkerboarded sync production sound, a track of voice-over if applicable, a track of ambience, two tracks of sound effects, a track of stereo left music, and a track of stereo right music. Remember to work on copies of your sequence as you mix down your tracks, in case you need to go back and remix. Refer to your NLE software documentation for directions on how to mix down tracks of audio. At this point, you may wish to make a digital audio tape back-up of your eight tracks. If you're working with a DV format, you can also consider outputting your eight-track audio mix back to a DV tape.

Make a copy of your eight-channel split track sequence for each different type of mix you want to create. To create a DM&E mix, mix the sync production sound and voice-over down to one track, and the effects and ambience tracks down to another track. Leave the music as is on the last two tracks. If you are recording your mix onto videotape that only has two channels, you'll need to make two outputs with matching timecode. *Be sure to send each channel to the VTR separately.* You can output the video at the same time, or do it in a separate pass if your system is capable of insert editing. Either way, it's good to have video on both tapes. To create a stereo mix, you need to mix the dialogue, effects, and stereo music left to channel one, and the dialogue, effects, and stereo music right to channel two. Be sure to balance your levels, since this different configuration can easily result in the dialogue and effects overpowering the music. Again, be sure to separately send each channel to the VTR.

Outputting to CD-ROM

If your video is intended for use within a game, interactive project, or corporate presentation, then your final edit will probably be output to CD-ROM. Even if your goal is a theatrical release, CD-ROM delivery can be useful for creating inexpensive, durable copies of short projects, electronic press kits, and trailers,

CD-ROM delivery is also useful for sending press copies of your project to Web sites and other electronic PR outlets. With your video on CD-ROM, a Web site or film festival won't have to go to the trouble of digitizing your work for electronic distribution. For this reason, CD-ROM delivery is ideal for submitting trailers to on-line film festivals and showcases.

On the downside, because of the performance limitations of most desktop computers, your video will be limited to a smaller size (usually 320 × 240 pixels or smaller) and possibly to a lower frame rate.

Once your final product is edited and finished, outputting to CD-ROM is a fairly simple three-step process:

1. Compress your video.
2. Arrange your compressed files on your hard drive.
3. Burn a CD-ROM using a recordable CD drive (CD-R).

At the time of this writing, you can pick up a decent 2x or 4x CD-R for $200–$300 dollars, and blank CDs for less than $1.00 each. If you don't have or can't afford a CD-R, then you'll need a way to move your files (which will be up to 650 megabytes) to a service bureau or computer that can burn your disk.

COMPRESSION

Just as video must be compressed before it can be played on your computer, video must be compressed before it can be put onto a CD-ROM. Unfortunately, CD-ROMs are even slower and smaller than a typical hard drive. Consequently, video must be very heavily compressed before you can put it on a CD-ROM. For best results, you'll want to make some decisions to find the best balance of image quality and small file size.

Know Your Audience

Like most forms of electronic delivery, your first concern when outputting to CD-ROM is to decide on the lowest-common-denominator hardware that a user will need to watch your video. A few years ago, it was pretty safe to assume that most users had slow systems with slow CD-ROM drives. Consequently, video was highly compressed using low-quality CODECs such as Cinepak. In addition, it was usually a good idea to cut your frame rate down to 12 or 15 frames per second, and possibly to reduce the size of your image even more, to something like 160×120.

Nowadays, it's pretty safe to assume that most users have a processor and CD-ROM drive that's fast enough for higher-quality video, but still not fast enough for full-screen, full-motion video. If your project is aimed at a very particular market, then you can usually make some educated guesses about the capabilities of your audience's hardware. For example, if you're creating video for an education product, you'll probably want to assume slower hardware, but if your target audience is a cartel of powerful CEOs, then they probably have faster, heavy-duty computing power.

Resize Your Video

No matter what compressor you're using, you'll have to re-size your video. 320 × 240 pixels is one quarter of the size of a full-screen video and is pretty much the accepted standard for CD-ROM video. Of course, you can always go smaller if you want to ensure good playback on any machine.

Your NLE or effects package should provide render controls that let you specify the size of your final output. Note that there is no overscanning when exporting to CD-ROM. In other words, the viewer will see the entire frame. If you want to conceal action outside of the Action Safe area of your screen, now is the time to crop your frame. Some applications let you crop and re-size at the same time. With others, you'll need to crop your video, save it in a loss-less format, and then perform another rendering pass to resize and compress (Figure 18.6).

Even if you haven't performed any actions that will affect the overscan area, note that some cameras might produce a black edge or border within the over-scan boundary. You'll definitely want to crop this out.

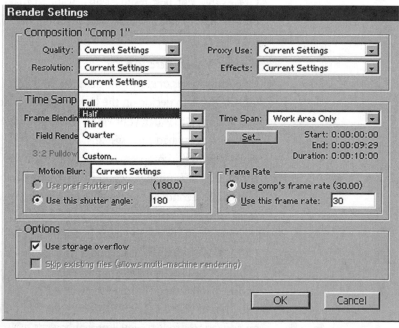

 Figure **18.6** *In most NLEs and effects packages, you can set the output size when you render your final movie. After Effects lets you easily define half, and quarter-size renderings from its Render Settings dialog.*

Compress Your Video

Once you've chosen your lowest-common-denominator platform, you're ready to make some decisions about how you'll compress your video. In the course of your production, you've probably become more comfortable with the use of QuickTime CODECs. In earlier chapters we discussed the DV CODEC that is used by digital video cameras, the MJPEG CODEC used by analog capture boards, and the lossless Animation CODEC that is ideal for moving video between applications.

There are also a number of CODECs built-in to QuickTime that are well-suited to compressing video for CDROM.

In the past, when the average CD-ROM drive operated at 2x or 4x, Cinepak was the only viable compression option. For playing on the greatest number of machines—new and old—Cinepak is still the best choice. However, Cinepak is a *very* lossy compressor. We only recommend using it if you're sure that your video will be played on older equipment. Cinepak is provided with QuickTime, and can be selected from the CODEC menu, just as you earlier selected the Animation CODEC.

The same holds true for the standard QuickTime Video compressor, which yields slightly larger files than Cinepak, but slightly better video.

TIP

Compressing
No matter what CODEC you choose, compressing can take a long time. You'll want to make sure that you've got everything right before you start compressing, and you'll probably want to perform your compression overnight.

Of all the CODECs suitable for CD-ROM use, MPEG1 produces the highest-quality output. However, smooth MPEG1 playback requires a fast computer. If you know your audience will be using fast G3s or Pentium IIIs, then go with MPEG1 compression. Note that MPEG1 is not built-in to QuickTime. You'll need to buy separate MPEG1 encoding software, such as Astarte's M.Pack or Heuris' MPEG Export Engine. See www.dvhandbook.com/mpeg for more details.

Currently, the Sorenson video compressor provides the best balance of quality, small file size, and reasonable system requirements. Though it will take a while to compress a video with the Sorenson compressor, you'll end up with a very tightly compressed file and an image whose high quality might surprise you. And, Sorenson video requires far less computing power for playback than does the higher-quality MPEG 1 compressor.

> ### How Much Will Fit?
>
> Calculating how much compressed video will fit on a CD can be difficult, as the final file size of a video is largely determined by the compressor you're using, as well as the quality of your video. Movies that have lots of moving images, or moving camera shots, will not compress as tightly as movies with more static shots. Before you commit to a particular compressor, perform some test compressions using scenes that are representative of the type of motion that is typical in your piece. From the resulting file sizes, you can try to determine how big your final project will be.
>
> If you have a lot of video and absolutely have to fit it on one CD, or if you have limited space because of other information that needs to go on the disc, you can limit the size of your movies by specifying a data rate. Divide the size of your disc—650,000 for a CD—by the length of your movie to determine the total KBps required to fit your movie onto a CD. Obviously, to fit a lot of footage onto a CD, you'll have to lower the data rate of your movie, thus sacrificing image quality. (See the following section for more information on data rates.)

Different CODECs have different idiosyncrasies. For example, some colors tend to become more saturated when compressed with the Sorenson CODEC. Consequently, you may want to make custom color adjustments tuned to the particulars of the CODEC. Also, because your computer monitor is a progressively scanned device, your CD-ROM-based video will look much better if it is de-interlaced.

To optimize your video for CD delivery, follow these steps:

1. Output a few representative samples of your video and compress them with your CODEC of choice. Select samples with varying lighting styles (day/night, overexposed, underexposed, etc.).
2. Make a copy of your final project. Because you might someday want to output to tape, or re-compress your video with another CODEC, you should keep a copy of your original project file.
3. Apply filters and color corrections *to the copy of your project* and output a final rendering using your desired CODEC. Remember also that since CD-based video is destined for display on a computer screen, you can freely use the entire RGB color gamut, rather than limiting yourself to

NTSC "broadcast safe" colors. If you've been frustrated by having to dull down your colors, now is your chance to beef them back up.

4. De-interlace your video. Most editing and effects apps include a de-interlacing filter.

5. If any of your footage was originally shot on film and then transferred to video via a telecine process, then you'll need to run those sections through an *inverse telecine* process to remove the 3:2 pulldown that was applied during telecine. Several programs, including Adobe After Effects, provide inverse telecine filters.

TIP

Stay Away from That Film Look!

That wonderful grain and texture that we all love in film is an anathema to the average video CODEC. No matter how nice it might look on your screen, don't go adding grain and noise to a movie that's destined for extreme compression. In fact, if you ended up with some particularly noisy video (from shooting in low light, for example), consider using a special grain killing filter like the one provided by the film-resolution version of DigiEffects' Cinelook.

If your video is destined for inclusion in a game or multimedia presentation, you'll need to weigh some additional concerns when choosing your CODEC. For example, if your video will be played back using a custom-authored application, then there may be CODEC limitations imposed by your programmer or authoring environment.

If you're producing video for a game, your video files might be competing with other videos, graphics, and software for space on the CD. Be prepared to sacrifice image quality for smaller files. Sometimes, game and multimedia developers use special CODECs, such as Smacker Technology's Smacker CODEC, which produce low-quality, full-screen, highly-compressed files. Consult your programmer for details on these custom CODECs.

Choosing a Data Rate

Some CODECs let you limit your movies to a specific data rate. In addition to helping you control file size, setting a data rate helps you tailor your movie to the throughput capabilities of a particular device.

The optimal data rate for CD-ROM output depends on the speed of your target device. Consult the chart below for details. Note, however, that your CD-ROM drive may not be as fast as it says it is. A 24x CD-ROM drive is not necessarily 12 times faster than a 2x drive. The 24x claim often refers to an ideal *burst speed* that the drive can achieve during certain operations, not a *sustained transfer* speed.

CD-ROM Speed	Safe Data Rate
2x	150–200 KBps
4x	250–300 KBps

If you're a Macintosh owner compressing movies for playback on a fast Mac, you can often push the data rate as high as 450 KBps. You should perform some tests on your target machine before you commit to these higher speeds.

If you're using the Sorenson CODEC, not only can you often get away with lower bit rates, you'll frequently get *better results* with lower bit rates. Experiment with settings as low as 50–75, or around 100 (Figure 18.7).

FIGURE
18.7   *The standard QuickTime Compression Settings dialog lets you set data rate and keyframe intervals for CODECS that allow such controls.*

Choosing a Keyframe Interval

One of the techniques that a CODEC employs to compress video is to only store pixels that change from one frame to another—a process called *temporal* compression. In compression terms, a *keyframe* is an entire frame that has been compressed *spatially;* that is, its color information has undergone some compression. The next frame is called an intermediary frame, or *i-frame,* and contains only the pixels that have changed since the previous frame. (They're called intermediary frames because they're the frames that come between keyframes.) Each successive i-frame contains only the pixels that have changed from the previous i-frame. The next *keyframe* contains a complete frame, which corrects for any errors or artifacts introduced in the intermediary frames.

Obviously, the more keyframes you have in a movie, the higher the quality will be, but the lower your compression ratio will be. Video with a lot of action will benefit from more keyframes, while clips that are more static can get away with very few keyframes (Figure 18.8).

Burn Your Disc

Once you've compressed your files, you'll simply need to organize them on your hard drive, and prepare your project for writing to CD. This process will vary depending on your CD writing software. Consult your manual for details.

If you're concerned about cross-platform playability, then you'll want to create a CD formatted with the ISO 9660 standard. Such disks will be playable from a Mac or a PC.

CREATING A VIDEO CD (VCD)

Though not very well-known in North America, in Europe and Asia the VCD format has quickly becomes as popular and prolific as VHS tapes. Introduced by Philips and Sony in 1993, VCD was a predecessor to DVD. The normal VCD format uses MPEG1 compression to store up to approximately 74 minutes of full-screen, full-motion NTSC or PAL video on a "normal" 650 MB CD or CDR.

VCDs can be played on special console VCD players (which are widely available in Europe and Asia), on some DVD Video players, and on most current Mac and Windows-based computers. VCDs have all the advantages of CD-ROM delivery, but with the extra advantage of full-screen video, and

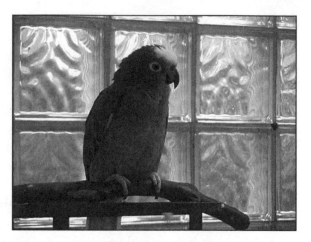

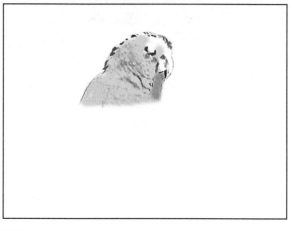

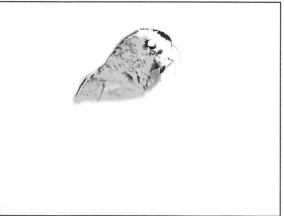

FIGURE

18.8
Movies are compressed temporally by storing only the pixels that are in the intermediary frames between keyframes.

more playback options. (Note that some console DVD players can't read CDRs, whether audio or VCD.)

In addition to the original VCD 1.1 specification, there are now several additional VCD formats, all of which fit on normal CDs or CDRs:

- VCD 2.0 can deliver NTSC and PAL video and provides hi-res, interactive menus àla DVD.
- VCD-ROM is a hybrid format that supports both computer data and VCD 2.0 data on the same disk.
- VCD-Internet is a VCD-ROM disc that includes video as well as links to control on-line or on-disc content, stored in the form of web pages. This format also includes drivers which allow the disc to play on any Mac or Windows machine without having to install special software.

Creating a VCD is pretty simple. As with CD-ROM and web delivery, you may want to do some test MPEG renderings to determine if your video needs any color correction. You might also want to experiment with de-interlacing your video, and you might need to crop the edges. After finishing your final edit and polish, you'll need to compress your video with an MPEG1 compressor. Since QuickTime doesn't ship with a built-in MPEG1 CODEC, you'll need to purchase one separately. If speed is of the essence, and you still have some money in your budget, consider buying a hardware MPEG1 encoder for faster compression.

Once your video is compressed, you can write it to a CDR using a standard CD recorder. You'll need software that can write VCD format such as Adaptec's Toast for Macintosh, or Easy CD Creator for Windows. If you're a Mac user, your best choice is Query Inc.'s Internet Disc Writer (a demo is included on the DV Handbook CD-ROM).

Note that with new 80 minute CDRs it is possible to store even longer videos on a VCD. Some companies offer even longer CDs (up to 130 minutes) using proprietary technology. See www.dvhandbook.com/vcd for more info.

An MPEG Compressor by Any Other Name

Not all MPEG compressors are created equal—some deliver substantially better (or worse) quality than others. In general, hardware compressors will yield higher-quality results than software compressors for any number or boring, technical reasons. If you can't afford a hardware compressor then you should at least compare sample output from several different software packages.

Outputting for the Web

Though presenting video on the Web was kind of a silly idea a few years ago, it's rapidly become a feasible means of video distribution. With cable modems and DSL connections, more users are accessing the Internet through high-speed connections, making the downloading of large video files more feasible. In addition to faster connections, running the latest compression and streaming technologies on today's faster desktop computers makes it possible to get video of very good quality.

Most of your concerns when outputting for the Web are the same as for outputting to CD-ROM. You need to pick a target audience, identify the CODEC that is best for that audience, and tweak and adjust the CODEC's settings to create the optimal balance of image quality and small file size.

You may have assumed that you'd already chosen your target audience simply by choosing to output for Web delivery. However, there are many different types of computers and connections attached to the Internet. As with CD-ROM, you need to consider the bandwidth capabilities of your audience. If you want as broad an audience as possible, you'll need to create very small, lower-quality files. If you know your audience will be using a faster connection, then you can go for a larger file with better image quality.

As with CD-ROM output, you'll need to resize, crop, and color correct your footage for your chosen CODEC.

Streaming or Non-Streaming?

Before you can select a CODEC, you need to decide how you want the user to access your movie. The easiest option is to simply upload the movie file to your server and place a link to it on your Web page. When the user clicks on that link, the movie file will be downloaded to his or her computer, and will play when it has been completely downloaded. The movie will not begin playing until the *entire* file has been transferred. Obviously, if your movie is 20 MB, then a 56K modem user will have to wait a while.

If you use the proper embed tags in your HTML, a user with a newer browser and the right QuickTime plug-in will begin playing a movie after enough of the footage has been downloaded. While playing, the browser will continue to download. Note that on a slow connection, a large file can still take a long time to begin playing. See www.dvhandbook.com/webdeliv-ery for more details.

If you're going to deliver a movie through a simple download, then you're free to use any type of compression that you want, as long as you're sure your intended audience can play such a file. Follow the CD-ROM compression guidelines outlined earlier.

On-Line Movie Theaters
There are a number of different "movie theater" sites that screen independent shorts and features. These are not only great venues for watching indie films (and great venues to which you can submit your own work), but they're also good showcases for different compression technologies. For a list of sites, check out www.dvhandbook.com/onlinetheaters.

Streaming video uses special compression to stream packets of video in real-time, on-demand to the viewer's computer. With streaming video, there's little or no waiting for the movie to start. As the streamed file is playing, the user's computer continues to download and buffer additional frames. Unfortunately, the compression usually required for streaming video results in significant image loss. However, since most users probably aren't willing to wait around to download dozens of megabytes, streaming video is probably the best alternative.

Your choice of streaming video format will depend largely on the service provider that is hosting your Web site. Video streaming requires special server software, and your ISP may not support video streaming. If they do, you'll need to find out what type of streaming they support, and download the appropriate compression tools.

Apple's QuickTime provides video streaming, and you can very easily create a streaming movie using Apple's QuickTime Pro player. First you'll need to compress your video using your CODEC of choice, usually Sorenson. Then open Apple's QuickTime Player and export the movie as a Hinted Movie. This will write out a new file with the information required for streaming.

QuickTime also provides support for *alternate data rates*. Alternate data rates allow you to post multiple copies of the same movie, each compressed with different settings. If you've provided for alternate data rates, then your server can take care of sending a file with settings appropriate to the user's connection speed (Figure 18.9).

For instructions on using other streaming technologies, consult your ISP.

QuickTime Pro
For an extra $30 you can upgrade your QuickTime player to QuickTime Pro, which provides the authoring and exporting options you need to create streaming QuickTime, Streaming QuickTime VR, and movies with alternate data rates.

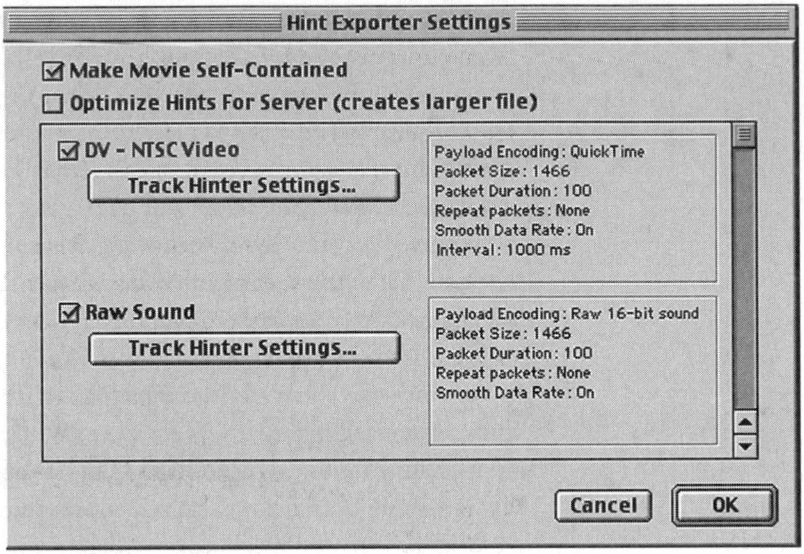

FIGURE 18.9   *You can create streaming QuickTime movies by exporting your compressed QuickTime file as a hinted movie.*

Depending on the design of your Web page, you might want to take advantage of other QuickTime features, such as the ability to display the initial frame of a movie on your page. For details, see www.dvhandbook.com/webdelivery.

Video streaming will require the user to have a special browser plug-in. Because downloading and installing a plug-in can be a bit of a hassle, it's better to consider formats that are more popular, such as RealMedia or QuickTime. The downside of the RealMedia format is that you must use the RealPlayer G2 interface to play audio and video clips—if you've worked hard designing your site, you may find its look intrusive (or just plain ugly).

Media Cleaner Pro

If you're outputting to Web or CD-ROM, you'll get much better results and have a much easier time if you buy yourself a copy of Media 100's Media Cleaner Pro. While we realize that we keep suggesting that you buy more and more software, this time we *really* mean it.

Media Cleaner Pro has become something of an industry standard for highly compressed video output. Media Cleaner's simple, wizard-driven interface will interview you about your output destination, analyze your movie, and automatically "clean" it for you. MediaCleaner does much more than picking optimal compression settings. It can also crop, resize, de-interlace, strip or add tracks, and much more.

If your budget is tight, Media100 also sells a "lite" version of Media Cleaner. With the ownership of Media Cleaner Pro, Edit DV, and Media 100 all under one roof, look for advanced Web video tools from Media 100 in the future (Figure 18.10).

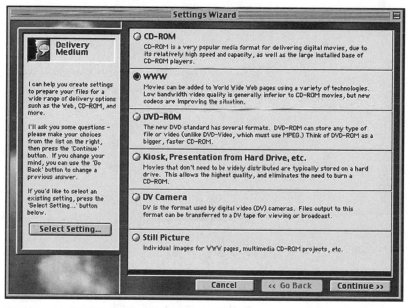

FIGURE **18.10**   *Media 100's Media Cleaner Pro includes compression wizards that determine your optimal compression settings through a simple interview.*

DVD Authoring

With the popularity of DVD soaring, and the installed base of players steadily growing, outputting to DVD is becoming a viable, cost-effective way to release your work. With its massive storage capabilities, and versatile, program mable interface structure, DVD provides a robust, high-quality delivery medium with a built-in simple authoring environment.

Unfortunately, though DVD players are becoming more popular, DVD mastering is still an expensive process involving equipment and software that may tax a small budget. However, despite its expense, if you can afford it, DVD is a great way to create short runs of high-quality copies for direct sales and distribution.

A DVD is, in essence, a much denser, higher-capacity compact disc. But, in addition to being able to store much more information (and the ability to store information on both sides), the DVD Video spec also defines interactive controls such as menus, buttons, chapters, hyperlinks, and random access. Consequently, creating a DVD involves much more than just compressing your video. You also have to author the menu environment. To do this, you'll need special software.

DVD Compression

DVDs are compressed using MPEG2 compression, a higher-quality variant of the MPEG1 spec that we discussed earlier. Once your project is edited and finished, you'll need to compress it into MPEG2 format. For this, you'll need compression software or hardware, and a lot of disc space.

Though you can buy software for compressing your DVD, you'll have to schedule a lot of time for your compression. Depending on the speed of your computer, software MPEG2 compression can take anywhere from 1 to 3 hours *per second* of video. Hardware MPEG2 encoders work much faster, but will cost you anywhere from a few hundred to a few thousand dollars, depending on the quality and features you demand.

You'll need a hard drive big enough to store your compressed files. A DVD can hold around 9 GB of data, but you probably won't use all of this unless you have a very long feature, or are planning on adding a lot of supplemental material. For authoring, you will probably want to use an external, portable drive, as this will make it easier to get your finished DVD files to a service bureau for duplication.

TIP

Content Is King
The biggest selling point for DVDs is proving to be the supplemental content beyond the feature film itself. Outtakes, gag reels, featurettes, original storyboards, rough special effects shots, director commentaries, and interviews with cast and crewmembers are all part of what makes a DVD better than a VHS tape. The latest trends include Web links and hidden bonus tracks.

DVD Authoring

Once you've compressed your files, you're ready to author the menus and interactivity that will form the interface for your DVD. Through special DVD authoring software, you'll use still images and short video clips to create the interface for your DVD.

Many packages such as Astarte's DVDirector Pro also include MPEG2 encoder cards, allowing you to buy a complete DVD authoring system for under $5000. For an updated list of DVD authoring software and hardware, check out www.dvhandbook.com/dvdauthoring.

Creating the Disc

It's important to understand that DVD Video is a different format than DVD ROM or DVD RAM. While you can buy a DVD RAM drive that lets you store and record on special DVD RAM media, this is not the same media or format as a DVD Video. In fact, both DVD ROM and DVD RAM have much smaller capacities than DVD Video.

Therefore, when your project is complete, you'll need to take your files to a special service bureau where they will be pressed onto DVDs.

Obviously, moving several gigabytes of data to a service bureau can be a bit tricky. If you authored your project on a single, external drive you can simply disconnect your drive and take it to your service bureau. Other options include copying the project to DLT tape. DLT tape drives are expensive, however, and your service bureau may not support them.

Pass the Buck

If all of this sounds too complicated, there are companies that will take your final video master and create a DVD for you. Services provided by these companies vary from simple MPEG compression to full mastering including interface authoring. Obviously, contracting out this type of work will be more expensive than doing it yourself, but it might be easier in the long run. For a list of DVD authoring companies, see www.dvhandbook.com/dvdauthoring.

Getting Your 35mm Film Release Print

High-quality video footage is the key to a successful tape-to-film transfer. Everything that looks bad on video is going to look worse on film, especially when projected. The resolution of 35mm is much, much greater than that of video: any underexposed blacks or over-exposed whites will read as large expanses of black or white nothingness, without the detail you would normally see in film. Also, any artifacts, noise, and other image flaws will be enlarged 25 times. If you shot your video properly—that is, if you took the time to light it like film, and set your video black and white levels properly when you created your videotape master—then you'll be giving your film recordist the best possible image, containing the most information. Avoid any sort of image processing that removes information, such as de-interlacing. Also, avoid any image processing that adds artifacts or noise, like boosting the video gain. If you're careful, the result of good DV footage transferred to film can look surprisingly similar to 16mm film.

Keep Your Crew Involved

Your director of photography and your editor probably know a lot more about film and video image quality than you do. Keep them involved throughout the whole process, from digital image enhancement, to on-lining your videotape, to film transfer

There are two ways to deliver your footage to the film recordist: digital files or videotape. We've already discussed how to best create a textless videotape master via a professional on-line session, or by doing it yourself. This is the easiest and most practical way to deliver your film to the film recordist. The other option is to deliver digital video files, usually QuickTime, Targa, or sequential PICT formats on a hard drive or high-capacity tape backup format. Talk to your film recordist before assuming that he or she can work with digital files.

The primary reason to deliver digital files is if you've done some effects work, such as color correcting or compositing, and do not wish to recompress those shots by going back out to tape. Titles should also be delivered digitally as high-resolution 2K files, or else they should originate on film via optical printing. (See Chapter 16). Talk to your film recordist about the way he or she prefers to have titles and effects shots delivered.

Reel Changes

If you're heading for a film transfer, you'll most likely have to break your project into 20- or 40-minute segments to accommodate reel changes. Talk to your film recordist about this as early as possible. Be sure to make these breaks at a hard cut, not a dissolve. Also, make sure they're at a natural lull in the soundtrack, not in the middle of a line of dialog or music—the edit at the reel change may not be seamless.

THE FILM PRINTING PROCESS

If you're planning to make a film print of your video, it's important to understand the traditional film printing process. 16mm and 35mm motion picture films are very similar to 35mm still film: the negative is exposed in the camera and the film is taken to a lab where it is processed to produce a print of the film. If you've ever compared a bad "one-hour photo" print to a professional print of the same image, then you know how different two prints from the same negative can look. Some film transfer companies have their own labs, others work closely with a nearby lab, or will work with the lab of your choice. Once you have a negative, you'll follow the same process as traditional film printing.

One-Light Prints

When a print is made from a film negative, the print is exposed using three lights—red, green, and blue—to create a full-color image. The lab takes the negative and determines the best RGB light settings for the entire film. The film is then printed using that setting, and the result print is called a *one-light print*, since the light setting remains the same for the entire print.

Color Timing

With color timing, a specialist at the lab watches the one-light print and determines different light settings on a scene-by-scene basis. Often the director and D.P. are present during this process. The negative is then re-printed using these special light settings. The result is a timed color print. In traditional film-making, several trial prints are made at this stage. The final, successful print is called the *answer print*.

By the time you have your videotape recorded to film, you should already have done a lot of color correction work (Chapter 15). Because these color adjustments have already been made, you may spend less time dealing with color timing than with a film-original project. In addition, your film recordist will have his or her own special formula for getting the best possible film print from your video.

TIP

Using an EDL as a Cut List
Having a list of where each edit occurs can be a big timesaver for your color timer and/or film recordist. Print out a simple A-mode EDL with clip names as a reference to help them quickly find the start of each shot and each scene in your film.

Release Print

Your answer print is used to make an intermediate print that will be used to strike release prints. The intermediate will either be a color *internegative* (IN) or an *interpositive* (IP). Figure 18.11 details this process. Because these intermediate prints are used to strike release prints, you can store your original negative away for safe keeping. If your intermediate print gets damaged, you can create a new one from your original negative.

Optical Soundtracks

Once you have a release print, a stripe of photo-active chemicals is added to the print next to the picture. A sound facility specializing in optical soundtracks will then take your audio master, either videotape or DAT, and record it onto the optical stripe on the film.

Film Math

Film is measured in frames and feet (hence the term footage*). 35mm film shot at 24 frames per second has 16 frames per foot. Typical film lengths are 50′ (about 30 seconds), 100′ (about a minute), 400′ (about 4.5 minutes), 1000′ (about 11 minutes), and 2000′ (around 22 minutes). 16mm film shot at 24 frames per second has 40 frames per foot. When companies quote prices for film, they may quote by the frame, by the foot, or by the minute.*

WHERE TO GET YOUR VIDEO TRANSFERRED TO FILM

At the time of this writing, there is a growing handful of companies that offer affordable video-to-film transfers, and a lot of companies that offer less affordable, high-resolution video to film transfers that typically cost between $2–$4 per frame. (For more on high-end film scanning, go to www.dvhandbook.com/2k.) The processes used by these companies vary greatly, but typically the price includes recording your videotape (or file) onto film stock, processing the negative, and a first print of the film, usually with an optical soundtrack added for an extra charge. Additional color timing and printing will be something you will have to work out with the lab. Here is a short who's who of affordable film recordists, how they do it, and how much it will set you back.

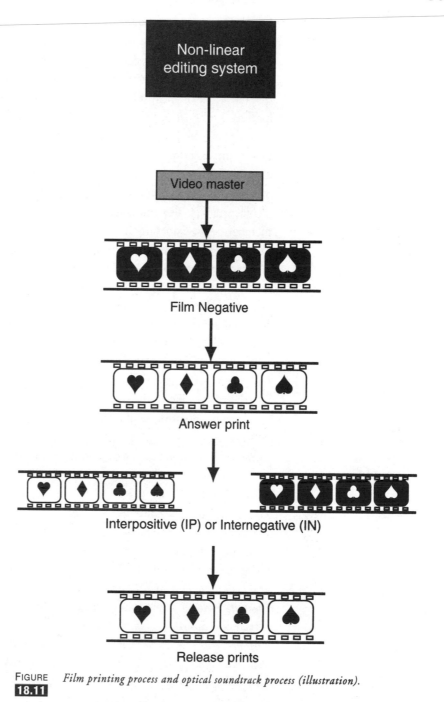

FIGURE
18.11   *Film printing process and optical soundtrack process (illustration).*

Four Media Company (4MC)

4MC, in Burbank, California, uses a process they developed in the early 1970s to make video to film transfers. Using an electron beam scanner, the videotape image is recorded by a special 16mm film camera that shoots one frame of red (R), one frame of green (G), and one frame of blue (B) for each frame of 24 fps film. A proprietary process is used to convert the 29.97 video frame rate to 24 fps film. 4MC will color correct the video beforehand, if necessary, although they resort to this rarely. The result is three 16mm color-separated *interpositives*. The three interpositives are combined into a single full-color RGB 35mm (or 16mm) negative, which is then used to strike a print of the film.

Since 4MC is also a film laboratory, they handle all processing of the film themselves. 4MC does not handle DV formats, so you will have to have your DV master transferred to another format, preferably Digital Betacam. You can deliver your project on D1, D2, Digibeta, BetaSP, or 3/4". Other formats will need to be transferred elsewhere. A 16mm transfer costs $180 per minute of finished film, and 35mm costs $425 per minute—both prices include the optical soundtrack transfer. A 90-minute video transferred to 35mm film will cost you $38,250. This price does not include the actual negative, which may cost upwards of $30,000 (for 35mm). If you don't purchase the negative, you'll have to go to 4MC's lab to strike all your prints, but in return, 4MC guarantees the safekeeping of the negative. This means that if anything happens to your original negative, 4MC will recreate it using the 16mm interpositives, which they keep in storage. 4MC has transferred video to film for *Hoop Dreams, The Blair Witch Project,* and many others.

TIP

High-Def Out

Getting high-def video into your computer is a lot easier and cheaper than getting it back out to tape. As a result, high-capacity optical tape storage is the method of choice for getting your high-def footage from your NLE to the film recordist. DTS, Exabyte, DLT, and even Jaz for very short pieces are all much cheaper than going to a high-def online suite. Be aware that just because your project is 16:9, doesn't mean it's high-def. If you used mattes or an anamorphic lens to shoot using a DV format, you can either deliver on tape or deliver digital files. Sony Image Works' high-def center, in Culver City, California, is specifically geared to transferring HD video to film, but you can also bump up your NTSC video to HD prior to transferring to film. The Cruise was shot on miniDV and bumped up to HD by the Sony Image Works' hi-def center before it was transfered to film. Read more about Sony Image Works at www.dvhandbook.com/HD.

Swiss Effects

Swiss Effects, in Zurich, is one of the most popular film recording solutions at the time of this writing. Films recorded at Swiss Effects include *The Saltmen of Tibet, Julien Donkey Boy,* and *The Bus Riders' Union.* Swiss Effects takes PAL video and increases the resolution to 2K/frame (considered the equivalent of film resolution). The 2K frames are displayed on CRT monitors and recorded directly to 35mm or 16mm negative. Striking the negative for a 90-minute feature film will cost about $35,000. A color-timed first print with optical soundtrack will cost an additional $15,000. Swiss Effects can work with labs in major cities around the world, so if you're based in New York and can't afford to go to Switzerland to oversee the printing of your negative, you can have the lab work done in New York. If your project was shot on NTSC, it will be transferred to PAL videotape prior to the negative recording process using one of several proprietary methods. Swiss Effects also offers on-line editing and a Web site with useful information from camera tests they've done.

TIP

Wedges
You can select representative frames from each scene, called wedges, and have them test-printed before you do the full transfer. This will usually cost anywhere from $200–$500.

Film Out Express

Film Out Express, in Glendale, California, transfers both videotape and digital files using a proprietary *kinescopic* process to do their film recording. A kinescope is a filmed image shot off a video screen. They offer a six-tiered price structure starting at $180 for a no-frills one-light print on Fuji 35mm stock, and achieve the 39.97 to 24 fps frame rate conversion by throwing out every 5th frame of NTSC video. That may sound scary, but it means you can get a first print for a little over $15,000 (about $20,000 with sound).

The next tier uses proprietary software to do a 30 fps to 24 fps conversion, and adds a one-light color correction pass for $230 a minute on 35mm Fuji stock. The same process on more expensive Kodak stock will cost $325/minute. For $280 a minute (Fuji) or $375/min (Kodak), you'll get specialized color timing on separate scenes. You can have them convert your sound to optical track for an additional $50/minute.

The top-level service starts with the $375/minute Kodak transfer described, but the film recordists will spend as much time as needed to digitally tweak the film to make it look as good as possible. This will run $150 per hour (of work time) extra and will require more turnaround time. Although they've been around for awhile doing shorter animation transfers for Disney and other big name clients, they've recently started doing transfers for long format projects. Look for their video-to-film transfer of the indie feature, *Boyd's Out*.

Conclusion

Believe it or not, over these last 18 chapters, we've been covering the *easy* part of film production. Now the hard part begins: selling your product. Hopefully, you have some idea of who might be interested in your final product. Or perhaps you have backers who are already committed to moving your project forward.

Odds are, though, that you have no idea what will become of your piece. Now is the time to make something happen. With independent film experiencing a resurgence in popularity, and with new delivery technologies such as the Web, CD-ROM, and inexpensive DVD production, there are many avenues you can pursue to sell your feature or documentary.

If you don't already have an "in," or know someone "in the business," then the best place to start is the film festival circuit. These days, *everyone* is hosting a film festival. Find out the entry requirements, raise the entry fees, and submit your finished product. If everything works well, you'll catch the eye of a distributor who will want to release your feature.

But, even if you don't get distribution, getting feedback from a live audience, other directors, and actors can be an invaluable—and fun—experience for improving your current project, or starting your next one.

In the end, your goal shouldn't be *selling* a story, but *telling* a story. If you feel you've successfully and effectively told the story you set out to tell, then your project has succeeded. Now, go tell another!

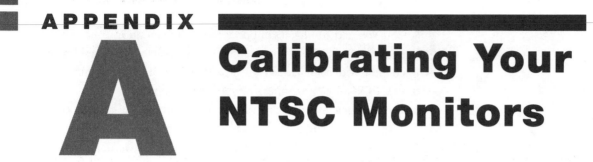

APPENDIX

A Calibrating Your NTSC Monitors

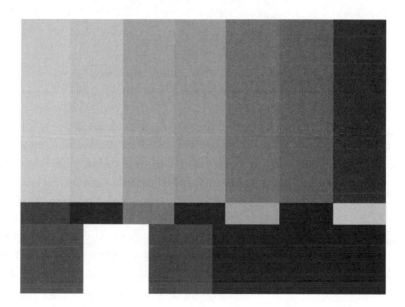

Before you start editing, it's important to adjust your NTSC monitor to ensure that it displays colors as accurately as possible. The easiest way to do this is with color bars, a regular pattern of colors and gray tones that can be used to adjust your monitor's brightness and contrast.

Many professional monitors and cameras can automatically generate color bars. Or, you can use editing packages like Final Cut Pro or Adobe Premiere to generate color bars. Though you can use these programs to record color bars to tape for playback on your NTSC monitor, it's better to feed the signal directly from your computer and into your monitor. Consult your editing package's documentation for details.

QuickTime Color Bars
You can find QuickTime movies of color bars on the DFH CD or at www.dvhandbook.com/colorbars.html.

Setting Up

Ideally, you'll want to calibrate your monitor in a dimly lit room. Try to get rid of any bright reflections on the monitor's screen. Before you start calibrating, turn the monitor on and let it warm up for a few minutes. Then, activate your color bars. Now you are ready to start. (See Color Plate 5 for an illustration of color bars.)

1. Your monitor should have a control labelled *Color* or *Chroma*. Turn this all the way down until the color bars are grayscale.
2. In the lower-right corner of the screen is a rectangle that is solid black. To the immediate left of this are three thin strips of gray. On your screen, these strips may look like a solid block of black. These gray tones, called *Pluge Bars*—or *Picture Lineup Generating Equipment*—will be your first adjustment. Adjust the brightness control on your monitor until the rightmost Pluge bar (see Figure A2) is barely visible. You should not see any difference between the left bar and the middle bar. You have just set the proper black level.
3. Now turn the contrast on your monitor all the way up. The white bar (second from the left at the bottom of the screen) will flare. Reduce the contrast until you have eliminated the bloom and can see a sharp edge between the white bar and the gray bars on either side. You have now set the white point for your monitor.

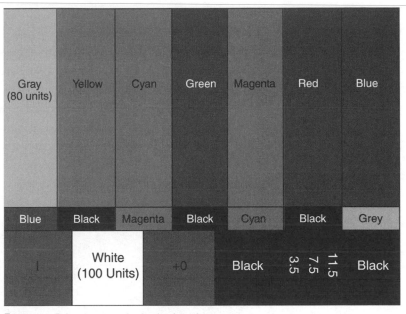

FIGURE
A.1   *Colors in a standard color bar chart.*

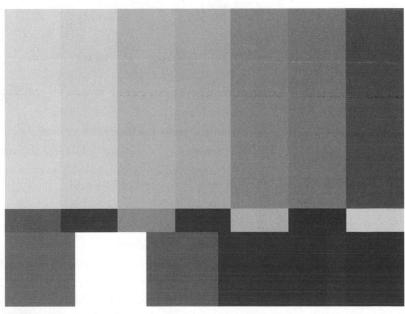

FIGURE
A.2   *Correct pluge bar.*

4. Many professional monitors have a *Blue Check* button or an equivalent that will shut off the red and green guns in the monitor. If you're using a television or non-professional monitor, you'll have to eyeball your color adjustments. Adjust your monitor's color controls until the yellow is a lemony yellow with no orange or green. The magenta bar should be pure magenta with no shifts toward red or purple. Your monitor is now calibrated.

5. If your monitor has a Blue switch, turn it on. (If your monitor doesn't have a blue switch, you can get some blue lighting gels and simply hold them up to your eye.) On a properly adjusted monitor, you will see alternating bars of equal luminance (see Figure A.3 and Color Plate 16).

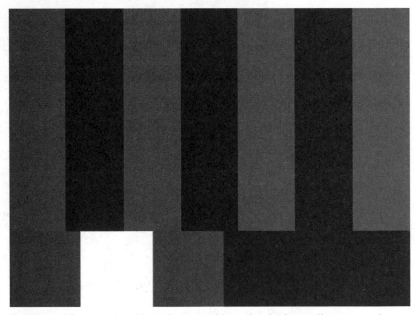

FIGURE
A.3   *On a properly calibrated monitor, blue-only color bars will appear as alternating shades of equal intensity.*

6. If your blue bars don't look correct, adjust the color settings on your monitor until the gray bar at the far left matches the sub bar that sits directly beneath it. Then do the same for the blue bar on the far right. If you have adjusted correctly, then the leftmost gray bar and the far-right blue bar will be equally bright.

7. Next, use the same process to adjust the cyan and magenta bars. When finished, the yellow, green, and red bars should appear completely black.

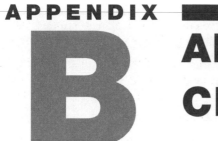

APPENDIX

B ABOUT THE CD-ROM

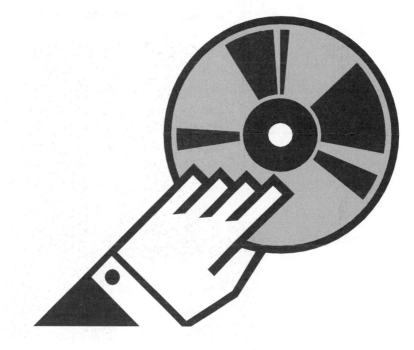

This CD contains files to assist you in your filmmaking ventures. There are three primary folders: TUTORIALS, DEMOS, AND EXTRAS. The contents of these folders are listed below. Please also refer to the system requirements contained in this document to insure that your system meets these requirements.

To use the items on the CD, you should select the folder you wish to use and then select the appropriate files. Again, be sure that you have all the necessary hardware and software to run these files.

- **TUTORIALS**: The tutorial folder contains support files and all necessary media for all of the Digital Filmmaking Handbook's tutorials. Some tutorials require you to create supplemental, accessory documents using Adobe Photoshop or After Effects. Demo versions of these apps are included in the Demos folder, however, these versions cannot save. If you don't have full versions of these programs, we recommend that you work through the tutorials to learn the steps, and then use the supplied, completed files for the rest of the tutorial. Some tutorials require the installation of demo plug-ins, also available in the demo folder.

- **DEMOS**: Demo versions of many popular editing and effects applications and plug-in are provided including the following:

  > Adobe: After Effects, Photoshop, Premiere 5
  > Atomic Power Corp.: Evolution for After Effects 4 and 3.1
  > Pinnacle Systems: Primatte, Commotion 2.0, Composite Wizard, Image Lounge (Mac only), Knoll Light Factory
  > Cycore Computers: Cult Effects Vol 1 (Mac only)
  > DigiEffects: Aurorix 2, CineLook, CineMotion (Mac only),
  > In:Sync: Speed Razor (Windows only)
  > Query: Internet DiscWriter 1.0.4 (Mac only)

- **EXTRAS**: Contains PDF production forms as well as a template document for creating "title safe" titles and graphics. For more extra goodies, check out http://www.dvhandbook.com.

SYSTEM REQUIREMENTS:

Mac 300 MHz G3 or better,128 MB of RAM, 100 MB+ of available hard-disk space Sound card (recommended); 16-bit video card (required); 24-bit or greater video display card (recommended), QuickTime 4.0 or higher, and Adobe Photoshop and After Effects.

Win Intel(r) Pentium(r) processor (required); Pentium II, Pentium III or multiprocessor system recommended. WIN 98 (32MB RAM) or WIN NT 4.0 or later (64 MB RAM) 100 MB+ of available hard-disk space, sound card (recommended); 16-bit video card (required); 24-bit or greater video display card (recommended), QuickTime 4.0 or higher, and Adobe Photoshop and After Effects.

Glossary

2-pop: The last two events in a countdown leader. After the "2" (as in "5, 4, 3, 2") there is a short pop that occurs instead of a "1." The "2-pop" is used for syncing audio and video when shooting non-sync sound.

3:2 pulldown A method for transferring 24fps film to 29.97 fps NTSC video. The film is slowed down by .1% and the first film frame is recorded on the first two fields of video, the second frame is recorded on the next three fields of video and so on.

3-point editing (See *Three-point editing*)

A/B rolling (see *checkerboard.*)

Accelerator cards: Custom hardware that can accelerate certain features such as 3D rendering, rendering of plug-in filters, or display of complex video.

Action Safe: The area of your image that will most likely be visible any video monitor. Essential action should be kept within the action safe area, as action that falls outside this area may be lost due to *overscan.*

Address A frame of video as identified by timecode information.

AES/EBU An acronym for the Audio Engineering Society and the European Broadcaster's Union; also a standard for professional digital audio that specifies the transmission of audio data in a stream that encodes stereo audio signals along with optional information.

Aliasing: The "jaggies," those stair-stepping patterns that occur on a diagonal or curved line on a computer or video display. Can be smoothed or corrected through *anti-aliasing* processes.

Alpha Channel: An 8-bit color channel (see *channels*) which is used to specify the transparency of each pixel in an image. An alpha channel works like a sophisticated stencil, and is the digital equivalent of a matte (see *matte*).

Alternate data rates When streaming QuickTime files from a web site, it is possible to specify several copies of the same movie, each optimized for a different data rate. The server will then decide which movie is best for the speed of the user's connection.

A-mode EDL An EDL sorted in order of master record in timecode.

Amp Short for ampere, a unit that measures the voltage of an electrical power source. (?)

Analog Information represented electronically as a continuous, varying signal. (See also *digital*.)

Anamorphic lenses: Special lenses that shoot a wide-screen image, but optically compress the image to a normal 4:3 aspect ratio. The widescreen image can be uncompressed by a projector fitted with a similar anamorphic lens, or by software that knows to stretch the image.

Animation compressor: A lossless QuickTime CODEC.

Answer print The final print of a film after color-timing.

Anti-aliasing: The process of eliminating "jagged" edges on computer-generated text and graphics. Anti-aliased graphics have their edges slightly blurred and mixed with background colors to eliminate the jagged, stairstepping patterns that can occur on diagonal, or curved lines.

Aperture: In any type of camera, light is focused by the lens, through an *aperture* and onto the focal plane. The size of the aperture controls how much light passes through to the focal plane. In addition to controlling the brightness of the exposure, the aperture controls the *depth of field* in the image. By balancing the size of the aperture (as measured in *f-stops*) with the *shutter speed* you can trade off between varying depth of field, and or the ability to better-resolve fast motion.

Array: See *RAID*.

Art director The person in charge of the execution of the production designer's vision who manages set construction, set dressing, props and scenic painting.

Aspect ratio The ratio of the width of the picture to the height. Aspect ratios can be expressed as ratios, such as 4:3, or as numbers, such as 1.33.

Assemble edit An edit onto a videotape that records over the entire tape, including the video track, the audio tracks, and the control track.

ATA: A type of hard drive interface. Not as fast as SCSI, but fast enough for DV.

ATSC Advanced Television Systems Committee - established to set the technical standards for DTV, including HDTV.

Attenuator: A circuit that lowers the strength of an electronic signal.

Audio compressor: A filter (or piece of hardware) that reduces the dynamic range of a sound to accommodate loud peaks.

Audio guide track A mixed audio track from the off-line final cut that is placed onto one of the audio tracks of the on-line master to serve as a guide during the on-line editing session.

Audio mixer A piece of hardware that takes several audio signals and mixes them together, allowing for the mixing of different sources. Mixers usually include some sort of equalization control.

Audio sampling rate: The number of samples per second that are used to digitize a particular sound. Most DV cameras can record at several audio sampling rates. Higher rates yield better results. Measured in kiloHertz, 44.1 kHz is considered audio CD quality and 48 kHz is considered DAT quality.

AVR Avid Video Resolution, a series of low and high-resolution codecs included with the Avid family of editing systems. AVR77 is the highest 2-field compressed resolution available although some Avid products offer uncompressed resolutions as well.

Axial One of several linear hardware-based on-line editing systems.

Balanced audio: A type of microphone connector that provides extra power. Sometimes needed if you want to have microphone cable lengths of 25 feet or longer.

Balancing light sources In a lighting setup with several different light sources, the process of making the color temperature of all the lights the same, either to match daylight or tungsten light. Usually this is done with CTO or CTB lighting gels.

Bandwidth The amount of digital information that can be passed through a connection at a given time. High bandwidth is needed for high-quality images.

Barn doors A set of hinged door-like flaps that attach to the front of a light and serve to control where the light falls.

Bars and tone A combination of *color bars* and *60 Hz audio reference tone*, usually recorded onto the head of each videotape. Used for calibrating video and audio levels.

Bin A film-editing term that refers to the place where the shots for a scene are stored. In software editing systems, bins can also be referred to as folders, galleries, or libraries.

Binary A system for encoded digital information using two components: 0 and 1.

Black and coded tape A "blank" tape that has been *striped* with a combination of a black video signal and timecode.

Black burst A composite video signal with a totally black picture. Used to synchronize professional video equipment. Black burst supplies video equipment with vertical sync, horizontal sync, and chroma burst timing.

Black burst generator A piece of video hardware that generates a black composite video signal, or black burst, used to sync professional video equipment and to *black and code* tapes.

Black level The black level defines the darkest a video image is allowed to get. Improperly set black levels can result in dull, greyish blacks.

Black wrap A heavy-duty aluminum foil with a matte black coating on one side used to block light. Can also be wrapped around light sources to make them more directional.

Blue spill A bluish light that is cast onto the back of a foreground subject due to a reflection from a blue-screen.

Blue-screen: A special screen, usually composed of blue cloth or backdrops painted with special blue paint, which is placed behind a foreground element. Blue-screen shots are those shots that you intend to later composite with other elements through the use of a chroma key function. Blue is used because most living animals have little naturally-occuring blue colors.

BNC Connector A connector used to carry composite video, component video, timecode and AES/EBU audio signals.

Boom: A long (sometimes up to 100' long) pole with a microphone at the end. Technically, a boom is a large, sometimes hydraulically controlled device, as opposed to a *fishpole*, a smaller, handheld pole. Increasingly, the term *boom* is used to refer to any stick with a mic on the end.

Bounce card A piece of white material, like foam core, used to create soft, indirect lighting.

Break-out box: A box that has connectors and ports for attaching video and audio peripherals. Usually provided with complex video digitizing systems.

Broadcast colors: Your computer monitor can display many more colors than can NTSC video. Broadcast colors are those colors that are safe – that is, they will display properly – for use in broadcast video. Many programs, such as Adobe Photoshop and Adobe After Effects, include special filters that will convert the colors in an image to their nearest broadcast safe equivalent. (See also *NTSC legal*).

Broadcast quality A somewhat vague term, referring to the minimum quality considered acceptable for broadcast television. Until the 1980s, 3/4" Umatic tape was considered broadcast quality, then Betacam SP was introduced and became the standard for broadcast quality. Today, Hi8 and MiniDV is often considered broadcast quality due to the fact that the final master is usually Digital Betacam.

BT. 601 A document that defines the specifications for professional, interlaced video standards as the following: 720 x 480 (59.94 Hz), 960 x 480 (59.94 Hz), 720 x 576 (50 Hz), and 960 x 576 (50 Hz) 4:2:2 YCbCr. Also called CCIR 601 and ITU-R 601.

Bumping up The process of transferring a videotape from a lower quality format to a higher quality format, i.e, bumping up miniDV tapes to DVCPro.

Byte: A unit of computer storage. How much one byte equates to depends on what you are storing. If you're just storing text, then a single byte can hold one character. For video or audio, what a byte holds depends on how your video is compressed and stored.

Camera negative After film stock is exposed in the camera and is processed, the result is the negative, also called the camera negative, which is usually transferred to video using a *telecine* process and then, after editing, is then used to strike the final print.

Candelas A measurement of the intensity of light.

Capturing: The process of moving video data from a DV camera into a computer. Because the camera has already digitized the data, the computer does not have to perform any digitizing.

Cardioid: The roughly heart-shaped pattern that a mic can "hear."

CCD: See *charge-coupled device*.

CCIR 601 (see BT. 601)

CDR **CD** Recordable. A special type of compact disc that can be recorded by the end user using a special drive. Standard audio or data formats are supported by most recording programs, along with Video CD, a special format that can store 70 minutes of full-screen, full-motion MPEG1-compressed video.

Century stand (see C-stand)

CG: Character generator. A special machine for creating titles and other text characters for inclusion in a video. Most editing packages include CG features.

CGI: Computer generated imagery. Used to refer to any effect that is created digitally, be it a composite, or a fully digital image such as a walking dinosaur. CGI is often used as a noun "we'll fill that spot with some CGI of a duck."

Channel: The color in an RGB image is divided into channels, one each for the red, green, and blue information in the image. When these channels are combined, a full-color image results. Certain effects are easier to achieve by manipulating individual color channels. Additional *alpha channels* can also be added for specifying transparency and selections (see *alpha channel*).

Charge-coupled device (CCD): A special type of chip that can convert light into electronic signals. A DV camera focuses light through a lens and onto a CCD where it is converted into electronic signals that can be stored on tape.

Checkerboard A way to arrange each piece of sound across a group of audio tracks so that no piece of sound is directly "touching" any other piece of sound, resulting in a checkerboard-like appearance. Also called *A/B rolling*.

Chroma key: A special key function that will render a specific color in a layer transparent. For example, if you shoot someone in front of an evenly-lit blue screen, you can use a chroma key function to render the blue completely transparent, thus revealing underlying video layers.

Chroma The part of the video signal that contains the color information.

Chromatic aberration: Color shifts and color artifacts in an image caused by faults in a lens, or by the camera's inability to register all three channels of color information. Single-chip video cameras are especially prone to chromatic abberation.

Chrominance The *saturation* and *hue* of a video signal. Although slightly different in meaning, this term is often used interchangably with the term *chroma* to refer to color.

Chyron A title identifying a speaker in a documentary that runs along the bottom of the screen, so-called after the Chyron character-generator popular in many post facilities. These I.D. titles are also known as *lower thirds*.

Cinematographer (see Director of Photography)

Cinepak: A QuickTime CODEC. Very *lossy* but ideal for delivery mediums with low data rates such as CDROM or the Web.

Clipping In digital media, an electronic limit that is imposed on the audio and/or video portion of the signal in order to avoid audio that is too loud and video that is too bright, too saturated or too dark. *Clipped blacks* are any blacks in an image that are darker than the set black level, or 7.5 IRE. *Clipped whites* are any whites that are brighter than the set white level, or 100 IRE. *Clipped audio* is any sound that goes into the red area on a VU meter. Clipped media is indicated by a flat line in a waveform view of the signal.

Close-up A shot where the subject fills the majority of the frame. If the subject is a person, the shot will consist primarily of their head and shoulders.

C-Mode EDL An EDL sorted nonsequentially by source tape number and ascending source timecode.

CMX A hardware-based linear on-line editing system. CMX-format EDLs are often the default for other editing systems.

CODEC COmpressor/DECompressor, an algorithm for compressing and decompressing video and audio.

Color bars A test pattern used to check whether a video system is calibrated correctly. A waveform monitor and vectorscope are used, in conjunction with color bars, to check the brightness, hue and saturation.

Color Depth The number of colors that a given video system can be displayed. The greater the number of bits-per-pixel that are used to store color, the higher the color depth.

Color sampling ratio In component digital video, the ratio of luminance (Y) to each color difference component (Cb and Cr). 4:2:2 means that for every four samples of luminance, there are two samples of chroma minus blue and chroma minus red. 4:2:2:4 indicates an additional four samples of the alpha channel or keying information.

Color spectrum The range of visible light which extends from violet to red.

Color temperature blue (CTB) A special color of lighting gel or camera lens filter that changes tungsten light to daylight.

Color temperature Light sources have different color temperatures, which are measured in degrees Kelvin. The color temperature of tungsten light is 3200°K and the color temperature of daylight is about 5500°K.

Color temperature orange (CTO) A special color of lighting gel or camera lens filter that changes daylight to tungsten light.

Color timing The process of setting the red, green and blue lights when creating a film print. Usually the color settings are timed to change with each significant scene or lighting change in the film.

Color-correction A post-production process to correct the overall color of a videotape master in order to get the best quality image, with an emphasis on enhancing skin tones.

Component video A video signal consisting of three separate color signals (or components), usually RGB (red, green, blue), YCbCr (Luminance, Chroma minus Blue, and Chroma minus Red), or Y, R-Y, B-Y (Luminance, Red minus Luminance, Blue minus Luminance.)

Composite video A video signal that contains all the luminance, chroma and timing (or sync) information in one composite signal.

Compositing: The process of layering media on top of each other to create collages or special effects.

Condensor: A type of mic that records sounds through a "capacitance" mechanism. Condensor mics require a power supply (usually in the form of a small battery). Because of the nature of their pickup mechanism, condensor mics can be made very small.

Conforming The process of meticulously recreating an off-line edit using, usually, higher quality footage with the aid of an EDL or cut list.

Continuity During a shoot, the process of keeping track of dialogue changes, actors' positions, wardrobe and props so that the footage from shot to shot, and day to day, will cut together. Usually the person in charge of continuity makes notes on a copy of the script and takes polaroids of the set.

Control track A part of the video signal that contains the timing, or synchronization, information, used to regulate the motion of the tape itself as it plays through a VTR.

Co-processors: Extra processors that are used to speed up a computer, or to perform special functions. See *accelerator cards*.

Coverage: Shooting all of the footage that will be needed to properly *cover* an event or scene.

CPU: Central processing unit. The box that contains the motherboard, peripheral cards and some storage drives. Also used to refer to the main processing chip that the system uses.

Cross-platform: Programs or hardware that come in different versions for different platforms. Ideally, the program's interface and features are identical from one platform to the next.

CRT monitor: The monitor attached to your computer. Short for Cathode Ray Tube.

C-stand A rolling metal stand designed to hold lighting accessories, such as flags and nets.

CTB (see Color Temperature Blue)

CTO (see Color Temperature Orange)

Cutaway A shot of something other than the main action or dialogue in a scene that is used to build the story and smooth rough edits.

D.P. (see Director of Photography)

Daisy chain: A group of storage devices that have been chained together so that each can be accessed independently.

DAT Digital Audio Tape, an audio tape format developed by Sony that records audio using a sampling rate of 48 kHz and is capable of recording SMPTE timecode information.

Data rate The amount of data that a particular connection can sustain over time. Usually measured in bytes/second.

DaVinci A professional digital color correction system.

Daylight Daylight is the combination of sunlight and skylight.

dBm: See *decibel milliwatt*.

dBSPL: See *decibel sound pressure loudness*.

Decibel milliwatt: A unit for measuring sound as electrical power.

Decibel sound pressure loudness A measure of the acoustic power of a sound.

Decibel: The standard unit for measuring sound. A subjective scale where one unit equals one increment of "loudness."

Degauss To completely erase all the information on a magnetic video or audio tape, using a demagnetizing device.

Depth of field A measure of how much, and what depth, of the image is in focus.

Destination monitor The monitor or window that displays an edited sequence as it plays, as opposed to the source monitor, which plays unedited source footage. Also called the *record monitor*.

Destructive editing: Any form of editing (either video or audio) that physically alters your original source material.

Device Control The ability of a piece of hardware, such as an edit controller or a CPU, to control a peripheral device, such as a VTR, via a remote control cable.

Diffuse light Light from a soft, undirected source, such as an typical household bulb.

Diffusion gel A semi-transparent piece of white plastic used to make a light softer.

Digital Information recorded electronically as a series of discrete pulses, or *samples*, usually using a *binary* system.

Digital zoom: A "fake" zoom which creates a zooming effect by enlarging the image on-the-fly. Unfortunately, when enlarging, the image is severely degraded.

Digitizing: The process of taking analog video information from a camera or deck and turning it into digital information that can be used by a computer.

Diopter An adjustment on the eyepiece of a camera that allows you to correct the focus of the eyepiece to match your vision.

Director of photography The film lighting and camera specialist responsible for the look of the photography and in charge of the camera and lighting crews.

Dissolve A transition in which the first shot is partially or completely replace by gradually superimposing the next shot.

Distressing A process of making objects on a set look aged or weathered.

DLT An optical tape back-up system, DLT tapes typically hold about 20gbytes of media.

DM&E Acronym for dialogue, music and effects, a four-channel, split audio mix that allows for easy remixing in case the audio needs to be dubbed to a foreign language.

Drag-and-drop editing A two-step editing method where the user selects a shot and drags it from one position and drops it in another position, for example from a bin to the timeline or from one position in the timeline to another.

Drive chassis: A box, mount, or rack for holding hard drives. Usually separate from the CPU.

Drop-outs A weak portion of the video signal which results in a problem in playback. *Hits* are small drop-outs that are only one or two horizontal lines in size, *glitches* are larger, where 5% or more of the image drops out. Large analog drop-outs can result in a few rolling video frames and large digital drop-outs can result in random "holes" across the screen.

DTV Acronym for Digital Television, the new digital television broadcast standard that will be adopted in the U.S. by 2006. DTV is an umbrella term that includes several subgroups, including HDTV and SDTV.

Dual stream-processing: The ability to handle up to two video signals at a time.

Dub A copy of a videotape, also known as a *dupe*.

Duvetine A black felt-like cloth used to block out unwanted light sources, such as windows.

DVD Digital video disc (sometimes called "digital versatile disc." An optical storage medium that is the same physical size as a compact disc. There are several different DVD standards and formats ranging from DVD-RAM (a rewritable format) DVD-ROM (a read-only format) and DVD-video (the format that is used for video releases).

DVE An acronym for *digital video effects*. The term comes from the professional linear video editing world and applies to what has become a fairly standard set of effects: wipes, dissolves, picture-in-picture, barn doors, and split screen, to name a few. Based on a trade name for a system sold by NEC.

Dynamic: A mic that derives its power from the pressure of the sound that is being recorded. Handheld mics are usually dynamic.

Edit controller A piece of hardware used in linear editing systems to control and synchronize multiple video decks.

Edit Decision List A list of all the edits in a project, identified by a chronological *event* number, source name, source in-point, source out-point, master in-point, and master-out point.

EDL (see Edit Decision List)

Egg crate A sectioned metal frame that attaches to soft light sources to make them more directional.

EIDE: A type of hard drive interface. Not as fast as SCSI, but fast enough for DV.

EIS See *electronic image stabilization*.

EISA slots: A type of expansion slot used in Windows-based computers.

Electret condensor: A cheaper, lower-quality version of the condensor mechanism.

Electronic image stabilization: Special circuitry in a camera that attempts to compensate for shaking and vibrating by electronically shifting the image to compensate for camera movement. Electronic image stabilization frequently results in a slightly blurred image.

Electronic zoom: Electronic controls that are used to zoom the lens in and out. These are the only zoom controls found on most pro-sumer camcorders.

EQ: See *equalization*.

Equalization: The process of adjusting the volume of individual *frequency* ranges within a sound. Equalization can be used to correct problems in a sound, or to "sweeten" or enhance the sound to bring out particular qualities.

Ethernet: A standard networking protocol for connecting computers together though one of several types of networking cable.

Exabyte A digital, optical tape –based storage system, used for backing up projects with large amounts of data. Exbabyte tapes typically hold XXX gbytes per tape.

Exposure The process of allowing light to enter the camera, exposing the film or video stock to light, which results in a recorded image.

Fade out A dissolve from full video to black video or from audio to silence.

Field dominance Hardware and software that play the field of video containing the odd-numbered scan lines first are known as *field one dominant*. Those that play the field of video containing the even-numbered scan lines first are known as *field two dominant*. Field one dominance is the norm.

Fields Each frame of interlaced video consists of two fields: one field contains the odd-numbered scan lines and the other field contains the even-numbered scan lines. In NTSC video, each field has 262.5 horizontal lines.

Film grain: Images are recorded on film by exposing the film's light-sensitive emulsion. Composed of chemical particles, the film's emulsion has a visible grain when projected. Many video producers try to mimic this grainy look to produce an image that looks more film-like.

Film recorder (see film recordist)

Film recordist The person responsible for transferring (or recording) video to film.

Filters: Special glass attachments that can be added to a camera lens to change the optical properties of the lens. Or, special pieces of software that can be added to a host application to perform special image processing functions.

Firewire: Apple's name for the IEEE-1394 specification.

Flag A black cloth held by a metal frame, used to block light.

Flats Large wooden "walls," used on a soundstage to construct the set.

Fluid head tripod: A special type of tripod head that is filled with hydraulic fluid that smooths the motion of the camera head.

Focal length The size of the angle of view of the lens, measured in millimeters. The smaller the number, the wider the lens. Zoom lenses have a range of focal lengths.

Focal plane: The area in a camera onto which light is focused. In a film camera, the film rests on the focal plane, in a digital video camera, the CCD rests on the focal plane.

Focus ring: A rotatable ring on the lens of a camera that allows for manual focusing. Ideally, you want a focus ring with distance markings so that you can perform more complicated manual focus effects such as *pulling* or *racking* focus.

Foley: The process of creating and recording ambient sound effects in real-time while watching the attendant video or film. Foley work is usually performed on a Foley stage equipped with special surfaces and props. Named for Jack Foley, the originator of the technique.

Footcandles A measurement of the amount of illumination falling on a subject, using the English measuring system. (See also *lux*.)

Fps Fps, or frames per second, is used to describe the speed at which film and video play. Film plays at 24fps, PAL video at 25fps, and NTSC video at 29.97 fps.

Fragmentation: When a hard drive has had many files deleted and replaced, it can become fragmented, which can slow its performance. At this point, it may need to be defragmented, or optimized.

Frame accuracy The ability for a device, particularly a VTR, to accurately perform edits on a pre-designated frame. Non-frame accurate VTRs may miss the mark by one or more frames.

Frame One complete film or video picture, each frame of video contains two fields. Moving images need at least 18 frames per second to appear as full-motion and 24 fps to allow for sync sound. NTSC video plays at 29.97fps and PAL video at 25fps.

Frame rate: When speaking of video or film recording, the number of frames per second that are recorded (and then played back).

Frequency An audio signal is made up of different frequencies, or wavelengths, which yield the high (or treble), mid and low (or bass) tones. The human voice resides mostly in the mid-tones..

Fresnel lens A lens attached to a light that allows for focusing of the beam of light.

f-stop: A measure of the size of a camera's aperture. The higher the f-stop, the smaller the aperture.

Gain boost A method of electronically increasing the strength, or amplitude, of an audio or video signal, resulting in a higher (OR LOWER? I FORGET) *signal-to-noise ratio*. In video, the image gets brighter but has more visible noise.

Gain The strength (or amplitude) of an audio or video signal

Garbage matte: A special matte used to knock out extraneous objects in a compositing shot. Garbage mattes are usually applied to a blue-screen shot before chroma-keying. They can be used to eliminate props, mic booms and other objects that can't be eliminated through keying.

Gate: A special type of audio filter that only allows a specific range of frequencies to pass.

Gel frame A metal frame that holds lighting gels in front of the light.

Glidecam: A camera-stabilizing mechanism similar to a Steadicam.

Globes The professional term for light bulb.

Green spill The same as blue-spill, except that it occurs with a green screen as a backdrop, rather than a blue screen.

Green-screen: Same as blue-screen, but used for those occasions where you need to have blue elements in your foreground.

Handheld: The typical handheld mic that used by rock stars, comedians, and wandering talk show hosts. Usually an omnidirectional, dynamic microphone.

Handles Extra footage at the head and tail of each shot to allow the editor room to add dissolves and manipulate the pacing of a scene.

Hard cut An edit from one shot to another without any sort of transition in-between, such as a dissolve.

Hard light Light from a direct, focused light source.

HDTV High-definition television, a subgroup of the new DTV digital television broadcast standard that has a 16:9 aspect ratio, a resolution of either 1280x720 or 1920x1080, a frame rate of 23.96, 24, 29.97, 30, 59.95 or 60 fps and either interlaced or progressive scanning.

HMI lights High powered arc lights used to simulate daylight. The lights at a baseball stadium are HMI lights.

Horizontal blanking interval The part of the composite video signal between the end of the image information on one horizontal scan line and the start of the image information on the next horizontal scan line.

Horizontal delay A display feature available on professional video monitors that shows the video signal offset horizontally so as to allow the editor to see and analyze the horizontal sync pulses. See also *vertical delay*.

Horizontal line resolution The number of vertical (THIS ALWAYS CONFUSES ME) lines in the visible portion of the video signal.

Horizontal sync The sync pulses in the video signal that regulate the movement and position of the electron beam as it draws each horizontal scan line across the video monitor.

Hot-swapping: Replacing a peripheral without shutting off the computer's power. Note: Not all peripherals are hot-swappable!

HSB: Just as colors can be defined by specifying RGB (red, green, and blue) values, colors can also be defined by specifying Hue, Saturation, and Brightness. Many color pickers allow you to switch to an HSB mode. For some operations, selecting a color is easier in one mode than in another.

Hue The shade of a color.

IDE drives: Hard drives that adhere to the IDE interface specification.

IE1394 (see Firewire)

IEEE-1394: A high-speed serial interface that can be used to attach DV cameras, storage devices, printers, or networks to a computer.

I-frame A video compression term. An intermediate frame between two keyframes. I-frames store only the data that has changed from the previous frame.

iLink: Sony's name for the IEEE-1394 specification.

Illumination The amount of light cast on a subject.

Inbetweening: The process of calculation (or interpolation) that is required to generate all of the frames between two *keyframes* in an animation.

Incident light Light coming from a direct source, such as the sun, a light, etc.

Infrared The area beyond red, outside of the visible part of the color spectrum.

In-point The starting point of an edit.

Insert edit An edit onto videotape which does not replace the control track and allows for the separate editing of video, audio and timecode.

Insert mode In most NLEs, a method of editing in the timeline that allows the placement of a shot between two shots without covering up what's already there. Instead, the second shot (and all the shots following it) move down to accomodate the new shot. (See also *overwrite mode*.)

Intensity (of light) The strength of a light source, measured in candelas.

Interface: The controls and windows that you use to operate a program.

Interlace scan The process of scanning a frame of video in which one field containing half the horizontal lines is scanned, followed by another field that contains the other half of the horizontal lines, adding up to a complete frame of video.

Interlaced (see Interlace scan)

Interleaving: The process of alternating data across multiple discs, as in an array.

Internegative An intermediary step sometimes necessary in film processing. The camera negative is printed and a new negative, the internegative, is made (or struck) from that print. The internegative (or IN) is then used to create more prints.

Interpositive An intermediary step sometimes necessary in film processing. The camera negative is printed and this print, called the interpositive (IP), is used to create a new negative. The release prints are then struck from that negative.

Iris: Synonymous with aperture. The iris is the physical mechanism that can be opened or closed to change the size of the aperture. "Irising down" for example, means to close down the iris (go to a higher f-stop).

IRQ: Special addressing information used by peripherals attached to a Windows-based computer. Each peripheral must have its own IRQ.

ISA slots: A type of expansion slot used in Windows-based computers.

ISO-9660 A format for writing CD-ROMs. Can be read by either Mac or Windows-based computers.

ITU-R 601 (see BT. 601)

JKL A way of editing using the J, K, and L keys on computer keyboard specifically programmed to allow for fast shuttling through clips in an NLE.

Kelvin scale A temperature scale used by scientists, similar to Celsius.

Key effect: Different types of "keys" can be used to remove the background from a video clip to expose underlying video. See *chroma key* and *luminance key*.

Keyframe interval When compressing video, the frequency at which a keyframe will occur.

Keyframe: When animating, you will explicitly define the parameters of an animated element by creating a keyframe. The computer will automatically calculate the changes that occur between keyframes (see *inbetweening*).

Kinescope A method of making a film copy of a videotape by recording the image off a video monitor.

LANC (or Control-L) A device control protocol most commonly found on consumer equipment and incapable of frame accuracy. (See also *RS-422* and *RS-232*).

Latitude The size of the grey scale ranging from darkest black to brightest white. The human eye sees more latitude than can be recorded on film or video.

Lavalier: A small clip-on mic. Usually an omnidirectional, condensor microphone.

Layback The process of transferring the finished audio back onto the master videotape after *sweetening*.

LCD: Liquid crystal display. The type of display used as a viewfinder on most cameras. In terms of cameras, LCD usually refers to a small, flip-out screen, as opposed to the optical viewfinder.

Lens: Usually a series of separate glass lenses, the lens on a camera is what focuses light onto the *focal plane* to create an image.

Letterboxing: The process of putting black bars at the top and bottom of the screen to change a 4:3 aspect ratio image to a wider aspect ratio image.

Light kit A set of professional lights, light stands and lighting accessories, usually contained in a heavy-duty carrying case.

Light meter A small, handheld device used to record the illumination at a particular location, usually measured in footcandles or lux, which can then be translated to f-stops.

Lighting gel Translucent pieces of special colored plastic used to change the brightness and color of a light source.

Linear editing Editing using linear media, i.e. tape to tape, as opposed to using random access media stored on a computer hard drive. All tape is linear, so linear media can be either digital or analog.

Locking picture The process of formally finalizing the editing of a film for story, so that the sound editors can start working without have to deal with any changes in timing.

Logging The process of recording the contents of each field tape using timecode, shot names and descriptions. The first step in the editing process.

Long Shot A shot that plays out over a long period of time.

Looping: The process of re-recording dialog in a studio. Called "looping" because the actor sometimes watches a continuous loop of the scene that is being re-recorded. Also known as ADR, for automatic dialogue replacement.

Lossless: Used to denote a form of compression that does not degrade the quality of the image being compressed.

Lossy: Used to denote a form of compression that degrades the quality of the image being compressed.

Lower thirds (see Chryon)

LTC An acronym for longitudinal timecode, a type of SMPTE timecode that is recorded onto the audio track of a videotape.

Luma clamping: see *luminance clamping*.

Luma Key: See Luminance key.

Luminance clamping: The process of clamping (or clipping, or scaling) the luminance value in a video signal. In video that has been luma clamped, luminance values over 235 are eliminated, frequently resulting in video with bright areas that look like solid blobs of white.

Luminance key: A special key function that will use the luminance values in a layer to determine the transparency of that layer. For example, a luminance key could be set to render the darkest areas of the layer transparent.

Luminance The strength (or amplitude) of the *grey scale* (or brightness) portion of a video signal.

Lux A measurement for the amount of illumination on a subject, using the metric scale. (See also *footcandles*.)

Master shot A wide shot that contains all the action in particular scene. Used as the basis for building the scene.

M-JPEG (see MJPEG)

MJPEG: A lossy, high-quality CODEC that can deliver full-motion, full-frame video. Almost always requires special compression hardware.

Montage In editing, the process of juxtaposing two shots against each other to arrive at an effect different than each shot would imply on it's own.

Motherboard: The main circuit board inside a computer.

Motion blur: When an object moves quickly, it will be look blurrier. Individual frames of video or film should show a certain amount of blur around moving objects. Motion blur is usually the result of average shutter speeds (1/60th to 1/125th of a second). Faster shutter speeds will result in less motion blur, slower shutter speeds will result in more. A lack of motion blur will result in stuttery, stroboscopic motion.

MPEG: A lossy, high-quality CODEC. Comes in several flavors. MPEG1 is used for the VCD format, MPEG2 is used for DVD format video. Both flavors are suitable for distribution of full-motion, full-frame video.

ND (see Neutral Density)

Negative cutter The person who physically cuts the film negative to conform to the final cut.

Neon light A light consisting of a glass tube filled with neon gas, which varies in color.

Kino-flo tubes Color-corrected fluorescent light tubes used to replace normal fluorescent light tubes when shooting at a location that will have fluorescent lights visible in the shot.

Net A large screen used to decrease the strength of the light falling on the subject, usually used for exterior shoots.

Neutral density A lens filter or lighting gel that tones down brightness without changing the color temperature.

NLE (see Non-linear editing system)

Non-destructive editing: Any form of editing (either video or audio) that leaves your original source material un-altered.

Non-linear editing system A digital editing system that uses a software interface and digitized audio and video stored on a hard drive which allows for random access, non-linearity, and non-destructive editing.

Notch: A special type of audio filter that can eliminate a specific, defined frequency of sound.

NTSC An acronym for National Television Standards Committee, NTSC is the broadcast video standard for North America and Japan, with a frame rate of 29.97 fps and 525 horizontal scan lines.

NTSC Legal The term NTSC legal refers to colors that fit within the NTSC guidelines for broadcast television. A vectorscope is used to determine if an image is within the NTSC legal color boundaries.

NTSC Monitor (see NTSC/PAL monitor)

NTSC/PAL monitor: The monitor attached to your camera, video deck, or NTSC outputs of your video digitizing system. Used to display the video you are eidting.

Omnidirectional: A mic that picks up sounds from all directions.

Off-line clip An off-line clip is one that has been logged but does not have any audio or video media attached to it, whether that is because it hasn't been captured yet or because the media has been deleted.

Off-line editing Off-line editing means working in a draft mode with the intention to eventually take the project to a better resolution and possibly, better videotape format, in order to do a final pass that will improve its look, quality and polish.

OIS See *optical image stabilization*

One-light print A one-light print is a film print created from the film negative that uses a single, constant, optimized light setting (i.e. one light) for the red, green and blue lights used to create the print.

Onion-skinning: Some animation programs can display semi-opaque overlays of previous frames. These "onion-skin" frames can be used as a reference for drawing or retouching the current frame.

On-line editing Creation of the final master videotape, whatever the means or format involved, usually conformed from the original production footage using an EDL.

Operating System: The low-level program that controls the communication between all of the subsystems (storage, memory, video, peripherals, etc.) in your computer.

Optical image stabilization: A special optical aperatus in a camera that attempts to compensate for shaking and vibrating by altering the camera's optical properties on-the-fly to compensate for camera movement. Because OIS doesn't alter your image data, there is no image degradation.

Optical viewfinder: The eyepiece on a camera that you look through to frame your shot. As opposed to the flip-out LCD viewfinder present on some cameras.

Opticals: Special effects that are traditionally added by an "optical" department. Usually, these are effects that are added through a separate optical printing pass. Lightning bolts, light flares, glows and halos are all traditional optical effects that can now performed through rotoscoping, or with the application of custom filters.

Out-point The end point of an edit.

Overexposure Overexposure refers to video or film that was shot with too much light or the wrong camera settings, resulting in a whitish, washed-out, faded-looking image.

Overlapping edit An edit where the picture ends before or after the sound ends. Also called an L-cut or a split-edit.

Overscan: All video formats scan more image than they need, to compensate for the fact that not all monitors and televisions display images at exactly the same size. To keep your action and titles within the visible area, you'll want to pay attention to the *action* and *title safe* areas of the screen.

Overwrite mode In most NLEs, a method of editing that allows the placement of a shot in the timeline that covers up anything that was previously occupying that space. (See also *insert mode*.)

PAL An acronym for Phase Alternate by Line, a television standard used in most of Europe and Asia, with a frame rate of 25fps and 625 horizontal scan lines, resulting in somewhat higher quality video than NTSC.

PAL Monitor (see NTSC/PAL monitor)

Pan: To rotate the camera left and right around the camera's vertical axis.

Parabolic: A special type of mic that can be used to record sounds from great distances.

Partitions: Logical divisions in a hard drive that make the drive appear to be more than a single drive.

Patch bay A rack of video and audio input and output connectors that makes it easier to re-configure the hardware in an editing system.

Pedastal: To raise the camera up or down.

Phono connector A medium-sized single prong connector used primarily for analog audio, especially headphones. Also known as 1/4" connector.

Pistol grip tripod: A tripod with a head that is controlled by a single pistol-grip mechanism. Such heads can be freely rotated around all axes simultaneously, making it very difficult to perform a smooth motion along a single axis.

Pixel: Short for *pic*ture *el*ement. A single point on your screen.

Platform: The computer hardware/OS combination that you have chosen to work on.

Plug-ins: Special effects and add-ons that can be added to a host application. See *filters*.

Polarizer A lens filter which polarizes the light coming into the lens. Can be used to increase saturation and to eliminate reflections in glass or water.

Post house: See *Post-production facility*.

Post-production facility: A service bureau that provides editing and other post-production facilities and services.

Practical light A light source that is both part of the scenery and a source of light for the camera.

Preroll The process of rewinding the videotape to a cue point several seconds prior to the in-point so that playback of the tape is stabilized and up to full speed when the tape reaches the in-point.

Prime lens: A lens with fixed focal length.

Prism: A special optical construct (usually a single piece of glass) that can split light into its component parts.

Production Board A hardbacked set of spreadsheets designed specifically for organizing film production.

Production designer: The designer who is responsible for the look of the entire production. They will supervise the set decorators, costumes and other visual artists.

Production Strip A removeable color-coded paper strip that fits into the spreadsheet layout of the production board and allows for easy re-organization.

Progressive scan A type of video display where each horizontal line is scanned consecutively from top to bottom, resulting in a full frame of video without the need for *fields*. (Compare to *interlaced scan*.)

Prop Short for property, a prop is any object on the set that is used by the actors, such as a knife, as opposed to set dressing and scenery which provide a backdrop for the action.

Proxy: A placeholder. Usually used in editing programs to take the place of video that has yet to be shot, or that has yet to be digitized at the highest quality.

Pull focus Pull (or pulling) focus is a technique used to change focal lengths during a large camera or subject move, such as a dolly. The camera assistant literally moves the lens to compensate for the camera/subject movement so that the subject remains in focus throughout the shot.

QuickTime: A software architecture for displaying and manipulating time-based data (such as video and audio) on a computer.

Rack focus A rack focus is a shot where the focus is set on an object in the background, then the focus is pulled, or racked, to an object in the foreground (or vice-versa). Exemplified by a shot of a billiard ball, then a rack focus to reveal the person holding the cue stick.

Radio cut An edit of a scene based on dialogue only, disregarding whether the picture works or not. The idea being that the result should play like an old fashioned radio show.

RAID: Redundant Array of Independent Discs. A group of hard drives that have been arranged to act like a single, very fast storage device.

RAM: Random Access Memory. The electronic memory inside your computer which is used to hold programs and data when working.

RCA Connector A small, single prong connector most commonly used to carry composite video and unbalanced audio signals.

Reaction A shot of a person in a scene as they react to the dialogue or action of the scene.

Real Media: A special streaming video and audio architecture created by Real, Inc.

Realtime A function, such as playback or recording, that occurs immediately and in real time, without the need for rendering and without any speeding up of the process, such as 4x (quadruple speed) recording.

Real-time editing: Editing that can happen in real-time. That is, effects and edits do not have to be calculated or rendered before they can be seen.

Reflective light Light coming from an indirect source, such as a bounce card, the sky (but not the sun), etc. (See *also incident light.*)

Reflector A shiny board or fabric used to redirect a bright light source, such as the sun.

RGB color space: The range of colors that can be displayed and recorded by your computer.

Room tone: The sound of the room in which a scene was recorded. During a shoot, the sound recorder will record roughly a minute's worth of the quieted location to create an "empty" sound with the right atmosphere. This sound will be used by the sound editor to correct audio problems.

Rotoscoping: The process of painting over existing frames of video or film. In DV production, rotoscoping is used for everything from painting in special effects, to painting custom-made mattes for compositing.

Rough cut An early edit of a project, as opposed to the final cut.

Router An electronic patching system for audio and video equipment.

RS-232 A serial device control protocol that allows for computers to control video decks and other hardware. RS-232 is most commonly used for low-end professional and consumer equipment.

RS-422 A serial device control protocol that allows for computers to control video decks and other hardware. RS-422 is the standard for professional equipment, uses SMPTE timecode and is capable of frame accuracy.

RT11 A floppy disk format used by high-end linear on-line editing equipment to store EDLs.

SAG Acronym for the Screen Actors' Guild.

Saturated colors The technical term for bright, bold colors is "saturated." For example, a true red is saturated, while pink and maroon are *desaturated* reds.

Saturation The amount of color in the video signal

Screen correction shot **A shot of a blue-screen or green-screen stage that has no actors in it and is used by compositing software to help create the matte.**

Scrim A lighting accessory used to tone down the brightness of a light. Single scrim dim the light by 1/2 f-stop and double scrims dim the light by a full f-stop. Half scrims are a half-moon shape, to allow for further manipulation of the light.

SCSI IDs: When using SCSI devices, each device on the SCSI chain must have its own, unique SCSI ID. A SCSI port can support up to 7 devices.

SCSI: Small Computer Systems Interface. An interface standard for connecting hard drives and other peripherals. Comes in many different flavors including SCSI-2, Ultra-SCSI, and Ultrawide-SCSI.

SDI An acronym for Serial Digital Interface, SDI is the professional digital video standard I/O protocol with a data rate of either 270Mbps or 360Mbps. (See also *Firewire.*)

SDTV An acronym for Standard Definition Television, a subgroup of the DTV digital television broadcast standard designed to replace the current NTSC standard.

Seamless edit A style of editing where the edits appear natural and do not call attention to themselves. A traditional Hollywood movie dialogue scene is usually seamlessly edited.

SECAM An acronym for *Sequential Colour a Memoire*, SECAM is the broadcast television standard for France, Russia and much of eastern Europe.

Sequence An assembly of shots edited together.

Sharpening: In a video camera, a special algorithm that is applied to the video image to make it sharper. With too much sharpening, strange artifacts will appear in the image.

Shooting ratio The ratio of the length of footage shot to the length of the final film. For example, a project with a 5:1 ratio would have shot five hours of footage for a one-hour long final project.

Shot list A list of the shots a director plans to shoot on a particular day of filming or taping. Usually a shot list is derived by carefully going over the script, the storyboard and blocking the scene with the actors in rehearsals.

Shotgun: A very directional mic that is often affixed to the front of the camera or to a boom or fishpole.

Shutter speed The speed of the rotation of the *shutter* inside the lens, measured in rotations per second.

Shutter: In a camera, the shutter opens and closes to control how long the focal plane is exposed to light. There is no physical shutter in a video camera, instead the camera's CCD samples light for an appropriate length of time, and then shuts off.

Sides A dialogue-only version of a script, used to make readings easier for actors.

Signal: Electronic information (video or audio) that is passed from one device to another.

Single-chip: A camera that uses a single CCD to gather all three (red, green, and blue) of the signals that will be used to create a full-color image.

Single-field resolution Some low-resolution CODECs cut down the size of the captured video files by discarding one field for each frame of video. The resulting single-field video plays fairly well but contains half the information of two-field video.

Sixty-cycle tone (60 Hz) Sixty-cycle tone, or 60 Hz tone, is used as an audio reference to calibrate the audio levels on editing equipment and speakers. Typically, the 60 Hz tone should fall at 0dB on a VU meter.

Skylight The ambient light from the sky, which consists of the reflected light of the sun. On a cloudy day there is no sunlight but there is still skylight.

Slating: When, recording the sound separately from the video or film, the process of holding a slate in front of the camera. On the slate are written the scene and take numbers. The top of the slate can be clapped to produce a distinct sound that will be used for syncing the audio and video.

Slow reveal A moving shot, often a pan or dolly, that reveals something slowly, such as a slow pan of a bathroom that reveals a dead person in the bathtub.

Slow-motion A shot that plays at a slower speed than full-motion film or video. Usually described as a percentage of full motion.

SLR camera: A *single lens reflex* camera. Unlike a camera with a separate viewfinder, in a SLR camera, you acutally look through the lens at your subject. A 35mm still camera with removable lenses is typically an SLR.

Slugline The first line of a scene in a screenplay that identifies whether the scene is interior or exterior, the location, and the time of day, all in upper-case letters.

SMPTE The Society of Motion Picture and Television Engineers, a standards organization who ...

Snow The image of a video signal that has no control track, also known as noise.

Soft light Light from a diffuse, often indirect light source.

SoftDV: The DV CODEC provided by Media100 for their EditDV line of video editing products.

Sorenson compressor: A lossy QuickTime CODEC with very good quality.

Source monitor The monitor or window that displays the unedited source footage, as opposed to the destination (or record) monitor, which plays the edited sequence.

SP-DIF Short for Sony/Phillips Digital Interface, a digital audio format used for consumer equipment.

Spin rate: Measured in revolutions per minute, the speed at which a hard drive spins.

Split-track dialogue Dialogue that is spread across several separate tracks, rather than mixed onto a single track. Usually split track dialogue has one track dedicated to each actor, or if the dialogue is *checkerboarded*, two tracks dedicated to each actor.

Spot meter A type of light meter that measures *reflective light* rather than *incident light*.

Spotting: Watching a locked-picture edit of your project with the intent of identifying all of the sound effect and music cues that will be needed.

Steadicam: A special camera mount that provides hydraulic, gimballed support for a camera. Allows steady, fluid motion of the camera.

Storage: Non-volatile storage that is used for long-term holding of programs and data. Usually magnetic or optical.

Storyboard editing A method of editing using thumbnails of each shot and organizing them in a bin, prior to drag-and-drop editing them into a sequence.

Streaming video Video that is downloaded, on-demand, iteratively to the viewer's computer.

Striped drives: Hard drives that have been indexed with special information so that they can be used as an array.

Strobing: The odd, stuttery motion caused by fast shutter speeds. Strobing appears because of a lack of motion blur.

Sunlight The light from the sun.

Super: To superimpose. Usually used to refer to the process of superimposing a title over an image.

Supercardioid: A very narrow cardioid pattern that indicates that a mic is very directional.

S-video (see Y/C video)

S-Video connector A proprietary cable that used to carry the Y/C video signal.

Sweetening The process of polishing the audio on a project by adding effects, equalizing and fine-tuning edits.

Switcher (see Router)

Sync Short for synchronization, the electronic pulses used to coordinate the operation of several interconnected pieces of video hardware. Also, the electronic pulses used to regulate the playback of the videotape in the VTR. See also *sync sound*.

Sync sound: Recording sound and video that are synchronized together, whether onto the same tape or by two or more separate recording devices.

TBC Acronym for *time base corrector*, an electronic device used to correcto video signal instability during videotape playback. Most modern professional VTRs have internal TBCs.

Telecine The process of transferring film to videotape.

Telephoto lens: A lens with a very narrow field of view (and, therefore, a long focal length). Telephoto lenses magnify objects in their field of view. Typically, lenses with focal lengths greater than 70 mm (equivalent to a 35mm film camera) are considered wide angle.

Termination: The last device in a SCSI chain must have a terminator, a connector that signifies the end of the chain, placed on it. Bad termination can result in the entire SCSI chain malfunctioning.

Textless master A videotape master that has no titles or any other text in it. Used for foreign language versions.

Three-chip: A camera that uses three separate CCDs to gather separate red, green, and blue data.

Three-point editing A method of editing where each edit is performed using an In and an Out point on both the source footage and the edited sequence. Once the editor enters three of the four In and Out points, the NLE or edit controller will automatically calculate the fourth In or Out point.

Three-point lighting The standard way to light a person using a strong directed key light, a diffuse, less intense fill light and a strong backlight.

Throughput: A measure of the speed at which data can be moved through a computer or storage system.

Tilt: To rotate the camera up and down around its horizontal axis.

Timecode Timecode is a numbering system encoded in the video tape itself. It measures time in the following format: hh:mm:ss:ff, where h= hours, m=minutes, s=seconds and f=frames.

Timeline A chronological display of an edited sequence in a non-linear editing system.

Title Safe: Another guide similar to the action safe area, the title safe area is slightly smaller. To ensure that your titles are visible on any monitor, always make certain that they fall within the title safe area.

Transcoder A device that changes the video signal from one format to another, such as from component to composite or from analog to digital.

Transfer mode: The type of calculation that will be used to determine how layers that are stacked on top of one another will combine.

Travelling matte: A matte (see *matte*) that changes over time to follow the action of a moving element. Travelling mattes are used to composite a moving element into a scene. In the digital world, an animated alpha channel serves the same function as a travelling matte.

Trim Mode The process of adjusting, or fine-tuning an existing edit in an NLE.

Tungsten light Light from an incandescent source, such as a household light bulb. Tungsten light is weaker than daylight and tends to have a warm cast.

Turnkey system: A video editing system that is preconfigured and assembled, and that provides everything you need to start working.

Tweening: See *inbetweening.*

UltraATA: A type of hard drive interface. Not as fast as SCSI, but fast enough for DV.

Ultraviolet The area beyond violet on the color spectrum, beyond the range of visible light.

Uncompressed video: Video that has not had any compression applied to it, either by the camera or by a computer.

Underscan A display feature available on professional video monitors that allows the viewer to see the complete video signal, including the sync pulses.

Unidirectional: A mic that picks up sounds from a particular direction.

USB: Universal Serial Bus. A standard for attaching serial devices such as keyboards, disk drives, and some types of storage. At the time of this writing USB video capture devices were just becoming available.

UV filter: A filter that can be attached to the front of the lens. Filters out excess ultraviolet light and serves to protect the lens from scratching and breaking.

Vacuum tubes: Before the invention of the CCD, video cameras used vacuum tubes to convert light into electronic signals.

VCD Video compact disc. A format for storing 70 minutes of full-frame, full-motion, MPEG1 compressed video on a normal compact disc or recordable compact disc.

Vectorscope A special monitor for calibrating the hue, or color information, in a video signal.

Vertical banding: Bright vertical smears that can occur in some video cameras when the camera is pointed at a very bright source.

Vertical blanking interval The period during which the video image goes blank as the electron beam returns from scanning one field of interlaced video to start scanning the next field. This "empty" space in the video signal is sometimes used to store VITC timecode, close-captioning and other information.

Vertical delay A display feature available on professional video monitors that shows the video signal offset vertically so as to allow the editor to see and analyze the vertical sync pulses. See also *horizontal delay.*

Vertical line resolution The number of horizontal lines in a frame of video.

Vertical sync The sync pulses in the video signal that control the field by field scanning of each frame of interlaced video.

VGA monitor: The monitor attached to your computer.

Video for Windows: A software architecture for displaying and manipulating time-based data (such as video and audio) on a computer.

Virtual memory: A process by which the disk space can be used as a substitute for RAM.

VITC Vertical Interleave Timecode, timecode that is encoded in the vertical blanking interval of the video signal.

VTR Video tape recorder, the professional term for VCR.

VU Meter: Volume unit meter. The volume meters on a sound recording device. VU meters help you gauge whether you are recording acceptable audio levels.

Wattage A measurement of the amount of electrical power used by a light, which determines the light's intensity.

Waveform monitor A special monitor for calibrating the brightness, or luminance, of a video signal. Waveform monitors are used to set the proper white and black levels.

White balance: When a camera has been calibrated to correctly display white, then the camera is *white balanced*. Once it is calibrated for white, other colors should display properly.

White level The peak level of the luminance (or grey scale) of the video signal, i.e., the brightest part of the image, usually set at 100 IRE.

Wide angle lens: A lens with a very wide field of view (and, therefore, a short focal length). Typically, the smaller the angle of the lens (measured in millimeters), the wider the angle. (BEN – i'm worried about

Widescreen: Standard NTSC or PAL video uses an aspect ratio of 4:3. Most film features are shot in a wider-screen aspect ratio. Some cameras include an option for shooting in a 16:9 aspect ratio. However, these modes are not actually any wider. Rather, they are just copped 4:3 images.

Wild sounds: Non-sync sounds recorded by hand "in the wild" using a portable recording system.

Wipe: A type of transition where one image is wiped over another.

XLR cable (see XLR connector)

XLR connectors: Three-pronged, balanced audio connectors for connecting mics and other recording equipment.

Y/C video Also called S-video (short for separate video), Y/C video has separate luma (Y) and chroma (C) video signals. (See also *component video* and *composite video*.)

YUV color space: The range of colors that can be displayed and recorded on digital video.

Zebra: Special lines that can be displayed in a viewfinder that indicate areas of overexposure in an image.

Zoom lens: A lens with variable focal lengths.

Zoom ring: Similar to a focus ring, but used for manually zooming the camera.

Index

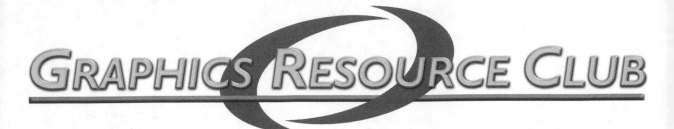
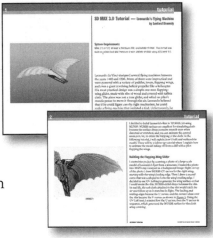